MAY 4 1999

338.973   Sloan, John W.,
S   1940-

         The Reagan effect.

$35.00

DATE			

THE REAGAN EFFECT

THE REAGAN EFFECT
ECONOMICS AND PRESIDENTIAL LEADERSHIP

JOHN W. SLOAN

UNIVERSITY PRESS OF KANSAS

Published by the University Press of Kansas (Lawrence, Kansas 66049), which was organized by the Kansas Board of Regents and is operated and funded by Emporia State University, Fort Hays State University, Kansas State University, Pittsburg State University, the University of Kansas, and Wichita State University

Library of Congress Cataloging-in-Publication Data

Sloan, John W., 1940–
    The Reagan effect : economics and presidential leadership / John W. Sloan
      p.   cm.
    Includes bibliographical references and index.
    ISBN 0-7006-0951-2 (alk. paper)
    1. United States—Economic policy—1918–1993. 2. Supply-side economics—United States. 3. Conservatism—United States--History—20th century. 4. Political leadership—United States--History—20th century. 5. United States—Politics and government—1981–1989. 6. Reagan, Ronald. I. Title.
HC106.8.S574   1999
338.973'009'048—dc21
                                          98-43844
                                              CIP

British Library Cataloguing in Publication Data is available.

Printed in the United States of America

10 9 8 7 6 5 4 3 2 1

The paper used in this publication meets the minimum requirements of the American National Standard for Permanence of Paper for Printed Library Materials Z39.48-1984.

To my son Patrick, who grew up during the 1980s

CONTENTS

PREFACE

As soon as Ronald Reagan was elected president in November 1980, I began thinking about writing this book. Since Reagan, as leader of the conservative movement, would be attempting to reverse liberal policies and to construct a conservative regime, I expected his presidency to be both significant and controversial. During the 1980s, I taught several seminars on the Reagan administration, and during the 1990s, I received three grants to conduct research at the Reagan Presidential Library in Simi Valley, California. Since 1990, each chapter in this book has been presented as a paper at a professional conference where my interpretations of the Reagan presidency were the targets—and the beneficiaries—of sharp criticism.

As I learned more about the Reagan administration, my initial evaluation changed considerably. I began this project with the working title *The Reagan Presidency: Political Success and Economic Decline*. After revising my outline six times, I came up with the present title, *The Reagan Effect: Economics and Presidential Leadership*. The change in title reflects the growing evidence that the Reagan presidency achieved both political and economic success.

My analysis of Reagan's leadership and economic policies is clearly different from most liberal and conservative judgments. Many liberals grudgingly conceded Reagan's political success, which they saw as a function of his skilled public relations staff and luck. Emphasizing Reagan's laid-back administrative style and his avoidance of details, most liberals denied that he was an authentic political leader. For them, Reagan's victories in the 1980s were built on illusions that would soon fade away. They predicted that the 1981 taxes would cause inflation and that the growing budget and trade deficits of the 1980s would lead to a decade of reckoning in the 1990s.

Instead, Reagan's tax cuts (and several later tax increases), combined with the revitalized efforts of the Federal Reserve Board, resulted in a formula that produced a rejuvenated economy capable of competing successfully in global markets and no longer threatened by inflation. Liberal arguments that the

United States was experiencing an economic decline and would soon be eclipsed by Japan and Germany were overwhelmed by indicators that the federal government's policies were prolonging the growth phase of the business cycle and creating more jobs than any of our competitors were generating.

The one major liberal claim that I found solidly supported by evidence was that there was growing inequality in the United States during the Reagan years. While the trend of income and wealth disparities accelerated, the Reagan administration condemned public policy efforts to deal with this problem. Since the quest for equality is such a vital component of the American political culture, I believe that Reagan's ridicule of attempts to promote social justice will lessen the chances of his being evaluated as a great moral leader by anyone other than his most conservative supporters.

My views also differ sharply from conservative ones. Conservatives are understandably proud of their leader, but in their quest to place Reagan on Mount Rushmore, they have attempted to elevate him to a mythical icon and have criticized most scholarly endeavors to analyze the nature of his political leadership and his achievements. For conservatives, Reagan had visions based on eternal truths that could not be compromised and that fundamentally changed the United States and the world. My study, however, suggests that Reagan succeeded partly by design, partly by compromise, and partly by muddling through. I point out that Reagan's visions contributed not only to record-breaking periods of economic growth but also to disasters—such as budget deficits, trade deficits, and the savings and loan debacle—that had to be dealt with by his successors.

My book also shines a light on Reagan's political leadership. He was not the Lone Ranger that a few of his conservative champions have created, nor was he the passive caricature painted by several of his liberal detractors. He was a unique political leader who combined an amiable, passive personality, a competitive urge to be liked and to win, an outstanding ability to communicate with the public, and a tenacious commitment to a few simple conservative ideas. The effectiveness of his leadership was based on his ability to attract and to use the talents of conservatives, pragmatists, and public relations experts. These three types of advisers provided Reagan with a mixture of skills that allowed him to enjoy the benefits of being a conservative conviction politician while, at the same time, successfully negotiating compromises and maintaining high public approval ratings.

Although Reagan was not able to construct a conservative regime, he was effective in economic policy making. For Reagan, economic policy—especially cutting tax rates—was the core area of his political leadership. This policy field was a strategic priority for him, inasmuch as in 1980 he was elected president largely because Jimmy Carter appeared so ineffectual in dealing with the stagflation of the late 1970s. Reagan's landslide reelection in 1984 was the result of the public's belief that his economic policies had provided prosperity.

But, in opposition to what Reagan proclaimed in his 1981 inaugural speech—namely, "In this present crisis, government is not the solution to our problem; government is the problem"—effective public policies were necessary to revitalize the American economy. Reagan's success was not only dependent on his tax reductions, it also relied on the Federal Reserve to control inflation and the International Monetary Fund to prevent the Third World debt problem from threatening the U.S. banking system. This is the great paradox of the Reagan presidency: his political achievements undermined the antigovernment perspective of the conservative movement.

I conclude that Reagan's impact, as opposed to his rhetoric and the aspirations of his conservative supporters, was not to displace the liberal regime created by the New Deal and the Great Society, but to weld his conservative orientation with the liberal one. The resulting merger is an awkward mix, and no one can be sure how long this hybrid regime will last. My study suggests, however, that neither the era of big government nor the need for effective public policies at the national and international levels is over.

1
CONTRASTING EVALUATIONS
OF THE REAGAN PRESIDENCY

Early evaluation of a modern president is a hazardous activity. The constantly changing appraisals of past presidents should caution us about making definitive judgments regarding a recently retired president and make us more open to opposing points of view. While Richard Neustadt in 1960 defined Dwight Eisenhower (1953–1961) as a political amateur, by the 1980s, the former general was being reinterpreted by Fred Greenstein as a surreptitious Machiavellian.[1] Appraisals change because more evidence comes to light and time allows us to separate durable achievements (Truman's Marshall Plan) from short-lived phenomena (Truman's scandals).

During Ronald Reagan's last years in the presidency, and in the years since he handed the office over to George Bush, journalists, politicians, and scholars have been busy assessing the impact of the Reagan administration. The evaluation of a two-term president is a monumental task because it requires an analysis of what role the president played in almost a decade's worth of national and international events. This problem was magnified during the Reagan era because history seemed to fast-forward during the 1980s. And Aaron Wildavsky has already labeled the 1980s a highly "contested decade" because of "the power of political polarization."[2]

That polarization has obviously influenced thoughts regarding the Reagan legacy. Taking the measure of a presidency is a highly subjective endeavor—and therefore open to ideological, partisan, and personal influences—because there is no agreed-upon formula or standard by which to judge presidential performance. The Reagan presidency will probably spawn more diametrically opposed perspectives than has any other presidency in American history. Conservatives talk of the Reagan revolution; they claim that Ronald Reagan come to power to change the United States and ended up changing the world.[3] Liberals argue that the 1980s were a period of self-delusion and national decline and that the reality was that Reagan's policies were detrimental to the long-term interests of the United States. While conservatives praise Reagan for most of the favorable outcomes of the 1980s, liberals blame him for most of the negative trends.

Both conservatives and liberals understand that the conclusions drawn from their debate over the significance of the Reagan era will be politically significant because they will influence future politics and policies. If the conservatives' argument that Reagan's policies were successful is the most compelling, then such policies should be continued. If liberals argue convincingly that his policies had major negative consequences, then they should be discarded. This debate is also important because it helps us to define ourselves as a nation as we near the end of the twentieth century.

During the 1980s, Reagan won a number of political victories, but since leaving office he has been losing the battle over evaluations of his political legacy. When Reagan retired in January 1989, he received a 68 percent approval rating in a *New York Times*–CBS poll, the best final review of any president in the post–World War II period. But by 1992, a *New York Times*–CBS poll found that 50 percent of the voters disapproved of the way Reagan had handled his presidency.[4] This decline in Reagan's popularity is partially explained by the large numbers of negative assessments of his presidency that have been forthcoming since his retirement. Liberals suggest that this means that we can now view the Reagan presidency more accurately as a first-rate public relations spectacle camouflaging a third-rate, sleazy political record. Conservatives argue, however, that these predominantly critical evaluations reflect the liberal bias of so many journalists and scholars.

The goal of this introductory chapter is not to resolve the ideological debates concerning the Reagan presidency by providing answers but to highlight some of the principal areas of dispute regarding Reagan's leadership and his economic policies that will be analyzed in subsequent chapters. My purpose, in short, is to exploit the initial ideological debates about the Reagan presidency in order to frame good questions to guide a more scholarly secondary analysis. To accomplish this task, this chapter first briefly assesses the relevance of early ideological evaluations of presidential performance, then offers a comparison of conservative and liberal evaluations of the Reagan presidency. Its conclusion defines the major issues of dispute concerning the Reagan record. My arguments are summarized in Table 1.1, below.

IDEOLOGICAL EVALUATIONS

One means of understanding the major issues involved in assessing a president is to compare the evaluations of conservative writers and liberal writ-

Table 1.1   Conservative and Liberal Evaluations of the Reagan Presidency

Subjects	Conservative	Liberal
Agreements	Carter was a failed president Reagan inherited a sick economy Reagan emphasized the value of individual freedom Reagan neglected the value of equality Reagan changed the nature of political debate Reagan restored the authority of the presidency Reagan's economic policies had strategic importance	Carter was a failed president Reagan inherited a sick economy Reagan emphasized the value of individual freedom Reagan neglected the value of equality Reagan changed the nature of political debate Reagan restored the authority of the presidency Reagan's economic policies had strategic importance
Reasons for Reagan's political success	An inspiring moral leader Authentic response to problems of the 1970s An economic growth that benefited the bulk of the population A vigorous and intelligent defense of U.S. national interests	Luck The abilities of other officials (e.g., James Baker, Paul Volcker) Reagan's abilities as an actor and speaker The public relations capabilities of the White House
Reagan's administrative skills	Set policy direction Chairman of the board Little concern with details Hire the best people Good-natured; faith in subordinates	Figurehead Lazy, superstitious, and uninformed Used and manipulated by his staff An administration pervaded by sleaze
Explanations for Reagan's decline in popularity since 1989	Biased cultural elites are trying to distort and destroy the Reagan legacy	Reagan's legacy has been weakened by kiss-and-tell memoirs The bills for Reagan's excesses will have to be paid for in the 1990s
Reagan legacy	A revolution in governing Outstanding economic growth Significant deregulation Overcoming the Vietnam syndrome U.S. victory in the Cold War	The temporary victory of illusion over substance A series of budget deficits that increased the national debt Increasing economic and social inequality The savings and loan crisis Exorbitant and wasteful military expenditures A weakening of the U.S. capability to compete successfully in the global economy

ers. Ideological beliefs give each of these groups the incentive, energy, and commitment to generate polemical analyses of a particular president. Contemporary polemicists rarely set a permanent agenda for evaluating a presidency; still, they structure the initial debate, and it is a safe assumption that each set of polemicists can identify most of the major successes and failures of a president. At a first stage of intellectual construction, the facts, anecdotes, and myths of a presidency, woven together by conservative and liberal writers, generate themes that help define the contours of an administration. Looking at an administration, usually from the outside, they provide the first evaluations of its successes and failures. Besides heat and smoke, polemical arguments can generate some illuminating insights into what a presidency was all about. By carefully comparing the major points developed by the two groups, one can reach a deeper comprehension of a presidency. In brief, although polemical evaluations of a president may provide few answers, they can help to construct important questions worthy of further study, and they compel the scholar to deal with conflicting facts and interpretations, thus preventing him or her from operating solely in a favored ideological comfort zone.

If this approach has merit, it should be especially valuable in analyzing the Reagan legacy. Reagan is often considered the most ideological president of the twentieth century. Both conservatives and liberals have powerful incentives to present their most incisive interpretations of the Reagan presidency to the public. For conservatives, Reagan was the first authentic adherent of their ideology to win the White House. He was their champion; he represented the movement; his success would validate their ideas; his failure might send them back to the fringes of the American political system. For liberals, Reagan was the conservative challenger to so much of what they believed in and had constructed since Franklin Roosevelt's New Deal. His success would undermine their intellectual foundations; his failure would validate their wisdom. Neither side had any difficulty in mobilizing its best ideological guns to fire away in support of or in derision of the Reagan presidency. This intellectual debate was also heightened by the self-consciousness brought about because the United States was entering its third century during the Reagan administration.

CONSERVATIVE EVALUATIONS

While most students of the Reagan presidency focus on his economic policy, some conservatives stress his moral leadership. Prior to the Reagan years, the modern conservative movement was largely identified with its vehement opposition to what it perceived as a liberalism that espoused a centralized, bureaucratic, secular, welfare-state philosophy. This liberal ideology, according to conservatives, was not promoting progress; it was cultivating individual moral decay and national decline. It was frustrating to conservatives that, even when Republicans such as Eisenhower, Nixon, and Ford were elected to the presidency, liberal policy trends continued to prevail. Conservatives were outraged that their passionately held beliefs were treated as reactionary by liberals and as childish by country-club, moderate Republicans. For conservatives, to hear their philosophy proudly proclaimed from the bully pulpit of the presidency by Ronald Reagan was exhilarating. Hence, conservatives praised Reagan "as the moral leader of a 'revolution' that was attempting to restore the values that had brought America greatness, reverse its decline, and reassert its mission in the world."[5]

The idea of Reagan as a moral leader has been developed in the writings of William Muir, a political scientist at the University of California at Berkeley and a former speechwriter for Vice President George Bush. Muir suggests that, whereas liberals like Richard Neustadt define presidential power as the ability to spur government to action, Reagan provided a moral leadership by reshaping the public philosophy that guides private and public behavior. For Muir, the key to the Reagan presidency was its rhetorical commitments. In Muir's words, "What was distinctive about the presidency of Ronald Reagan (1981–1989) was the centrality of its character-shaping purpose. It was organized to achieve a moral revolution—moral in the sense of affecting the animating ideas of the American people, a revolution in the sense of returning the nation to its intellectual starting point."[6]

For Muir, ideas count, and morally correct ideas count the most, because people have the ability to recognize the truth when they hear it. The presidency offers a unique and powerful forum to articulate moral truths. As president, according to Muir, Reagan extolled the moral advantages of the philosophy of freedom over the philosophy of equality. Muir declares that the central conflict in American politics has been the rivalry between liberty and equality. In that contest, Reagan was able to demonstrate verbally that the philosophy of equality led to a centralized and paternalistic state that squashed individuality.

Whereas liberals saw selfishness and crass materialism in Reagan's message, Muir suggested that human nature is divided between good and evil and that Reagan's message was that "the ethical measure of individual human worth was spiritual, signifying the victory within of good over evil; that a society organized around private exchange fortified the individual in his spiritual battle; that reciprocity provided countless compulsions to please others; and that a welfare society robbed individuals of the demands to reciprocate that fortified them in their inner battles with their worse side."[7] The conservative columnist George Will expressed a similar idea when he wrote that Reagan's "aim has been to restore the plain language of right and wrong, good and evil, for the purpose of enabling people to make the most of freedom."[8] By using such plain language, Reagan identified with the public; by avoiding such moral language, liberals distanced themselves from the way the public speaks.

According to Muir, the philosophy of freedom was the guiding force that directed the Reagan administration toward its major policy achievements. He writes, "The cuts in the federal budget, the domestic and international stabilization of the dollar, the reduction of income tax rates, 'revenue neutral' tax reform, the increase in voluntarism, the reforms in social policy, the emphasis on excellence in education combined with an insistence on infusing moral values into school curricula, the withdrawal of the central government from some of its former regulatory and fiscal responsibilities, the adherence to free trade and resistance to protectionism—all became part of the president's agenda because they reinforced his moral objectives of preparing Americans for the task of living free."[9]

The ever-optimistic Reagan believed that most individuals—and especially Americans—could meet the challenges of living free. With freedom, most citizens would choose to lead moral and productive lives. As a conservative populist, Reagan encouraged citizens to rely on themselves instead of becoming dependent on bureaucrats. One of the sources of Reagan's political strength and popularity was that he seemed to have more faith in people's abilities—not only their entrepreneurial talents but also their willingness to help one another—than liberals did.

By acting in accordance with his political beliefs, Reagan established himself as a conviction politician—that is, an elected official who actually believed what he was saying and doing. In several of his farewell speeches, the president stressed that "a revolution of ideas became a revolution of governance on January 20, 1981." In comparison to previous decades, the subject of policy debates during the 1980s changed from which federal programs should be launched or expanded to which ones could be cut and by how much. A *New York Times* reporter wrote in 1986, "If the President leaves a single legacy, it is that he appears to have almost totally eliminated for years to come any discussion of new social-welfare initiatives."[10] In his final *Economic Report,* Reagan claimed that his administration had reversed a fifty-year liberal trend of turning to the federal government for solutions to problems. Edwin J. Feulner, president of the Heritage Foundation, asserts that Reagan changed the political landscape in much the same way that Franklin Roosevelt did in the 1930s. Feulner writes, "Presidents leave lasting legacies by establishing new frameworks for public policy debates. Franklin D. Roosevelt's policies culminated with Lyndon B. Johnson's Great Society programs twenty-one years after FDR's death. The new framework that Mr. Reagan created has spawned a generation of new institutions staffed by young people who have abandoned the delusion of their counterparts in the 1960s. Just as the Roosevelt era gave way only seven years ago, the full flower of Ronald Reagan's era will come in the next century."[11] Conservatives are hopeful that the Reagan policy legacy will be reinforced by his appointments to the federal courts, who were carefully screened to assure their loyalty to the president's philosophy.

Conservatives were particularly proud of what the Reagan presidency was able to achieve economically. Edwin Meese, perhaps the leading conservative in the administration, stressed that "since the economic agenda was the centerpiece of the Reagan program, an accurate understanding of what it meant in terms of taxes, budgets, deficits, and other outcomes is essential to any judgment of the President's place in history. The economic program was the first matter the administration tackled, and it dominated discussion of domestic politics for years. It was the most consistently attacked and most ardently defended of all the President's initiatives."[12] Conservatives point out that the "misery index" (the unemployment rate plus the inflation rate) was 20.7 percent at the end of the Carter presidency and only half that figure by the close of the Reagan tenure. Reagan succeeded in getting Congress to pass the Economic Recovery Tax Act of 1981 and the Tax Reform Act of 1986, which together reduced the top federal marginal income tax rate to less than half the level that prevailed before he was elected. According to supply-side theory, reducing tax rates for all groups, and removing six million low-income families from the income tax rolls, strengthened incentives to work, save, and invest. The trough of the 1981–1982 recession, labeled the Carter recession by Reagan supporters, was reached in November 1982; it was followed by an economic expansion that lasted until July 1990. This period of economic growth lasted ninety-two months, more than twice the average length of expansion periods since World War II. By 1990, the gross national product (GNP) was 31 percent above the 1982 GNP in real, inflation-adjusted terms. Between 1982 and 1990, real disposable per capita income increased by 18 percent, and the economy added 18.4 million jobs.[13] In brief, for many conservatives, the key element of Reagan's leadership was the success of his economic policies in overcoming the stagflation of the 1970s and in providing the formula for sustainable economic growth.

From the conservative point of view, the Reagan years were a period in which the rich got richer and the poor got richer. They frequently quoted John Kennedy's metaphor that a rising economic tide lifts all boats. A tripling of the Dow Jones to 3,000 and a drop in interest rates by two-thirds produced jobs and benefits for the many, not just the few. In response to liberal charges about the "unfairness" of the Reagan tax cuts, conservatives such as Republican Bill Archer point out that, in 1981, the wealthiest 5 percent of Americans accounted for 35 percent of total tax receipts; by 1988, that figure had climbed to 46 percent. During the same period, the proportion of tax revenue contributed by the lower half of American earners dropped from 8 percent to 6 percent.[14]

In short, from the conservative viewpoint, Reagan delivered a prosperity that left citizens better off. Moreover, despite complaints from liberals, the Reagan prosperity of the 1980s was neither unfair nor based on greed.

For many conservatives, Reagan's defense policy was as important and successful as his economic policy. They believe that the combination of Reagan's moral crusade against the "evil empire" of communism and his huge defense buildups led to the victory of the United States in the Cold War. Reagan's moral leadership and his willingness to expand and to use military power brought about the dismemberment of the Soviet Union and the collapse of the idea of communism as an attractive alternative to democracy and capitalism.

In 1980, it certainly did not look as if the United States would win the Cold War by 1990. Indeed, during the 1970s, conservatives were arguing that the United States was in grave danger of losing the superpower struggle with the Soviet Union. While the Soviets were rapidly expanding their military capabilities and confidently proclaiming the historical inevitability of worldwide communism, the United States, weakened by its self-imposed defeat in South Vietnam, was no longer articulating its moral superiority over communism; nor was it matching the Soviet military expansion. Instead, America's foreign policy was based on the appeasement-type policy of détente, which succeeded only in restraining the United States from protecting its vital interests. During the 1970s, the Soviets expanded their influence into Afghanistan, Angola, Cambodia, Ethiopia, Grenada, Laos, Mozambique, Nicaragua, South Vietnam, and South Yemen. The United States, according to conservatives, was blocked from vigorously responding to these Soviet moves because of post-Vietnam psychosis and cuts in the military budgets.

All that changed when Reagan was elected. R. Emmett Tyrrell compares Reagan's "epochal" foreign policy achievements with Franklin Roosevelt's. Whereas Roosevelt's presidency overcame America's tradition of isolationism, the Reagan presidency broke the post-Vietnam paralysis of neoisolationism.[15] That break was largely reflected in the priority given to defense buildup as the Reagan administration channeled $2 trillion into the Pentagon. Reagan's belief in the moral righteousness of the United States encouraged him to use our military and intelligence capabilities to combat communism in Afghanistan, Angola, Grenada, El Salvador, Nicaragua, and Libya (Lebanon is usually left off the list). His opposition to the deterrent strategy of mutually assured destruction (MAD) and his faith in U.S. technology led him to promote the

Strategic Defense Initiative of 1983 that eventually induced the Russians to accept significant arms reduction agreements. His reputation as a staunch anti-communist provided him with the freedom to negotiate a new and more meaningful détente with the Soviet Union. No paradox of the Reagan presidency is greater than the fact that Reagan, who assumed office as a bitter critic of previous efforts to negotiate agreements with the Soviet Union, left office having had more summit meetings with his Soviet counterpart than any previous president.[16] When Reagan stepped down in January 1989, *U.S. News and World Report* wrote, "in one of history's exquisite ironies, it was a cautious new détente with what he had once called the 'evil empire' that became a linchpin of the Reagan legacy."[17]

Conservatives are outraged by what they consider the deliberate distortion of the Reagan presidency by the cultural elites in America. Since Reagan left office, the number of books and articles negatively evaluating his presidency has far outweighed the few that have presented a positive view. This led William Randolph Hearst, Jr., the owner of a large newspaper chain, to write in 1991, "I have a strong hunch that a systematic and high-powered campaign to discredit Ronald Reagan's record as president is currently in full swing. Having twice failed to prevent his election by overwhelming margins—as well as the election of his chosen successor—liberal intellectuals and academics, I suspect, set out to rewrite the history of the Reagan years and debunk his achievements in domestic and foreign affairs."[18] At the 1992 Republican convention in Houston, many conservatives distributed posters that pictured a 1940s movie photo of Reagan about to be hung by what the poster called "The Liberal/Media Lynch Mob." Conservatives claim that the decline of Reagan's popularity is due to the deliberate lies of such liberal authors as Lou Cannon, Bob Schieffer, Laurence Barrett, Sidney Blumenthal, and Haynes Johnson, who have worked to change the public perception of the 1980s from a decade of economic growth to a decade of illusion and greed.

This liberal campaign against the Reagan presidency, according to conservatives, is motivated by the fact that Reagan's ideas, policies, and successes constitute a lethal threat to the self-esteem of liberals. Reagan shocked the liberal establishment by accusing it of being elitist and antipatriotic, by demonstrating that his populist brand of conservatism could attract many young and working-class voters, by confirming that God was not dead among American voters, and by illustrating that an old conservative could rejuvenate the office of the presidency.

The strongest attack on alleged media bias against the Reagan presidency was launched by Edwin Meese, who wrote that

those with a different agenda—more governmental authority over people and institutions, greater centralized power in the federal government,
and therefore higher taxes—have attempted to distort history and substitute their own mythology for what actually happened during the Reagan Presidency. These people have tried to lessen the significance of their
defeat by decrying the "decade of greed" (although private philanthropy
and volunteer service rose to unprecedented heights) and the politics of
"envy" and class warfare (although all segments of the economy benefitted from the Reagan growth policies), and by criticizing the Reagan
defense buildup as costly and unnecessary (although it caused the collapse of communism and enabled the United States and our allies to
sweep to victory in the Persian Gulf War). The purpose of these revi-
sionist pundits is to erase from public memory the achievements and the
lessons of the Reagan years, and to fill the ensuing vacuum with the policies and practices of the 1970s—which caused the very problems that
Reagan erased. . . . The apostles of negativism are seeking to disparage
the Reagan record of the 1980s in order to deceive future generations.[19]

Conservatives recognize that the stakes of this interpretive conflict are high.
The battle over the Reagan legacy is really a struggle to determine America's
future. If the Reagan administration is perceived by the public as being successful, that increases the possibility of new conservative leaders inheriting
Reagan's mantle and continuing his policies into the next century.

Although conservatives desperately want to promote a positive perception
of the Reagan presidency, this has not prevented them from voicing selective
criticism against what they believe were his administration's failures. When
Reagan left office, several conservatives noted that, for all the talk about the
Reagan revolution, the New Deal and most of the Great Society were still
largely intact, and little of the Religious Right's social agenda—such as restricting abortion and allowing prayer in the schools—had been enacted into law.
In trying to explain why the administration failed to legislate so much of its
agenda, some conservatives blame Reagan's pragmatic political appointees,
such as James Baker and Richard Darman, who conspired to prevent the president from being his true conservative self. Others blame Reagan himself,
whom they accuse of being more concerned with maintaining his own popularity than with working hard and fighting for conservative causes. Com-
bining both criticisms, David Boaz from the Cato Institute writes, "President
Reagan's detachment from the process of governing may explain the disjointed
policies of his administration and the gulf between rhetoric and reality. Some
of his appointees successfully carved out the policies widely believed to be his;

others ignored them or pursued policies that were clearly antithetical to them. But the successes are almost random rather than the result of a careful presidential attention to the agencies or policies involved."[20]

George Will attributed the absence of fundamental policy changes during the 1980s not to Reagan's lack of personal commitment to fight for conservative causes but to the constraints of public opinion. In Will's words, "The Reagan years have involved a rolling referendum on government. The results are clear, and they are not what conservatives wanted. Americans want lower taxes and a high level of services. Big surprise. Big deficit. The deficit is the numerical expression of a cultural phenomenon—the American determination to live beyond our means, to consume more than we produce."[21]

Other conservative writers criticized Reagan for not doing enough to institutionalize conservative thinking in American society. While praising his conservative judicial appointments, they were angry that the president did nothing to ensure that a committed conservative would succeed him in the White House. Most members of the conservative movement considered George Bush a country-club Republican who would inevitably compromise and betray their principles—and from the conservative perspective, that is precisely what Bush did in 1990 when he accepted an increase in taxes. The conservative fear is that much of what Reagan accomplished will be undone by a Democratic president working with a Democratic-controlled Congress, thereby reducing the significance of the 1980s to the "Reagan Interlude."[22] Under those circumstances, the Reagan presidency will have been only an aberration, a period when the growth of the liberal welfare state was merely slowed down.

Thus, in 1987, Paul Weyrich, president of the Free Congress Foundation, argued that Reagan had not produced the lasting change that Franklin Roosevelt, or even Margaret Thatcher, had been able to bring about. In Weyrich's opinion,

> When Roosevelt governed, he created a power base for his politics that endured long after his death. He forged a coalition that lasted more than 50 years by creating programs [such as Social Security] that in turn created new constituencies for the liberals. . . . Mrs. Thatcher's privatization programs created new constituencies for her conservative party. Slum dwellers living in public housing suddenly became Conservative voters when they were allowed to purchase their own apartments and actually own them. . . . By contrast, President Reagan's policies have created no new conservative constituencies. On the contrary, the same old liberal establishment is in place, just waiting for the election of the next Democratic President.[23]

R. Emmett Tyrrell argues that another reason conservatives failed to con-
solidate their gains was Reagan's unwillingness or inability to create a conservative counterculture to challenge the prevailing liberal Zeitgeist. Given
Reagan's background in radio, movies, and television, it is surprising that he
did not do more, according to Tyrrell, to institutionalize conservative thinking in the media, as Franklin Roosevelt and John Kennedy had. Tyrrell stresses
that politics is waged in the culture (books, movies, television) as well as at
the polls. At the end of the Reagan years, universities, the arts, and the media
were as dominated by the liberal perspective as they had been before Reagan
took office. Whereas New Deal and New Frontier themes were reinforced by
the media, Reagan did nothing to counteract the influence of Dan Rather and
Oliver Stone.[24]

A few conservatives also criticize Reagan for not doing more to control rising budget deficits. Whereas many Reagan supporters accept the administration position that the budget deficits and soaring national debt were solely
Congress's fault, others concede that Reagan must share a major portion of
that responsibility. William Safire suggests that Reagan refused to spend the
political capital necessary to cut domestic spending in order to finance his
defense buildup. Safire writes, "like Lyndon Johnson, but on a grander scale,
[Reagan] preferred red ink to a hard choice between guns and butter. A
Democratic Congress shares the blame, but the Reagan refusal to reduce the
rate of spending increase burdened the coming generation with a whopping
cost of debt service."[25] Similarly, George Will points out that even if Congress
had accepted each of the Reagan budget proposals beginning in 1982, the
aggregate deficits would have been only $90 billion less than the actual
increase in the national debt during these years, which totaled over $1.1 tril-
lion. Will concluded that Reagan "presided over a debilitating feast as the
nation has eaten much of its seed corn."[26]

Still, Safire predicts that realistic historians will judge Reagan as a "near-
great first term President who tired and faded in the stretch." Safire criticized
Reagan for the issueless 1984 presidential campaign, for increasingly distanc-
ing himself from decision making, for harboring "a soft-hearted self-delusion
that hostages could be ransomed with arms and nobody would notice," and
for a late fixation on the imagery of peacemaking to ensure his "place in history."[27] Like many conservatives who were shocked to see Reagan embracing
Mikhail Gorbachev and kissing babies outside the Kremlin, Safire feared that
Gorbachev had duped an aging Reagan—who seemingly felt compelled to
make progress toward peace in order to warrant a favorable historical evaluation. Using a biting conservative analogy, Safire wrote, "In Mr. Reagan's late
life-crisis, personality swallowed policy. Like the failing Roosevelt with 'Uncle

Joe' at Yalta, the American president saw himself and his Soviet counterpart as individuals of personal charm and power able to leap historical chasms, rather than as temporary leaders of antithetical movements able to make adjustments to lessen tension."[28] Thus, by the end of Reagan's second term, some conservatives felt that the president had become a threat to the nation's national security.

LIBERAL EVALUATIONS

Future historians will probably find it ironic that liberals had such difficulty taking Ronald Reagan seriously. Although Reagan proved to be a far greater threat to liberalism than Senators Robert Taft, Joseph McCarthy, and Barry Goldwater, liberals continually underestimated him. Their most frequent response to Reagan was ridicule. Clark Clifford allegedly called Reagan an "amiable dunce." Jokes about Reagan's ignorance, factual errors, laziness, and beliefs in myths and astrology proliferated during the 1980s but did little to reduce the president's popularity. Indeed, Reagan frequently (and cleverly) co-opted this humor to his own advantage. What liberals did not understand was that, by jeering Reagan, they were alienating voters and lowering expectations of what such a lazy, ill informed actor could possibly achieve. No politician ever gained more mileage from merely avoiding catastrophe than did Ronald Reagan.

For the liberal historian Arthur Schlesinger, Jr., Ronald Reagan's political success can be partially explained by the cycles of American history. The 1980s were analogous to other decades characterized by private concerns—the 1920s and 1950s—destined to be succeeded by periods in which a greater interest in public purposes prevailed.[29] Reagan's rhetoric about the individual pursuit of private wealth and his dismissal of governmental efforts to promote the collective welfare were compatible with the conservative temper of the cycle. Whereas Reagan's message sounded idealistic to conservatives, it sounded "mean-spirited" to liberals. According to Irving Howe, the editor of *Dissent,* "the dominant ethic of individual selfishness would be collective beneficence. . . . The ideological right kept shrilling that nothing good could come from government, and did its best to prove it."[30]

When Garry Wills reviewed Reagan's memoirs, he ridiculed the president's unreflective accounts of his White House experiences by describing him as "Mr. Magoo"—the kindly, bumbling, nearsighted cartoon character. According to Wills, "Mr. Magoo, blind and optimistic, loudly describes the happy things going on around him while the viewer sees him surrounded by perils, destruction, and violence. So while Reagan fondly described this period as one continual sequence of virtuous acts, businesses were taking corruption in defense contracts to spectacular new heights, robbing the H.U.D. treasury, and using government-backed saving and loan banks as their private kitties."[31] But Reagan, like Mr. Magoo, neither saw nor acknowledged the damage he caused.

Liberal pressure-group leaders pointed out what they saw as damage left in the wake of the Reagan presidency. They claimed that he had the worst record among modern presidents in the fields of civil rights, the environment, and concern for social justice.[32] For many liberals, the increase in homelessness was as potent a symbol of the Reagan presidency as the Hoovervilles were of the Hoover presidency.

After observing Reagan for a number of years, Robert Wright, a political analyst for the *New Republic,* presented his final thoughts on the departing president in January 1989. Wright doubted that any future historians would uncover Reagan's "hidden-hand" political skills in the way Professor Fred Greenstein did for President Eisenhower. While both chief executives delegated a considerable amount of authority, "in Eisenhower's case, the president did the delegating. In Reagan's case, tasks are delegated *to* him—tasks like going to the Kennedy Center." Moreover, according to Wright, whereas Eisenhower determined the direction of his administration, "the Reagan administration was, in the final years, an ongoing struggle among advisors for the soul of a man who was virtually brain dead. The fact that things worked out no worse than they did is either a tribute to the institutional sturdiness of the presidency or proof of the existence of God."[33]

Wright concludes that it is absurd to debate the Reagan legacy, because the president has no legacy in the traditional sense of the term. "The . . . 'Reagan Legacy,' " according to Wright, "implies that the consequences of this administration's actions can meaningfully be attributed to Reagan; that within his brain have resided coherent policy strategies that have succeeded (or failed) by virtue of their correspondence to (or inconsistency with) the real world."[34] But in Wright's view, there were no coherent policy strategies in Reagan's brain; nor did his mind have any understanding of the real world. Wright denies Reagan a legacy because this detached and ignorant president was not personally directing anything; he was not aware of what his administration was doing; nor was he cognizant of the consequences of his administration's behavior.

However, most liberal observers believe that Reagan did have a legacy, and they agree with conservatives that its most important effect was on the economy. From the liberal point of view, Reagan's economic policies provided a false prosperity in the 1980s and presaged a decade of reckoning in the 1990s. The good times of the 1980s were fueled by consumer spending and debt designed for immediate gratification at the expense of the future—party now, pay later. Reagan's political success was based on the unsustainable economic policy of overborrowing and underinvesting.

While Reaganites claim that, beginning in 1983, their supply-side tax cuts launched the country's longest peacetime expansion, liberals counter that this period of growth was powered by the defense buildup and accompanying deficits in a Keynesian manner—that is, aggregate demand was stimulated. As for the seventeen million new jobs created during the Reagan administration, liberals argue that these new jobs were the result of so many baby boomers entering the labor force and so many wives compelled to work outside the home in order to supplement their husbands' stagnating income.[35]

During the Reagan presidency, the United States' national debt increased from $914 billion to $2.6 trillion. The total national debt accumulated under the nation's first thirty-nine presidents more than doubled under its fortieth, Ronald Reagan. When Reagan was inaugurated, it cost us $71 billion a year to service the national debt; when he left office, debt service had soared to over $150 billion annually. This increase in debt service more than offset the savings achieved by the 1981 cuts in social expenditures. Liberals assert that Reagan's tax cuts and his defense buildup were largely responsible for this fiscal insanity, which will inevitably reduce the living standards of this generation's children.

In addition, liberals claim that the Reagan budget deficits were both qualitatively and quantitatively different from those of earlier years. In qualitative terms, the Reagan deficits financed operational expenses, which "left a smaller share to fund the investments, from education to airport construction, that are essential to future economic growth."[36] The lack of public investment meant that part of Reagan's legacy was a "silent rot," as so much of our public infrastructure deteriorated during the 1980s. From a quantitative point of view, the Reagan deficits amounted to a larger proportion of the nation's GNP than ever before in peacetime. The liberal economist Benjamin Friedman writes, "On average since 1980 the federal government's borrowing has absorbed nearly three-fourths of all net saving done by American families and businesses combined. As a result, the share of the nation's income devoted to net investment in new plants and equipment has been lower than at any time since World War II."[37] The largest creditor of the federal debt has been the Social Security trust fund, which by 1992 had used its surplus funds to purchase nearly $1 trillion in U.S. Treasury bonds—thus mortgaging the future benefits of retired citizens to fund the current operations of the U.S. government.[38] Finally, much of this debt is held by foreigners; paying it off will also contribute to lowering our living standards in the near future.

Liberals have pounced on the supreme irony that the architects of Reaganomics created what they feared most—the Keynesian Frankenstein of large and permanent budget deficits. These deficits allowed us to enjoy a self-indulgent prosperity for a short period. Writing during the 1991 recession, one liberal columnist characterized the economic growth of the 1980s as "a drug-induced high, and the drug was debt. We looted this country's past prosperity, mortgaged its future and gloried in the accomplishment." But after the borrowing binge, "it is the Morning After in America. Let the hangover begin."[39] Whereas Reagan inherited an inflation-battered economy from President Carter, he left as his legacy a deficit-burdened economy for President Bush.

A few liberals "solve" the riddle of Reagan's fiscal irresponsibility with a conspiracy theory—namely that, after 1982, budget deficits were a deliberate policy of the administration. This interpretation was first put forward in 1983 by Democratic Senator Daniel Patrick Moynihan, who argued that Reagan's advisers had a hidden agenda—to place a lid on the growth of the welfare state. That lid would be strengthened by massive budget deficits and the mobilization of the nation's citizens as an overpowering bloc vote against any increase in taxes.[40] Politically, this strategy placed the Democrats in a box throughout the 1980s. Thus, there may have been method to Reagan's fiscal madness.

The liberals' most passionate accusation against Reagan is that his policies increased the problem of inequality in America. Liberals claim that Reagan championed the value of individual liberty while neglecting the value of equality. Such an ethos bred a hospitable environment for the likes of Ivan Boesky and Michael Milken, but not for millions of poor children. Many liberals believe that Reagan's legacy of neglecting or even encouraging inequality will be more difficult and painful to overcome than his budget deficits. Just as the federal government cannot continue to incur large budget deficits without eventually paying an enormous economic price in terms of declining living standards, the nation cannot allow inequality to condemn perhaps as much as a third of its citizens to a life of hopeless despair without inevitably paying a painful price in terms of untrainable workers, crime, violence, and instability. Increasing inequality is politically unsustainable.

As David Broder wrote, "History will not deal kindly with the [Reagan] administration's deliberate efforts to slow down or reverse the two previous decades of steady progress in reducing poverty and discrimination. It is not just Ed Meese and Brad Reynolds pushing Justice Department lawyers into court battles to reopen settled issues of civil rights enforcement. It was Reagan himself signaling moral indifference to the struggle for equality."[41] Similarly, Jesse Jackson pointed out in January 1989 that, during the eight years of the Reagan presidency, "The gap between the haves and have nots has widened. We have witnessed the most economic polarization in our history. . . . Our glitter is brighter, but our foundation is weaker."[42] A Democratic congressman charged that "the President, by expressing no sympathy for the disadvantaged yet cutting tax rates for the affluent by nearly two-thirds, followed a career path that was the reverse image of Franklin D. Roosevelt's: While FDR was born rich and grew to be a tribune for the underdog, Mr. Reagan was born poor and grew up to champion the rich."[43] Following the bloody aftermath of the Rodney King case in 1992, Leonard Silk wrote, "The Los Angeles riots should serve as a reminder that economic growth is no cure-all. America's problems of race and poverty, crime and family disintegration festered and worsened during the Reagan years of growth. These problems cannot be solved by trickle-down economics but will need to be addressed directly. . . . Most important of all is a heightened national concern for those left behind by national economic progress, and a recognition that progress will cease and give way to anger, despair and retrogression unless the nation acts to repair the growing split between rich and poor, white and black."[44]

Liberals have accumulated a mountain of statistics attempting to prove that the majority of Americans were not—to paraphrase Reagan's 1980 challenge to President Carter—better off as a result of Reagan's policies. Benjamin Friedman points out, for example, that in 1983, the first year of the Reagan recovery from the 1981–1982 recession, the average worker in business earned $281 per week. By 1990, the average worker was receiving just $267 per week in 1983 dollars. However, while the chief executive officers of the nation's 300 largest companies made an average of twenty nine times what the typical manufacturing worker made in 1980, by 1990, the multiple was ninety-three to one.[45]

To the dismay of Reagan supporters, liberals have succeeded in conveying their image of the 1980s to the public, creating a heightened sense of middle-class grievance and helping Governor Bill Clinton win the 1992 presidential election. That image is based on the liberal view that the Reagan administration practiced trickle-down economics in which the emphasis was on extending privileges to the already privileged while the middle class endured rising taxes and stagnating income. In a January 1992 *New York Times*–CBS poll, when asked who had suffered most from the policies of the federal government in the past ten years, 46 percent said the poor and 43 percent said the middle class. When asked who had received the most benefits, 82 percent said the rich.[46]

Toward the end of the Reagan presidency, liberals raised a new accusation—that Reagan's policies were contributing to the decline of the United States. There was great irony in this charge, because Reagan had been elected in 1980

promising to revive the nation's will and power in its superpower confrontation with the Soviet Union. By the end of the decade, it was clear that the
Soviet Union was a declining power—indeed, by 1991 it ceased to exist. While
conservatives claim that our Cold War victory was largely a function of Reagan's defense buildup and his moral crusade of declaring the superiority of
capitalism and democracy over communism, liberals respond that the breakdown of communism was not the result of Reagan's Pentagon spending $600
for toilet seats but was largely due to communism's own internal contradictions, which were finally allowed to publicly manifest themselves because of
the reforms instituted by Mikhail Gorbachev. From the liberal point of view,
Reagan was merely lucky that Gorbachev came to power in 1985. In the
words of one liberal columnist, "If he [Reagan] was dumb, superstitious,
childish, inattentive, passive, narcissistic, and oblivious, how come he won the
cold war? . . . The answer . . . is Mikhail Gorbachev. Reagan, always lucky, was
never luckier than to find himself president at just the moment when a Soviet
leader decided to lift the pall of fear and lies from his empire, thus permitting
the system's accumulated absurdities and contradictions to come into plain
view and to shake it to pieces."[47]

While liberals argued that Reagan should not be given any credit for the
United States' victory in the Cold War, they blamed him and his policies for
handicapping our nation in its attempt to compete successfully with a rising
number of trading states in the emerging global economy. According to liberals, by focusing on the Cold War, Reagan failed a major test of leadership—
he did not foresee that the country's economic security would increasingly be
determined by its ability to match the export capabilities of countries such as
Japan and Germany. The United States was not able to meet the challenges
of the new international system that was replacing the Cold War system
because its levels of savings and investments were considerably below those
of rival trading countries. Unlike the research and development policies of
Japan and Germany, most of the public research and development investments
in the United States were directed at increasing military strength, not at
enhancing commercial competitiveness. And because of the continuing decline
of America's public education system, a large proportion of its potential labor
force was woefully unprepared to fill the types of jobs opening up in a modern
economy confronting global competition.[48]

During the 1980s, the United States had high interest rates because its savings rate was so low and the federal government was running such large budget deficits. High interest rates caused the value of the dollar to rise, which
contributed to a mounting trade deficit as U.S. exports became more expensive and foreign imports became cheaper. In 1987, the U.S. trade deficit

peaked (for the 1980s) at $152.13 billion. That same year, we suffered a negative trade balance with Japan of $52.09 billion. The liberal economist Charles Schultze pointed out that "At the end of 1982, the United States was a net creditor abroad in the amount of $260 billion; by the end of 1990, America was a net debtor to the tune of $360 billion."[49] Arthur Schlesinger concurred: "The United States under Ronald Reagan has lived considerably beyond its means—an indulgence made possible by the influx of capital into the American economy. In half a dozen years he marvelously succeeded in transforming the United States from the world's largest creditor to the world's largest debtor. . . . Reaganomics has left the republic, in Felix Rohatyn's words, 'a first-rate military power and a second-rate economic power.' "[50] In January 1989, liberal columnist Robert Wright suggested that the best metaphor to describe the effect of Reagan's policies was a "national anabolic steroid." In Wright's words, "He [Reagan] inherited a country subdued by stagflation and frightened by Vietnam, and left it economically and militarily virile. Unfortunately, steroids . . . have side effects, and already our national testicles are starting to shrink: not only are the Reagan budget deficits beginning to emasculate the Pentagon—they are also undermining our long-term economic health, which as Eisenhower stressed, is the foundation of national security."[51]

Liberals are frequently astounded when conservatives praise Reagan as an inspiring moral leader. For many liberals, Reagan was a hypocritical politician who preached morality but practiced sleaze, who championed traditional family values but was distant from his own children, and who extolled religion but believed in astrology and did not attend church. Liberals do not see any moral model in a politician who, while cutting the tax rates for the very rich, suggested that ketchup could fulfill the vegetable requirement in the school lunch program.

For an administration ostensibly committed to the traditional values of law and order, the record of the Reagan presidency was not inspiring. During the 1980s, over 110 Reagan political appointees were accused or convicted of unethical or illegal conduct. There were major scandals involving the Justice Department, the Department of Housing and Urban Development, the Environmental Protection Agency, defense contractors, the regulation of the savings and loan associations, and, of course, the White House itself in the Iran-Contra affair. By the end of the Reagan presidency, Attorney General Edwin Meese—deeply implicated in the Wedtech scandal—was spending more time as a potential defendant than as a prosecutor. Hodding Carter charged that "wretched is the only word to use for the petty thieves, moral midgets, and grand poltroons who pockmarked the administration from beginning to end. . . . Indictments, convictions, forced resignations, slippery evasions, and a general contempt for the rule of law were hallmarks of the Reagan years. Not since Warren Harding had so many federal officials so thoroughly ignored the admonition that public service is a public trust."[52]

The Democrats never succeeded in tying Reagan personally to this corruption, a fact that enhanced his reputation as the Teflon president. But it seems evident that scholars will hold Reagan to a higher standard than the public did concerning the improprieties perpetrated by his political appointees. A president takes an oath "to take care" that the laws be faithfully executed. It appears that Reagan was extremely lax in this regard.

By heaping so much ridicule on Reagan, liberals have created a paradoxical problem for themselves: how can they account for Reagan's political success? Liberals answer that question in several ways. One particularly weak argument is that Reagan was successful because he was lucky. The element of luck can hardly be relied on to explain why Reagan was elected governor of California and president of the United States. A second response is to account for Reagan's success in terms of the capabilities of other officials. Thus, James Baker was responsible for early achievements in 1981; David Stockman negotiated the cuts in the federal budget; Paul Volcker lowered the inflation rate; George Shultz negotiated the INF Treaty with the Soviet Union; and Mikhail Gorbachev caused the collapse of communism. From this perspective, Reagan was merely an ignorant bystander to everything that was achieved in his administration. This argument is also not likely to hold up under scrutiny.

The third and most persistent liberal explanation is that Reagan's political success was based on the outstanding public relations capabilities of the White House. Under the guidance of public relations experts such as Michael Deaver, David Gergen, and Roger Ailes, the White House understood how to exploit Reagan's acting skills and amiable personality to maintain his popularity. Two scholars concluded that "no president in modern history has so effectively managed the media as Ronald Reagan."[53] As an actor—it was a mistake to call Reagan an ex-actor—the president was an excellent master of national ceremonies. The White House became a theater and propaganda machine where symbols and images were more important than substance. Reagan's popularity was maintained as an end in itself, at the expense of dealing realistically with painful problems such as the budget deficit and the savings and loan crisis.

After thinking about the public's acceptance of illusions during the 1980s, Maureen Dowd wrote, "In many ways, Ronald Reagan is more interesting as a phenomenon than an individual, more for what he says about us than what he says about himself. To what extent do we prefer myth to reality, the comfort of strong convictions at the expense of facts? To what degree do we become complicit in believing black is white, if we are emotionally attached to a politician who tells us it is so? Do we crave a king who is beyond criticism and oblivious to it?"[54]

Hence, from the liberal point of view, Reagan's political success was largely built on the illusions created by the public relations practitioners of the Deaverized White House. Reagan might believe his illusions, and highly skilled public relations officials might keep the president popular by filling media space with flags and balloons, but these assets would not solve any of the hard problems of the period. Indeed, the ascendancy of public relations advisers had the effect of increasing the tendency to avoid confronting issues that would threaten the president's popularity. With the strategies of campaign thinking pervading the Reagan White House, governing became as trivialized as elections have become. Reagan's political success in relying on campaign-style thinking meant that the United States became less capable of confronting, debating, and resolving major problems.[55]

Because, according to liberals, Reagan was so dependent on illusion, once he left the White House, the process of deglamorization was rapid. The decline in Reagan's popularity since 1989 has not been due to liberal bias, but has been the result of reality finally—in the absence of the White House fog machine—peeping through illusionary mists and registering on the national conscience. Reagan has mockingly been compared with the Wizard of Oz, with the numerous kiss-and-tell memoirs performing the function of Toto pulling the curtain aside and revealing a bumbling old man. Haynes Johnson described the growing disillusionment with the Reagan presidency in these words:

> Some people, in retrospect, would conclude that they had been had. Reagan, the wizard, had deceived them. The pictures he had painted for the country had taken on a life of their own; they had replaced reality. It was the *pictures* they had believed in. . . . Now Reagan would be gone and people were left with the memory of how he had made them feel better. His departure was like the end of a fireworks display when the colors and trails and sparks fade, leaving nothing but a dark sky.[56]

For all the ridicule liberals have directed at Reagan, there have also been some begrudging positive evaluations of his administration. First, some liberals have conceded that Reagan restored the authority of the presidency. After a series of failed presidencies, the job was beginning to be perceived as impossible, beyond the capabilities of any mortal. Reagan demonstrated that the roles of the office were manageable and that a person could even have some fun fulfilling them. *Time* magazine's Laurence Barrett wrote, "Reagan's four immediate predecessors presided over a frightening decline in presidential authority. Neither Lyndon Johnson, Richard Nixon, Gerald Ford, nor Jimmy Carter could manage two full terms. . . . Yet Reagan not only arrested the presidency's slide, he reversed it."[57] Lou Cannon concurred in his judgment and wryly noted, "The great irony about Reagan, who has spent much of his life trashing government, is that he made people feel better about their government and better about the presidency."[58]

Second, some liberals have developed a greater appreciation of Reagan's leadership skills. They recognize that, in both domestic and foreign policy, Reagan demonstrated that he was one of those rare conviction politicians who knew when and how to compromise. It was also obvious that Reagan had dominated the national agenda during the 1980s. Hodding Carter suggested that, "for a reputedly passive man, he had a more pervasive impact on the country than anyone since Franklin D. Roosevelt."[59] Arthur Schlesinger claimed that "Reagan is the triumph of a man who earnestly believed in something. . . . He went up and down the country expounding his gospel, and eventually the cycle turned from public purpose to private purpose, and it was his time. I don't think it was a triumph of packaging; it was a triumph of commitment. . . . I think Reagan is proof of the power of conviction politics."[60] In brief, some liberals have challenged the self-serving liberal explanation that Reagan's political success was solely, or mainly, a function of his public relations staff's being able to market his acting skills.

Similarly, some liberals have recognized weaknesses in the argument that Reagan's achievements can be explained solely, or mainly, by the capabilities of his subordinates. In response to this assertion, Robert Samuelson skeptically asks, "how did such a dopey president (tolerant of 'cronyism' and 'sleaze') manage to have so many competent subordinates? And if the president was merely manipulated by his subordinates, how was it that he repeatedly ignored their advice in many areas—the budget deficits being the best example?"[61] Samuelson's questions suggest that Reagan may have had some unique and effective administrative skills that were not understood. Maybe Reagan wasn't dopey; perhaps instead of being manipulated by his staff, Reagan was using them to achieve his political purposes.

Finally, some liberals are willing to entertain the idea that Reagan deserves more credit for contributing to the United States' victory in the Cold War. Since the late 1960s, liberals have become inhibited in their willingness to defend vigorously the national security interests of the United States because of painful memories of Vietnam. Reagan was able to employ force effectively in such places as Libya, Grenada, and Afghanistan without getting bogged down in no-win quagmires, which was extremely important for the self-confidence of U.S. foreign policy makers. In the words of Stuart Eizenstat, a former Carter aide, "the sense that America was paralyzed in projecting its power after Vietnam was ended by Reagan. . . . Future Administrations will no longer be inhibited by Vietnam; future Administrations will have more leeway in projecting United States economic and military power without running into the constant argument of Vietnam."[62]

There is a good possibility that the rigid Soviet system was no longer capable of responding effectively to the vigorous challenge offered by the Reagan administration. Of course, the president was fortunate that Gorbachev came to power in 1985, but Reagan was intelligent enough to take advantage of the opportunities opened by the new Soviet leader. Reagan was also brave enough to risk alienating his conservative supporters by believing that he could do business with the new leader of the "evil empire." Reagan was never the warmonger that liberals feared he was; indeed, he was far more committed to peace and ending the threat of nuclear war than liberals could have imagined.[63]

CONCLUSION

The premise of this chapter has been that an ideological presidency like Reagan's would elicit the best polemical efforts of the best conservative and liberal writers. Such efforts would frequently be inaccurate because partisanship often distorts judgment. However, each set of writers may be providing us with grains of truth and insight. Most importantly, by comparing conservative and liberal evaluations, we can frame the major issues of the Reagan presidency, thus setting up a more scholarly analysis of these issues in upcoming chapters.

Conservatives and liberals disagree fundamentally about what kind of person Reagan was and what kind of political leadership he provided. Scholars should be open to the notion that Reagan's personality and intelligence may be more enigmatic than the simplified caricatures that conservatives and liberals have drawn. The important questions are: How did Reagan's personality affect his political behavior? What kind of political leader was he? What was the nature of his administration style? Where and why did it work successfully? Where and why did it fail? Was Reagan "used" by his staff, or did he use them? Why was the liberal opposition to Reagan's political challenge so ineffectual during the 1980s?

Both sides agree that economic policy was the strategic priority of the Reagan presidency and that a valid evaluation of Reagan's political leadership should focus on this subject. Since Reagan came into office largely because of the stagflation in the late 1970s, he should be judged mainly on the ability of his economic program to produce positive results. The questions that need to be addressed are: What were the economic consequences of the Reagan presidency? Who was responsible for the soaring budget deficits of the 1980s? Did some officials in the Reagan administration have a political purpose—a hidden agenda—in deliberately running up large budget deficits in order to stifle any new liberal policy initiatives? Who benefited from the economic growth of the 1980s? Did economic and social inequality increase because of Reagan's policies?

Although both sides agree that Reagan was conservative, our understanding of his presidency may be helped if we analyze his ideological predispositions more carefully. Was Reagan really a conservative? And since there are a variety of conservatives, what kind of conservative was he? Was Reagan more of a populist than a conservative? Did Reagan's inclinations as a performer seeking applause dilute his conservative orientation? How committed was he to the policy proposals of different types of conservatives?

Whereas Reagan and his supporters claimed during his administration that the United States was standing taller because of his policies, liberals asserted that the country was declining because of them. The big questions generated by this debate are: Did Reagan's policies renew the United States' will and power, or did they hasten the decline of the nation? Did his policies inhibit the United States' ability to compete successfully in the post–Cold War international system of trading states?

These are only a few of the many questions that can be generated by trying to evaluate the Reagan presidency, and scholars should be open to the proposition that Reagan had, like all modern presidents, multiple and conflicting legacies. Moreover, the 1980s were, in Lou Cannon's phrase, "a period of national renewal and national excess."[64] Where conservatives see idealism, liberals see greed. Where conservatives see visionary leadership, liberals see blind stupidity. Where conservatives see economic growth, liberals see inequality. Where conservatives see national renewal, liberals see national decline. Where liberals see social injustice, conservatives see envy. It is not likely that any scholarly analysis of the consequences of the Reagan presidency will agree with the entire list of ideological positions taken by either conservatives or liberals. But that is what makes evaluating the performance of a modern president such a challenging activity.

This book is not a comprehensive study of the Reagan presidency. It is an attempt to answer in a scholarly manner the questions raised by the polemical debates between conservatives and liberals concerning Reagan's political leadership and his administration's economic performance. Chapter 2 explains how the failures of the Carter presidency set the stage for Reagan's political and economic success. It also discusses why the Democrats were so ineffective in opposing Reagan.

Chapter 3 deals with the variety of factions in the conservative movement and their relationship with Reagan. It stresses that Reagan became the leader of the conservative movement while maintaining his political independence by appointing pragmatists and public relations experts to a number of key positions.

Chapter 4 describes how Reagan's personality affected his decision-making style. It includes a short summary of Reagan's life, his personality characteristics, and how his advisers provided him with a blend of administrative talents that enabled him to be a conviction politician, achieve policy goals through pragmatic compromises, and maintain high public approval ratings.

Chapter 5 explains how Reagan achieved so much success in his first year by persuading Congress to pass his budget reductions, tax cuts, *and* funding for a defense buildup. However, this chapter also sets forth how much blundering and compromise occurred during Reagan's "honeymoon." Because it provides detailed insights into Reagan's governing style, this is the longest chapter in the book.

Chapter 6 summarizes the contribution of tax policy to Reagan's political success. This policy area, to which Reagan was personally committed, efficiently served his political purposes (uniting the Republican Party and placing the Democrats on the defensive) throughout the decade.

Chapter 7 discusses the Reagan administration's responsibility for the savings and loan disaster. Although Reagan was usually skillful at enjoying the benefits and avoiding the costs of being an ideological leader, in this case, his conservative vision—which espoused deregulation—helped to produce a multibillion-dollar mess that had to be cleaned up by the Bush presidency.

Chapter 8 depicts how the Reagan presidency dealt with trade imbalances, protectionist pressures in Congress, and Third World debt problems. It emphasizes that his administration handled foreign economic policy with more pragmatic flexibility than most scholars of the 1980s acknowledged.

Chapter 9 is particularly important, because it analyzes the major economic achievement of the Reagan presidency, namely, the construction of a policy regime that prolonged the growth phase of the business cycle by lowering the threat of inflation. What conservatives usually neglect when they discuss this achievement is that it was not simply the result of fulfilling Reagan's supply-side visions. Success also required compromise, tax increases, and the efforts of a Carter appointee as head of the Federal Reserve, Paul Volcker. Ironically, in this important policy achievement, government—usually the bugaboo of conservative credo—was part of the solution.

Chapter 10 criticizes the Reagan presidency for contributing to the growing inequalities in the United States. It argues that Reagan's reputation as a moral leader was tarnished by his efforts to delegitimize policies attempting to promote social justice.

Chapter 11 concludes that the net effects of Reagan's political leadership, both domestically and internationally, were positive. His leadership did not bring about a conservative revolution, but it did create a hybrid regime of liberal and conservative policy commitments. The New Deal, the Great Society, and the Reagan revolution make up a strange "goulash" that the public finds appetizing despite its ideological inconsistency.

2

PREPARING THE STAGE FOR REAGAN: CARTER'S FAILURE AS A POLITICAL LEADER

Since Jimmy Carter has been so successful as an ex-president, considered by many to be deserving of the Nobel Peace Prize, it is difficult to remember how ineffectual he seemed in the Oval Office. But it is necessary to revive memories of the late 1970s, because the seeds of understanding the behavior of the Reagan presidency lie in the negative evaluations of the Carter administration. Reagan's presidency was as much a reaction to Carter's experiences as Franklin Roosevelt's was to Herbert Hoover's. If Carter had been planted as a "mole" in his own administration by conservative Republicans to deliberately wreck his presidency and prepare the way for Reagan's political successes, he could hardly have been more effective in accomplishing that feat.

The idea that Carter paved the way for Reagan is not new. Peggy Noonan writes, "There was no Reagan without Carter. Only four years of steady decline and lack of clarity could have lurched the country over to this . . . actor."[1] Michael Foley suggests that "Reagan's election, his political agenda, his style of leadership and the level of success achieved in his term of office was to a large extent attributable to President Carter. Without Carter, the presidency of Ronald Reagan would be unimaginable, not just because the latter simply followed the former in time, but because . . . Carter prepared much of the ground for Reagan and provided many of the prior conditions that Reagan was later to capitalize on."[2] Thus, a number of scholars have mentioned one or two ways in which Carter forged a path for Reagan, but that subject was not the focus of their studies. It *is* the focus of this chapter.

My purpose here is not to present a comprehensive review of the Carter administration but to analyze how his presidency set the stage for his successor. Consequently, some of Carter's successes, such as the Camp David Accords and the Panama Canal Treaty, will not be dealt with. Instead, the following sections examine Stephen Skowronek's theoretical explanation for Carter's failure, the context of the late 1970s during which Carter served as president, the leadership style of Jimmy Carter, and Carter's political ineffectiveness.

STEPHEN SKOWRONEK'S EXPLANATION: CARTER AND THE POLITICS OF DISJUNCTION

Stephen Skowronek provides us with theoretical guidance to explain the role of the Carter presidency in setting up that of his successor. In *The Politics Presidents Make,* Skowronek presents a historically based model for comparing the leadership efforts of chief executives from John Adams to George Bush. The author asserts that the leadership style of presidents is the major force that transforms American politics. Constitutionally, the United States has three coequal branches of government, but in reality, according to Skowronek, "it is the presidency that stands out as the chief point of reference for evaluating the polity as it moves through time and space; it is the executive office that focuses the eyes and draws out the attachments of the people. Unity, energy, and visibility combine in the presidency to place its incumbents foursquare at the intersection of the received order of things and current demands for change; and, so exposed, the president becomes the lightning rod of national politics, attracting and objectifying contending interpretations of the existing state of affairs."[3]

Skowronek stresses that the office of the presidency creates compelling incentives that impel its incumbents to engage in large leadership projects that inevitably threaten existing governing arrangements. The political system is often disrupted and sometimes transformed by the "battering ram" of order-shattering, order-affirming, and order-creating presidential decisions. In their attempts to secure a prestigious place in history by undertaking "great and arduous enterprises," presidents find their authority to act constantly challenged. A president's authority depends on the warrants he can derive from the moment at hand to justify deeds and earn the legitimacy of the changes brought about. For Skowronek, a successful president wins the interpretive battle over the meaning of his actions; his narrative prevails over the opposition's. The disruptions his leadership has caused are vindicated because they are compatible with his message.

Skowronek's major contribution is a model of structures of presidential authority that cyclically repeat themselves in political time. The author classifies presidents according to whether they were opposed or affiliated with the prevailing regime. Regimes (the dominant political orthodoxy, such as the

New Deal) are defined in terms of whether the previously established institutional arrangements are vulnerable or resilient. The resulting table allows scholars to compare presidents in different time periods facing similar leadership challenges (see Table 2.1, below).

In the first cell of this typology, a president comes to office opposed to a vulnerable regime. His task is to repudiate the failing political order and reconstruct a new one. Paradoxically, the power to recreate order depends on the authority to repudiate it. The authority to reject the declining established commitments of ideology and interests is the most decisive of all political resources for the exercise of leadership, because it combines message and action, intention and consequence, in the reconstruction of political order. Skowronek places Thomas Jefferson, Andrew Jackson, Abraham Lincoln, Franklin Roosevelt, and Ronald Reagan in this box. In the author's words, "These presidents each set out to retrieve from a far distant, even mythic, past fundamental values that they claimed had been lost in the indulgences of the received order. In this way, the order-shattering and order-affirming impulses of the presidency in politics become mutually reinforcing. As the president's initial political warrants dovetailed with the inherently disruptive exercise of presidential powers, the interplay of power and authority generated its own supports for independent action. The order-creating capacities of

Table 2.1   Recurrent Structures of Presidential Authority

Previously established commitments	Presidential political identity	
	Opposed	Affiliated
Vulnerable	Politics of reconstruction:	Politics of disjunction:
	Thomas Jefferson Andrew Jackson Abraham Lincoln Franklin Roosevelt Ronald Reagan	John Adams John Quincy Adams Franklin Pierce James Buchanan Herbert Hoover Jimmy Carter
Resilient	Politics of preemption:	Politics of articulation:
	John Tyler Andrew Johnson Woodrow Wilson Richard Nixon	James Monroe James Polk Theodore Roosevelt Harry Truman Lyndon Johnson

Source: Stephen Skowronek, *The Politics Presidents Make: Leadership from John Adams to George Bush* (Cambridge, Mass.: Belknap Press of Harvard University Press, 1993), p. 36.

the presidency were realized full vent in a wholesale reconstruction of the standards of legitimate national government."[4]

Opposition leaders in resilient regimes engage in what Skowronek calls the politics of preemption. The programs of these presidents are designed to split the dominant coalition. Presidents who identify with the existing resilient regime are engaged in the politics of articulation. Their task as "orthodox innovators" is to continue and fulfill the policy agenda of reconstructionist presidents such as Andrew Jackson or Franklin Roosevelt.

For our purposes, the most interesting category is presidents affiliated with a declining regime. Presidents in this category—John Adams, John Quincy Adams, Franklin Pierce, James Buchanan, Herbert Hoover, and Jimmy Carter—are typically portrayed as being politically incompetent. Skowronek provides a deeper, structural explanation for their failures. These presidents are confronted with an "impossible leadership situation," doomed to find their activities fail because of a dismal choice: "To affirm established commitments is to stigmatize oneself as a symptom of the nation's problems and the premier symbol of systemic political failure; to repudiate them is to become isolated from one's most natural political allies and to be rendered impotent."[5] The politics of disjunction are destined to fail because the president can neither fully support the integrity of the existing regime nor strongly repudiate it. In this no-man's-land, the president is subjected to a withering cross fire from proponents of the declining regime and increasingly rabid supporters of a new one. His authority to control the political definition of his activities is denied, which means that he is unable to establish credibility as a leader. The foreordained failure of presidents performing the politics of disjunction creates the conditions for the next stage in the cycle of political time, namely, the politics of reconstruction. According to Skowronek, "Through their hapless struggles for credibility, they become the foils for reconstructive leadership, the indispensable premise upon which traditional regime opponents generate the authority to repudiate the establishment wholesale."[6]

It is ironic that the presidents who assume office in this ungovernable situation usually have weak ties to the establishments they represent. As semi-outsiders, these leaders often propose major departures from the standard formulas and priorities. But Skowronek claims, "The political impact of these departures is disjunctive: they sever the political moorings of the old regime and cast it adrift without anchor or orientation."[7] These presidents also attempt to legitimize their authority by claiming special expertise in resolving the pressing problems of the day. Skowronek suggests that "the reification of technique as the central justification for political action—the elevation of proper administrative methods into a political cause and the claim of special insight into the mechanics of government—is a hallmark of the politics of disjunction."[8] The reification of technique cannot compensate for the absence of a programmatic consensus; it is the final and futile refuge of leadership ambitions that cannot be sustained by a governing coalition.

Carter was a nominal affiliate of a vulnerable, declining New Deal regime whose experience followed the doomed pattern of late-regime affiliates. Skowronek summarizes Carter's role in fulfilling the conditions for Reagan's succeeding politics of reconstruction in these words:

> Acting on his precious formulas for rejuvenating the machinery of liberal government, Carter placed himself at the center of dissension over the substantive commitments of the national government. . . . Caught between the problematic expectations of his liberal constituents and the mushrooming critique of the insurgent conservatives, the man who had promised to make liberal government work again became the leading symbol of its collapse. Initiatives heralding the revitalization of the old order served instead to stigmatize it as utterly barren of hope for the future, and Carter's search for credibility yielded the precise opposite of what he intended. Indicted by his own standards, Carter's leadership offered a prima facie case for an even more decisive break with the past. He became a caricature of the old regime's political bankruptcy, the perfect foil for a repudiation of liberalism itself as the source of all the nation's problems.[9]

THE 1970s

By the end of the 1970s, the American people's confidence in their ability to deal with the major problems of the day was shattered. Political assassinations, political corruption, the defeat in South Vietnam, OPEC-dictated oil price increases that raised the cost of a barrel of oil from $4 in 1973 to $37 in 1980, the collapse of the exchange-rate system, the kidnapping of our embassy in Iran, the Russian invasion of Afghanistan, and the frightening economic news about budget deficits, inflation, and unemployment led many citizens to fear that the United States was declining. After the Kennedy assassination in 1963, a series of failed presidencies only added to the cycle of hope and gloom. Presidential candidates could exploit the problems of incumbents during the campaign, but once in office, they could not govern effectively. Whereas in the 1960s, problems seemed solvable (the 1964 Civil Rights Act) and great tasks manageable (traveling to the moon in 1969), in the 1970s, the country lost faith in its ability to deal with crime, education, inflation, poverty, competition with the Japanese, Third World nationalism, and the containment of communism.

Underlying much of this despair was a decline in productivity. From 1947 to 1973, the average annual increase of output per worker hour had been 3 percent, but from 1973 to 1979, it dropped to 0.8 percent. The lessening of productivity occurred in many nations, but whereas in other industrialized countries the decline went from fast to modest growth, in the United States it collapsed from modest to almost zero growth. The result was stagnation in standards of living for more than half the population in a country that expects economic progress. Government figures indicated that "growth in real GNP per capita was cut to one-half the 1948–73 rate, to a 1.1 percent annual rate between 1973 and 1981. Real median family income showed no growth despite the growth in the proportion of two-earner families. A real differential began to show up in the 1970s, however, with the lowest groups in the distribution of income faring the worst. The poverty rate increased from 11.1 percent in 1973 to 14.0 percent in 1981."[10]

A number of explanations were offered to account for the downturn: an increase in the female proportion of the labor force, decreasing growth of capital per worker, stifling government regulations, mammoth increases in oil prices, and the growing proportion of the economy devoted to services. Conservative market-oriented economists argued that the slowdown reflected the inadequacy of Keynesian economics and that what the country needed were public policies that would increase the incentive to save and invest. Michael Boskin, a Stanford economist, wrote, "Among all explanations advanced, the decline in incentives to produce wealth and income is perhaps the most important. The reasons for this decline include high and rising inflation, which increased uncertainty in returns to investment and saving; rising marginal tax rates, especially on the returns to savings and investment, aggravated by the interaction of inflation and the unindexed tax system; and the growth of government regulation, which increased costs and uncertainty in long-term investment planning."[11]

The economic problem felt most severely by the public was inflation. During the 1970s, the price level as measured by the Consumer Price Index (CPI) doubled; this was four times as large an increase as occurred during the 1960s. In 1979 and 1980, unemployment rates went up along with the CPI. The double-digit inflation rates in 1979 and 1980 were devastating for the Carter administration and one of the major reasons that Reagan was able to win the presidential election. James Alt reports that "by 1979 the cost of living was seen as the most important problem facing the country by 60 percent of the public; it was the seventh straight year it had led the list, beating Watergate, energy and unemployment in turn."[12] The fact that inflation was condemned by the public and politicians yet continued to spread like some insidious plague heightened fears that the government had lost its ability to protect the purchasing power of the currency.

Accelerating inflation also had the effect of shoving taxpayers into higher marginal tax brackets, thus forcing them to pay more taxes even though they were not enjoying real income gains. The proportion of the population subject to very high marginal tax rates quadrupled between 1965 and 1980. When the effects of bracket creep were combined with the increases in Social Security taxes, many families found themselves struggling with less disposable income. Hence, there was a growing alienation from the tax system, highlighted by the passage of a property tax–cutting constitutional amendment in California known as Proposition 13 on June 6, 1978. "By 1980," according to Boskin, "the United States tax system had reached a crisis, creating pressure for fundamental tax reform. . . . Our tax system was widely perceived to be pro-consumption and anti-saving, in a society that had an extremely low saving rate."[13]

The economic conditions at the end of the 1970s set the stage for Reaganomics, with its emphasis on supply-side tax cuts to promote economic growth and monetarism to control inflation. In 1980, interest rates were high (the prime rate reached 21.5 percent) and the budget deficit doubled from the previous year to $59 billion. High interest rates were partially blamed on the crowding-out effect of the federal government's borrowing to finance its budget deficit, which borrowing amounted to almost 36 percent of the $348 billion in U.S. credit markets.[14] The Carter administration was overwhelmed by economic trends that saw unemployment grow, industrial production decline, and the dollar fall in value.

The liberal-Keynesian formula of economic growth and moderate inflation financing the incremental growth of social programs no longer worked. The declining productivity and rising inflation of the 1970s terminated this self-perpetuating system. In the long run, Keynesianism collapsed into stagflation—a condition of high inflation and high unemployment that Keynesianism could neither explain nor provide a policy remedy for.[15] In brief, both the public and the politicians were ready to pursue different economic strategies.

The 1970s were also hard on the unity, philosophy, and effectiveness of the Democratic Party. Franklin Roosevelt's New Deal had created a coalition of workers, southerners, farmers, ethnics, minorities, and intellectuals that made the Democrats into the majority party, the organization most likely to control Congress and the presidency. Its philosophy was based on the idea that the federal government had the expertise and compassion to tax, spend, and regulate society in order to bring about maximum employment and social progress. By the mid-1960s, liberal Democrats could claim an impressive list of achievements. Their foreign policy had rebuilt the war-torn economies of Europe and Japan and contained communism; their Keynesian-inspired economic policy had prevented a depression and was promoting cycles of economic growth, low inflation, and high employment marred only occasionally by mild and short recessions; their domestic policies had promoted civil rights, health care for the elderly and the poor, federal aid to education, and a large variety of welfare programs.

But by the end of the 1960s and into the 1970s, the prospects for the Democrats darkened considerably. The war in Vietnam was lost and had severely split the party; the war against poverty, initiated with such high hopes, degenerated into trench warfare, with some progress but no major victories; school integration produced "white flight" and a decline in public education; the crime rate soared; welfare dependency increased; and the economy that liberals in the 1960s believed they could "fine-tune" with the help of the Phillips curve became a constant source of worry in the 1970s. The slowdown in the economy meant that Democrats could no longer finance the expanding budgets of their New Deal and Great Society programs. "Declining growth rates," according to Steven Gillon, "created a zero-sum game where further expansion of the welfare state required shifting resources among groups."[16]

The Democrats found it difficult to adapt to the altered environment of the 1970s. Older liberals tried to maintain the FDR coalition, while newer liberals felt that an alliance of campus, ghetto, and suburbs could constitute a new majority. The new liberal strategy was tested by George McGovern's 1972 campaign and was buried by the Nixon landslide. There were racial, cultural, and regional cleavages within the broad-based Democratic Party that could be exploited by the opposition. The sons and daughters in many working-class families went to college and became more culturally liberal and more economically conservative than their parents. Perceptive politicians such as Richard Nixon and George Wallace discovered a number of wedge issues, such as law and order, busing, abortion, and prayer in schools, that appealed to the more culturally conservative Democrats, thus splitting the party. As the economy soured in the 1970s, "A working class threatened by inflation had little sympathy for 'the powerless' who demanded their tax money. . . . Just as ominous, a struggling middle class watched as inflation consumed much of its purchasing power. By the early 1970s, postwar prosperity along with many successful Democratic programs had created a growing middle class, which now fought to protect its hard earned status."[17] In this new milieu, many members of the working and middle classes viewed Republican promises of lower taxes, law and order, and deregulation as being more compatible with their interests than were liberal Democratic programs.

The Democratic Party was hurt as much by its successes as by its failures. Decades of economic prosperity helped many laborers move up into the middle class, thus weakening a major constituency of the Democratic Party and increasing the market for those attracted to Republican calls for cuts in taxes. Civil rights programs aided many blacks but also alienated many white voters and allowed the Republicans to become increasingly competitive in the formerly solid Democratic South. Gillon points out that, "despite the massive mobilization of black voters since passage of the Voting Rights act in 1965, the increase of white registration between 1960 and 1980 surpassed black by almost five to one. The mobilization of southern blacks and the defection of white southerners from the Democratic Party dramatically transformed the demographic composition of the Democratic coalition in the south."[18] Even the Democratic victory of forcing Nixon to resign because of the Watergate scandal had unforeseen costs, in that it fueled the public's paranoia about how corrupt politicians and government are.

By the end of the 1970s, liberal policies were seen as a major cause of high taxes, budget deficits, inflation, and stifling bureaucracies. Democrats were shocked that populist conservative allegations that a liberal elite was benefiting from policies that hindered social mobility were being accepted by a growing proportion of the electorate. Skowronek writes, "By 1976, the liberalism of Roosevelt had become a grab bag of special interest services all too vulnerable to political charges of burdening a troubled economy with bureaucratic overhead. . . . The energies that once came from advancing great national purposes had dissipated. A rule of myopic sects defied the very notion of governmental authority."[19] The historian Alonzo Hamby suggests that liberalism "increasingly became open to attack as a conglomerate of diverse special interests—labor unions, blacks, feminists, homosexuals, environmentalists, disarmers, counterculturalists—that had little support in the larger body politic and no compelling vision of a general public interest."[20]

Blinded by sectarian squabbles, liberal Democrats allowed conservatives, long associated with privileged interests, to make the stronger claim for representing the public interest. By pandering to narrow constituencies, the Democrats lost the ability to mobilize majorities. During the 1930s, Roosevelt had articulated a vision and a program when the bulk of the citizenry was needy, but no Democratic leader was able to construct a similar project for the 1970s and 1980s, when the majority was middle class and the issues were more morally ambiguous. The Democratic Party's problems and ineptness are painfully revealed in a series of statements by E. J. Dionne.

> When the poor are seen as a "special interest" while the wealthy are not, something very peculiar has happened to the national political dialogue. When such values as family and work are perceived as the exclusive province of one party to the political debate, the other party has clearly made some fundamental blunders. When the party of racial harmony creates conditions that encourage racial division, something is awry in its program. When constituencies who had gotten jobs, gone to college, bought houses, started businesses, secured health care, and retired in dignity because of government decided . . . that "government was the problem"—when this happened, it was clear a political revolution was in process.[21]

Thus, when James Earl Carter was inaugurated on January 20, 1977, as the thirty-ninth president of the United States, he was likely to be challenged and constrained by a troubling economy and by an intellectually exhausted and fragmented political party.

THE CARTER PRESIDENCY

The failure of the Carter presidency was overdetermined. For Skowronek, Carter had assumed a doomed mission: he was attempting to rejuvenate rather than repudiate a declining liberal regime. Others believed that Carter lacked the political skills to govern successfully during the difficult and uncertain times of the 1970s. Whatever the case, the challenge for any study of the Carter presidency is to explain why such a good, intelligent, and hardworking man failed so miserably in office.

Jimmy Carter looked far more promising in 1976 when he transformed himself from "Jimmy Who?" to president. The son of a peanut farmer in Plains, Georgia, a graduate of the Naval Academy, a naval officer who worked under Captain (later Admiral) Hyman Rickover as a nuclear submariner, governor of Georgia from 1970 to 1974, Carter defeated a number of more liberal Democratic candidates in 1976 to win the Democratic nomination for president. The fifty-two-year-old Carter was an ideal candidate in a country still affected by Watergate and the defeat in South Vietnam. Carter was an "outsider"; he had nothing to do with the "mess in Washington." He was a religious Southern Baptist who solemnly promised to never tell a lie and to fulfill all his campaign promises.

Carter was considered a liberal in the South because he was committed to the civil rights of blacks, but he was also conservative in that he promised to balance the budget within four years and to do away with unnecessary bureaucracy and government regulations. He felt that government could be revitalized if the executive branch installed zero-based budgeting, as he had done as governor of Georgia, and if it streamlined the bureaucracy by reducing the number of federal agencies from 1,900 to 200. He pledged major reforms of the tax and welfare systems, and he vowed to replace the realpolitik of Henry Kissinger's foreign policy with an approach that stressed moral purpose, human rights, less fear of communism, and more concern with aligning the United States with progressive forces in the Third World. Bert Lance tried to clarify the debate about Carter's political identity by saying, "Jimmy may campaign liberal, but he governs conservative."

Carter's experiences in 1976 foreshadowed problems that would plague his presidency. The self-inflicted wounds of the *Playboy* interview, in which Carter gratuitously criticized Lyndon Johnson and admitted that he frequently had "lust in his heart" for women, demonstrated a lack of political wisdom. Party professionals were dismayed that Carter blew most of his thirty-three-point lead over President Gerald Ford in the summer of 1976 and was able to win in November by a margin of only two points. Carter would have heavy Democratic majorities in the House and Senate, but his influence over Democratic congressmen would be limited by his lack of electoral coattails. In the congressional elections of 1976, the Democrats gained only one additional seat in the House and one in the Senate. The resulting 95th Congress had 292 Democrats and 143 Republicans in the House; the Senate was composed of 62 Democrats and 38 Republicans. The president-elect ran ahead of only twenty-two successful House Democrats and only one successful Senate Democrat.[22] Hence, there were early anxieties among Democrats about whether Carter was ready for prime time.

There was also a "fuzziness" about his leadership and political identity. Was Carter a liberal or a conservative, a populist or a technocrat, a politician or a preacher? Theodore Lowi captured the paradox of Carter's position when he wrote, "In 1976 Jimmy Carter ran against the party he wanted to lead and against the government over which he would preside."[23] Skowronek makes a similar point: "It is Jimmy Carter's peculiar genius to treat his remoteness from his party and its institutional power centers as a distinctive asset rather than his chief liability in his quest for a credible leadership posture. . . . This curiosity afforded neither the regime's outsider's freedom to oppose established interests nor the regime's insider's freedom to support them."[24]

Carter's Leadership Style

The new president's views on leadership were largely influenced by his religious beliefs and his training as an engineer. Every aspect of Carter's behavior was affected by his deeply held religious beliefs. He often quoted a line from Reinhold Niebuhr that encapsulated the former governor's grim view of political leadership: "The sad duty of politics is to establish justice in a sinful world." According to Gillon, "For Carter, 'the people' were his flock and he was the shepherd elected to protect them from the narrow interest groups scheming to corrupt their democratic institutions."[25] Considering himself to be a virtuous leader, Carter felt that he could communicate directly with the public and decipher what was best for it in the long run; he didn't need the Democratic Party or interest groups to serve as intermediaries.

As a trained engineer, Carter expected to lead through mastering the mechanism of government rather than through rhetorical eloquence. Rickover had insisted that submariners be fully knowledgeable about a variety of tasks on their ships, and Carter attempted to apply this philosophy in the White House. Professor Erwin Hargrove writes, "For Carter the cognitive aspect of political style was most strongly manifested in his drive for competence. He wished to understand thoroughly the issues for which he assumed primary responsibility, and he characterized his cognitive processes as those of an engineer."[26] The problem here was that Carter assumed responsibility for a multitude of issues, which meant that the cognitive demands on him were overwhelming. No president labored harder than Carter to understand deeply such a wide variety of issues.

Carter thought that it was his duty to search for hard problems, study them diligently, then seek comprehensive solutions to them. He was ambitious and tenacious and expected to be politically rewarded for his unconventional behavior in tackling the most difficult issues. He sought to achieve major reforms in the policy areas of energy, welfare, tax, urban development, hospital cost containment, and the environment. His successes in negotiating an accord between Israel and Egypt at Camp David and in passing the Panama Canal Treaty through a skeptical Senate were truly personal triumphs. James Sterling Young asserts that Carter believed that "the point of presidential leadership . . . was to achieve good policy. In a political system that was tilted in favor of policies that were expedient, constituency-oriented, costly, and good for the short run, it was the president's job to push for policies that were problem-solving, goal-oriented, cost-effective, and best in the long run."[27] Similarly, John Burke claims that Carter's "leadership style . . . sought long-run, cost-effective policy solutions that were goal oriented rather than defined by immediate political problems and considerations and that looked to the nation's common good rather than the particular interests of constituency groups. . . . Carter's 'politics as public goods' leadership, as Hargrove terms it, or his vision of a 'trusteeship' presidency, as Charles O. Jones characterizes it, set a different tone from the incremental and political concerns of a Johnson or a Nixon or the skillful projection of a public image as a public program, which his successor was to employ."[28] The tragedy for Carter was that such noble intentions and prodigious efforts led to more failures than successes.

Carter had the analytical skills to recognize that the liberal regime was no longer economically viable. A slowdown in economic growth and existing budget commitments were placing old liberal aspirations on a collision course with present economic realities. True to his leadership perspective, Carter did not shirk his responsibility in analyzing this problem and trying to formulate a solution. Constrained by his moral code and analytical capabilities, Carter was not afforded the luxury of avoiding painful trade-offs by selecting "voodoo" remedies.

In an overreaction to the Nixon administration and complaints about an imperial presidency, Carter decided that he would not have a chief of staff in the White House and would reconstitute the Cabinet to its proper role as the president's top tier of advisers. By not selecting a chief of staff, Carter was, in reality, taking on the onerous and time-consuming duties of being chief of staff himself. The new president would be the hub of a circle of advisers who would report directly to him. Carter's administrative system, according to Hargrove, "called for diversity of advice within a collegial setting emphasizing homework and knowledge."[29] The Democratic Party could certainly provide diversity.

As an outsider who had never served in Washington, Carter was overly dependent on his advisers from Georgia. Major advisers from his home state included Hamilton Jordan, his principal political adviser; Jody Powell, his press secretary; Bert Lance, director of the Office of Management and Budget (OMB); James McIntyre, who replaced Lance because of a scandal in September 1977; Frank Moore, congressional liaison; and Griffin Bell, a conservative who became attorney general. For his national security adviser, Carter appointed Professor Zbigniew Brzezinski, an expert on the Soviet Union whom Carter had met during meetings of the Trilateral Commission. Most of Carter's non–White House appointments came from the liberal wing of the Democratic Party. Former senator Walter Mondale was chosen as vice president to be an expert on and a liaison with Congress, the Democratic Party, and labor. Carter's decision to staff his administration with both insiders and outsiders was probably designed to increase its representation and flexibility;

instead, it augmented its unmanageability. Rather than being praised for appointing a wide variety of Democrats, Carter was criticized, according to Sidney Milkis and Michael Nelson, as "an irresolute leader who was eager to accommodate all sides."[30] For the most part, Carter's appointments were individually talented but collectively ineffective.

Instead, Carter's White House advisers developed many of the problems associated with collegial systems. Burke notes, "They put a heavy burden on the president's time and attention and called for unusual interpersonal skills, which Carter was unable to provide, in mediating differences and maintaining teamwork. . . . Meetings of the Cabinet proved unproductive, forcing Carter to work individually with Cabinet members or in task forces and placing increasing authority for coordinating the policy process on the White House staff, which was ill-equipped to handle it."[31] The lack of a chief of staff until mid-1979—combined with the fact that neither Stuart Eizenstat, as head of the domestic policy staff, nor Brzezinski had the authority to control the centrifugal forces of the presidency—meant that the Carter administration frequently appeared to be at war with itself. The numerous publicized disputes within the administration—between Cyrus Vance and Brzezinski, Mondale and Griffin Bell, Eizenstat and Patrick Caddell (Carter's pollster), McIntyre and all the liberal appointees—projected the deflating image that Carter could not lead his own team.

The usual White House procedures did not compensate for Carter's handicaps as a leader and decision maker; they magnified them. Thus Carter's system did not help him establish priorities nor help him impose order. The president was inundated with time-consuming details that should have been settled at lower levels. Midway through his presidency, forty advisers were reporting directly to Carter, and he was reading 300 to 400 pages a day. This problem was recognized but could not be solved. Brzezinski reports that "whenever I tried to relieve him of excessive detail, Carter would show real uneasiness, and I even felt some suspicion that I was usurping authority."[32] In Carter's commitment to "conquer the office," he felt compelled to master the details of a wide variety of subjects.[33] By submerging himself in trivia, he lost sight of the big picture.

This lack of strategic vision was noted by Carter's contemporaries. He was ridiculed for monitoring the White House tennis courts. In 1978, Emmet John Hughes, a journalist who had been an aide in the Eisenhower White House, wrote, "there has been no President since Hoover so absorbed and fascinated as Carter by the 'machinery' of his government and the monitoring of all its details. There has been no President since Hoover so devoted to 'running a desk' with an industry decreed by a presidential work-ethic of exhaustive briefings and exhausting hours."[34] Perhaps no chief executive learned more about how the government works and understood less about how a president succeeds.

Carter's Political Ineffectiveness

Carter's leadership style and his decision-making procedures often combined to make him appear ineffectual. His labors were woefully inefficient in terms of producing positive results. Carter's intelligence and hard work seemed capable only of publicizing how complex and difficult his problems were; his lack of political skills meant that he could not provide solutions. Hargrove provides the most perceptive critique of Carter's leadership style:

> Carter did not manage the seamless web of purpose, politics and process smoothly. His strategic leadership had a disjointed character in which discrete decisions jarred and jostled each other. He fastened too much on particular decisions without relating them to decisions that had come before and those that would follow. . . . He reversed his course often in response to immediate situations. . . . Constant reversals in economic policy confused everyone. Carter did not know how to extract a strong strategic sense of direction from a welter of discrete decisions. The decisions rather than the direction were his focus.[35]

This focus on individual decisions and neglect of direction meant that the Carter administration often appeared to be adrift, buffeted by shifting political winds, with no clear set of priorities. Unlike that of most modern presidents, Carter's leadership project could not be captured in a catchy phrase such as the New Deal or the Great Society. When Carter failed to provide a unifying theme, the Republicans stuck him with one—Carter was the personification of failed liberalism. This labeling was effective but unfair, because Carter's decision-making style did not adhere to any ideology. Indeed, as Stephen Hess suggests, "many of Carter's policies seemed inordinately at cross purposes. Complicated tax proposals belied attempts at tax simplification, new social programs compromised the vision of a balanced budget, the creation of new federal departments [Energy and Education] scuttled the promise to reduce the size of the bureaucracy. The Domestic Policy staff proposed a liberal task and OMB pursued a conservative one."[36] In other words, because the president lacked a guiding political philosophy, his policy recommendations fluctuated between the liberal and the conservative.

Carter believed that if he diligently searched for the best solution to a problem, he had the intelligence to find it. He resented that his decisions had to be sold to politicians who were less knowledgeable and less moral than himself. Their petty interests frustrated him. The fact that other politicians did not consider their interests petty and were not moved by Carter's appeals to morality and the public interest caused him constant grief. Only a politically naive person could believe that good policy would automatically sell itself.[37] What Carter considered a higher form of leadership seemed to many other politicians merely a sanctimonious attitude.

Unlike most politicians, Carter liked substantive discussions about important issues but disliked debates about political feasibility. However, in stressing how nonpolitical he was, Carter unintentionally created incentives for the media to focus on the role of politics in his decisions. When the media found evidence of political concerns in Carter's behavior, it made him look like a hypocrite. Because of Carter's holier-than-thou attitude, no president ever received less credit for negotiating a compromise. A Carter-engineered compromise tended to be viewed as "politics as usual"—the very thing he was pledged to change. A member of his own administration was quoted as saying that he did "good things badly."[38] Carter's moral posturing had the effect of reducing the effectiveness of his political activities. When he engaged in personal attacks against Senator Edward Kennedy during the 1980 Democratic primaries and Ronald Reagan in that year's presidential election, the result was to raise the issue of his own "meanness." The press quickly changed its image of him from Christian Carter to Jungle Jimmy.[39] Charles Jones points up the president's leadership dilemma when he writes that "Carter's style and techniques suggest that his first instincts were to try to make Washington less political. Failing that, he was forced to engage in the very behavior that upset him. It is understandable that problems developed for him, both in pursuing his natural instincts and in trying to be somebody else."[40] In brief, Carter was not effective when he was himself nor when he tried to act like a conventional politician. That did not give him much opportunity to be productive.

In publicizing the standards of efficiency and honesty by which it wished to be evaluated, then selecting the most difficult issues to address, the Carter presidency was setting the stage for its own downfall. The more Carter stressed his competence, the more incompetent he looked. The more he pointed out that there were no easy answers, the more it looked like he had no answers at all. The more he pronounced that he was a moralist and not a politician, the more he appeared to be neither. "The final irony," according to Hargrove, "was that he became the scapegoat for all unresolved national and international problems. Everybody—politicians, the public, interest groups, and media—piled on him."[41] Whereas the ridiculing of Reagan often did not work, the caricaturing of Carter paid dividends for the Republicans. No one accused Carter of being a Teflon president.

Carter's problems were aggravated by his administrative system. The absence of a chief of staff for the first two and a half years of his administration reinforced Carter's inability to establish priorities. And when Carter finally did establish a chief of staff in July 1979, he appointed Hamilton Jordan to the position, even though this young Georgian lacked the organizational aptitude for the job. Moreover, the organizational structure of the Carter White House did not shield the president from issues and problems that should have been handled at lower levels.[42]

Carter lacked both the Washington experience and the political wisdom to make political judgments about policy decisions. The president desperately needed help here, but his determination to keep top decisions in his hands prevented him from delegating authority and seeking more assistance. This meant that Carter was frightfully exposed and alone in the making of too many decisions. Whereas most modern presidents have used certain advisers as lightning rods (think of how Reagan used David Stockman, Caspar Weinberger, and James Watt), Carter's style all too often highlighted himself as the scapegoat when things went wrong. And because Carter's decisions often appeared to be directionless, he did not even get credit for having the courage to take on so much responsibility.[43]

Both Carter and his staff were deficient in the political skills needed to deal effectively with Congress, especially during their first year in office. Thomas "Tip" O'Neill, the Speaker of the House, believed that Carter was the smartest public official he had ever encountered in terms of the range and depth of his knowledge about policy. However, O'Neill complained that Carter did not know how Congress worked and wasn't interested in learning. The new president naively expected Congress to adjust to his style of leadership. Nothing reveals Carter's ineptness more sharply than his attempt in February 1977 to cancel nineteen water and dam projects, including several in Louisiana, the state represented by Senator Russell Long, the chairman of the Finance Committee. Additionally, O'Neill and many Democratic congressmen found that Frank Moore, Carter's congressional liaison, "didn't know beans about Congress." But O'Neill was particularly enraged by what he considered the arrogance and ignorance of Hamilton Jordan, whom he nicknamed "Hannibal Jerken." The Speaker claims, "When it came to helping out my district, I actually received more cooperation from Reagan's staff than from Carter's."[44]

By not taking advantage of its "honeymoon" period with a Democratically controlled Congress in 1977, the Carter administration became trapped by a reputation of failure from which it never escaped. Even Hamilton Jordan later conceded that, "by the end of the first year there were a number of perceptions about the Carter administration. Fair or unfair, the perception was that he didn't know how to deal with the Congress, that he was not successful in getting things through the Congress, that he was surrounded by too many people from Georgia who were in over their heads, and that he was overwhelmed by all the details of issues in his presidency. . . . Those perceptions never changed."[45] That negative image weakened the leverage of the Carter administration in every bargaining situation after 1977.

Carter's administration was equally ineffective in dealing with the Democratic Party. The Democratic Party and its constituent groups were not willing to coalesce behind Carter and follow him in a new style of politics. They liked the traditional way of the New Deal and the Great Society. They wanted more; Carter was offering them less. For them, liberal progress had been temporarily derailed by the Kennedy assassination and the Vietnam War. After eight years of Republican leadership, it was time to complete the liberal agenda. Each liberal constituency felt that it had supplied the margin of victory for Carter in 1976, and each threatened to withdraw its assistance unless his administration rewarded it in terms of recruitment and policies. Blacks, Hispanics, women, environmentalists, and labor unions wanted their people appointed to administrative positions, and they demanded big increases in social spending.

After Reagan defeated Carter in 1980, Hamilton Jordan was extremely bitter about the disloyalty of so many of the administration's political appointees. He charged that many of them felt more obligation to their constituencies than to Carter. When Carter made decisions that gave their constituency groups less than what they demanded, these officials would frequently publicize their disapproval. Moreover, by not instituting White House control over personnel decisions, thus allowing Cabinet secretaries to hire many of their own people, the administration internalized "the chaos and fragmentation out in the party." In Jordan's words, "The way we were going to deal with all those people was by having a black and an hispanic and a woman and an environmentalist and a consumer type. So in trying to reach out and be able to stay in touch with all the moving parts of the party, we almost created the same set of tensions within our . . . administration. . . . We didn't stress the loyalty factor enough. The Reagan administration has done a much better job of that than we did."[46]

After Carter's defeat, Eizenstat viewed Carter as a transitional president valiantly attempting to induce the Democratic Party to adapt to the milieu of the 1970s. Carter was the nominal leader of a party that was philosophically based on aid to various factions and that had a particular concern with helping low-income and disadvantaged groups. But how could the Democrats maintain their majority rule when labor and the poor were a declining proportion of the electorate? In Eizenstat's words, "What you had is an institution . . . whose constituent members refused to recognize the economic realities, [and who] continued to make maximal demands on the administration, and therefore governance became very difficult for a Democratic President at a time of high inflation and inadequate resources."[47] Eizenstat praises Carter for recognizing that the Democratic Party had to move beyond Great Society liberalism because economic conditions could no longer finance it, but he concedes that his boss was never able to construct a compelling vision to transform enough traditional Democrats. The Democratic Party was not going to be revived by civil service reform and zero-based budgeting.

What did excite many traditional Democrats, at least for a while, was Senator Edward Kennedy. Kennedy's challenge to Carter's leadership exacerbated the philosophical, religious, and regional cleavages in the Democratic Party. In December 1978, at the midterm Democratic Party convention in Memphis, Kennedy told a cheering crowd that the party ought to "sail against the wind" of public opinion and reject "drastic slashes" in domestic expenditures. The senator declared, "The party that tore itself apart over Vietnam in the 1960s cannot afford to tear itself apart over budget cuts in basic social programs."[48] In May 1979, Kennedy proposed a $100 billion national health plan several weeks before Carter presented his less comprehensive health program. That same month, when enraged motorists were enduring long lines at the gas pumps to buy gasoline selling at over a dollar a gallon for the first time ever, polls showed Kennedy leading Carter among Democrats by two or three to one. Kennedy was even leading the president in the South.[49] The bubble of Kennedy's popularity burst quickly after he formally announced his candidacy for the Democratic nomination in November 1979. A few days after Kennedy became a candidate, the Iranians took over the U.S. embassy in Tehran, and the nation rallied around the president, doubling his public approval rating to 61 percent. When the press reminded the public about the Chappaquiddick scandal, and Kennedy was not able to duplicate the inspiring campaigns of his fallen brothers John and Robert, Carter was able to defeat his liberal antagonist. But the fact that a morally blemished politician like Ted Kennedy could command more support than Carter in 1979 spoke volumes about the lack of rationality in the Democratic Party and the dearth of political skill in Carter's leadership.

In his last two years in office, Carter was whipsawed between liberal criticism that he was too conservative and Republican complaints that he was too liberal. Carter could not even constrain the clamoring constituents of his party by raising the specter of Ronald Reagan; the former actor was a source of derision, and the consensus was that he would be rejected by the voters, just as Barry Goldwater had been in 1964. Nor did Carter have the adroitness to build a governing coalition in support of his policies.[50]

Throughout most of his term in office, Carter was also criticized for the contradictions of his policies. As a candidate, he had promised to cut the military budget, but he soon found himself compelled to promote major increases in defense expenditures. His assertions that he could achieve more cooperation with the Soviet Union were denied by its invasion of Afghanistan in late 1979. His administration's response to the energy crisis, which he declared constituted "the moral equivalent of war," was eventually so delayed and watered down that it was satirized by the acronym MEOW. His belief in human rights and in the idea that the United States could develop a better relationship with progressive forces in the Third World was undermined by the Ayatollah Khomeini in Iran and the Sandinistas in Nicaragua.

According to Hargrove, Carter "wished for new balance between equity and efficiency in domestic programs, for a fiscally responsible economic expansion and for subordination among nations through cooperation. He deliberately incorporated these contradictions into his political appeals and in so doing embodied in his presidency the contradictions of public policy of the 1970s. This incorporation was accomplished by the confidence that hard issues could be resolved by goodwill and homework."[51] It did not work. Carter saw the contradictions and tried to reconcile them, but they ended up overwhelming his presidency. Two political scientists summarized the policy history of the Carter presidency in two bleak sentences: "Carter's first hundred days were characterized by attempts to act on a laundry list of campaign promises. The thrust of his presidency became increasingly blurred as he set deadlines, ran into obstacles, retreated, then changed directions."[52] Because of the way Carter was positioned, even when he responded to the policy preferences of the times—such as increasing the defense budget or signing a tax bill in 1978 that cut the rate on capital gains—he did not receive any credit. Indeed, Carter's policy changes were usually belittled as "too little too late" and "flip-flopping."

Carter's economic policy was especially prone to this criticism. In the election year of 1976, the unemployment rate was a little over 7 percent, inflation was under 6 percent, and the federal government had a budget deficit of about $66 billion. During the campaign, Carter promised to lower the unemployment rate, reduce inflation, and balance the budget within four years. As a Democrat, Carter felt that his first duty was to propose a $30 billion economic stimulus program, which was less than half of what union leaders advocated. With so many unemployed, Carter's economic advisers were not worried that the stimulus package would generate more inflation. However, when the economy grew faster than expected early in 1977, Carter withdrew the consumption-inspired $50 rebate portion of his program. This initial flip-flop created immediate doubts about the economic and political wisdom of the Carter administration.

Inasmuch as Democrats are prone to see unemployment as a more significant economic problem than inflation, it took several years before Carter reluctantly decided that inflation would have to be addressed. The CPI rose 6.5 percent in 1977, 7.7 percent in 1978, 11.3 percent in 1979, and 13.5 percent in 1980. By not attacking inflation in 1977, the administration allowed rising prices to gather a momentum that would prove electorally lethal in 1980. If the administration had employed budget cuts and a tighter monetary policy in 1977, the economy might have encountered a mild recession in 1978, but with economic recovery and low inflation, it would have been in better shape in 1980. This strategy was not pursued, however, because most of Carter's economic advisers underestimated the inflationary forces operating in the economy and were fearful that any strong attempt to control inflation would result in rising unemployment, which would cause suffering among Democratic constituencies. Carter responded to this dilemma by being tentative, by splitting the difference in terms of the advice he received from conservatives such as Secretary of the Treasury Michael Blumenthal and OMB Director James McIntyre and from more liberal advisers such as Charles Schultze, Walter Mondale, and Stuart Eizenstat. Hargrove explains the president's predicament in these words: "Carter's economists could not give him a policy strategy for the inflation problem that he could pursue as a Democratic president. The centrist political strategy did not work, either with Democratic interest groups or with diffuse publics."[53]

Carter began targeting inflation in 1978. He set up a Council on Wages and Price Stability (COWPS), directed by Barry Bosworth, to monitor wages and prices. The goal was to use public pressure (jawboning) on business and labor to voluntarily keep their prices and wages below the average of the previous two years. The program was bitterly opposed both by business, which suspected that this was a forerunner to mandated controls, and by labor, which feared that restricting wages would turn out to be the principal means of curbing inflation. Republican economists ridiculed wage and price controls by claiming that invoking such a policy was like commanding the tides to stop moving. Jawboning was a total flop; COWPS merely ended up publicizing the inflationary figures, thus making the administration look even more impotent. Similarly, the moderate budget cuts the administration undertook were, according to Eizenstat, "enough to make all the constituencies mad without accomplishing the desired result."[54]

Ironically, the most effective decision Carter made in confronting inflation was to appoint Paul Volcker as chairman of the Federal Reserve Board in July 1979. Volcker believed that inflation was the major threat to the health of the economy and was therefore willing to take strong and unprecedented steps to subjugate it. On October 6, 1979, the chairman announced a new monetary policy that would emphasize controlling the supply of money and credit instead of interest rates. Volcker's strategy of tightening the money supply caused interest rates to soar during the election year of 1980; only after the recession of 1981–1982 did the inflation rate finally drop back to acceptable levels. Fighting inflation with monetary weapons meant rising unemployment during an election year; it opened up an opportunity for Reagan to appropriate what has traditionally been the Democratic Party's best issue—full employment—and attract a significant portion of the labor vote. Carter's electoral support from union households decreased from 59 percent in 1976 to 49 percent in 1980. According to Dionne, "Working class voters weighed Carter's policies of retrenchment against Reagan's buoyant optimism and decided that Reagan really did sound more like Franklin Roosevelt than the Democratic nominee."[55] Thus, in the 1980 election, Carter absorbed much of the political heat for the rise in interest rates, inflation, and unemployment levels, and in the 1984 election, Reagan received much of the political reward for taming inflation and overseeing a robust economic recovery.

By 1980, the political identity and direction of the Carter presidency had become blurry, but its failures were clear. Richard Neustadt, the foremost presidential scholar, wrote, "Watching President Jimmy Carter in early 1979 sparked the question, is the Presidency possible?"[56] Throughout Carter's four-year term, his presidency exhibited a propensity for self-inflicted wounds, from the vetoing of nineteen water projects in 1977 to the grain embargo and Olympic boycott in 1980.

Carter had hoped to legitimize his leadership on the basis of his competence. But the economic, political, and international situation in 1980 indicated that, for all of Carter's hard work, the public felt that conditions had deteriorated since he had entered office. His personal identification with so many problems that did not get solved—the energy issue, welfare reform, the tax system, inflation, and especially the kidnapping of U.S. embassy personnel in Tehran—made it easy for the Republicans to campaign against Carter in 1980. By that year, the public had less faith in government programs than in 1976, and the target of much of their alienation was Carter.[57] Reagan exploited this sentiment by asking voters, "Are you better off now than you were in 1976?" Carter's leadership projects were rejected by the voters because, according to Foley, "they evoked an image of passivity; of a leader attempting to mobilize a people downward to lower expectations, when their traditions and culture were rooted in progress and optimism."[58] Reagan would not make that mistake.

By the end of the 1970s, Carter was vulnerable to the accusation that he was passively presiding over the decline of the United States. His "leadership" style was to explain to the public the complexity of problems, the limits of U.S. power, and the need for sacrifices. In 1980, the country seemed unable to preserve the purchasing value of its currency, to supply gasoline for its motorists at a reasonable price, to check Soviet aggression, or to maintain the safety of its embassy officials. James Baker later wrote, "The Iranian hostage crisis . . . contributed greatly to the election of Ronald Reagan in 1980. Jimmy Carter's inability to secure the release of American diplomats held hostage by Iran for 444 days had become a metaphor for a paralyzed presidency and the decline of American power throughout the world."[59] The indictment in 1980 by Norman Podhoretz, a former Democrat who had become a neoconservative, was even more comprehensive.

> Carter, as the . . . President of a country . . . whose military power was declining in relation to the Soviet Union, whose economic power was declining in relation to the Japanese, whose moral standards were declining in relation to its own past . . . had only two choices in trying to win reelection. Either he could say that things were not so bad as they seemed or he could say they were beyond anyone's control [the result of vast historic forces]. If he took the first course, he would be laughed out of the race; but since his opponent was promising to *do* something about the decline of the country, the second course would only work if he could persuade the voters that the effort to change things was so dangerous that no responsible person would ever think of making it.[60]

Carter was not able to sell this argument, and in 1980 he became the fifth straight president who failed to serve two terms. Reagan defeated Carter in forty-four states.

CONCLUSION

From the perspective of Reagan, the Carter presidency was a perfect predecessor (see Table 2.2, below). Carter's bitterly disappointing performance set

Table 2.2   President Carter Paving the Way for President Reagan

President Carter (1977–1981)	President Reagan (1981–1989)
Overreaction to Nixon and the imperial presidency	Effective reaction to Carter's problem
No chief of staff until 1979	Strong chief of staff
Weak staff—overly dependent on members from Georgia	Strong staff of conservatives, pragmatists, and public relations experts
Allowed Cabinet secretaries to hire own staff	Exercised more White House control over political appointees
No unifying philosophy	Unifying philosophy of conservatism
Ambivalent ties to divided party	Strong ties to unified party
Hit the ground stumbling	Hit the ground running
Never established legislative priorities	Established legislative priorities: tax cuts, budget cuts, and defense buildup
Never established social base	Strong anchor in conservative movement
Ambivalent ties to liberal regime	Repudiation of the liberal regime and attempt to create a conservative one
Drowned in details	Strategic vision and priorities
Lack of resilience	Resilient—successfully rebounded from 1981–1982 recession and Iran-Contra scandal
Directionless, zigzagging	More conservative consistency
Crisis of confidence, malaise	Optimism
Velcro presidency—blame stuck to Carter	Teflon presidency—Reagan used lightning rods effectively: David Stockman, Caspar Weinberger, and James Watt

the stage for Reagan's politics of reconstruction by bolstering the latter's authority to repudiate the liberal regime. This insight was recognized intuitively by many observers in the 1980s but was analyzed at a deeper level by Stephen Skowronek. Skowronek classified Carter as a president affiliated with a vulnerable regime practicing the politics of disjunction. The politics of disjunction is doomed because it denies its leader the kind of political identity and authority that a president needs to attract mass support. Carter came into office trying to rejuvenate a tired liberal regime through a combination of hard work and administrative reforms. The president failed, according to Skowronek, because "locating the salvation of the nation in the machinery of the government, Carter was unable to anchor his leadership project in any bedrock of constituency support."[61] Carter did not possess the authority to reform the declining regime or to create a new one. His dilemma was that the order-affirming and order-shattering targets of his decisions were virtually the same. This accounts for Carter's ambivalence toward liberalism, the Democratic Party and its constituencies, Congress, and Keynesian economics. Carter was impeded as much by his ostensible allies as by his opponents. By diligently attempting to renew the liberal regime, he hastened the collapse of both the regime and his presidency.

Skowronek argues that Carter was programmed to fail because he was chained to a sinking regime. But the record indicates that the probability of Carter's downfall was increased by his political ineptness. There are some fine scholars who argue that Carter was less incompetent than he appeared, but that evaluation is reminiscent of those who claim that Wagner's music is better than it sounds. Perhaps it is most accurate to say that Carter showed great skill as a campaigner in gaining the Democratic nomination, average skill in barely defeating President Ford, and exceptionally poor skills in the Oval Office. The ex-governor of Georgia came to Washington, D.C., in 1976 as an outsider with few friends and left four years later still an outsider with even fewer friends. Carter was a bundle of contradictions: he combined great intelligence with a lack of political wisdom, hard work with ineffectiveness, attention to detail with propensity for error, and moral commitment with a reputation for flip-flopping. His overreaction to the pathologies of the imperial presidency demonstrated that there were at least equal dangers from the imperiled presidency. By not employing a chief of staff at the beginning of his administration, Carter reinforced his disinclination to establish priorities. By not scoring legislative victories during his honeymoon period, he became imprisoned by the image of a loser, a perception that burdened the rest of his time in office. Carter's decision-making style, which often tried to placate everyone, ended up pleasing no one. His fatally delayed anti-inflation policy managed to be ineffective against rising prices while it antagonized most Democratic constituencies and delivered its economic and political benefits to Reagan. No president, with the notable exception of Herbert Hoover, had less political success to show for his immense efforts.

Carter tried to communicate that the United States now lived in an age of uncertainty and limits but succeeded only in conveying his limitations for the job of president. In highlighting his own incompetence to deal with the complex problems of the day, he became the personification of a paralyzed presidency and of spent liberalism. Carter's leadership style was incompatible with what the Democrats needed most—a maestro to rebuild the party. His style was personal, moral, issue oriented, difficult to grasp, and not likely to inspire. His pessimism clashed with our sanguine political culture, and his complex message did not resonate with public opinion. He left himself open to attacks (by Kennedy on the Left and Reagan on the Right) that he was blaming the

American people for the nation's problems. He became vulnerable to the lethal charge that he lacked the qualities of leadership that constitute the essence of what we expect in a president. In brief, Carter's failures fulfilled the conditions that allowed Reagan, as the leader of the conservative movement, to enter from stage right.

RONALD REAGAN AND THE CONSERVATIVE MOVEMENT

In 1980, Professor Alan Wolfe, a liberal sociologist, published an open letter to conservatives warning them to be prepared for frustration after their candidate Ronald Reagan won the presidential election. Wolfe predicted that "Ronald Reagan will be as much a letdown to you as John Kennedy and Lyndon Johnson were to me." The liberal professor suggested that ideologues "raised the issues" and "supplied the energy" for presidential campaigns, but their goals were inevitably betrayed by politicians. In Wolfe's words, "The problem is that the president you elect will not even attempt to achieve them [your goals], leaving you with a few symbols and even fewer crumbs, hoping to appease you the way our presidents tried to 'cool out' the radical left."[1]

The relationship with his ideological supporters also presents problems for the president. Although a chief executive certainly enjoys advantages in having zealous followers, he is likely to encounter a greater number of disadvantages. Ideologues are less likely to appreciate a president's need to compromise in a governmental system with built-in checks and balances. They are usually too demanding that their leader be confrontational, less sensitive to his need to establish priorities, and overly anxious to press their leader to do too much too fast. This pressure by his conservative constituents presents the president with a dilemma: he can either satisfy their demands, thus alienating the majority of the public who are not highly ideological, or he can dilute ideological goals in order to maintain broad support, thus antagonizing his core ideological followers. For a president, ideological constituencies are probably the most difficult to service. Given the nature of their demands and their condemnation of compromise, they are seldom satisfied.

I argue that Reagan was usually able to enjoy the advantages of being a conviction politician, leading and uniting the multiple sects of the conservative movement while avoiding most of the pitfalls of being its acknowledged head. Before Reagan assumed office, few observers thought such leadership was possible. In January 1981, a liberal journalist offered the president-elect the following warning:

> When you think about it, your real problems will come from your conservative friends—from conflicts between the Old Right and the New Right, the ones who were with you from the start fighting the new boys—and from those who simply know what God wants better than you do. A lot of these people actually believe that you were elected on the strength of their philosophy. To them, you are a means and not an end. Such people are most concerned with such doctrinal purity, and you never will be able to live up to their standards. . . . Hell hath no fury like an ideological purist scorned.[2]

To lead and personify the conservative movement while maintaining the broad public support necessary to be an effective president was a terribly difficult task. Nevertheless, this book presents the case that Reagan successfully handled one of the major challenges of the modern presidency, namely, how to project both narrow and broad appeal.

THE CONSERVATIVE MOVEMENT

What we are concerned with in this chapter is not a comprehensive history of the modern conservative movement but rather an analysis of the significant features of that movement that affected its interaction with President Reagan. The rise of modern conservatism in the United States can be viewed as a phenomenon largely generated by ideas and frustrations. The ideas that pervade modern conservative thought include liberty, competitive markets, private property, community, and religion. Clinton Rossiter stresses that "the preference for liberty over equality lies at the root of the Conservative tradition, and men who subscribe to this tradition never tire of warning against the 'rage for equality.' "[3] Conservatives claim that liberals have become obsessed with equality. This futile quest results in a centralized state that threatens liberty, private property, and prosperity. Under liberalism, the goal of the state becomes the redistribution of wealth through confiscatory taxes and social welfare policies that inevitably destroy community.

The frustrations of modern conservatives derive from living in a society where, until recently, so much of the culture, philosophy, and politics was dominated by liberalism. Conservatives frequently felt that their ideology was being ignored or ridiculed by academics and the media. In the field of political philosophy, the dominant view was that, although there was a legitimate conservative perspective in Western civilization associated with Edmund Burke, in the United States there was no Burkean tradition to defend. There was no authentic American conservative political philosophy because, as Louis Hartz had "proved," the United States' political tradition was essentially liberal.[4] In universities, it was easier to find a course on socialism than on conservatism. Thus, many liberals were free to regard conservatives as a fringe element of cranks and Neanderthals.

Obviously, conservatives view themselves more positively. From their perspective, as endlessly repeated in their speeches and essays, they have engaged in an epic struggle and have risen from a despised minority to a vanguard ready to lead the nation back to—and forward to—greatness. According to conservative columnist George Will, "Since the 1950s, when the conservative movement coalesced out of many exasperations, conservatism has been on a long march, transforming itself from an ideology of protest to a philosophy of governance."[5] We can arbitrarily date the beginning of this long march to 1955 when William Buckley began the *National Review* and proclaimed in its first issue that conservatives were "a minority standing athwart history and yelling, Stop!" At the same time, one of Buckley's mentors, Frank Meyer, portrayed American conservatives as a beleaguered "remnant," defending the barricades of freedom against a domestic liberal establishment and the foreign threat of Russian expansionism.

The conservative resurgence of the 1980s was largely fueled by a reaction to the alleged failures of liberalism in the 1960s and 1970s. Liberalism and its chosen economic strategy of Keynesianism were severely wounded in a number of countries by the stagflation of the 1970s. Norman Thomas writes, "The resurgence of conservatism [in the United States, Great Britain, and Canada] has been a response to the inability of the Keynesian welfare state simultaneously to maintain real economic growth at levels sufficient to finance the rapidly increasing expenditures of its social service programs and to control inflationary forces unleashed by the oil price shocks of 1973–74 and 1979–80. The welfare state had its theoretical foundations in Keynesian conceptions of economic management that involved the use of the state to enforce individual well-being and equality."[6] These liberal foundations were also challenged by Friedrich Hayek's dictum that "government cannot act in the general interest." Conrad Waligorski summarizes the conservative condemnation of governmental intervention and support of unfettered markets:

> The chief conservative indictment of government is that intervention interferes with the operation of the spontaneous market. Conditions in

the market are the best that can be because individual self-interest impels people to make the most efficient use of resources to further their self-interest. . . . Without market controls and cost allocations to identifiable individuals, bureaucratic use of someone else's money ensures that it is wasted. The ostensible purpose of public programs is always subverted to serve the interests of those initiating or administering the program, while taxpayers and supposed beneficiaries at best receive no real benefits and in most cases lose freedom, dignity, and the chance to participate in competitive markets.[7]

The economic slowdown and soaring budget deficits of the 1970s conditioned a wider variety of people to be more receptive to this conservative message.

But the conservative complaints against liberalism were not limited to the field of economics. Conservatives believed that a seductive and self-righteous liberal establishment had spread its influence from government to the media and universities. George McGovern might have been overwhelmingly defeated in 1972 by the electorate, but American society was increasingly being subjected to the liberal Zeitgeist. For conservatives, liberal domination of the culture meant that its ethos stayed in control even when liberal candidates lost elections. When Republican presidents Eisenhower, Nixon, and Ford were in office, the liberal agenda of increasing the powers of the federal government at the expense of the states, along with a foreign policy that was seeking détente with the Soviet Union, continued to be implemented. Republican presidents only slowed the pace of fulfilling the liberal policy agenda; they lacked the conservative conviction to reverse it. Nothing exasperated conservatives more than losing even when they won.

The fear of betrayal by the Republican Party prompted some conservatives to advocate the creation of a third party, but most conservatives had enough political experience to realize that such efforts would probably not be successful. It would be easier to dominate the Republican Party with a conservative candidate like Reagan than to engage in the quixotic quest of constructing a new party. Nevertheless, Richard Viguerie stressed that the New Right would "put philosophy before political party."[8] He even warned President Reagan in 1981 that "never again will conservatives lie down for a Republican President, like they did for Nixon and Ford."[9] In brief, this fervent belief in principle over party suggested that many conservatives were demanding that the Republican Party and Reagan be the instruments of achieving their ideological goals.

Many conservatives believed that the advancement of the liberal agenda would lead to socialism and the end of freedom. An editor of the *National*

Review, Joseph Sobran, wrote, "The ideological form of socialism in America has been liberalism; its political vehicle has been the Democratic Party. . . . It brings us socialism piecemeal, dividing politics into discreet 'issues' and choosing the collectivist option at every turn. Modern liberalism is careful not to embrace socialism *in toto,* but it has no way of drawing the line against total collectivization, and doesn't want to."[10] Because of the growth of liberalism, according to Sobran, "The cancer of socialism has metastasized among us."[11]

Despite their growing influence, conservatives still talked as if it were dangerous to challenge the liberal establishment. Conservative polemics were peppered with phrases like, "No one dares say. . . ." For example, R. Emmett Tyrrell wrote, "there are many truths about American public life that we dare not utter. One is that American public life is thoroughly dominated by the personae and ideology of Liberalism. Another is that today's Liberalism has become radicalized."[12] The conservative's view of the pervasive power of the liberal establishment was nicely articulated by Joseph Sobran:

> The left controls the media, the judiciary, the universities that count; it can magnify its own signals and muffle the right's. It has even succeeded in making its own vocabulary the rhetoric of public discourse. . . . How is the right, as a system of communication, supposed to coalesce? Its lines of communication are in disrepair, under constant threat of sabotage. . . . Imagine a society divided into two classes of people, one of which had telephones while the other didn't. Then you will begin to get the picture. Conservatives lack telephones in today's culture.[13]

Since conservatives attributed so much power to liberals, many of them had no qualms about blaming leftists for most of what was wrong in America by the end of the 1970s. Liberals were blamed for going into Vietnam without the will to win; the humiliation of the Iranian capture of our embassy in Tehran; high and rising taxes; unbalanced budgets that were causing inflation; overregulation of business, which reduced our capacity to compete internationally; social engineering through forced busing, affirmative action, and employment quotas; increased welfare dependency; the decline of traditional family and religious values; the deterioration of public schools; and the rise in the crime rate. By the end of the 1970s, according to the right wing, not even the fog machine of the liberal establishment could hide its bankruptcy and the ineptness of the Carter presidency in dealing with the nation's domestic and foreign policy problems. For many conservatives, Carter became a potent symbol as reflected in Tyrrell's words: "The historic failure of the Carter administration revealed the crack-up of American Liberalism for all to see."[14] Indeed, the collapse of the Carter administration and the failure of Senator Ted Kennedy's campaign in 1980 demonstrated to conservatives (and others) that liberalism was exhausted, bereft of new ideas, and totally incapable of providing effective leadership.

The failures of liberalism created an opening for conservatives to expand their influence. They felt ready to lead and to replace the liberal governing philosophy with a conservative one. High taxes and concerns about too much regulation induced corporate managers and entrepreneurs to contribute money to conservative organizations and think tanks. The Business Roundtable was created in 1972, the Heritage Foundation in 1973. Established conservative think tanks, such as the American Enterprise Institute (AEI), the Hoover Institution, and the Center for Strategic and International Studies at Georgetown University, grew rapidly in the 1970s.[15] Ideologically committed, well financed, facilitated by the latest techniques of direct mail and communications, conservatives felt that they were riding the crest of a political wave, their truths spreading like a "prairie fire." By the 1980s, conservatives believed that they were ready to implement their policy agenda. According to William Schambra, "We no longer ask ourselves *the* question that dominated national politics for fifty years . . . : What major new programs should the federal government undertake in order to bring about a more equitable distribution of resources in America? . . . Instead, we ask ourselves today how we can shore up the 'small societies,' state and local governments, and private associations—and how they can be brought to assume many of the burdens heretofore borne by the federal government. And today we ask ourselves how we may re-stimulate the production of resources in America, rather than how we may insure that resources are equally distributed."[16]

Conservatives believed that although liberal policies had been able to mobilize electoral majorities known as the FDR coalition, by the end of the 1960s, these policies had gravitated too far to the Left. Liberalism had become radicalized and, therefore, alienating. Such policies, by catering to the projects of leftist intellectuals reflecting the concerns of special interests, now antagonized many voters and made them available for conservative mobilization. Liberals in the early 1960s could attract citizens in support of extending the vote to blacks, but later liberal proposals for forced busing and affirmative action programs alienated more groups than they attracted. New Right activists argued that they had populist messages that could construct a conservative majority by appealing to patriotic Americans who wanted a more vigorous defense of national interests, workers and middle-class citizens burdened by high taxes, people frightened by inflation, small businessmen overwhelmed by governmental regulations, Christians outraged by secular humanism in the public schools and by sex and violence in the media, and parents opposed to forced busing.[17]

One cannot help noticing how much the conservative movement has mimicked what it calls the liberal establishment. What conservatives once criticized they now duplicate. They now have their own research foundations, journals and magazines, pundits, and talk show hosts. There is even a "new class" of conservative policy analysts working at subsidized think tanks such as the Heritage Foundation whose research findings (ideologically directed conclusions) inevitably support private enterprise and market solutions while condemning big government. Richard Viguerie said it succinctly: "all the New Right has done is copy the success of the old left."[18] And conservatives in the 1980s hoped that Reagan would emulate the success of Franklin Roosevelt.

VARIETIES OF CONSERVATIVES

In reacting to the liberal establishment, in mobilizing the resentments of many different kinds of voters, the conservative movement evolved into a variety of sects and organizations. What is called, for convenience, the conservative movement is actually a complex cocktail ranging from Catholic William Buckley to Protestant fundamentalist Pat Robertson, from libertarians who want to decriminalize the use of drugs to Christian rightists who want the state to impose the strictest forms of censorship, from Nobel Prize winners in economics such as Milton Friedman to supporters of tobacco subsidies such as Senator Jesse Helms, from Pulitzer Prize–winning columnists such as William Safire and George Will to Congressmen Jack Kemp and Newt Gingrich, from respected scholars Robert Nisbet and James Wilson to acid-penned polemicists Patrick Buchanan and R. Emmett Tyrrell. Table 3.1, below, provides thumbnail sketches of the major types of conservatives that influenced the Reagan presidency.

The first group can be called traditional conservatives, or the Old Right. These conservatives believed that New Deal liberalism and its subsequent mutations had derailed the United States from its traditions of personal freedom and community stability. According to J. David Hoeveler, traditional conservatives "were united by a conviction that the roots of decay in the West lay in the disorders of the modern mind. The Old Right provided conservatives with an edifice constructed variously on theology, metaphysics, or culture."[19]

The key spokesman for this group was William F. Buckley, Jr. More polemicist than philosopher, Buckley attempted to reconcile the conflicting ideals of individualism, the market economy, community, tradition, and anticommunism.

Table 3.1 The Variety of Conservatives During the Reagan Presidency

Types of Conservatives	Principal Spokespeople	Principal Institutions	Major Complaints	Major Goals	Major Disappointments in the Reagan Administration	Major Achievements of the Reagan Administration
Traditional	William Buckley George Will	*National Review*	Liberalism was ending U.S. capacity to preserve its ideals and protect itself from communism	Individual freedom Defeat of communism	Failure to balance the budget INF Treaty with the Soviet Union	Lowering tax rates Articulating conservative values Reducing inflation
New Right	Richard Viguerie Paul Weyrich Howard Phillips Phyllis Schlaffly	Direct mailing lists Committee for the Survival of a Free Congress Conservative Caucus Eagle Forum	Liberalism, with its emphasis on equality of results, was stifling the American dream	Gain control of the Republican Party Make the Conservative Republican Party the majority party Create a conservative establishment that could rule the way the New Deal did	Failure to gain control of Congress Pragmatists prevented Reagan from being Reagan Failure of the Bork nomination Reagan did not groom a conservative successor	Lowering tax rates 90 months of economic growth
Supply-siders	Jude Wanniski Robert Mundell Jack Kemp	*Wall Street Journal*	High tax rates were stifling the economy and entrepreneurial activity	Lower tax rates	Reagan signed several tax increase laws	Lowering tax rates 90 months of economic growth
Neoconservatives	Irving Kristol Norman Podhoretz Michael Novak	*Public Interest Commentary*	Liberals claimed that U.S. foreign policy was morally equivalent to the Soviet Union's behavior New Class	Proclaim the moral superiority of the U.S. over the Soviet Union Reverse the decline of U.S. power Vigorously defend U.S. interests	INF Treaty Failure to overthrow the Sandinistas	Defense buildup Calling the Soviet Union an "evil empire"
Christian Right	Jerry Falwell Pat Robertson	Moral Majority National Christian Action Coalition	Moral decline of U.S.	Overturn *Roe v. Wade* Allow prayer in schools Pass antipornography legislation Challenge secular humanism in schools	Failure to overturn *Roe v. Wade* Failure to legalize school prayer	Articulating Christian and family values

Born to a millionaire Texas oilman and a gentle southern mother and educated at elite schools in the Northeast, Buckley was the proud outsider—a Catholic in a Protestant nation, a southerner among northerners, a conservative among liberals, an elitist among populists. His *National Review*, launched in 1955, was for many years the principal forum wherein liberal ideas and practices were attacked and conservative ideas and practices were debated and promoted. Buckley's "conservatism was a matter of style as well as philosophy, of rhetoric as well as program, of cultural habit as well as ideology."[20]

Buckley was not capable of weaving the various strains of conservatism into a logically coherent philosophy, but he did believe passionately that conservatism was best equipped to defend American ideals against modern liberalism and international communism. He was convinced by Whittaker Chambers, an ex-communist, that the chief threat of communism was its spiritual appeal. Although nominally atheistic and materialistic, communism promised a millennial victory that was insidiously seductive to those alienated and atomized by modern life. Liberalism, Buckley felt, was incapable of mobilizing the national will to counter and defeat the Red menace. With its emphasis in the 1950s on the "end of ideology," liberalism, in Buckley's eyes, exacerbated the problems of different social groups and weakened the capacity of the nation to defend its vital interests. There were truths worth fighting for, but the pragmatic and accommodationist spirit of liberalism anesthetized the legitimate passions of the American people. Liberals were too prone to accept moral relativism; they did not understand that there were many moral issues that could not be compromised. The secular philosophy of liberalism could not provide the fighting faith that America desperately needed. Conservatism, according to Buckley, could.[21]

The second conservative grouping can be labeled the New Right. New Right leaders were more likely to be political activists and polemicists than philosophers. The list of New Right organizations includes Paul Weyrich's Committee for the Survival of a Free Congress, Howard Phillips's Conservative Caucus, Phyllis Schlaffly's Eagle Forum, John Dolan's National Conservative Political Action Committee, and Jesse Helms's National Congressional Club. According to Stephen L. Newman, "The New Right is less a political movement than a collection of constituencies mobilized around such highly charged issues as abortion, school prayer, and the now defeated Equal Rights Amendment. The term 'New Right' was first applied to these groups in the mid-1970s by journalist Kevin Phillips and was quickly adopted by conservative activists who saw the opportunity to create a powerful network. . . . The New Right network is largely the result of their efforts to forge a hard-line conservative coalition, bringing pressure to bear on the moderate Republican establishment."[22] But such a network of organizations allows a number of leaders to maintain their top positions and their ideological priorities.

New Right activists stress that although they share many of the economic and foreign policy ideas of traditional conservatives, they believe that it is necessary to expand the appeal of conservatives to issues that can attract "ethnic and blue-collar Americans, born-again Christians, pro-life Catholics and Jews."[23] In 1980, Richard Viguerie, whose direct-mail skills did so much to construct and expand the New Right, wrote, "We are determined to achieve our goal of organizing the conservative middle-class majority in America. We are convinced that such a new American majority is an idea whose time is now."[24] Thus, within a few decades, conservatives had evolved from the ignominy of their image as an insecure fringe element to the heady atmosphere of being capable of leading a new electoral majority and electing their candidate to the presidency.

The most intriguing feature of the New Right was its effort to cast itself as populist. As populists, New Right activists attempted to replace the "country-club" image of the Republican Party by getting rid of moderates like George Bush. New Right populists also stressed that liberal programs, with their emphasis on equality of results, were actually hindering the traditional American value of equality of opportunity. As they saw it, liberal policies that utilized government controls and high taxes inhibited the fulfillment of the American dream by bringing about the inflation and bureaucratic nightmares that haunted the middle class. While liberals were warning about the limitations of economic growth and the fragility of the environment, New Right populists were proclaiming the unlimited possibilities of people's capitalism. Populist politicians such as Reagan, Jack Kemp, and Newt Gingrich suggested that the initials of the Grand Old Party (GOP) now stood for the Grand Opportunity Party because it was promoting lower taxes, less governmental regulation, enterprise zones, and school vouchers. New Right populists declared that they represented the needs of ordinary citizens while, according to Tyrrell, "New Age liberalism was in essence nothing more complicated or noble than a running argument with life as it was led by normal Americans."[25] To be labeled elitist in America is a handicap. And unlike in the 1950s and 1960s, conservatives now considered themselves typical Americans; liberals were now a minority of weirdos.

A third group of conservatives consisted of supply-siders. It included, for example, economics professor Robert Mundell, business consultant Arthur Laffer, newspapermen Jude Wanniski and Robert Bartley, and politician Jack Kemp. During the 1970s, these men came to the conclusion that Keynesian economics, the system based on manipulating aggregate demand, was intellectually bankrupt because it could neither explain nor provide a policy remedy for the stagflation of the decade. They proposed a new system or, more accurately, repackaged an old idea in classical economics. The old idea was Say's law, which states, "Supply creates its own demand." The new packaging was the Laffer curve, originally scribbled on a napkin, which could explain and sell supply-side economics. Supply-siders argued that the liberal welfare state had created powerful disincentives to economic growth. By lowering tax rates, you could increase the motivation to work longer, increase savings and investments, and produce more. Through the Laffer curve, it could logically be shown that reducing taxes would actually increase revenues. Hence, one did not have to fear that cutting taxes would increase the budget deficit. Indeed, the key to balancing the budget was to slash the oppressive tax rates and allow the incentives to encourage entrepreneurial activity. Whereas liberals tended to believe that only a few possessed entrepreneurial skills, supply-siders asserted, in a populist vein, that many possessed those qualities. And while liberals were critical of entrepreneurial "greed," supply-siders viewed entrepreneurs as the heroic source of economic growth.

Sidney Blumenthal suggests that "supply-side economics was an example of the [conservative] Counter-Establishment in motion, an intricate meshing of media, money, and ideas."[26] The ideas were developed by Robert Mundell and Arthur Laffer; they were publicized by the *Wall Street Journal*; and Jude Wanniski's book on supply-side economics, with the immodest title *The Way the World Works,* was financed by the Smith-Richardson Foundation. Supply-side ideas and optimism were offered at a time (the late 1970s) of great pessimism and uncertainty. The Keynesian consensus was breaking down, and the budget seemed to be spiraling out of control. Supply-siders were the religious zealots who had found the Holy Grail; they had rediscovered the truth that had been buried by liberalism and Keynesian economics. Their insights could save the Republican Party and reinvigorate Reagan's presidential campaign by avoiding the conventional castor-oil strategy of austerity (budget cuts and tax increases) to balance the budget and, instead, provide a politically costless (no painful trade-offs) rationale to cut taxes, stimulate the economy, avoid inflation, and balance the budget. In Blumenthal's words, "The doctrine restated the free-market myth with verve and originality. In an era when the 'limits to growth' were proclaimed, the gnostic supply-siders made claims to knowing the secret of endless wealth: the magic of the marketplace. And in an era when political solutions to fundamental problems were widely considered nearly impossible because of a 'zero-sum' paralysis of interest groups, supply-siders declared that their formula required only a willingness to implement it for the world to be saved."[27] In brief, the supply-siders' prescription would make us free and rich.

Neoconservatives constituted the most combative component of the modern conservative movement. "Neoconservative" was first used by Michael Harrington, a socialist, as a term of rebuke to a set of social scientists, literary critics, and journalists who were intellectually migrating from the Left to the Right. In their youth, many of these intellectuals had identified with the interests of the working class, but in the 1970s they became champions of bourgeois values, defending capitalism and writing op-ed essays for the *Wall Street Journal*. Many of their leaders, such as Irving Kristol and Norman Podhoretz, came from Jewish backgrounds and had gone from being radicals (Trotskyites) in the 1930s to Hubert Humphrey and then Henry Jackson Democrats in the 1950s and 1960s, finally becoming Republicans in the 1970s after George McGovern won the Democratic nomination in 1972. Their favorite form of combat was the essay in such journals as the *Public Interest,* edited by Kristol, and *Commentary,* edited by Podhoretz, and in the editorial pages of the *Wall Street Journal.* The residue of their former radicalism was reflected in their use of class analysis and in their dark aspersions about what liberals were really trying to accomplish. From the neoconservative point of view, since the Vietnam War, the liberal movement had become a kind of Stalinist fellow traveler incapable of vigorously defending our national interest against the aggression of the Soviet Union. Kristol wrote, "Though they [liberals] continue to speak the language of 'progressive reform,' in actuality they are acting upon a hidden agenda: to propel the nation from that modified version we call 'the welfare state' toward an economic system so stringently regulated in detail as to fulfill many of the traditional anticapitalist aspirations of the Left."[28] Fulfillment of the liberal agenda, according to neoconservatives, would surely lead to economic stagnation and dictatorship.

As former Democrats, many neoconservatives have felt a need to justify their switch of allegiance to the Republican Party. Their explanation has been that they maintained their loyalty to the liberal, anticommunist ideals of Truman and Kennedy, but that they were driven from the Democratic Party when it was taken over by leftist radicals in 1972. Podhoretz expressed his alienation from the Democratic Party in these words:

> In foreign policy, liberal Democrats up until 1968 believed in the use of American power to contain the spread of Communism in general and Soviet expansionism in particular; in economic policy they believed in growth as the means to general prosperity; and in social policy they believed in eradicating discrimination against individuals as the best route to social justice. In each of these areas the radical movement repudiated the liberal position. In foreign policy, it attacked the use of American

power to contain Communism as politically ill-advised and morally wrong; in economic policy, it attacked growth as destructive of the quality of life of working people and of the quality of the physical environment; and in social policy, it attacked equality of opportunity as an instrument of "tokenism."[29]

Neoconservatives believe that the liberal orientations that prevailed in the 1960s and 1970s brought about overwhelmingly negative results for the United States. Détente did not encourage more moderate behavior on the part of the Soviet Union; instead, the Soviet Union became more aggressive in Afghanistan. Carter's human rights policy did not bring democracy to the Third World; instead, according to Jeane Kirkpatrick, it helped to undermine the pro-U.S. authoritarian regimes of Iran and Nicaragua, turning them into regional threats to our vital interests. Keynesian fine-tuning of the economy did not stabilize the business cycle; it brought about stagflation. The shift in emphasis from equality of opportunity to equality of results did not culminate in a higher level of community; it fostered increasingly hostile relations between men and women, blacks and whites, gays and straights. Kristol attacked the effects of liberal welfare policies on the poor by suggesting that they had made "the child fatherless, the wife husbandless, the husband useless."[30] In brief, liberal policies were usually counterproductive; they made problems worse.

If liberal programs inevitably fail, why are they constantly proposed? Neoconservatives answer this question by arguing that such policies serve the interests of what they call the "New Class"—social scientists, urban planners, and bureaucrats. Members of the New Class have developed vested interests in designing, promoting, and directing welfare programs. They are the prime beneficiaries of these programs and the welfare dependency that results from them.

After painting this bleak picture, it can come as no surprise that neoconservatives rejected Carter and were attracted to Ronald Reagan. Liberalism was causing the decline of the United States. It simply did not acknowledge that the United States was engaged in a life-or-death struggle with the Soviet Union. As Jeane Kirkpatrick was fond of pointing out, liberalism weakened the resolve of the nation by talking about the "moral equivalence" of the opposing superpower's foreign policies. But how could there be moral equivalency when the United States was cultivating capitalism and democracy and the Soviet Union was promoting communism and tyranny? The country desperately needed a leader who believed that the United States was morally superior to the Soviet Union, that capitalism could outproduce communism in both consumer goods and weapons, and that we had to act like a superpower by vigorously defending our national interests. The neoconservative reasons for believing that Reagan could reverse the decline of the United States are summarized by Podhoretz: "In general, the high hopes I entertained for Reagan were stimulated by his evident conviction that the decline of American power—American military power, American economic power, American political power—was neither inevitable nor irreversible. We had, Reagan suggested, lost or forgotten the principles through which we had become the most productive, the most prosperous, the strongest and the most respected nation on earth; it was up to us to rediscover and rededicate ourselves to them, and he proposed to lead us in this adventurous undertaking."[31]

During the 1970s, the conservative movement added a major new component to its alliance—the Religious Right. Members of the Religious Right felt compelled to abandon their traditional nonpolitical stance because they sensed that the country was experiencing a moral decline due to the fact that so many of its leaders were guided by the secular ideology of liberalism. Religious leaders such as Jerry Falwell felt that because most religious people were not active in politics, a godless minority had been able to dominate the moral majority. The results of liberal domination of the policy process were catastrophic: the divorce rate had soared to 40 percent, pornography dominated the media and was all too available to seduce children, the feminist movement was threatening the traditional family, the widespread use of drugs was destroying lives and causing a rise in the crime rate, abortion was available on demand, the Internal Revenue Service was interfering with Christian schools, and the public schools were dominated by "secular humanism."[32] According to Falwell, "In the last several years, Americans have literally stood by and watched as godless, spineless leaders have brought our nation floundering to the brink of death. . . . It is now time for moral America to band together in a collective voice and make the difference in America by exerting to make their feelings known. The godless minority of treacherous individuals who have been permitted to formulate national policy must now recognize they do not represent the majority. They must be made to see that moral Americans are a powerful group who will no longer permit them to destroy our country with their godless, liberal philosophies."[33] Similarly, television evangelist James Robison proclaimed, "I'm sick and tired of hearing about all the radicals and perverts and liberals and leftists and Communists coming out of the closets. It's time for God's people to come out of the closets, out of the churches, and change America."[34] In 1980, Pat Robertson announced, "We have enough votes to run the country."[35]

Propelling the Religious Right were cultural anxieties caused by social changes associated with the 1960s. From their perspective, liberal elites were forcing them to become strangers in their own country. Their children were being forced to integrate with minorities; their beliefs were being oppressed in the schools by secular humanism; their ideas were being ridiculed in the media. The result was a seething resentment that was soon mobilized by television evangelists and New Right activists.

In Michael Liensch's study of the New Christian Right, he concluded that it "is best understood as an alliance of conservative preachers. Although its leaders publicly boast of its mass membership, they privately admit that the primary constituency is several thousand ministers."[36] These ministers were largely brought together by New Right activists such as Paul Weyrich, Howard Phillips, and Richard Viguerie. As a result of meetings between New Right and Christian Right leaders, new organizations were created at the end of the 1970s, such as the Religious Roundtable headed by Edward McAteer and the Moral Majority directed by Jerry Falwell. As a result of the alliance with conservative activists, the Christian Right in 1980 became very active, producing liberal candidate hit lists, moral report cards, and Christian political action manuals. Lienesch concludes that the New Christian Right "in spirit . . . is extreme and passionate, uncompromising, totally committed, and at times apocalyptic."[37] Stephen Newman suggests that "its fundamentalist partisans are on a symbolic crusade reminiscent of the temperance movement; theirs is a campaign to redefine the values at the core of public life."[38]

The Christian Right supported Reagan in the hope that he would imbue public policy with Christian values and reverse the moral decline of the nation. Their leaders expected that Reagan would appoint conservative judges to the federal courts and reverse *Roe v. Wade*, outlaw pornography, and break the monopoly of secular humanism in public school curricula. They also wanted Reagan to pressure Congress and the states to pass constitutional amendments forbidding abortions and allowing prayer in the schools. Most of all, they desired a president who would articulate their values from the bully pulpit of the White House, which would give them the respect they craved.

SPLITS AMONG CONSERVATIVES

This short review of the conservative movement reveals that it was composed of numerous organizations, each with its own leaders, each stressing the issues that were most important to its members. The conservative movement created a Tower of Babel with many sects speaking in different tongues. While conservative leaders certainly recognize the need for cooperation among their organizations in order to combat the still potent powers of the liberal establishment, the passionate style of their politics, the fear that compromise will lead to betrayal, and the stress of allegiance to principle over political party combine to reduce the capacity for effective interaction and increase the probability of strife. Kevin Phillips, a conservative columnist, expressed his skepticism about the future unity of the movement by writing, "by what dynamics can conservatism continue to encompass populists, Tories, libertarians, ordinary middle-class Americans, religious fundamentalists, farmers, and free-market philosophers?"[39] Blumenthal predicts that Reagan's conservative coalition will be less stable than FDR's, because the latter was bound together by material interests in what the federal government could provide—social security, public works, and so forth. Mutual interests are easier to satisfy than the ever-sharpening demands of conservative groups. In Blumenthal's words, "To maintain its momentum, the Counter-Establishment has a constant need to elaborate its ideology; only an incessant agitation keeps the wheels turning. But conservatives can never resolve their own differences by an appeal to party loyalty, which must be secondary. The Hobbesian permutation, where each faction wars against all, always remains a possibility."[40]

The modern conservative movement was created with an ideology whose components were in conflict with one another. Within the Christian Right there were differences among fundamentalists, evangelicals, and charismatics. Supply-siders were split over the issue of whether the United States ought to return to the gold standard. Traditional conservatives argued among themselves how rapidly the budget ought to be balanced and whether raising taxes should be used to achieve that goal. And among neoconservatives, there were disputes about what should be given initial priority in the Reagan administration—economic recovery or confronting communism.

The fault lines within the conservative movement were obvious: religious conservatives against free-spirited libertarians; supply-siders against the fiscally orthodox; longtime loyalists against the more recent converts.[41] Many traditional and religious conservatives resented the neoconservatives as ex-Democrats and opportunists who harbored liberal ideas concerning prayer in the schools, a woman's right to an abortion, trade union rights, and the welfare state. There were also disputes over tax cuts in which New Right activists demanded that the reductions should be targeted toward families, while some supply-siders asserted that they should be aimed at lowering the rates on capital gains. Arthur Schlesinger caricatured Reagan's coalition as being composed of "one wing devoted to getting government off our backs, the other to putting government in our beds."[42] Similarly, John Lukacs wrote, "The conservatives argued against big government, yet they favored the most monstrous of government projects: laser warfare, biological warfare, nuclear super-bombs. They were against the police state, yet they were eager to extend the powers of the F.B.I. and the C.I.A. . . . They stood for the conservation of America's heritage, yet they were usually indifferent to the conservation of the American land."[43] Clearly, the conservative movement was both helped and hindered by its stress on ideology. Ideology aided the movement in mobilizing the resentments of millions of citizens, but it also increased the probability of splits within the movement.

CONSERVATIVE PERSONNEL

However much leaders of the conservative movement might argue about ideological issues, they were in agreement that the Reagan administration ought to fill its political appointments with their members. Conservatives stressed that they had not only the ideas to govern but also the dedicated personnel to operate the machinery of government. Appointing nonconservatives would only assure the watering down and failure of the Reagan revolution. Conservatives repeated the dictum that "people are policy" and that the Heritage Foundation, the AEI, the Hoover Institution, and the Center for Strategic and International Studies could supply the newly elected Reagan presidency with lists of qualified conservatives. Throughout the Reagan years, conservatives measured their progress by counting the number of political appointments they attained in comparison to the number received by regular Republicans. Their goal, domination of the commanding heights of the Reagan administration, was never achieved. By denying conservatives hegemony, Reagan increased his flexibility for political leadership.

Although the Reagan presidency did appoint more conservatives than any previous Republican administration, they received only a minority of political appointments. Although it is not always easy to classify a political appointee as either a conservative or a regular Republican (for example, how would you designate Caspar Weinberger?), Thomas Langston estimates, based on biographical sketches in the *Congressional Quarterly Weekly Report* in 1981, "that approximately 69 of 350 appointees profiled there came to work for the Reagan administration with conservative credentials, as opposed to backgrounds in regular Republican politics."[44] Blumenthal reported that, by 1985, the Heritage Foundation had placed thirty-six of its people in the administration, including James Watt as secretary of the interior and William Bennett as chairman of the National Endowment for the Humanities and then as secretary of education; Murray Weidenbaum of AEI was chairman of the Council of Economic Advisers, and AEI's James Miller was, first, chairman of the Federal Trade Commission and, later, director of the Office of Management and Budget (OMB); the Hoover Institution had fifty of its scholars in the administration; and the Center for Strategic and International Studies counted eighteen of its members in government positions.[45]

The top-profile conservatives in the Reagan presidency were those who had served him in California when he was governor. Edwin Meese was not appointed chief of staff, but he did receive the counselor position, with Cabinet-level status, and was put in charge of policy development. In Reagan's second term, Meese served as attorney general. Some movement conservatives were initially opposed to Caspar Weinberger's selection as secretary of defense because he had served as director of OMB in the Nixon administration. They were afraid that he would live up to his old nickname of "Cap the Knife," but when Weinberger constantly championed big increases in the defense budget, his new name because "Cap the Shovel," and he became a conservative favorite. Lyn Nofziger failed to receive the position of press secretary and served as a White House political aide for a year. William Clark served in the State Department, as National Security Council (NSC) adviser, and then as secretary of the interior.

Given the high visibility of economic issues in the Reagan years, surprisingly few supply-siders were appointed. David Stockman was considered a supply-sider when he was named director of OMB, but he soon betrayed that ideology in the William Grieder interview and by supporting tax increases to balance the budget. Supply-siders had wanted Lewis Lehrman, owner of the Rite Aid drugstore chain, to be secretary of the treasury, but Reagan appointed Donald Regan from Merrill Lynch. Norman Ture and Paul Craig Roberts were both placed in the Treasury Department (undersecretary for tax and economic affairs and assistant secretary for economic policy, respectively), but both resigned in 1982.

Neoconservatives were more successful in foreign policy. Jeane Kirkpatrick was named ambassador to the United Nations but was stymied in her efforts to become either NSC adviser or secretary of state. Norman Podhoretz had wanted to head the U.S. Information Agency, but Charles Wick, a friend of the Reagans, got that job. Reagan did appoint Elliott Abrams, Podhoretz's son-in-law and former aide to Senator Henry Jackson, as assistant secretary of state for Latin American affairs. Richard Perle, another former aide to Jackson, became assistant secretary of defense. Kenneth Adelman, a former student of Jeane Kirkpatrick, was appointed director of the Arms Control and Disarmament Agency. Dr. Ernest Lefever was nominated to be the assistant secretary for human rights, but because he had spoken so disparagingly about

U.S. efforts to promote human rights overseas, his nomination was rejected by a thirteen-to-four vote in the Senate Foreign Relations Committee.

When movement conservatives saw that they were not going to dominate the Reagan administration, they consoled themselves with the notion that they were establishing the credentials of a younger generation of conservatives who would go on to play more significant roles in future presidencies. The model was FDR's administration, which had trained numerous young lawyers who then influenced policy making for the next thirty years. Conservatives claimed that the Reagan years was their time to be "credentialed" in the Washington establishment. Although Republican regulars might still be dominant, the future would be different, as predicted by the head of the Heritage Foundation, Edwin Feulner:

> Conservatism is emphatically *not* the old Republicans. . . . It's a case of trend lines. Conservatives are in an up trend. Republicans are in a down trend . . . the Republicans are quietly becoming not the dominant element. . . . Our infrastructure was never built up in the Nixon administration. By and large Reagan relied on the Establishment to staff his administration. Our bright young people hadn't had the on-the-job training to be really credible. Ten years from now it will be very different. Next time around, there might be fifty percent conservatives—an order of magnitude larger. You won't be counting the James Watts one at a time.[16]

This optimistic view was countered by the perception in Washington that conservatives were frequently outmaneuvered by the pragmatists within the Reagan administration. James Baker's staff clearly outperformed Meese's. Within a year of the beginning of the Reagan presidency, Baker had increased his power, while Meese's influence had declined. Many conservatives, such as Martin Anderson and Paul Craig Roberts, became frustrated and resigned. Scandals were associated with a number of conservatives, such as Richard Allen, James Watt, Anne Burford, and Meese himself, and gave rise to the "sleaze factor" issue. The Iran-Contra scandal was particularly damaging during the second administration.

CONSERVATIVE CRITICISMS OF THE REAGAN ADMINISTRATION

Throughout the eight years of the Reagan presidency, conservative leaders complained about his leadership but never deserted him. Their motivation was revealed by John Lofton, an editor for the *Conservative Digest:* "The history of the conservative's relations with Ronald Reagan is trying to hold his feet to the fire he himself lit."[47] Conservatives had a vested interest in fanning the fires of conflict and confrontation; as a president, Reagan usually did not. Based on his impassioned speech delivered repeatedly over two decades about the threat of communism and the dangers of big government, many conservatives "expected President Reagan's arrival in Washington to be like Carrie Nation's in a saloon."[48] But instead of smashing furniture, the amiable Reagan appeared to be too accommodating to the ways of Washington. The problem was symbolized for conservatives on December 10, 1980, when the president-elect passed up the annual banquet of the AEI to attend a private dinner party in Georgetown hosted by Katherine Graham, owner of the *Washington Post.*

The conservatives were not pleased when Reagan, during the 1980 Republican convention, had negotiated with former president Gerald Ford about the vice presidency, but they were shocked when he selected George Bush, the epitome of the moderate, country-club Republican, as his running mate. While this move promoted party unity, conservatives feared that Reagan had neglected an opportunity to groom a conservative successor. After Reagan was elected, conservatives complained that he appointed too many moderate mercenaries and not enough Reagan revolutionaries. While pragmatists viewed the hiring of a variety of Republicans as a means of broadening the president's political base, this was frowned upon by conservatives as a typical Washington procedure that would water down Reagan's programs.

What particularly set off the alarm bells of conservatives was Reagan's selection of James Baker, instead of Ed Meese, as White House chief of staff. Since Baker, a pragmatist who had worked for Ford and Bush, was a Washington insider with no ties to the conservative movement, conservatives could not fathom why the president had put him in charge of White House operations. From their perspective, Baker would control access to Reagan and thus be in a position to screen conservative advice from reaching the president. Baker immediately became their chief villain, a "liberalizing Rasputin" who encouraged Reagan to adjust to, rather than confront, the liberal establishment. Following Baker's advice, Reagan flip-flopped on many of his conservative principles and became, in the conservative mind, "Carterized." When Baker directed Reagan's 1984 reelection campaign, the conservatives accused him of running an issueless popularity contest that never tried to receive a mandate from voters to launch new conservative initiatives. With Baker at the helm, the administration was, according to Howard Phillips, "unprepared to grab problems by the neck. If Reagan continues this way, he'll be very popular—and very irrelevant."[49] In 1982 Phillips complained, "Baker's group calls the plays, and Reagan runs with the ball. Baker only understands negotiating and compromise. What he is doing is destroying Reagan's reputation for integrity and principle."[50] In a *Time* magazine interview, Richard Viguerie revealed that it was precisely Baker's skills that conservatives felt were his major vice: " 'Jim is a reasonable person who sits down with the opposition and works things out,' complains Richard Viguerie . . . who considers such reasonableness a weakness. In Viguerie's view, Baker 'doesn't understand confrontation politics.' "[51]

In Reagan's second term, when the president fired Donald Regan as chief of staff and replaced him with Senator Howard Baker, another moderate, Viguerie again whined, "You can't fight a revolution without revolutionaries. In Washington, putting Howard Baker in charge of the White House is called a master stroke. Out in the real world, it's what they call running up the white flag."[52]

It was frustrating for conservative leaders that the Reagan presidency would be classified as a conservative regime and evaluated in terms of what a conservative government could accomplish, when conservatives constituted only a minority faction within the administration. This situation was exacerbated by the power given to pragmatists such as James Baker, who forged alliances with public relations figures such as Michael Deaver to restrain Reagan's conservative instincts. In James Watt's telling phrase, moderates in the White House were not letting "Reagan be Reagan." Conservatives were sure that Reagan was one of their own, and if only he were freed from pragmatic bondage, he would act accordingly. But after hearing all these public and private complaints, Reagan never freed himself from his pragmatic advisers. It is significant that Reagan appointed four chiefs of staff during his eight years in office and not one of them was a movement conservative.

Conservatives also griped about how the Reagan administration dealt with a number of issues. The Christian Right, for example, was bitterly disappointed that its moral issues were placed on the back burner in 1981 when the administration was mainly concerned with economic policies. They and other conservative leaders were also angry when Reagan nominated Sandra Day O'Connor for the Supreme Court because she was not militantly opposed to abortion. For religious conservatives who compared the *Roe v. Wade* decision to Auschwitz, this choice was reprehensible. In response, Patrick Buchanan wrote in his column: "The White House boys have just made the most basic mistake you can make in politics: They have compromised the vital interests of the President's most ardent followers, to score brownie points with their political enemies. A frivolous campaign promise has been kept, and a solemn written commitment violated."[53] Early in 1982, conservatives were embarrassed by how ineptly the administration handled the issue of tax exemptions for religious schools. In this situation, popularly known as the Bob Jones case, moderates were angry that the White House, under the leadership of Meese, initiated an effort to reverse a decade of Internal Revenue and federal court rulings; then conservatives were outraged when the administration, in response to a storm of protest, reversed itself and sought legislation to guarantee that tax benefits not be allocated to schools that discriminate.[54]

Many conservatives, but especially supply-siders, were disturbed in 1982 when Reagan signed a $98 billion tax increase in order to reduce the budget deficit. In August 1982, thirty conservatives met in Washington to voice their opposition to the tax increase. The group included Congressman Jack Kemp, former White House aides Martin Anderson and Lyn Nofziger, Irving Kristol, and former supply-side Treasury officials Norman Ture and Paul Craig Roberts. Roberts was quoted as saying, "There were more Reaganites in that room than there are in the Administration, and ten times as many as there are in the White House."[55] After the 1982 tax increase was signed by Reagan, William Buckley wrote, "The collapse of Reaganomics is testimony to a failure of nerve and understanding."[56]

Conservatives were also critical of Reagan's foreign policy. The New Right was especially upset that the president was not supporting Taiwan as much as they expected. Senator Jesse Helms argued that State Department officials and White House aides were causing Reagan to "imitate" the "disastrous foreign policies of Carter and Kissinger." Howard Phillips angrily added that "Conservatives had no stake in Reagan's foreign policy. Neither does Ronald Reagan, though I'm not sure he knows it."[57] Although compromise was unprincipled from the conservative point of view, it was politically successful in that it maintained our support for Taiwan without breaking our ties with China.

Neoconservatives were also critical of Reagan's foreign policy. While praising the president's unabashed assertions of U.S. moral superiority over the "evil empire" of communism, they were disappointed that the administration's deeds did not live up to the standards of its rhetoric. Podhoretz deplored Reagan's first significant foreign policy decision, lifting Carter's grain embargo against the Soviet Union. He also criticized the president for a very weak response to the Polish crisis of 1981–1982. In both of these cases, Podhoretz charged, echoing a George Will gibe, that the administration appeared "to love commerce more than it loathed communism." Reviewing Reagan's foreign policy during his first term, Podhoretz believed that it merely continued the strategy of containment and détente, which, from the neoconservative point of view, was the policy of the liberal establishment. Neoconservatives had expected a more aggressive policy aimed at winning the Cold War. (In a profound way, Reagan's endorsement of the Strategic Defense Initiative [SDI] partially fulfilled that expectation.) Podhoretz also feared that Reagan in his second term might be "lured by seductive fantasies of what historians in the future might say of him as a peacemaker" into accepting détente with the Soviet Union as his policy. The problem, in Podhoretz's words, was that "Reagan, while perhaps more swayed by ideological convictions than most professional politicians, showed in his first term (as he had already demonstrated when Governor of California . . .) that . . . he was more politician than ideologue. As such he would go only so far, and no farther, against the pressures of public opinion, and the resistance of the media and the permanent government; he would wherever possible cut his political losses after doing anything risky or unpopular; and in the face of serious opposition, he would usually back down even from a policy to which he was personally devoted."[58] This was a fairly accurate characterization of Reagan's political style of leadership, and it indicated that he would not allow himself to be steered by his ideological followers. Reagan would navigate his own course.

Reagan's foreign policy during his second term continued to disappoint most conservatives. The Sandinistas remained in control of Nicaragua, and the administration was caught trading arms for hostages with the terrorist state of Iran. But what infuriated a wide range of conservatives was the administration's increasing belief that it could conduct business with Mikhail Gorbachev, who had come to power in 1985. The pictures of Reagan and Gorbachev developing a personal relationship in a series of summit meetings, along with the successful negotiation of the Intermediate Nuclear Forces (INF) Treaty, helped Reagan recover from the Iran-Contra scandal, but they frightened conservatives, who maintained their bedrock conviction that it was perilous to trust the Russians. As relations with the Soviet Union improved, Secretary of State George Shultz replaced James Baker as the conservatives' chief pragmatist villain within the administration for successfully negotiating the INF Treaty. By the end of 1987, Howard Phillips charged that Reagan was "fronting as a useful idiot for Soviet propaganda."[59] William Buckley concluded, "Any way you look at it, our foreign policy is a mess."[60] Within several years, the Russians left Afghanistan, the Sandinistas were voted out of office, the Berlin Wall came tumbling down and Germany was reunited, the states of Eastern Europe regained their sovereignty, the Soviet Union disintegrated, and the idea of communism collapsed. Some mess.

A surprising conservative criticism of Reagan, given his Hollywood and television background, was that he did nothing to create a conservative counterculture to challenge the prevailing liberal Zeitgeist. Tyrrell stresses that politics is waged in the culture (universities, books, movies, and television) as well as at the polls. Whereas Democratic presidents had gotten their messages across to the public in books and movies like *The Grapes of Wrath* and *PT-109*, the Reagan message was frequently lampooned by the media in such programs as *All in the Family* and *M*A*S*H*. In Tyrrell's words, "Despite all the chatter about Reagan's bringing Hollywood to the banks of the Potomac, there was never an effort to create a Republican Camelot or a *Sunrise at Campobello*."[61]

A major conservative criticism of Reagan paralleled a liberal view—namely, that the president was a hands-off executive who frequently did not know what was going on. By not being familiar with the details of policy, Reagan often conveyed the impression that he was not committed to a program. His laid-back, amiable style suggested that he was not focused on dealing with all the crises that conservatives felt he should be. Conservatives could not comprehend why Reagan allowed himself to be surrounded by mushy compromisers. Although Reagan was obviously competitive enough to energetically rebound from four straight primary defeats in 1976, in the conservative view, the lethargic, intellectually passive side of his personality prevailed too often. Reagan seemed to be enjoying himself and in no hurry, while conservatives were anxious, after so many years in the wilderness, to take advantage of their moment in power. These anxieties were multiplied by the fact that Reagan had barely survived an assassination attempt, and conservatives had no obvious successor. Conservative frustration frequently surfaced in morbid humor, as when Judge Robert Bork's nomination to the Supreme Court was rejected by the Senate in 1987 and one conservative responded, "This never would have happened if Reagan were still alive."[62]

The politically correct way for conservatives to criticize Reagan was to blame the people who advised him for constructing a comfortable cocoon around him that prevented Reagan from being his conservative self. Only a few conservatives made the obvious point that a president has the freedom and authority to construct and to interact with his advisory system. In 1982, a conservative from California wrote, "The real problem in Washington today from a conservative's standpoint is not James Baker . . . ; the problem is a president who refuses to take the time to understand policy and is therefore unable to take command himself. The one person who is scuttling Reaganism is Dutch Reagan. . . . Not in this century has there been a chief executive so uninformed about his administration's policies and so unconcerned about that lack of information. . . . He is oblivious to the continual bickering within his administration, and keeps himself deliberately removed from it."[63] At the end of the Reagan presidency, a scholar at the Hoover Institution wrote, "The incredible internal diversity of the administration has turned Reagan's winning personal qualities—the aw-shucks, all-American charm, the unintense, non-analytical intellectual style, the breezy moralism—into a crippling liability for a president. This was one administration that really required a firm hand at the helm and a clear mind and penetrating vision at the top if it was to get anywhere. Ronald Reagan has many virtues, but they don't include the intellectual power and moral insight needed to pull the complex strands of the nation's politics together in a coherent political whole."[64]

Conservatives complained about Reagan's administrative style because they felt that he was not using his time and resources as efficiently as he should to fulfill their agenda. Liberalism had been in power for so long; there were so many liberal programs to repeal. There were also so many conservative policies to enact and administer in order to reverse the decline of the United States. Conservatives wanted Reagan to institutionalize a rightist regime in the way FDR had created a liberal one that lasted long after he died. What frightened conservatives was that almost everything Reagan accomplished could be undone by some future Democratic president and a Democratic Congress.

CONCLUSION

What is called the conservative movement is actually a loose alliance of organizations motivated by a variety of ideas, principles, and grievances. This movement evolved from a ridiculed minority in the 1950s to a major player in the politics of the 1980s. But conservatives confronted a number of problems in transforming themselves from a philosophy of protest to a philosophy of governance: their leaders were often in competition with one another; their ideas and priorities were not always compatible; their ability to cooperate in support of a political leader and his programs was in doubt. Because of their obscure origins and sudden success, conservatives oscillated between being an insecure group that felt it was ignored, ridiculed, persecuted, and betrayed and being one that was supremely confident that it possessed the eternal truths and was ready to provide uncompromising leadership for a national revival.

Reagan became the leader of the conservative movement primarily because of his ability to articulate its ideas with a rare blend of eloquence and humor. He could speak for the many brands of conservatives and broaden their movements' appeal. Reagan could not only rally the convinced in the choir, he was able to attract former liberals, ethnics, and working-class Democrats. The challenge for the Reagan presidency was whether it would be able to satisfy the huge expectations of conservatives—who demanded that the liberal regime be destroyed and replaced by a conservative one. Many conservatives were seriously concerned whether Reagan's administrative arrangements and easy-going decision-making style—the focus of the next chapter—could lead them to the promised land.

4

PRESIDENT REAGAN'S ADMINISTRATIVE FORMULA FOR POLITICAL SUCCESS (AND A FEW DISASTERS)

Many studies of the presidency suggest that, given his awesome responsibilities, the president should be the best-informed person in the nation. No one would argue that Ronald Reagan was that person during his two administrations. And yet Reagan experienced more political success in terms of electoral victories, public approval, and policy achievements than several of his predecessors and successors who were undoubtedly better informed than he was. A fundamental chore of any study of the Reagan presidency is to explain how that administration achieved a significant amount of success, even though it was led by a man who possessed few of the leadership qualities stressed in the presidential literature. Even Richard Neustadt is reduced to the intellectually weak argument that Reagan was the luckiest president since Calvin Coolidge.[1]

A major part of the explanation for Reagan's success—and for several of his disasters—can be based on analyses of his relationship with the White House staff. Thanks to a relatively large number of revealing "kiss-and-tell" memoirs by members of the Reagan administration, each of which paints a similar portrait of his detached leadership style, we already know a great deal about his managerial behavior. Much of what we have learned makes it easier to relate President Reagan's managerial style to the failure of Iran-Contra than to the more numerous political victories he enjoyed. And it is highly unlikely that we are going to discover sometime in the future, when the Reagan Presidential Library makes its holdings available to scholars, that Reagan was duplicating Eisenhower's hidden-hand style of political leadership.[2]

This chapter analyzes Reagan's managerial style in terms of how he attracted the support of, and interacted with, three types of staff members:

conservatives, pragmatists, and public relations experts. It is my argument that the chronic conflict among these officials served the political purposes of President Reagan. In support of this thesis, I briefly describe those aspects of Reagan's personality that are relevant for understanding his unique leadership style, analyze the strengths and weaknesses of the three types of staff members recruited by the Reagan presidency, and portray how Reagan interacted with his staff. The principal arguments are summarized in Table 4.1, below.

RONALD REAGAN: PERSONALITY AND PHILOSOPHY

Reagan's most important personality characteristic was his optimism. With the notable exceptions of having an alcoholic father and being diagnosed with Alzheimer's disease in 1994, Reagan has led a charmed life. He was born on February 6, 1911, in Tampico, Illinois, but was raised in Dixon, Illinois. His mother was a devoted member of the Disciples of Christ Church who taught her son how to perform—reciting poetry and acting in plays—at an early age.

Table 4.1   President Reagan's Personality and Administrative Style

Reagan's Personality Characteristics	Consequences of Reagan's Administrative Style
Optimism	Faith in his subordinates; faith that his programs would eventually work; faith that every problem had a solution; an expectation that his staff would provide solutions, not problems
Stubbornness	Pushing for the conservative agenda; allowing Reagan to play the role of a conviction politician and maintain the support of movement conservatives; facilitating the ability of pragmatists to negotiate the best available deal
Friendly but impersonal	Facilitated Reagan's ability to use the talents of his three kinds of staff
Intellectual passivity	Detached management style; dissipated responsibility and deflected political heat; provided a plausible denial in the Iran-Contra scandal; minimized the need for Reagan to take sides in the struggle among conservatives, pragmatists, and public relations types; maximized the stakes in the struggle among the three groups; allowed pragmatists to negotiate arrangements without Reagan realizing how much his values might have been compromised
Persistent performer	Because of his role-relevant experience in Hollywood, Reagan was prone to accept the advice of public relations experts and stress his public role; for Reagan to perform best, his mind could not be cluttered with facts; an informed Reagan was often a less effective performer

In 1932, Reagan graduated from Eureka College, a Disciples of Christ Church school, with a C average. After graduation, in the midst of the depression, he soon found a job as a radio announcer in Iowa. As a sports announcer, he accompanied the Chicago Cubs to California for spring training in 1937 and was granted a screen test. He was hired by Warner Brothers and subsequently made fifty-four movies over the next twenty years. Reagan's movie reputation was that of an easy-to-direct actor who quickly learned his lines because of his photographic memory.

In Hollywood, he married Jane Wyman, became president of the Screen Actors Guild, and was active in politics as a Democrat supporting his hero, Franklin D. Roosevelt. Jane Wyman became a bigger star than her husband and divorced him in 1949. Three years later, Reagan married Nancy Davis. In 1954, as Reagan's acting career fizzled, he was hired by General Electric to be the host of its television series. He also agreed to travel around the country speaking to GE employees, an experience that developed his skills in political rhetoric.

In 1964, after GE canceled his contract, Reagan delivered a very successful speech in support of Goldwater's campaign that was broadcast on national television. A group of California millionaires were so impressed by this speech that they agreed to finance Reagan's 1966 campaign for governor of California against the Democratic incumbent Pat Brown (Reagan had joined the Republican Party in 1962). Ultimately, both Reagan and his millionaire backers saw him as a prime candidate for the presidency.

Reagan defeated Brown in 1966 and was reelected in 1970. He retired from the governorship in 1974, and in 1976 he ran in the Republican presidential primaries, narrowly losing to President Gerald Ford. Four years later, he was elected president. In brief, Reagan's life seemed to confirm his mother's religious belief that God has a positive plan for each of us. Like Voltaire's Candide, Reagan always expected things to work out for the best, which helped him to be happy and self-confident.

As an optimist, Reagan was prone to think that there was a solution— usually a simple one—to any problem. As an ideologue, he was likely to assume that the solution was compatible with his conservatism. Reagan was optimistic about America, markets, religion, heroes, and the military; he was pessimistic about the federal government's ability to resolve problems. He had faith in his instincts and his staff and felt, therefore, that there was no need to search for facts or agonize over alternative solutions. In his worldview, good intentions led to good results; he never second-guessed himself. This perspective was protected by his ability to screen out from his consciousness dissonant facts that did not confirm his ideological expectations. Given the way his mind worked, Reagan was incapable of experiencing cognitive dissonance. Hence, Reagan was generally a happy and secure person; he did not have the low self-esteem associated with James David Barber's concept of the passive-positive personality.

Reagan was also a "conviction politician." Even those who ridiculed Reagan's convictions often conceded that they were honestly held. Reagan's beliefs were derived not from books but from his life experiences and from his mythical perceptions of American history. In Reagan's mind, "we the people" of the United States had discovered long ago the right values and the correct answers to all the big questions. The eternal truths of individual liberty and limited government had been verified by our nation's history. Since these values were both morally correct and proven in their practical application, no one could be more stubborn in their defense than Ronald Reagan. The contemporary problems of the nation were due to our having been seduced off the righteous path by leftist liberals who had overtaxed and overregulated the nation's citizens. The obvious solution was to return to the traditional values that had served us so well. Thus, Reagan's vision of the future was derived from the past. As explained by Sidney Blumenthal, "the dreams Reagan had of the future were not prophetic, for the future appeared only in the guise of the past. What he recollected was not really history, but fable. His wisdom was not illuminated by a precise memory or erudition, but by archetypical stories in which he always placed himself."[3]

Since there were only a few simple truths and Reagan already knew them, he felt no need to engage in any rigorous intellectual activity. Most of the president's aides learned that he thought anecdotally, not analytically. His photographic mind meant that he easily memorized the speeches written for him. In addition, he had inherited his father's ability to tell stories and to interject quips that could substitute for—and camouflage—a lack of substantive knowledge. He was content to see the big picture, to point out the right direction, and leave the details to his subordinates. The explanation that the president was not a detail man became a mantra for Reaganites and implied that possessing detailed information was only for smaller minds and Jimmy Carter.

Reagan's intellectual passivity was legendary among his staff. One of them told two journalists that "Ronald Reagan is not a stupid person . . . but he was the least curious person that I have ever met."[4] A former campaign manager, John Sears, said that it was part of Reagan's "habit to operate on the surface without a plan of how to get from here to there."[5] Lou Cannon, a longtime observer of Reagan, wrote, "Most of the time, President Reagan was intuitively keen but intellectually lazy. . . . He did not know enough. And he did not know how much he didn't know."[6] Peggy Noonan, a speechwriter for Reagan, admitted, "There were times when I would see the earnest young people in the middle levels of the administration trying to get someone to listen to their thoughts . . . and see the sunny president who did not seem to know or notice, and I would think to myself . . . that the battle for the mind of Ronald Reagan was like the trench warfare of World War I: Never have so many fought so hard for such barren terrain."[7] But the most perceptive observation was made by the journalist David Broder: "Reagan, as everyone must know by now, is the living refutation of Francis Bacon's aphorism that 'knowledge is power.' He knows what he thinks and has the power of his own beliefs. But he treats knowledge as if it were dangerous to his convictions. Often it is."[8] Obviously, Reagan did not fulfill Richard Neustadt's presidential job description of being his own political intelligence adviser in order to discern his personal power stakes in each of the many issues he had to decide.

Watching Reagan as an actor or as a politician, one realizes that he was a persistent performer, an affable man with a competitive urge to win and to be loved because he was acting in a morally correct way. In the movies, he always wanted to play cowboy heroes. As president, he enjoyed playing the ultimate hero who saved the nation from the internal threat of big government and the external threat of the "evil empire" of communism. Reagan was a moralist without being a prude; he led a happy crusade that did not call for any sacrifices.

Reagan loved to receive applause and to make people laugh. As a performing salesman, he sold religion, sports, Hollywood, General Electric, the conservative ideology, and himself. Success came to Reagan not because of his hard work but largely because of his attributes as a performer: his voice, his good looks, his sense of humor, his charm, and especially his ability to attract others to work hard for him.[9] As a performer, and as a populist, he sought to appeal to as wide an audience as possible. Unlike many movement conservatives who stressed their exclusivity, Reagan, the former Democrat who frequently quoted FDR, was an inclusive political leader who succeeded in enlisting the support of a wide variety of people. While Reagan's opponents constantly underestimated and ridiculed him for being an actor, he frequently triumphed precisely because he was an actor who believed in his performance.

In terms of his political behavior, Reagan was always classified as a conservative, but he was less rigidly conservative in policy behavior than many people believed. His conservatism could be diluted by his desire to receive applause, by his inattention to detail, and by his management style, with its extensive delegation of authority to subordinates, many of whom were more moderate than their boss. It was natural for the laid-back and eternally optimistic Reagan to delegate a considerable amount of authority to underlings and feel assured that his intentions would be implemented. Indeed, Reagan had such faith that his commands would be carried out that he never felt any need to verify whether staff behavior was fulfilling his conservative agenda.

Finally, although nearly everyone agrees that Reagan was a very likable person, there is also a consensus that only Nancy Reagan was close to him. Reagan was always friendly and courteous but rarely open and intimate with aides. He could be as friendly with a doorman as with an aide who had served him for years. James Baker told Peggy Noonan that Reagan was "the kindest and most impersonal man I have ever known." She concludes that Reagan was "a power source" that was "cool at the core."[10] In 1979, Reagan was willing to follow John Sears's advice to release one of his closest aides and friends, Michael Deaver. This demonstrates an essential paradox in Reagan's leadership style: though very dependent on his staff, by considering none of them indispensable, he perhaps unknowingly reduced their potential power over him.

Working with Reagan was like making a movie. A group of actors, directors, writers, cameramen, and so forth would labor together intensely for a period of time, complete the project, then split up and form a new team to make a new movie. It is possible that once aides recognized how little Reagan understood and appreciated their efforts on his behalf, they felt free to vent their frustrations by writing memoirs that, despite all their protestations of admiration for the man, ultimately paint an unflattering portrait of him.

REAGAN'S WHITE HOUSE STAFF

Like any president, Reagan had the kind of White House staff he wanted. It was composed of three types of individuals: conservatives, pragmatists, and practitioners in the field of public relations. (This categorization is not rigid; it does not mean that an adviser characterized as a conservative could not also have pragmatic inclinations.) Under Reagan, the interaction of these three groups was conflictual, but it was also politically effective because each provided the president with vital services. The conflict among these disparate staff members existed whether the White House was organized in the troika system of the first administration or the more centralized system of the second. And it continued through a whole series of personnel changes. Such conflict was simply endemic to Reagan's management style. It seems somewhat ironic that a leader who extolled the values of community created a White House environment characterized by "backstabbing and knifing each other and anonymous sources killing each other with . . . gossip."[11] In such a hostile environment, one sought protective alliances.

The most tightly knit group was the conservatives—bound together by ideology, by Adam Smith ties, and by a commitment to Ronald Reagan. Conservatives such as Edwin Meese, William Clark, Martin Anderson, Edwin Harper, John Svahn, Gary Bauer, Jeane Kirkpatrick, and Peggy Noonan provided the energy and the ideological direction for the Reagan presidency. Their chief weakness was that they often lacked the federal government experience and the policy knowledge of their chief adversaries, the pragmatists, headed by James Baker. Consequently, although Reagan always kept a cluster of conservatives around him, he frequently selected pragmatists for the most important positions—especially the position of White House chief of staff. Nor were the conservatives as skilled as the pragmatists in the art of public relations, a fatal flaw in Reagan's highly image-conscious White House.

Conservatives oscillated between feelings of arrogant grandeur and whimpering insecurity. At times they felt that their historical moment had come; they had put Reagan into power, and he would lead a conservative revolution that would change the United States and the world. At other times they were the helpless victims of a Bush-Baker cabal, aided by the liberal media, that was denying them the fruits of their victory by isolating and misinforming the president. Thus, the conservative James Watt, secretary of the interior, charged that the pragmatists were not letting Reagan be Reagan. For conservatives, Reagan was not being his true self whenever he appointed a pragmatist to a key office (selecting George Shultz as secretary of state in 1982), signed a tax increase (in 1982 and 1983), transacted a legislative compromise with the Democrats (Social Security reform in 1983), or negotiated a diplomatic arrangement with Mikhail Gorbachev (the INF Treaty in 1987).

While the pragmatists and public relations experts argued that the Reagan administration had to accommodate political realities, the conservatives advocated that the president should militantly pursue a broad range of economic, social, and foreign policy goals. It made no sense to hoard the president's popularity; it should be used to reverse the misguided policies the United States had pursued since the 1930s. Conservatives were convinced that the Great Communicator could circumvent Congress and the media to mobilize an increasingly large majority (an electoral realignment) to fulfill their agenda,[12] and they were in a hurry (especially after the nearly successful March 1981 assassination attempt). They felt that their views had been excluded and ridiculed (as Neanderthal) since the 1930s; they were more alienated and more anxious to change the America of the 1980s than were the pragmatists and, to their dismay, Reagan himself. The happy and accommodating Reagan agreed with the conservatives' dissatisfaction with the America of the 1980s, but he did not share their rage.

The conservatives' strategy did not work because they remained a minority within the administration; they could not attain allies, could not successfully manipulate the media, and could not enlist the full support of the president. Too many conservatives had loyalty tests—were you with us in 1968 and especially in 1976?—that served to exclude potential allies. Conservative proposals and rhetoric were frequently untempered by concerns for political feasibility and public relations. In the second administration, Patrick Buchanan, the director of communications, strenuously objected to Donald Regan's aides' watering down Reagan's conservatism into their "Constructive Republican Alternative Proposals (CRAP)."[13] And he conveyed what he thought about Deaver and public relations by labeling Deaver "Lord of the Chamber Pot."

The conservative role and dilemma were best personified by the experiences of Edwin Meese. A dedicated conservative who served Governor Reagan in California and played a major role in the 1980 campaign, Meese had expected to be named White House chief of staff. Instead, Michael Deaver, Stuart Spencer, and Nancy Reagan convinced Reagan that Meese lacked the organizational skill to run the White House. In Mrs. Reagan's eyes, Meese was an example of a "jump-off-the-cliff-with-the-flag-flying conservative who is so rigid in his beliefs that he would rather lose than win a partial victory."[14]

In the first Reagan administration, an original and innovative structure (the troika) was created in which Meese was named counselor to the president, James Baker was made chief of staff, and Deaver was designated deputy chief of staff. Meese and Baker negotiated an arrangement whereby the former was in charge of formulating policy and the latter handled operations. In their bargaining, Meese gained Cabinet-level status for himself and control over the National Security Council (NSC) staff and the domestic policy staff. Although Meese seemed to emerge with greater stature under these arrangements, Baker achieved control over the real levers of power. Because there is no clear demarcation between formulating and implementing policy, effective power usually shifts toward those with operational responsibility. According to a Baker partisan, "Baker had cheerfully given Meese every position he wanted in return for one function: control of all the people and paper flowing to President Reagan. This secured Baker's position; in a bureaucracy like the White House, paper flow . . . is power, because it determines what the president knows about and therefore what he does."[15] A veteran of several administrations, Alexander Haig, later wrote, "There are three main levers of power in the White House: the flow of paper, the President's schedule and the press. Meese did not get a firm grip on any of these."[16] Obviously, Baker's more sophisticated knowledge and experience in White House politics had helped him negotiate an arrangement that placed himself in a powerful position to reduce the influence of Meese in the first administration.

Meese's behavior also contributed to his limited role and diminished reputation. Although the lawyerly Meese was frequently designing organizational charts, he was notoriously disorganized. Meese took on much more work than he could handle. A statement often heard in the White House—and repeated to the press—was that once Meese put a document in his bulging briefcase, it was lost forever. Whereas Baker's staff performed in a highly competent manner, Meese's top appointments—Richard Allen to be NSC adviser and Martin Anderson to head the Office of Policy Development—were generally considered "ineffectual," and both were quickly replaced.[17] Their poor performance, and especially Allen's involvement in a bribe scandal, reflected badly on Meese's judgment. One Reagan official later wrote,

As counsellor to the president, Ed Meese was the most conspicuously mediocre man in American life. . . . Although he usually wore an Adam Smith tie, he confused Reaganomics with the interests of the last business group to visit his office, particularly if it was from California. Meese had a poor sense of priorities and was a terrible manager. He would often be speaking to some 4-H group at a time an important issue was being resolved. Memos would pile up in his in-box for months without being answered. His concept of management was to revise organization charts, issue executive orders, and arrange for presidential pep talks.[18]

Meese's judgment came into question on a number of occasions. In August 1981, he failed to awaken Reagan and inform him that the United States had shot down two Libyan planes. In January 1982, he talked Reagan into reversing a tax policy that had prohibited tax breaks for schools practicing segregation, a decision that caused an enormous amount of negative publicity and eventually had to be reversed. During the 1981–1982 recession, when hunger became an issue and the public relations staff was attempting to show how compassionate the president was, Meese suggested that some people went to soup kitchens voluntarily "because the food is free."[19] In the second administration, while serving as attorney general, Meese almost got himself indicted because of his involvement in the Wedtech scandal. No wonder Meese was known in the White House as a "roving mistake in search of a title."[20] In an administration that was dominated by public relations sensitivities, Meese was destined to experience trouble.

Nevertheless, there was never any public indication that Reagan was dissatisfied with Meese. Reagan demonstrated his support by appointing him attorney general and by accepting Meese's recommendations for the Supreme Court, including the ill-fated Robert Bork and Douglas Ginsburg. Meese resigned in the summer of 1988.

Whereas the conservatives were the most vociferous in proclaiming that Reagan was one of them, the pragmatists could point out that the president continually selected a pragmatist to head the White House as chief of staff: James Baker, Donald Regan,[21] Howard Baker, and Kenneth Duberstein. And each of these pragmatists helped Reagan focus on and achieve a limited number of strategic goals: the 1981 tax cut, the defense buildup, tax reform in 1986, the INF Treaty with the Soviet Union, and the election of George Bush. While condemned by zealous conservatives for being philosophical spoilers, pragmatists claimed that their cool finesse was largely responsible for the political successes of the Reagan presidency. The pragmatists also asserted that it was their restraining influence that may have prevented more loose-cannon types, exemplified by such conservative fanatics as John Poindexter and Oliver North, from causing lethal damage to the Reagan presidency. Moreover, the pragmatists stress that, after the Iran-Contra scandal, when the administration was experiencing its greatest peril, Reagan turned to former senator Howard Baker to help save his presidency. Reagan's selection of a pragmatist like Senator Baker, a villain to the right wing because of his support of the Panama Canal Treaty, indicated the president's understanding that he needed the kind of services pragmatists could provide.

Within Reagan's White House and administration, pragmatists supplied the Washington experience and the know-how to get things done. They understood that their lack of personal ties to Reagan left them vulnerable to attacks from movement conservatives and that they were frequently the ones who had to tell the president things he did not like to hear. The Reagan pragmatists were conservatives, but they were not engaged in a crusade; they were playing an endless game whose object was not all or nothing but to win as often and as much as possible. They had played it before; it would go on whether they won or lost a particular phase. Compromise at the opportune moment was not forbidden; it demonstrated a sophisticated understanding of the political process. But by emphasizing their sophistication and their experience in previous administrations, they often enraged movement conservatives.

Many pragmatists had experiences in the imperiled presidencies of Richard Nixon and Gerald Ford. From the outside, they had watched the burdens of the office overwhelm the Jimmy Carter presidency and reduce it to impotence and despair. They were determined to avoid the mistakes that had destroyed recent chief executives and to prove that the presidency, when skillfully managed, could be successfully run. These pragmatic attitudes were largely exemplified by James Baker and his chief assistant, Richard Darman.

In 1970, Texas Congressman George Bush asked his country-club friend James Baker, a successful corporate lawyer, to help run his Senate campaign. Bush lost that race to Lloyd Bentsen, but Baker discovered that politics was more exciting than corporate law. In 1975, Rogers Morton, secretary of commerce under President Ford, recruited Baker as an undersecretary. At Morton's suggestion, Ford chose Baker as his chief delegate hunter for the 1976 Republican Party convention, and it was Baker who orchestrated Ford's narrow nomination victory over Governor Reagan. Ford was so impressed by Baker's skills that he named him chairman of his election campaign. In 1980, Baker ran the Bush campaign, which eventually placed the latter on the ticket with Reagan. Baker received the task of preparing Reagan for his debate with President Carter, and his successful performance of this job impressed Reagan, his wife, Michael Deaver, and Stuart Spencer. Hence, President-elect Reagan "opted for talent over ideology" in selecting Baker as his chief of staff, a decision that disappointed Meese and his conservative supporters.[22]

Baker assembled an excellent staff headed by his deputy, Richard Darman, and he quickly learned how to communicate with Reagan by using short sentences and effective anecdotes to illustrate his points. In interviews with the press, Baker stressed that Reagan was the visionary leader, while his role was to advise the president as to what was politically feasible. As chief of staff, Baker was aware of the John Sears lesson (Sears was fired after the 1980 New Hampshire primary victory): overestimating your own influence by underestimating Reagan's stubbornness and pushing him too hard would backfire.[23] Baker let it be known that he was not in agreement with the entire Reagan program, but he was in charge of negotiating and implementing most of it. One of his aides was quoted as saying that Baker was "a conservative who never bothered to memorize the theology."[24]

By advertising that he was not a fervent believer in the president's program, Baker was, in effect, announcing that he was a member of a team that other moderates in the administration and Democrats could do business with. Not being a true believer, Baker found it easier to forge compromises. Aided by Darman, Baker exhibited great skill at weaving coalitions across ideological lines. As a negotiator, he earned the respect of his opponents by demonstrating a detailed knowledge of their concerns and by being true to his word. He was not motivated by hate; nor did he deny the honor of those who held different positions. Baker believed that, in the American game of politics, "only fools turn adversaries into enemies."[25] According to William Niskanen, Baker's political strategy was quite simple: "Do something for every element of your own coalition. Don't alienate any group. Avoid policy proposals that might lose. Cut losses quickly. Focus on conditions between now and the next election."[26]

The fruits of Baker's negotiating labors included the 1981 budget and tax cuts, the Saudi arms sale in 1982, the tax increase in 1982, and especially the bipartisan Social Security compromise in 1983. However, Baker told a *Time* reporter in January 1985 that orchestrating Reagan's forty-nine-state victory in the 1984 election was his proudest accomplishment. In Baker's words, "I've never denied I like the game. . . . I've won and I've lost. Winning is better."[27]

Nevertheless, Baker remained a villain to conservatives, who always complained that the victories he arranged for the president were too few and often watered down. Sometimes when a weary Baker complained to his ally Michael Deaver about what it would take to stop conservative sniping, Deaver would reply, "Ronald Reagan is the only conservative you have to worry about."[28]

One of the factors that made Baker and Deaver natural allies was Baker's skill in manipulating the press. As soon as Baker knew that he was going to be chief of staff, he began to cultivate the press by calling up journalists who had covered him in 1976 and during the 1980 campaign and letting them know that he would be available in the White House. Unlike Meese or Donald Regan, Baker understood that media relations is a necessary game of give-and-take. He always made sure that reporters came away from a Baker interview with juicy tidbits, even if they could not be attributed to Baker. He planted the image of Meese as "poppin' fresh—the Pillsbury doughboy," which helped undercut Meese's authority. When Baker wanted to change the president's mind about an issue, he might have an aide leak the notion that friends of Reagan feared he was hurting himself by being too rigid. Thus, the stage would be set for Baker, Deaver, and Nancy Reagan to work on the president to change his mind on a particular issue and demonstrate his flexibility. In 1982, one reporter estimated that Baker saw twice as many newspeople as Deaver and Meese combined and that "many regular correspondents are agreed that Baker is the most adroit leaker in the White House."[29]

But just when the Baker-Deaver axis appeared to achieve hegemony in the White House, Reagan proved that he was the chief executive who could make the final decision. In late 1983, Baker and Deaver negotiated an arrangement whereby Baker would replace William Clark as national security adviser and Deaver would become chief of staff. However, the leading conservatives in the administration—Edwin Meese, William Casey, William Clark, and Caspar Weinberger—were able to meet with the president and reverse the decision.[30] The conservatives hoped to place Jeane Kirkpatrick in the NSC position, but

Secretary of State George Shultz objected, and Robert McFarlane was selected by Reagan.

The third group attracted to the Reagan White House was made up of those skilled in the art of public relations. Led by Michael Deaver, David Gergen, Larry Speakes, Richard Wirthlin, and Roger Ailes, these people knew how to use Reagan's acting skills to maintain his popularity. The public relations practitioners used their expertise to make Reagan look good. They generally knew when and how to make him appear tough or compassionate, proud or humble, involved or uninvolved. Although Reagan started off in January 1981 with a comparatively low public approval rating of about 50 percent, which dipped to the mid-thirties during the 1981–1982 recession and after the Iran-Contra scandal in late 1986, the president was far more popular than any Democrat, as evidenced by the 1984 landslide, and he finished his second term with a 65 percent approval rating. The least controversial aspect of the Reagan presidency is how effectively it utilized public relations.

There is a natural inclination to view public relations as a subordinate, tactical function in the White House. But one of the keys to interpreting the Reagan presidency is understanding that public relations was a strategic factor; it probably influenced more decisions than any other element in the administration. It is worth stressing that Reagan (and Mrs. Reagan) felt closer to Deaver, his public relations specialist, than to any of his policy advisers. One former Reagan aide was quoted as saying, "It was a Deaverized White House. . . . Everything was public relations. . . . Public relations was the reality."[31] Similarly, Larry Speakes, Reagan's deputy press secretary, said, "Almost everything we do is still determined by whether we think it will get on the network news shows in the evening."[32] Peggy Noonan satirized this orientation by writing:

> When I was in the White House, TV was no longer the prime means of receiving the presidency, TV in a way *was* the presidency . . . and decisions were made with TV so much in mind, from the photo-op to the impromptu remark on the way to the helicopter, that the president's top aides who planned the day were no longer just part of the story—it was as if they were the producers of the story. They were the line producers of a show called the White House, with Ronald Reagan as the President. And this wasn't particular to that White House, *it was simply a trend that achieved its fullness in the Reagan era.*[33]

All presidencies attempt to manage the news in order to influence public opinion, but the Reagan administration—supported by Republican Party money and organization—proved to be exceptionally successful at this. Whereas Kennedy had the attractive personality and the Nixon administration had the public relations techniques, Reagan had both in abundance. Reagan's media advisers had witnessed the debilitating consequences of the credibility gap in the Johnson and Nixon presidencies and the inept use of communication techniques in the Ford and Carter administrations. They felt that the chronic dilemma of the contemporary presidency is that its performance cannot match the public's expectations. The public confuses the president's prominence in the media with the president's power to resolve problems. Reagan's media advisers responded to this problem by developing methods that could satisfy many of the public's expectations symbolically rather than substantively. They also believed that the president could not lead the country if he could not communicate with it. In Mark Hertsgaard's words, "Both Deaver and Gergen recognized that to engineer mass consent in the modern media age, the government had to be able to present its version of reality to the public over and over again. Neutralizing the press, by limiting journalists' ability to report politically damaging stories, was necessary but not sufficient. The press had to be turned into a positive instrument of governance, a reliable and essentially non-intrusive transmitter of what the White House wanted the public to know."[34]

The public relations tactics used by the Reagan presidency included severely reducing the number of regular press conferences; presenting well-planned, coordinated themes of the day and/or week to repeatedly convey the president's message to the public; prepackaging attractive visuals; having members of the administration speak in one voice; and stage-managing Reagan's speeches to take advantage of his communication skills. This last strategy utilized Reagan's ability as an actor while camouflaging his lack of knowledge regarding policy.[35]

In Reagan's first administration, the man in charge of packaging the president was Michael Deaver. Deaver had first joined Reagan's team in California in 1967. When Governor Reagan's chief of staff, William Clark, was being driven crazy by phone calls from Nancy Reagan, he assigned the task of responding to her requests to Deaver. Ironically, Deaver's relationship with Mrs. Reagan became his "ultimate chip" in the struggle for Reagan's mind. Whereas Deaver possessed the professional skills to be the choreographer in chief, Mrs. Reagan was "the supreme authority on her husband's needs as a performer."[36] Together, they saw the president more often than anyone else did. They became a team dedicated to making Reagan comfortable and making him look good. This meant that he could not be overworked; his public appearances had to be carefully orchestrated. Just how bad Reagan could appear when his advisers could not control the setting was strikingly demonstrated in the ex-president's testimony in March 1990 at the Poindexter trial.

Deaver and Mrs. Reagan believed that they had to compensate for Reagan's weaknesses by protecting him. For Mrs. Reagan, this guardian role became more manifest after the March 1981 assassination attempt. In her words, "I now understood that each day was a gift to be treasured, and that I had to be more involved in seeing that my husband was protected in every possible way."[37] While the failed assassination made the conservatives anxious to move ahead more quickly with their agenda, it made Mrs. Reagan more concerned about safeguarding her husband. A clash in priorities was inevitable.

Deaver and Mrs. Reagan felt that the president was sometimes ideologically rigid, naive, overly trusting of his subordinates, and too reluctant to fire anyone. They lobbied the president to soften his stance toward the Soviet Union, to slow down the increase in military spending, to pursue a diplomatic solution in Nicaragua, to cancel his trip to Bitburg, and to fire Edwin Meese, Raymond Donovan, William Clark, Helene Von Damm, Richard Allen, William Casey, and Donald Regan.[38] This is not to say that Reagan always agreed with their recommendations, nor does it imply that Mrs. Reagan and Deaver were "closet liberals"; but it does suggest the parallel interests of the pragmatists and the public relations specialists at the expense of the conservatives.

Deaver and Mrs. Reagan saw their role in terms of protecting the person of Ronald Reagan from the sharp edges of his conservative instincts and his conservative advisers. Deaver would explain to Mrs. Reagan that Richard Wirthlin's polls provided survey evidence that the president's performance ratings rose when the public saw him and Congress working together to resolve problems. Such cooperation was threatened by hard-line presidential speeches. Mrs. Reagan accepted this reasoning. A close friend of the Reagans was quoted as saying, "She has been the force to say, 'This is too strident, this is too difficult for people to follow, it's politically not doable. . . .' She often feels that many of these people are out to hurt the President, and they're only in there for themselves. . . . When her own antennae go up, and she spots somebody trying to use Ronald Reagan for the benefit of his own philosophy, she'll fight like a tiger."[39] In brief, as the guardian of her husband, Mrs. Reagan was extremely sensitive about anyone's exploiting Reagan's popularity, an attitude that made her deeply suspicious of conservatives who were constantly exhorting the president to take bigger risks for their causes. The goals and tactics of the pragmatists and public relations officials were simply more compatible with Mrs. Reagan's emphasis on safeguarding her husband's image.

In response, conservatives argued that, by trying to make Reagan look good and flexible, Deaver and Mrs. Reagan made him appear weak and malleable. By constraining his conservative instincts and isolating him from his conservative advisers, they were not allowing him to be the great president he was capable of being. The Hollywood-inspired feel-good type of conservatism advocated by the public relations people meant that presidential resources were used more to keep Reagan's ratings up than to implement the conservatives' policy agenda. Thus, Reagan did not steadfastly and unyieldingly press to balance the budget, end abortion in the United States, allow prayer in the classroom, and defeat communism in Central America and Cuba, as the hardline conservatives wanted him to.

REAGAN'S ADMINISTRATIVE STYLE:
HIS INTERACTION WITH HIS STAFF

The conflict among conservatives, pragmatists, and public relations practitioners caused pain and frustration for each group, but it caused Reagan minimal grief. Finding the squabbling among these groups unpleasant to contemplate, he typically denied its existence.[40] More importantly, the interaction among the three types of staff members provided Reagan with a blend of administrative capabilities that proved functional for Reagan's presidency. Thus, Reagan was able to appear to be a conviction politician, achieve a limited number of domestic and foreign policy goals, and maintain a fairly high approval rating.

The chief organizational problem in managing the Reagan administration was conceptualized by Bert Rockman: "How can organizational structures, systems, and strategies be developed for a committed [to major policy changes] presidency and a detached president?"[41] The solution was to stress the president's public role, an orientation that enhanced the functions of the public relations staff. Reagan became the star salesman of his presidency, a role he was both able and happy to play. In 1984, Steven Weisman reported that "White House aides estimate that he spends 80 percent of his time selling his programs and only 20 percent of his time actually shaping them."[42] As an actor, Reagan was uniquely capable of exploiting media trends both in the election campaigns and in governing. Whereas a president more knowledgeable about policy and more personally concerned with resolving problems would have recognized the limitations of public relations activities, no one believed the illusion of public relations as reality more readily than Reagan did. His principal role-relevant experience had been in Hollywood, where he had seen John Wayne become a war hero even though Wayne had never been in the military. In Reagan's mind, illusion created reality.[43]

Ronald Reagan was more impressive in public than in private. He was not a hard worker; he did not possess an analytical mind; he did not possess substantive knowledge concerning the issues he had to make decisions on, nor was he inclined to ask penetrating questions about subjects he needed to know about; and he did not like to supervise, punish, or fire subordinates. David Stockman claims that the president did not understand the difference between constant dollars and current (inflated) dollars.[44]

During Reagan's eight years in office, there were significant changes in White House personnel and structures but very little, if any, change in the president himself. His style of leadership remained the same because it was derived from his personality and his role-relevant experiences. That style had produced success in California and a landslide victory in 1980. He optimistically believed that his approach to decision making would continue to work effectively in the White House.

For Reagan, his rhetoric pointed out the correct direction, and it was up to his subordinates to fill in the details. Whereas Richard Neustadt's ideal president (FDR) had believed that knowledge of the details was necessary for a leader to have a personal impact, Reagan never felt this way, even about issues he claimed he cared about (Iran-Contra, SDI, the budget). Reagan considered himself the chairman of the board who had assembled "the best people" to carry out the job. But it would be difficult to find many analysts of the presidency who believe that Edwin Meese, William Clark, Raymond Donovan, Caspar Weinberger, Richard Allen, Robert McFarlane, and John Poindexter were the best people available for their jobs.

Reagan probably read fewer policy memos than any president since Calvin Coolidge. Domestic policy memos were usually limited to two pages; foreign policy papers were usually no more than five pages. Reagan also received clippings from old conservative friends and read several conservative magazines.

One area in which Reagan was highly active was responding to letters addressed to the president. In a rare expression of initiative, Reagan arranged to have about 50 of the approximately 200,000 letters the White House received each week brought to his attention. Reagan would then personally write letters to those fifty people and sometimes try to help a select few if they were having problems with the federal bureaucracy.[45] In this way, Reagan revealed his compassionate side, his concern for the individual, and his desire to play the role of a hero as he once did as a lifeguard back in Dixon, Illinois. However, this activity also contradicted his image of being focused on the big picture.

At meetings with his advisers and Cabinet officials, Reagan was usually quiet except for his trademark bantering. He was most pleased when his advisers had forged a consensus about a particular problem, because that meant that he would not have to choose between positions advocated by quarreling advisers. Most aides agreed that they felt free to debate openly in front of him. They also claimed that he was a good listener, although a few voiced concern that because he was hard of hearing he might not have heard everything being said. Alexander Haig observed, "Because of his habitual cheery courtesy, it is at times difficult to know when he is agreeing or disagreeing, approving or disapproving."[46] Based on a series of interviews with Reagan aides, Leslie Gelb writes, "At most meetings, the President sits quietly. If he offers an opinion, he seldom sets forth his underlying reasoning. Often he keeps his own counsel entirely."[47]

One of Reagan's favorite aphorisms was that he wanted his aides to provide "solutions, not problems." This expectation, a function of his optimistic nature, is useful in explaining the major breakdown of Reagan's decision making in the Iran-Contra affair. In this case, most of the advice he received from the Departments of State and Defense concerned how difficult it would be to gain the release of the hostages. However, William Casey, Robert McFarlane, John Poindexter, and Oliver North provided a "solution" that appealed to the compassionate and staunchly anticommunist president. Their "neat idea" would free the hostages, forge a new strategic tie with moderates in Iran, and circumvent congressional prohibitions on aiding the Contras to overthrow the Sandinistas in Nicaragua. When Shultz and Weinberger criticized the obvious pitfalls in this policy, Reagan allowed the locus of this decision making to become even more secretive.[48]

The presidency carries with it the supreme capability of acquiring information. But Reagan rarely asked questions of his staff and seldom demanded further information before making a decision. In 1984, a *Time* reporter wrote, "Reagan's curiosity, even after three years at the epicenter of events, seems stunted. He is something of a military buff, but last fall during his tour of allied fortifications along the 38th parallel [in South Korea] . . . he did not ask a single question of his U.S. military guide. White House aides cannot remember an instance when the President has asked that they form an *ad hoc* group to help thrash out a puzzling policy question."[49] Nor did Reagan feel the need to reach outside the White House for alternative and competing sources of information and policy advice. Apparently, Reagan never endured the anxieties experienced by many previous presidents who worried whether they had sufficient information to make a rational decision when confronted with a potentially explosive issue. Reagan simply had faith that everything would work out successfully.

Those who worked under Reagan have expressed astonishment at his passive administrative style. The president's secretary wrote, "He was never the initiator. He never even asked me to get Mac Baldridge or Bill Casey on the phone just because he hadn't heard from them in a while. He would make decisions as they were presented to him."[50] David Stockman recalled pre-inauguration meetings with Reagan: "We had a few informal sessions with the President-elect, during which he simply listened, nodded, and smiled. 'We have a great task ahead of us,' he would say, but he never finished the sentence. He gave no orders, no commands, asked for no information, expressed no urgency. This was startling to me."[51] Donald Regan was also surprised. As treasury secretary during the first administration, Regan was befuddled that the president never met with him privately to explain what goals he was expected to accomplish. Since Regan was accustomed to management by objective, where officials have in writing what is expected of them, he wondered how one could accomplish a task if the task was not defined. What Regan finally figured out was that, as a member of the Reagan administration, one did not receive specific instructions from the president; instead, one had to read Reagan's speeches for policy guidelines. In Regan's words, "The President seemed to believe that his public statements were all the guidance his private advisers required. Ronald Reagan's campaign promises *were* his policy. To him, in his extreme simplicity of character and belief, this was obvious. . . . Once I had grasped that principle, I understood that I was free to interpret his words and implement his intentions in my field of policy and action according to my best judgment."[52]

For those who harbored traditional views of leadership, Reagan's presidency was difficult to decipher. To Alexander Haig, "the White House was as mysterious as a ghost ship; you heard the creak of the rigging and the groan of the timbers, and sometimes even glimpsed the crew on deck. But which of the crew had the helm? . . . It was impossible to tell."[53] Peggy Noonan was equally perplexed by how the "disengaged" president ran the White House. After interviewing numerous White House colleagues, she came to a metaphysical conclusion—that "the *idea* of Reagan ruled" like a giant balloon over Macy's Thanksgiving parade. For Noonan, "the idea of Reagan" had been formulated in twenty years of speeches. She believed that competing groups in the White House were struggling to implement different components of Reagan's philosophy.[54]

Although Noonan's imagery may make one smile, its functional aspects should not be underestimated. Reagan's ideas attracted the support of a number of talented people, and his administrative style encouraged them to work for his causes. There is no indication that Reagan's laziness caused his subordinates to work less hard; on the contrary, it probably caused them to work harder. Terrel Bell, Reagan's first secretary of education, stresses how diligently he labored because he knew that conservatives like Meese were planning to eliminate his department. Bell suggests that Reagan "worked us hard so he could do his job and still be relaxed. . . . He had a laid-back style, but this did not mean he was not effective. Indeed, it enabled him to be effective."[55] The consequences of Reagan's management style are also implied in Stockman's words: "He [Reagan] conveyed the impression that since we all knew what needed to be done, we should simply get on with the job. Since I *did* know what to do, I took his quiet message of confidence to be a mandate. If the others weren't going to get his administration's act together, I would."[56] And no one toiled more zealously in 1981 to fulfill the conservative objectives of the Reagan administration than David Stockman. Hence, Reagan's detached style encouraged officials to take initiatives, to pick up the ball and run with it.

Reagan's administrative procedures induced the contending White House factions to fight one another rather than pressure the president. The competition for Reagan's approval was severe, because the winners received a relatively free hand to make decisions in certain policy areas. Each group accused the other of "using" the president by taking advantage of his trusting disposition and his inattention to detail.[57] Nancy Reagan was acutely sensitive on this point, and for good reason: Reagan was the most "usable" of presidents. For example, Terry Deibel points out that "Reagan's very remoteness from the diplomatic process allowed foreign policy professionals—working, say, on the Philippine transition or on southern Africa—to exert their talents, bringing the president on board when the pieces fell into place."[58]

What is often overlooked is how the competing staff groups were serving Reagan's interests. Generally speaking, when policies pushed by one faction were successful, Reagan would share the credit, but when they failed, he could avoid responsibility. Whereas the hands-on management style of Carter resulted in his being blamed for much of what went wrong in his administration, Reagan seldom suffered for mistakes or controversial decisions made on his behalf. Aided by the Deaverized White House, blame was deflected to Stockman for cruel budget cuts, to Weinberger for the skyrocketing defense budget, and to James Watt for the lack of concern over the environment. Reagan's management style provided him with the ultimate plausible denial. It also minimized the need for Reagan to take sides in the conflicts among his staff, while it maximized the stakes in the struggles among the three groups. In brief, the stage was set for historians and political scientists to argue over who was using whom.

Thus, Reagan's presidency oscillated between pragmatism and ideological purity, without suffering the negative consequences of flip-flopping as Jimmy Carter's did. Although Reagan reversed himself on taxes, Panama, Taiwan,

Lebanon, and the Soviet Union, he was able to maintain his image as a conviction politician. Reagan's staff provided him the opportunity to pursue conservative objectives by pragmatic skills and means. As governor of California, he ran the same type of operation, which supports the thesis that Reagan "gets exactly the kind of staff support his low-key, risk-averse and reactive administrative instincts demand."[59] Frances Clines suggests that the "basic dynamic of the Reagan Administration" was to have pragmatists such as James Baker make the necessary "accommodations on a pressing issue while the President accepts them privately and continues a tougher grade of public rhetoric."[60]

The pragmatists usually provided compromise solutions, whereas the conservatives often advocated proposals that led to greater strife. Under these circumstances, the pragmatists, aided by their public relations allies, usually prevailed. This raises the question of why the conservatives did not complain more or even drop out of the administration. Conservatives generally remained Reagan supporters because the president was often pursuing conservative policies and because he was granting them more influence than any previous president. Moreover, because of his charm and reputation, Reagan could obtain their support rather cheaply. Peggy Noonan mentions four conservatives who were reassured of their importance and ties to the president by the simple act of Reagan winking at them during White House meetings, and she wistfully notes, "We made so much of those winks."[61] Who else but Reagan could have earned so much loyalty from so little effort?

To assert the functionality of Reagan's management style is not to deny that there were serious flaws in the president's process of decision making. The combination of Reagan's optimism and lack of attention to detail meant that he had no true way of measuring whether his policies were working. Because he saw no need for it, there was no reality testing. Reagan had an almost infinite capacity to live contentedly within his myth-dominated world. According to one of his aides, "You have to be careful with him. If you had nine bad items to tell him and one good one, he would latch on to the tenth favorable item and discount the other nine. The blind spots are very troubling."[62] In Reagan's mind, unpleasant facts could be avoided; contradiction could be denied; anecdotes could overcome facts; movie illusions could substitute for history; unpleasant realities could be blamed on a hostile press. The simple truths that made Reagan a conviction politician could blind him to the facts that his tax cuts were not leading to balanced budgets, that the deregulation of the savings and loan industry was leading to a fiscal catastrophe, and that he was trading arms for hostages in the Middle East. In brief, Reagan was usually serene because of his propensity to allow simple, comforting truths to become comprehensive truths.

Reagan's serenity was preserved by his dislike of experts and by the protection of his staff. Donald Regan wrote, "Reagan's personality and his infectious likability are founded on a natural diffidence. He hesitates to ask questions or confess to a lack of knowledge in the presence of strangers—and thanks to the way his staff operated, nearly everyone was a stranger to this shy President except the members of his innermost circle."[63] It should also be noted that no economist entered that innermost circle of advisers, despite the centrality of economics in Reagan's program. Whereas such economists as Arthur Burns, Walter Heller, and Alan Greenspan became major advisers in the Eisenhower, Kennedy, and Ford administrations, no economist achieved that status in the Reagan presidency. Indeed, Reagan believed himself knowledgeable about economics because he had majored in it at Eureka College, and he felt free to denigrate the profession with one of his oft-repeated jokes: "those fellows have a Phi Beta Kappa key on the end of their watch chains, and no watch." Reagan's decision-making style was also demonstrated before the 1986 Reykjavik meeting with Gorbachev: "In preparation for the Iceland summit, Reagan did not study the history and nuances of America's arms-control strategies; instead, he practiced ways to sell Gorbachev on SDI. To get himself into the right frame of mind, he read Tom Clancy's *Red Storm Rising,* a potboiler about a non-nuclear war between NATO and the Soviet bloc."[64] In short, Reagan had trouble with experts because they often told him things that were not compatible with his ideological predispositions. Experts, and especially economists, dealt with probabilities, but their arguments were frequently not persuasive to the president because Reagan's life was full of improbables. From Reagan's optimistic point of view, long odds were no obstacle in the pursuit of his goals. Fortunately, this propensity was constrained by Reagan's belief that no great sacrifices were needed to achieve his goals. He did not lead the nation into any impossible wars. Even Reagan's stubbornness could be turned around, as it was in early 1984 when he withdrew the marines from bomb-scarred Beirut.

Those closest to Reagan appreciated what a valuable asset he was, but they also felt that he needed an unusual amount of sheltering for a leader. There was something vulnerable about Reagan that made his staff feel the necessity of creating a comfortable cocoon around him. He was rarely allowed to handle issues and situations on his own. In 1984, David Broder wrote, "Foreign diplomats and members of Congress have found that an invitation to meet with the president is really a summons to a committee session with the president surrounded by members of his staff, his Cabinet, and often Vice President Bush. . . . As they describe the sessions, the president often does little more than offer an opening word of welcome, then settles back to listen as the others discuss the matter before them."[65] The staff recognized that, in the real world of private negotiation, Reagan's lack of knowledge would be a liability; it would make him look uninformed and uncommitted.

The surprising solution to this problem was to keep Reagan uninformed. To educate this president would not necessarily have been compatible with increasing his capacity for rational decision making. When Reagan studied hard for the first Mondale debate in October 1984 and for his first defense of the Iran-Contra conflict in November 1986, the results were disastrous. In her memoirs, Mrs. Reagan blamed her husband's poor debate performance— "the worst night of Ronnie's political career," in which he was "tense, muddled, and off-stride"—on the way he had prepared.

> He told me he felt "brutalized" during the rehearsals, and that his mind was so jammed with facts and figures that he hadn't been able to focus on what Mondale was saying. Ronnie has always been an inspiring leader who outlines broad themes and visions, but his staff had spent weeks cramming him full of details and statistics. Instead of letting Ronnie lead with his strengths, they tried to turn him into somebody he wasn't. . . . "What have you done to my husband?" I said to Mike Deaver angrily, back at the hotel. "Whatever it was, don't do it again!"[66]

What Mrs. Reagan calls "brutalized," others might label the process of being well briefed. To be brutalized by facts is to suggest that one has a low threshold for processing information. In any case, Roger Ailes replaced David Stockman as Reagan's tutor for the second Mondale debate, and Ailes supplied the president with a script of quips instead of attempting to fill his head with facts. Reagan responded by defeating Mondale in the second debate with a fine performance.

The key point here is that to fill Reagan's mind with information was to clutter it; the more facts he had, the less likely it was that they could be reconciled with Reagan's simplistic ideology. This leads to a counterintuitive proposition: the more informed Reagan was, the less likely he was to perform effectively. Thus, in some ways, being uninformed was not only bliss for Reagan, it was necessary for him to function with conviction.

CONCLUSION

This chapter has analyzed the personality-driven consequences of President Reagan's administrative style. It argues that Reagan's management style was more effective than it appeared to many professors and journalists. My contention is that Reagan unmindfully "used" his staff to a much greater degree than is generally understood. Reagan was able to attract and utilize the talents of three types of personnel—conservatives, pragmatists, and public relations experts—whose combined efforts largely explain the political success of the Reagan presidency. As chief executive, Reagan mobilized the energy, political skills, and public relations techniques of these three groups with a balancing-act strategy that destroyed the emerging conventional wisdom of the 1970s that the presidency was no longer manageable. For a conviction politician, the major problem is how to balance moral zeal with political finesse. Reagan's staff provided the blend of skills to solve this problem. My point here is not that Reagan was conscious of this balancing-act strategy—it is difficult to prove what the president was knowledgeable about—but rather to indicate that this was simply how it was done.

The most controversial point that emerges from this study is the idea that, for Reagan to perform best, his mind could not be cluttered with facts. For Reagan, details were excess baggage; they weighed him down. An informed Reagan was often a less effective president because his capacity to act as a conviction politician was reduced. This view runs counter to all the literature on the presidency from Richard Neustadt to Alexander George. In brief, although it is usually dangerous for a president to be uninformed and uninvolved, operating at a certain level of ingenuousness was functional for Reagan. This unique attribute of Reagan's political style will be demonstrated in the following chapter, which explains how his administration achieved the most successful first year in office since FDR's in 1933.

5

THE FIRST YEAR:
HIT THE GROUND RUNNING

The modern president confronts a series of leadership challenges. A newly elected president has already demonstrated that he has the campaign skills to win both his party's nomination and the general election. After these victories, the next challenge concerns governing. Can the new chief executive take advantage of his first few months in office, the so-called honeymoon period, and induce Congress to pass a significant portion of his program, thus establishing his professional reputation as someone who possesses the governing skills to be president? From the candidate's many campaign promises, can he select the few that will receive public and congressional support? During Franklin Roosevelt's first 100 days in office in 1933, he successfully pressured Congress to pass thirteen major pieces of legislation, creating a standard of performance—probably an impossible one to duplicate—by which each subsequent president has been measured.

The public expects political leadership from its presidents, but the political system provides limited opportunities for such performance. One such opportunity is the first few months in office, during which the new president can attempt to ride the momentum of his electoral mandate, lead a Congress that now contains more of his partisans than it will after the next congressional election in two years, exploit a public opinion approval level that is probably destined to decline, and enjoy the initially friendly coverage of the media, whose reporting is likely to become more adversarial as his term progresses. According to Elisabeth Drew, "When a new President takes office, there is much talk about a 'honeymoon,' but the term does not really describe what occurs. What actually happens is that a line of credit is extended to the new President; the opposition, having heard the voice of the electorate and interpreted it in a certain way, lies low and waits; those within the President's party who have misgivings remain silent; and permanent floating Washington, with its seemingly infinite ability to adjust, adjusts."[1] The key point is that the honeymoon is a temporary period of indefinite duration that provides the new president with a window of opportunity that will not remain open for long. Failing to take advantage of this opportunity will damage the president's professional reputation and thus restrict his bargaining leverage for future success. Hence, how a president begins governing significantly influences how successful his performance will be.

In 1981, President Reagan did not flunk this leadership test. He "hit the ground running" and created a new standard of performance to measure how well presidents exploit the temporary advantages that exist during their first few months in office. The purpose of this chapter is to explain how Reagan and his advisers achieved early success by establishing their strategic priorities and focusing their efforts on getting Congress to pass them. It also analyzes some of the consequences of Reagan's budget and tax cut victories. As we shall see, these political triumphs entailed costs in terms of policy rationality and soaring budget deficits.

STRATEGIC GOALS OF THE REAGAN PRESIDENCY

The Reagan administration came into office determined to avoid the mistakes of the Carter presidency. Whereas Carter had appointed the inept Frank Moore, a Georgian with no Washington experience, to head his congressional liaison office, Reagan named Max Friedersdorf, who had worked in the congressional liaison offices of Presidents Nixon and Ford. Whereas Carter had located the congressional liaison office in the Old Executive Building, Reagan moved it to the more prestigious East Wing of the White House. In contrast to Carter, who squandered his honeymoon by overwhelming Congress with a barrage of legislative proposals, many of which were never passed, Reagan established his strategic priorities: a three-year tax cut, budget reductions, and a major defense buildup. Dealing with other issues, such as foreign policy and social policy (abortion), was postponed, much to the frustration of Secretary of State Alexander Haig and the leaders of the Religious Right. Reagan's White House advisers, Edwin Meese as counselor, James Baker as chief of staff, and Michael Deaver as deputy chief of staff, worked together to make sure that the president's time and resources were efficiently focused on getting Congress to pass the economic program. According to Kenneth Duberstein, Reagan's chief lobbyist in the House of Representatives in 1981, "If you can rivet public attention on one or two things, you have a less difficult time focusing the congressional mind-set. So the economic recovery program became the agenda. When Reagan spoke to the nation on television, or did a photo opportunity, or met with members of Congress, it was always on the economic recovery program."[2]

Since Reagan was a conviction politician, it was probably easier for him to derive his legislative priorities from his fundamental beliefs than it was for other presidents. He believed that liberalism was a misguided ideology because it had led the nation into the dead end of the welfare state. His remedy was to renew the American dream of individual freedom by supply-side tax cuts, budget reductions to reverse the growth of the welfare state, and a steep rise in defense expenditures that would allow us to defend vigorously our interests against communism. In Reagan's optimistic worldview, a retreating welfare state would promote both the economy and the moral order. No modern president came into office with a clearer set of priorities than did Reagan.

But no chief executive assumed office needing more help from his advisers in turning his simple ideas into politically feasible programs than did the former governor of California. As an actor and rhetorician, Reagan was an expert at selling his ideas and an amateur at implementing them. He knew little about Washington, D.C., Congress, the bureaucracy, the budget, and the tax code. The new president needed the aid of a vigorous staff system.

The political advice that Reagan received in 1981—with the exception of cutting Social Security—was almost flawless. By generally following his staff's recommendations, Reagan achieved notable success. But when that record is reexamined, we can see that this political triumph was disastrous in terms of virtually eliminating the federal government's ability to balance the budget in the near future. Exploiting the advantages of the honeymoon period required haste, and that atmosphere was not conducive to rational policy making.

Reagan's campaign to dominate Congress was as skillfully scripted as his electoral campaign. The new president was as carefully stage-managed as the candidate had been. Reagan's projection of self-confidence and direction contrasted positively with the flip-flops of the Carter presidency. In March 1981, Elisabeth Drew wrote that the first few months of the new administration were successful because Reagan was "dominating the argument, keeping the opposition off base, and riding public opinion, while at the same time shaping it."[3] It was not hard to convince the American people in December 1980 that there was an economic crisis when interest rates were over 20 percent, the inflation rate was 13 percent, and there were fears of an impending recession. But it would take some skill to convince the public and Congress that Reagan had received an electoral mandate to remedy these problems with his risky and untested economic program.

The strategic thinking of the early Reagan administration was influenced by a twenty-three-page report, labeled the "Dunkirk Memo," written by two

Republican congressmen, Jack Kemp and David Stockman, in mid-November 1980. The principal author was thirty-four-year-old Stockman, who hoped that this document would help him be appointed director of the Office of Management and Budget (OMB). It did. But the major purpose of the memo was to warn the euphoric winners of the 1980 election that they must quickly gain control over several major economic problems, or those problems would rapidly overwhelm the new administration. The alarmist tone of the memo was set in its first sentence: "The momentum of short-run economic, financial, and budget forces is creating an economic Dunkirk during the first 24 months of the Reagan Administration." To create a crisis atmosphere, Stockman painted an ominous picture: there was at least a 50 percent chance of a recession in 1981; a recession would cause budget deficits to spin out of control, because welfare policies had "now become an automatic coast-to-coast soup line that dispenses remedial aid with almost reckless abandon"; Carter's fiscal-year 1981 budget was already hemorrhaging and would probably produce a deficit of over $50 billion; Paul Volcker, chairman of the Federal Reserve Board, was regulating the supply of money in an erratic and thus destabilizing manner; and the Reagan presidency faced a "regulatory time bomb" because the bureaucracy was filled with "McGovernite no-growth activists" who were set to implement environmental, energy, and safety regulations that would raise compliance costs for industries by $100 billion.[4]

Stockman admonished Reagan that the rising budget deficit, sluggish economic growth, and fears of inflation would split the budget-balancers and supply-siders in the Republican Party and erode "our capacity to govern successfully and reverse the economy before November 1982." Thus, the Reagan revolution in public policy and the Republican realignment of the electorate would be thwarted, just as Margaret Thatcher's strategy (she became prime minister in 1979) appeared to be in Great Britain. To avoid this calamity, Stockman advised Reagan to launch bold policies of supply-side tax cuts and major reductions in the budget within the first six months of his presidency. The key to holding the Reagan coalition together was a budget cut that "projected" a balance by fiscal-year 1984, because that would legitimize voting for a tax cut by both Republicans and southern Democrats. Without the protection of a projected balanced budget, a vote for the largest tax reduction in U.S. history would look reckless, since it would raise fears about inflation. The top goal was enactment of the three-year tax cut that was designed to spur economic growth, but the administration sought to make sure that a credible budget policy was passed first to calm concerns about inflation on Wall Street and in Congress.[5]

Reagan's first year was also influenced by another document entitled "The Initial Actions Project." This fifty-five-page planning document was largely written by Richard Wirthlin, the president's pollster; Richard Beal, Wirthlin's associate; and David Gergen, who was director of communications in the Ford White House. It was designed as a practical guide for the first few months of the Reagan presidency. The report was not officially completed until January 29, 1981, but its essential recommendations were presented to the president-elect at Blair House in mid-December. Wirthlin's polling data and analysis reinforced the Stockman-Kemp recommendation that the administration ought to focus its resources on the economic recovery program. The final report warned that "no American president since F.D.R. has inherited a more difficult economic situation." Most Americans were pictured as being dissatisfied with the direction in which the country was being led and hopeful that the new president could redirect public policy. The authors suggested that, to take advantage of that opportunity, the new president engage in a brisk but not frantic pace of activity to convey a sense of urgency but not panic. Reflecting their knowledge of Reagan's skills, they advised the president to explain his program in "simple, straightforward, and understandable" terms. To avoid being "Carterized," the president was urged "to restore a sense of stability and confidence, to demonstrate that there is a steady hand at the helm."[6]

The authors of the "Initial Actions Project" studied the first 100 days of five newly elected presidents, gong back to FDR, and came up with several conclusions. First, "The personality of the President as seen by the general public and the opinion-makers is strongly etched in the first 100 days, and the personality he presents is something that carries through his Presidency."[7] Second, the early days of a new presidency offer a rare and golden opportunity to establish the central thrust of an administration. Third, these initial months are also a period when a new administration is particularly prone to make major blunders, as evidenced by Kennedy's Bay of Pigs and Carter's errors in presenting his energy program. Therefore, the report correctly stressed, "How we begin will significantly determine how we govern."[8]

According to Lou Cannon, Reagan liked Wirthlin's report because it appealed to his conception of leadership and his belief that the nation faced its most threatening economic crisis since the depression. It was a fact that disoriented some conservatives and enraged some Democrats, but "Reagan's enduring model for presidential performance in times of economic crisis was his first political hero, F.D.R."[9] And that meant that Reagan wanted "to hit the ground running" as successfully in 1981 as his hero had in 1933. Since Reagan personified the conservative movement, his staff argued that his landslide election victory (in a three-way race) was a mandate for the conservative policies he had championed for several decades. Unlike most new chief executives, Reagan had developed his convictions and commitments *before* he came into office.[10] Hence, there was less difficulty in deciphering what Reagan most wanted to emphasize in office than in, say, the Carter or Clinton presidency. The problem in formulating the economic program was that there were conflicts among Reagan's commitments that he, being by nature optimistic and prone to avoiding details, was not aware of.

Reagan's economic advisers consisted of an uneasy alliance of three types: supply-siders, monetarists, and budget-balancers. Supply-siders believed that the top priority should be to cut marginal tax rates, since that would significantly influence the incentives to produce, to save, and to invest. Their assumption that slashing tax rates would immediately produce a surge in economic activity freed them from the fear that tax reductions would increase the budget deficit and/or accelerate the rate of inflation. The chief dread of the monetarists was inflation; their remedy was that the Federal Reserve Board should be encouraged to ensure a slow, steady growth of the money supply that would not expand faster than the growth of goods and services. The budget-balancers were traditional conservatives who worried that the flood of red ink was causing stagflation and would eventually bankrupt the United States.[11] Blending the advice of these three groups, the administration argued that it could employ fiscal policy to stimulate economic growth and balance the budget by 1984 while using monetary instruments to restrain inflation.

A few days before the inauguration, Alan Greenspan, a top economic adviser during the transition, was quoted as saying, "The basic problem that faces the new administration is to lower rates on long-term bonds," because they reflect inflationary expectations. Greenspan predicted that if the administration could demonstrate that it was slowing the growth of federal expenditures and moving toward a balanced budget, "the markets will immediately lower the long-term inflation premium."[12]

The official who obtained the authority to move the Reagan economic program as quickly as possible was David Stockman, the new director of OMB. The young, indefatigable Stockman gave up his congressional seat and began his career in the administration as a dedicated supply-sider but quickly became a fervent budget-balancer. Stockman considered himself a revolutionary and was deeply committed to helping the new president achieve the goals of what was already being called the Reagan revolution. Stockman's "Grand Doctrine" (his term) was a minimalist state relying on market rationality for progress and requiring the elimination of dozens of programs and the curtailing of Social Security and Medicare. Partly to his dismay, but appealing to his ambition and ability to take advantage of opportunities, Stockman quickly saw that he was in a position to play a leading role in formulating Reagan's program. In Stockman's words, "I soon discovered that it would be up to me to design the Reagan Revolution. December [1980] brought hints, suggestions, and circumstantial evidence that the Californians— including the most crucial Californian—were neither equipped nor inclined to launch the kind of sweeping anti-statist revolution implied in the supply-side platform."[13]

Stockman blamed Edwin Meese for all the frantic activity, endless meetings, and lack of understanding about what it would take to launch the Reagan revolution.[14] Although the economic indicators were worsening at the end of 1980, the economic team and program were not being organized with any urgency. Stockman was also troubled by the few informal meetings he had with the president-elect in which Reagan generally listened, nodded, and smiled but neither issued orders nor requested information. Stockman stressed that "the President-elect . . . seemed so serene and passive. He conveyed the impression that since we all knew what needed to be done, we should simply get on with the job. Since I *did* know what to do, I took his quiet message of confidence to be a mandate. If the others weren't going to get his administration's act together, I would."[15] Consequently, he submitted a memo to Meese and James Baker on December 19, 1980, outlining a blueprint for commencing the economic recovery program within a few weeks of the inauguration. His action plan was accepted.

Stockman gloried in his role as the administration's point man for Reagan's economic program. He later bragged that Meese did not understand what a broad mandate the young revolutionary had received. According to Stockman, Meese "believed that broad policy would be made in the cabinet and its departments with presidential review and approval. The government's technical budget and auditing work, as he called it, would go on in O.M.B. He granted me a much greater charter than he realized."[16] What Meese did not fathom was that the early political success of the Reagan presidency was largely dependent on the credibility of the numbers and forecasts generated by OMB. What was a technical task to Meese was going to take a lot of political skill and perhaps more than a trace of creative accounting. The more Stockman learned about the budget, the more he understood that federal expenditures were programmed by law to increase at an accelerating rate. With each *honest* revision of the budget figures, he found that more had to be cut in order to project a balanced budget in fiscal-year 1984. This created enormous incentives for faulty and overly optimistic assumptions.

Stockman fully understood the need to move expeditiously before the battered Democrats could reassemble and to provide assurance to markets that, finally, reasonable economic policies were being pursued. His job of operationalizing the president's commitments into a budget document was enormous, because Reagan as a campaigner had spoken in generalities (e.g, eliminating fraud, waste, and abuse). The closest Governor Reagan came to quantifying his program was the speech he gave in Chicago on September 9, 1980, based on economic data provided by Martin Anderson and Alan Greenspan. That speech promised a balanced budget by 1983, but Stockman disagreed with its assumptions about continuing high inflation and believed that its "numbers were worthless."[17]

To accomplish the task before him, Stockman engaged in weeks of feverish activity in late January and the first few weeks of February. The director of OMB considered his labors to be mainly ministerial, that is, transforming the doctrine into budget figures. In doing this, however, Stockman soon discovered that the economic program "was riddled with political contradictions." To reconcile these contradictions, there should have been tough meetings to clarify the trade-offs among Reagan's goals. But in the administration's haste to maintain its political advantages, there was no time for such meetings. The official most likely to see the urgency of such consultation, James Baker, was also the one most reluctant to call for it, because of his association with George Bush's criticism that Reaganomics was based on "voodoo economics." Nor was Reagan likely to order such a debate, since he never believed that there was any incompatibility among his goals.

Years later, Stockman blamed himself for the costly lack of a policy debate at this time.

> The main reason there was no debate was that the remaining variable in the policy equation was the domestic spending cut, and in the mind of the plan's architect—me—that remained almost infinitely elastic. The domestic spending cut could be sized modestly or massively, depending upon what was required to make everything else add up. . . . The size of the spending cut number was where ideological doctrine and political possibility should have had their showdown. But the showdown never happened. The pace was so hectic that the White House never really knew what the domestic spending-cut number was. The linchpin of the plan was shrouded in a haze of rapidly changing figures.[18]

In the mad rush to project a balanced budget, Stockman created the magic asterisk. The asterisk was used as a "temporary plug" to fill in budget lines when actual cuts could not be specified. Officially, the asterisk meant "future savings to be identified." The magic referred to the elasticity of the dollar amounts the asterisk could signify; it could cover whatever it would take to reach a balanced budget by 1984. As we shall see, the asterisk eventually stretched to cover a gap of unspecified expenditure cuts of $44 billion. Stockman later claimed that "the circumstances of this accounting invention were slightly more innocent than what eventually materialized. I'd never believed we could review the entire $740 billion federal budget before February 18. So I contemplated two more budget-cut packages to be transmitted to Congress later."[19] The first package was known as the "March revisions" and was expected to result in minor cuts of about $10 billion per year. Stockman wanted the major reductions to come in the second package, which would involve sweeping reforms of middle-class entitlement programs: Social Security, Medicare, and federal retirement pensions.[20] Thus, from the budget director's perspective, the magic asterisk secretly signified future budget cuts from some very popular programs.

The combination of haste and overloading responsibilities on Stockman created a decision-making situation in which blunders were likely to be made. One egregious error involved an agreement between Stockman and Caspar Weinberger, the secretary of defense, concerning increases in the defense budget. After a long day, a very tired Stockman met with the secretary of defense and Frank Carlucci, the deputy defense secretary, on the evening of January 30, 1981, in Weinberger's office. Stockman favored a reasonable rise in defense expenditures. Weinberger had been budget director under President Nixon, when his nickname had been "Cap the Knife," but now he was under pressure from conservatives such as Senator John Tower, the new Republican chairman of the Armed Services Committee, to demonstrate how committed he was to a massive buildup of the military. In addition, Weinberger's political hero was Winston Churchill, who had fought such a lonely and valiant battle during the 1930s for British rearmament and an end of the appeasement policy toward Hitler's Germany. The new defense secretary saw himself playing a similar Churchillian role in the 1980s, leading the charge for a massive increase in defense expenditures and reversing the policy of détente toward the Soviet Union.[21] To reverse what they considered the military decline of the United States, many Republicans—and especially Weinberger—advocated that the Reagan administration should exploit public support for defense budget increases, because history suggested that such support would be temporary and would not last longer than a few years. And indeed, it did not.

Hence, when Stockman and Weinberger met on January 30, they were in agreement that the Reagan defense program should enjoy the benefits of real growth over the next five years. The first problem they discussed was that the administration had not yet decided what inflation rate estimates should be included in the economic forecast. This obstacle was easily sidestepped by agreeing to estimate future defense budgets in constant 1982 dollars. When the economic policy makers finally worked out an estimate on future inflation, Stockman would just add the amount for inflation to each year's defense expenditure.[22]

The second issue was agreeing on what the real growth per year in defense expenditures should be. During the campaign, Reagan had called for 5 percent per year, but there were hawks in the transition defense task force and in the administration who were advocating 9 percent growth. The problem was compounded by the fact that Soviet aggression in Afghanistan in late 1979 had induced President Carter to become far more hawkish in his last two defense budgets. As Hedrick Smith explains, "When Reagan called in his 1980 campaign for five percent real growth in defense spending over several years, Carter's defense budget level was $142 billion a year. But by the time Reagan took office, Carter's defense level had jumped to $176 billion in 1981; it was set for $200.3 billion in 1982 and projected to grow five percent a year on top of that into the mid-1980s. This was more than Reagan promised."[23] No matter. Since Carter was pictured as the Neville Chamberlain of the 1970s, the political reality was that Reagan's real growth figure for defense had to be significantly higher than his predecessor's.

In the meeting with Stockman, Carlucci argued for an 8 or 9 percent increase. In response, according to Stockman, "I suggested we split the difference down the middle and go with an interim 7 percent real growth increase. A fully developed Reagan defense budget could be worked out later in the spring and then we'd get the real answer."[24] Weinberger said that 7 percent was still "pretty lean," but he agreed with that figure.

The final issue seemed misleadingly minor and technical, namely, designating the base year from which the administration would initiate the 7 percent real growth calculation. A tired Stockman readily accepted Carlucci's recommendation that the administration start with the 1982 level of expenditure (instead of 1980) as the base, which would include the previously accepted $32 billion supplement to Carter's last two defense budgets (approximately $6 billion to the fiscal-year 1981 defense budget and $26 billion to the proposed fiscal-year 1982 defense budget). The meeting then ended, and so did Stockman's chances of reducing budget deficits.

It took several weeks for Stockman to realize the magnitude of his mistake. He, whose mission was to balance the budget by 1984, had agreed to a five-year defense budget of $1.46 trillion, when inflation estimates were factored in. By 1986, defense expenditures were projected to reach $368 billion dollars. As explained by Stockman, "We had taken an already-raised defense budget and raised that by 7 percent. Instead of starting from a defense budget of $142 billion, we'd started with one of $222 billion. And by raising that by 7 percent—and compounding it over five years—we had ended up increasing the real growth rate of the . . . defense budget by 10 percent a year between 1980 and 1986. That was double what candidate Ronald Reagan had promised in his campaign budget plan."[25]

Stockman would later argue that these numbers constituted a temporary estimate and that harder numbers would be decided on later in the spring, after there was sufficient time for review. But that never occurred. "Instead what happened," according to Stockman, "was the top line [7 percent compounded growth], plus the inflation added to it, was parceled out to the military . . . and they [*sic*] in a matter of 60 days built a whole program down to the last $600 ashtray to spend it. Once that got wired into this massive bureaucracy and its correlates in Congress and the defense community, it was hard to ever do anything about it."[26] Weinberger and the military now had a tremendous advantage in their battles with Stockman. After the agreement of January 30, whenever Stockman recommended a change in the military budget, he was requesting a cut in previously accepted raises in defense spending—precisely the type of decision that Reagan was least likely to make. Thus the defense budget was being driven more by bureaucratic politics than by rational policy analysis.

Important decisions could also be thrown off track by public relations considerations. On February 10, Stockman addressed the president and the Cabinet about the budget issues that had to be decided within four days. The budget director was worried that he had been able to locate only about $71 billion of the then estimated $129 billion in reductions it would take to reach a balanced budget by 1984. Reagan was not troubled by this daunting task, again stating simply, "We're here to do whatever it takes." But the discussion quickly turned from the question of where the more difficult cuts of $58 billion should come from to the bad press the administration was receiving for the reductions that had already been decided upon. Stockman explained that eventually more programs would be targeted for budget hits but that, so far, he had not cut Social Security, veterans' benefits, Head Start, Supplemental Security Income, and summer jobs programs for ghetto youth. Missing Stockman's essential point that in a subsequent round of budget cutting these programs would be reduced, but sensing an effective response to Democratic charges of unfairness and liberal media bias, participants at the Cabinet meeting quickly decided that the administration ought to publicize this information. Meese proposed that Stockman meet with him, Press Secretary Jim Brady, and Dave Gergen after the meeting and write up a press release for the next day. When this group met later that morning, Stockman insisted that these programs would eventually have to be pared down, but he was not able to head off Meese's determination to score a propaganda victory. Newspapers the next day reported that the Reagan administration had decided not to cut seven social programs (Meese had added two more). The consequence of this public relations–driven decision was ruefully noted by Stockman: "The fact was these seven programs accounted for $240 billion of baseline spending— more than 40 percent of the domestic budget. And we had just neatly built a fence around them. Henceforth people would wave these newspaper clippings in our face over and over."[27]

Doctrinal disputes also inhibited the Reagan economic team from formulating realistic forecasts. Supply-siders, such as Paul Craig Roberts and Norman Ture, argued for the largest growth in current-dollar GNP (real GNP plus inflation), because that would demonstrate the powerful effect of the tax cut. Since real GNP growth had historically averaged about 3 percent annually, supply-siders expected their miracle cure to average about 5 or 6 percent. The monetarist members, especially Beryl Sprinkel, demanded the lowest possible figures for money GNP. After all, the Reagan administration was pledged to slash the double-digit inflation rates that had eroded public support for Carter in 1979 and 1980. The budget-balancers were represented by Murray Weidenbaum, chairman of the Council of Economic Advisers. As a professional economist, Weidenbaum wanted estimates that he could publicly defend, which meant lower annual economic growth rates than desired by supply-siders and higher rates of inflation than preferred by monetarists. Higher inflation was especially important to Weidenbaum because that would generate more revenue to balance the budget.

The president was scheduled to deliver a speech to Congress on February 18 outlining his economic program, and Stockman was responsible for providing the economic forecasts to support that program. With the clock ticking, Stockman became anxious that he would not be able to forge a consensus forecast among the three schools of thought. In early February, according to Stockman, "We now went into a white heat of pressure. The forecasting sessions, which formerly had been crucibles of intellectual and ideological formulations, degenerated into sheer numbers manipulation. The supply-siders yielded a tenth of a percentage point toward lower real growth; the monetarists yielded a tenth of a percentage point toward higher money GNP. . . . Round after round it went."[28] The difficulty and delay of reaching an agreement caused Stockman to lower his standards. He no longer wanted the most accurate forecast; he simply had to have an economic forecast that the president could employ in his upcoming speech. In a refrain that would be used more than once in 1981, any errors born out of haste and expediency could be corrected later.

On February 7, Stockman made a deal with Weidenbaum. If Weidenbaum would consent to keeping the real growth estimate "reasonably high," Stockman would accept Weidenbaum's higher inflation figures. When the group reconvened, Weidenbaum's forecast caused consternation among both the supply-siders and the monetarists. One of them challenged Weidenbaum: " 'What model did *this* come out of, Murray?' Weidenbaum glared at his inquisitor a moment and said, 'It came right out of here.' With that he slapped his belly with both hands. 'My visceral computer.' "[29]

Stockman then compelled the group to accept Weidenbaum's numbers, which became known as the "Rosy Scenario." According to Stockman, "The new Weidenbaum forecast added $700 billion in money GNP over five years to our previous consensus forecast [that had been negotiated between the supply-siders and the monetarists]. Nearly $200 billion in phantom revenues tumbled into our budget computers in one fell swoop. The massive deficit inherent in the true supply-side fiscal equation was substantially covered up."[30] Political expediency was causing the Reagan administration to use almost as many phony numbers in governing as it had used during the campaign.

On February 18, within a month of being inaugurated, President Reagan presented his blueprint to change the direction of the United States in a nationally televised speech to Congress and in a widely distributed document entitled *America's New Beginning: A Program for Economic Recovery*. The administration was recommending the largest budget cuts ever proposed by a president because "the uncontrolled growth of government spending has been a primary cause of the sustained high rate of inflation experienced by the American economy. Perhaps of greater importance, the continued and apparently inexorable expansion of government has contributed to the widespread expectation of persisting—and possibly higher—rates in the future."[31]

Using figures provided by OMB, Reagan's economic program was proposing a $659.5 billion budget for fiscal-year (FY) 1982 with a budget deficit of $45 billion. The president requested nondefense reductions totaling $41.4 billion in eighty-three major programs. He also asked for an additional $200 billion in cuts stretched out over the next three fiscal years, which would decrease the federal government's share of the GNP from 21 percent in FY 1981 to 19.3 percent in FY 1984. By FY 1984, based on very optimistic forecasts, the administration predicted a balanced budget and modest surpluses thereafter, because revenues would be rising rapidly in response to the tax cut incentives. The budget reductions were designed to constrain the growth of federal spending rates from the 16 percent trend that had prevailed during the last few years under Carter to about 7 percent over the next few years and to only about 5 percent by 1984. The defense program was projected to expand from one-quarter to one-third of total expenditures. To protect him-self from Democratic accusations that his budget cuts were unfair, Reagan pledged in his speech, "We will continue to fulfill the obligations that spring from our national conscience. Those who, through no fault of their own, must depend on the rest of us, the poverty stricken, the disabled, the elderly, all those with true need, can rest assured that the social safety of programs they depend on are exempt from any cuts."[32] The protected social safety net pro-grams, costing about $216 billion in FY 1982, were Social Security; Medicare; supplemental income for the blind, the aged, and the disabled; veterans' pen-sions, school lunch programs, Head Start, and summer youth jobs.

Although Reagan would have preferred that his tax cuts for individuals be retroactive to January 1, 1981, to raise more revenue he proposed that tax rates be lowered by 10 percent on July 1, 1981; a second 10 percent on July 1, 1982; and a third 10 percent on July 1, 1983. The net effect would be a 5 percent cut in 1981 income taxes, a 15 percent cut in 1982 taxes, a 25 per-cent cut in 1983 taxes, and a 30 percent reduction in 1984 taxes. Marginal rates, ranging from 14 to 70 percent in 1980, would eventually be lowered to between 10 and 50 percent.

The Reagan tax bill also offered businesses faster depreciation tax write-offs (retroactive to January 1, 1981) in order to stimulate investment. In the pres-ident's proposal, cars and light trucks used in business could be depreciated over three years; machinery and equipment over five years; and factories, stores, and warehouses over ten years. Under tax laws in 1980, most business equip-ment was depreciated over seven to twelve years, and it could take up to forty years to write off some buildings. Together, the individual tax cuts and the lib-eralized depreciation allowances would cost the Treasury about $300 billion by FY 1984 on a "static" basis—that is, discounting the new revenues that would be gained from economic growth spurred by supply-side tax cuts.[33]

Reagan's February 18 speech was received enthusiastically by many con-gressmen. After all the uncertainties and despair of the Carter presidency, here was a political leader who was sure of himself and his plan. The optimistic and confident Reagan boasted, "We're in control here. There is nothing wrong with America that together we can't fix." He issued a challenge to Democrats to come up with a better approach than his: "Have they an alternative which offers a greater chance of balancing the budget, reducing and eliminating infla-tion, stimulating the creation of jobs and reducing the tax burden? And if they haven't, are they suggesting we can continue on the present course without coming to a day of reckoning in the near future?"[34]

But once the Reagan economic program was publicized, it was subject to sharper criticisms. Democratic politicians stressed that the president's program was unfair to the poor. Economists emphasized that the plan was based on unrealistic expectations. New administrations are usually staffed by people whose euphoria about winning the presidency is likely to fuel overly optimistic projections. As Herbert Stein, who served in Nixon's Council of Economic Advisers (CEA), explains, "They think that the world is different because they are in office and that problems that seemed difficult under the old regime will yield easily to their presence and their wisdom."[35] After achieving the impossible dream of attaining the White House, how hard could it be to quicken the rate of economic growth, slow down the pace of inflation, and balance the budget within a few years? When Reagan assumed office, this anticipated euphoria was amplified because his administration contained a higher than usual percentage of ideological true believers who interpreted Reagan's election as a mandate for a revolution in policy. And lest we forget, Reagan, who might have been expected to be the most realistic member of his administration because of his age, was actually the most enthusiastic and unrealistic. Indeed, Stockman complained to Hedrick Smith "that Reagan had trouble understanding that Stockman's projections already included the best recovery Reagan could dream of; Reagan kept expecting more good news on top of the Rosy Scenario."[36]

There were inconsistencies in the Reagan economic program that administration officials could not see because of their fervent ideological beliefs. This was especially true of the supply-siders. Elisabeth Drew was told by one White House aide that discussions about economic assumptions within the administration were more like "a religious debate" than "a scientific debate."[37] Lou Cannon reported, "Supply-siders believed that these reforms would produce unprecedented economic growth in which . . . increased productivity would generate so much new wealth that government revenues would actually increase. The evidence for this proposition was skimpy, resting chiefly on the disputed outcome of a far more limited tax cut during the Kennedy administration. The supply-siders, however, thought the validity of their economic doctrine self-evident. Many of them expressed their convictions with an evangelical fervor more appropriate for a religious crusade than an economics discussion."[38] Reagan's roseate thinking was revealed in his reply to a reporter's question on February 19: "There's still that belief on the part of many people that a cut in tax rates automatically means a cut in revenues. And if they'll only look at history, it doesn't. A cut in tax rates can very often be reflected in an increase in government revenues because of the broadening of the base of the economy."[39]

Most liberal economists scoffed at Reagan's tax cut proposal, which was based on Arthur Laffer's curve. Keynesians stressed that there was no evidence that the economy's reaction to revenue reductions would be as strong or as quick as claimed by supply-siders. A Brookings Institution economist, Henry Aaron, lampooned the supply-side remedy as a quack cure by stating: "Laffer is the Laetrile of economics."[40] George Will perceptively defended the supply-side proposal by writing, "Kemp-Roth links an emotionally rational act (cutting taxes of the investing class) to a politically palatable act (cutting everyone else's taxes)."[41] The liberal economist Lester Thurow argued that Reagan's tax cut was more Keynesian than most people thought, because across-the-board revenue reduction would first stimulate demand and then supply. This criticism was vehemently denied by Treasury Secretary Regan, who emphasized that the administration's tax cut differed from past demand-oriented proposals because it targeted more benefits to those in upper tax brackets, the people most likely to save and invest.[42]

The Reagan recovery program was based on unrealistic assumptions that a number of negative economic trends would suddenly turn positive. For example, in an economy that was showing signs of slowing down, the administration estimated that real GNP would grow by 4 to 5 percent over the next four years. In May 1981, Thurow wrote, "This explosion in output is predicted for an economy where growth in productivity has been gradually slowing down since 1965 and has in fact been negative during the last three years. The Reagan administration assumes that productivity is going to return to a 3 percent rate of growth almost instantly, but what will make that happen? Such an increase in productivity has never happened before in our history, and there are good technical reasons for believing that it will not happen now."[43] This unprecedented expansion of economic growth and productivity was also projected to be accompanied by a decline in the money supply. While publicly supporting the Federal Reserve Board's policy of gradually reducing the growth in the supply of money, the administration was also assuming an average rate of growth of nominal GNP of 11.7 percent between 1980 and 1984. Rudolph Penner pointed out, "Between 1976 and 1980, the money value of GNP grew at an average annual rate of 11.2 percent. The question arises whether a more rapid growth of nominal GNP can be financed over the next four years with a significantly slower growth of the money supply. . . . If nominal GNP were to grow one percentage point less per year than is assumed by Mr. Reagan, 1984 GNP would be $150 billion lower than the number now underlying the budget estimates. Receipts would be lowered by $30 to $40 billion."[44] Skeptical questions like this and the inability of the administration to answer them satisfactorily created doubts in financial markets and set the stage for the recession that kicked in during the late summer of 1981.

STRATEGY

The administration's strategy required focusing on the country's economic problems and mobilizing support for the president's legislative remedies. Reagan's success in 1981 depended on convincing majorities in Congress that economic conditions were intolerable and that he was offering them the only possible solution. The traditional approach to economic policy making—repeatedly characterized by Reagan as tax and spend—had brought the nation to the worst economic crisis since the depression. With public opinion polls showing that the American people were becoming increasingly alarmed about their economic future, many congressmen were receptive to the president's proposals.

Whereas Carter had difficulty providing coherence to his legislative programs, Reagan's priorities could be contained within his budget proposal. That made them easier to sell to both the public and Congress. And since Congress must deal with the budget every year, it also simplified the problem of constructing a legislative strategy. In the words of Earl Walker and Michael Reopel, "By choosing the economy, [Reagan] added simplicity to both policy making and the policy process. All social and domestic issues were discussed not in terms of need, or values, but in budget recommendations—how much can be cut back without causing an uproar."[45] The best overview of Reagan's legislative strategy in 1981 was provided by Allen Schick.

> Ronald Reagan asked a lot of Congress in 1981, but he asked it to do little. He kept his priorities clear and succeeded in spacing the major budget battles throughout the year. . . . He did not clutter the legislative calendar with peripheral issues. As a conservative bent on scaling down the federal government, President Reagan did not have an ambitious legislative program; he wanted Congress to legislate less. . . . Other than "must" legislation (such as expiring authorizations), Congress handled few nonbudget issues in 1981. There were fewer recorded votes in the House and Senate than in any other year since 1971. The number of bills signed into law by Ronald Reagan was barely half the amount enacted during Jimmy Carter's first year in office.[46]

The administration's strategy was also based on portraying its economic program as a bold change of direction that it was firmly committed to for the long term. Reagan's economic advisers were convinced that erratic shifts in policy direction in the Carter administration had caused uncertainty that unsettled both business and consumers. The Reagan prescription to stabilize volatile markets was to provide a consistent, pro-business regime of low taxes, slow and steady growth in the money supply, balanced budgets, and less regulation. A major key to restoring business confidence was to convince markets that here was an administration that would not stray off its designated track.

After Reagan's economic program was launched, the major political decisions were largely made by the Legislative Strategy Group (LSG). The LSG was created in late February to coordinate the administration's activities to pass the program. Composed of senior White House officials, it was co-chaired by James Baker and Edwin Meese, but it met in Baker's office and he emerged as its directing officer. Baker's aide Richard Darman served as the liaison for all papers coming from the White House staff, and Craig Fuller was the contact for information rising from the Cabinet departments. In 1981, the LSG was the place where information was processed and strategies were discussed concerning how best to guide Reagan's legislative program through Congress.[47] As the president's program sailed through Congress, the LSG's political operations received rave reviews. Hedrick Smith reported, "In contrast to the Carter White House, Mr. Reagan's political team is widely praised as well-organized, purposeful, attentive and usually ahead of the Democrats in tactics."[48] Thomas "Tip" O'Neill, the Speaker of the House, later wrote, "All in all, the Reagan team in 1981 was probably the best-run political operating unit I've ever seen."[49] Such positive evaluations helped to elevate the status and power of Baker over Meese in the White House.

The LSG agreed to follow a recommendation made by David Stockman and Republican Senator Pete Domenici, the new chairman of the Senate Budget Committee, to use the reconciliation process to achieve Reagan's budget cuts. Reconciliation procedures were based on Section 310 of the Budget and Impoundment Control Act of 1974. This legislation had set up a budget committee in each house and created a timetable calling for two budget resolutions. The authors of this reform bill had intended reconciliation to operate at the end of the budget process, namely, in the second budget resolution. The first budget resolution, which sets tentative targets, is supposed to pass in May; the second resolution sets binding budget targets and is scheduled to pass in September. According to Richard Fenno, "As planned by the architects of the 1974 reform, reconciliation legislation would be used, at the end of the budget sequence, to 'reconcile' existing laws with the spending ceilings and the revenue totals prescribed in the final budget resolution. Whereas budget resolutions do not carry the force of law, a reconciliation bill would change the law and would, thereby, provide enforcement of budget decisions. The reconciliation procedures called for the Budget committees to 'instruct' each standing committee to report legislation that would implement budgetary prescriptions within its jurisdiction. Then, each Budget Committee would package the prepared legislation, without change, into a single reconciliation bill."[50] Thus, reconciliation is both a procedure and a bill; it can change both budget appropriations and statutory law.

The use of the reconciliation process as part of the first budget resolution was first employed by the Carter administration in the spring of 1980. When credit markets reacted negatively to Carter's initial FY 1981 budget proposal, he tried to move toward a balanced budget by cutting his recommendations and pressuring Congress to use the reconciliation process in the first budget resolution. This innovative procedure, fiercely resisted by standing committee chairmen in both the House and the Senate, resulted in a reconciliation bill that called for $4.6 billion in cuts and $3.6 billion in revenue increases.[51] This established the precedent that Stockman planned to exploit for far more extensive budget cuts and changes in funding formulas in the FY 1982 budget.

The reconciliation process provided a number of advantages for the Reagan administration. First, it was an action-forcing mechanism that could compel congressional committees to obey spending ceilings. Second, in Schick's words, "As used in 1981 the reconciliation instructions required the affected committees to report spending reductions for each of the next three fiscal years, thereby enabling Reagan to achieve multiyear cutbacks in one measure."[52] The president's economic advisers believed that multiyear cuts in both the budget and taxes would convey the consistent message necessary for markets to respond favorably in terms of high investment and low inflation. Finally, the reconciliation process would provide the administration with a major bargaining advantage. Unlike the usual procedure for changing statutes, in which legislation is created by various standing committees and comes to the floor in a variety of bills, the reconciliation process meant that the budget cuts would arrive on the floor in a single package. Instead of many painful votes, there would be only a few.

Despite the advantages provided by the innovative use of the reconciliation process, the Reagan administration was confronted with numerous obstacles in steering its legislative agenda through Congress. By picking up 12 seats in the Senate in the 1980 elections, the Republicans controlled that body (53 Republicans to 47 Democrats) for the first time since 1954. But many Republican senators, including the new majority leader Howard Baker and the new Budget Committee chairman Pete Domenici, were skeptical about the promised effects of supply-side tax cuts. The Democrats lost 33 seats in the House in the 1980 elections but still retained majority control with 243 Democrats and 192 Republicans. More ominous for the Reagan agenda was that whereas the Republicans occupied 44 percent of the seats in the House, the new Speaker Tip O'Neill allocated them only 40 percent of the seats on the Budget Committee, 34 percent of the seats on the Ways and Means Committee, and 31 percent of the seats on the Rules Committee.[53] If the Democrats in the House maintained their discipline, they could kill Reagan's program in these committees and prevent it from reaching the floor. Hence, for Reagan's program to pass Congress, the Republicans would have to maintain the highest levels of discipline in both chambers and attract the votes of several dozen southern Democrats in the House.

Republicans in the White House and Congress felt that they must produce results to retain their new majority status and set the stage for gaining control of the House in the 1982 elections. To establish their credentials to govern for the public, most congressional Republicans felt that they had to accept the political leadership of President Reagan and adhere to party discipline in both committee and floor votes. This was especially true in the Senate, where every Republican member was newly placed in a position of authority as chairperson of either a committee or a subcommittee. Given their slight majority in the Senate, any Republican defections were likely to be costly. In Senate Majority Leader Baker's words, "We are a team, the president is the quarterback and we are his blockers and we can't say now we don't like the plays."[54] The big plays were to pass the budget and tax cuts as quickly as possible.

However, this strategy of concentrating on Reagan's economic program antagonized social conservatives, who correctly observed that their issues were being neglected. Conservative spokesmen such as Richard Viguerie blamed James Baker and Howard Baker—but not Reagan—for the postponement of social issues on the legislative agenda. John Lofton, editor of *Conservative Digest,* angrily said, "This is the classic 'Give them rhetoric and hope they don't watch what we do.'"[55] But Reagan's legislative priorities were supported by such staunch Senate conservatives as Strom Thurmond of South Carolina, Jake Garn of Utah, and Jeremiah Denton of Alabama.

In 1981, the degree of Republican unity was exceptionally high, and the percentage of Democratic defectors was close to normal. One congressional scholar noted that "House Republicans averaged nearly 98 percent support on seven key votes; Senate Republican averaged 97 percent on nine key votes."[56] Hedrick Smith reported, "Neither Eisenhower, nor Nixon, nor Ford had achieved that party discipline. Such solid Republican voting had not been equaled since the hardheaded rule of 'Czar' Joe Cannon, Republican Speaker in 1910. Nor was Reagan ever again to muster such Republican unity."[57]

As for the Democrats in Congress, the intellectual foundation of their opposition was largely laid by liberal pundits and Keynesian economists. They criticized the president's program as unfair, unproven, and inflationary. Multiyear tax cuts coupled with a big boost in defense spending would overwhelm the proposed budget reductions and accelerate inflation. Immediately after Reagan introduced his legislation, Carl Rowan wrote, "America will soon learn that while Mr. Reagan's plan is bold, it is neither fair nor humane, and that a lot of cruelty is covered up in glib clichés."[58] The liberal economist Robert Lekachman suggested that "no one can say with complete certainty that this voyage into unchartered economic waters will end on the rocks, but one thing should be clear. . . . The benefits of [Reaganomics] will accrue quickly and massively to stockholders, corporate executives and other affluent types. The costs will affect the poor, the unemployed, the young, the female and the black."[59] Walter Heller, the Keynesian economist who served as President Kennedy's chairman of the CEA, argued that the supply-siders were making a false analogy when they claimed that Reagan's tax cuts would operate as successfully as Kennedy's did in 1964. According to Heller, "Savings stimulated by the 1964 tax cut came from real marginal rate cuts in a non-inflationary environment, not illusory ones that high inflation in the Eighties will snatch away."[60] Moreover, Heller ridiculed how unrealistically optimistic Reagan's economic plan was. The president's program was based on projections that real GNP would surge ahead at a 4.5 percent rate from 1982 to 1985, investment would leap from 10.5 to 14.5 percent of GNP, and inflation would drop from 11 to 5 percent a year. Nothing in the historical record or in the scholarly literature of economics indicated that these roseate estimates were possible.

The Democrats in Congress, however, were not able to exploit the arguments of their intellectual supporters as skillfully as they might have in the past. In the early months of 1981, congressional Democrats were still shell-shocked from their defeat in the 1980 elections, ineffectively led by new party leaders, unsure of the validity of their party's ideas, in partial agreement with Republican proposals that taxes and the budget should be pared down, and fearful that the 1982 congressional elections could lead to further Republican gains. No wonder that the word used most often to describe the Democrats was "disarray." Democrats were divided over whether they should act like a majority party and recommend alternatives to the president's program or respond like a minority party and try to delay and dilute the program's passage by publicizing its weaknesses. Barbara Kellerman notes that "the story of Reagan's success during his first nine months in office is also the story of a generally emasculated and disorganized opposition. The Democrats lacked a leader. Jimmy Carter vanished into the Georgia countryside; Robert Byrd, who was not . . . a strong leader even as head of the majority party, was even less consequential now that Senate Democrats were in the minority; and Tip O'Neill seemed to be out of his element as leader of an obstructionist opposition."[61]

As a result, the Democratic response to Reagan's thrust was frequently disorganized, sometimes supportive, occasionally obstructive, and almost always ineffective. These ambivalent orientations were reflected in the statements and behavior of congressional Democrats. In December 1980, Democratic Representative Henry Reuss said, "Our own prescriptions having proved ineffective, Democrats are likely to be charitable towards Republican economic policies, no matter how zany."[62] In February 1981, Representative David Obey of Wisconsin, a liberal Democrat, said, "I personally think it would be a political mistake if we don't give the administration an opportunity to test its views. There is a mandate for the administration to proceed with significant budget cuts and significant tax cuts."[63] In the spring, Senate Minority Leader Robert Byrd announced that he was going to vote for the Reagan budget because he felt that the public wanted the president's program to be given the opportunity to work. In the House, where the Democrats had their best chance to thwart Reagan's initiatives, Tip O'Neill's behavior was especially ambivalent. On the one hand, O'Neill stressed the inequities in Reagan's proposals; on the other, he promised not to use his power as the Speaker to prevent the president's program from reaching the floor of the House for a vote. According to Kellerman, "Since the generally accepted view was that delays would help opponents of the budget cuts, it was clear that by relinquishing control of the legislative schedule, O'Neill had given away one of his strongest cards." Later, one of his advisers sought to explain the Speaker's decision: "What the Democrats did . . . was to recognize the cataclysmic nature of the 1980 election results. The American public wanted this new President to be given a chance to try out his programs. We weren't going to come across as being 'obstructionists.' "[64] Moreover, during the April Easter recess, while the White House and Republican leaders were mobilizing their troops for upcoming votes, O'Neill and Dan Rostenkowski (the new chairman of the Ways and Means Committee) traveled to Australia and New Zealand. In short, the Democrats appeared to be paralyzed by the fear that the popular president would be able to frame them as "obstructionists," thus placing the blame for continued economic troubles on them. Finally, as Kellerman points out, "the Democrats were not entirely averse to letting the president have his way because if Reaganomics proved to be a disaster, he and his party would take the blame."[65]

To take advantage of the Democratic disarray, the Reagan administration used a well-coordinated two-track strategy. On one track, the communication skills of Reagan were utilized in several speeches and in low key appeals to southern Democrats at the White House or Camp David. The other track was taken by Lyn Nofziger, assistant to the president for political affairs, and his deputy, Lee Atwater. While Reagan played the role of nice cop in his dealings with the Democratic legislators, Nofziger's operation played tough cop, bringing the budget and tax conflicts into the home districts of vulnerable Democrats so that they would be more susceptible to the president's gentle persuasion. In April 1981, Nofziger directed a campaign in fifty-one congressional districts, forty-five of them in the South. This operation mobilized the efforts of the Republican National Committee, the National Conservative Political Action Committee, the Moral Majority, business political action committees, and local civic clubs. Atwater explained, "The premise of the operation is that political reforms and the impact of the media have made it so that a Congressman's behavior on legislation can be affected more by pressure from within his own district than by lobbying here in Washington."[66]

Because southern Democrats were the most vulnerable, they were subjected to the most pressure. In the 1980 elections, southern Democrats lost eight of their seventy-seven seats in the House, along with four of their sixteen Senate seats. Moreover, Reagan had run ahead of many southern Democrats in their own districts, which made them worry that the president would campaign against them in 1982. To defend their interests, a group of forty-seven southern Democrats organized themselves into an organization called the Conservative Democratic Forum, better known as the "Boll Weevils." The most prominent Weevils came from Texas, a state that Reagan had carried by more than 600,000 votes while Democrats were winning nineteen of twenty-four congressional seats. Texas Democrat Charles Stenholm was the leader of the Conservative Democratic Forum. Two other Texas Democrats provided valuable support for the Reagan program: Phil Gramm cosponsored the budget bill, and Kent Hance cosponsored the tax bill. This enabled Reagan to portray both measures as "bipartisan bills" in his television speeches.

At a White House breakfast on June 4, Louisiana's John Breaux expressed a major anxiety of the Boll Weevils—that in cooperating with Reagan, they were alienating themselves from their own party and then might have to confront the president campaigning against them in 1982. Reagan responded in a widely quoted statement: "I could not oppose someone who supported my principles. I could not look myself in the mirror if I campaigned against you."[67]

The result of the administration's pressure was to mobilize support among most southern Democrats for Reagan's program. Charles Stuart shows that "on the four substantive roll call votes on the 1981 tax cut, Southern Democrats supported the cut by margins of 71 percent, 54 percent, 88 percent, and 96 percent, respectively. Northern Democrats opposed these votes by margins of 72 percent, 93 percent, 60 percent, and 65 percent."[68]

The role of Reagan's impressive communications skills in getting his economic program enacted in 1981 helped to establish his presidential style, which emphasized the White House as the "bully pulpit." His speeches, delivered in his own inimitable, avuncular style, could make a partisan message sound bipartisan; appear confident and compassionate without sounding arrogant; reinforce his conservative credentials as a "conviction politician" while appealing to independents and working-class Democrats; and make chronic problems appear solvable by employing traditional, time-tested, commonsense remedies. In Kellerman's words, Reagan "spoke of cooperation rather than conflict, of cutting waste instead of funds, of protecting the truly needy while at the same time attending to what really had to be done. Above all, his message relied on the power of positive thinking. President Reagan seemed convinced that if only we followed where he led, everything would turn out just fine."[69] Given the populist logic of Reagan's speeches, only selfish interests and narrow-minded bureaucrats could oppose his proposals.[70]

Reagan not only sold his message to the American people, he employed his persuasive capabilities on a number of congressmen. According to Cannon, "During the first hundred days of his presidency, Reagan held 69 meetings with 467 members of Congress, prompting some of them to say that they had seen more of Reagan in four months than they had of Carter in four years."[71]

Ironically, the efficacy of Reagan's efforts was enhanced after he was shot on March 30. Because of Reagan's bravery and publicized wit, the near tragedy of a life-threatening gunshot wound was turned into a universally acclaimed personal triumph by his skilled public relations staff. In mid-March, the president's public approval rating, according to the Gallup poll, was 60 percent. His disapproval rating was 24 percent, which Samuel Kernell points out was "the lowest approve-to-disapprove ratio the Gallup Poll had ever recorded for a president in his second month in office."[72] After the failed assassination attempt by John Hinckley, Reagan's approval rating went up by seven points and his disapproval score declined by six.[73] The seventy-year-old man had met a severe test of courage and was now elevated to the status of a real-life hero. Especially for conservatives, this episode enlarged Reagan's mythic credentials; the conservative "Camelot" was not ended by an assassin's bullet. It would be more difficult for Democrats in Congress to oppose a heroic president rather than an ex-actor who had merely played heroic roles in the movies. Journalists reported that Reagan's courage had either extended his honeymoon or granted him a second one.

Once James Baker and Michael Deaver saw that Reagan was going to recover, they were able to turn the assassination attempt into a political opportunity. Each of Reagan's quips at the hospital—telling Nancy he "forgot to duck" and writing a note to the doctors who were about to operate on him expressing hope that they were Republicans—was widely publicized. Within four weeks from the time he was bleeding internally with a collapsed lung in the emergency room of George Washington Hospital, Reagan was addressing a joint session of Congress.

The president's slow recuperation after the March 30 shooting—during which his working hours were curtailed by doctor's orders that were strictly enforced by his wife—had another important consequence; it helped to reinforce the notion among senior White House staffers that they could run most of the administration's affairs without the active, personal participation of Reagan. Thus, what could have been a formative learning period for the new president became a shakedown cruise for his staff. In Cannon's words, "Reagan's political success in the months after the shooting reinforced the view of the Californians that Reagan could operate in Washington without changing his ways. . . . Reagan was so popular and so politically successful during the six months following the shooting that he had absolutely no motivation to alter his approach."[74] Hence, both the president and most of his top aides became comfortable with an administrative arrangement in which Reagan knew relatively few of the details of his programs. Democrats observed that, in meetings, Reagan mainly read from his index cards, did not seem to know the details of his own legislation, and frequently looked over to Meese or Baker concerning how to respond to a question. Even House Republican Minority Leader Robert Michel was quoted as saying, "The President's really not as well posted on the specifics and on the machinery as Johnson, Nixon, or Ford, who used to be more intimately involved in how it all worked. . . . Sometimes I think, 'My gosh, he ought to be better posted. Where are his briefing papers?' "[75] The budget director wrote, "For all practical purposes, he'd been out of the loop completely since inauguration week."[76] Blissfully uninformed about such crucial items as the forecast debate and Stockman's error in agreeing to massive increases in the defense budget, Reagan could pressure Republican congressmen to support an emergency increase in the debt ceiling, promising them that once his economic program was passed, they would never have to do that again. The price for this situation was lamented by Stockman: "I had simply failed all along to reckon with a crucial fact of life: the President would inevitably be called upon to make on-the-spot tactical decisions and compromises. But if he didn't understand the big picture, how would he make the right decisions?"[77] Stockman had been hoisted on his own petard.

THE BUDGET

By March 10, the Reagan administration was requesting total cuts of $48.6 billion in the FY 1982 budget. For Stockman, the task of projecting a balanced budget by 1984 was becoming more onerous. In March, Stockman was horrified to find that baseline spending was almost $10 billion higher per year than OMB had estimated in its February 18 white paper. This meant that more budget cuts were required. But the bulk of the easier cuts had been agreed upon in February; by March, the more seasoned Cabinet secretaries were fighting harder and more skillfully against further reductions in their departments' finances.

Stockman was disgusted to discover that members of the Reagan administration and Republican congressmen did not share his commitment to budget cutting. The budget director felt strongly, for example, that the federal government should not be spending $20 billion a year to finance the repair or building of local city streets, county roads, bridges, or mass-transit systems. In his view, local improvements should be paid for by local taxes. But Drew Lewis, the secretary of transportation, was able to forge an alliance with conservative Senator Alfonse D'Amato and moderate Senator Arlen Specter to preserve most of these subsidies. Stockman later lamented, "In the end, the transportation sector of the pork barrel never even knew the Reagan Revolution had tilted at it."[78]

Another case in point involved Secretary of State Alexander Haig fighting a $10 million cut in his department's payroll that would eliminate 591 people from the 22,000-person agency. After hearing Haig's hyperbolic protest— "Mr. President, if you accept the O.M.B. proposal, your entire foreign policy will go right down the drain"—Reagan split the difference and suggested a cut of 295. Haig later won the restitution of another 130 personnel. "By 1986," according to Stockman, "the State Department budget would be *50 percent bigger* in after-inflation dollars than the 'compromise' level Haig reluctantly agreed to that day."[79] When Stockman proposed to slice about 2,000 officials from the Justice Department's 54,000 employees, Attorney General William French Smith angrily responded that his department represented "the internal arm of the nation's defense" and that even though his budget was less than one percent of the Defense Department's allocation, "dollar for dollar we provide far more actual security to the American people."[80] Stockman scoffed at Smith's argument concerning the "Internal Defense Department," but Reagan thought it had merit and restored about half the cut employees.

Stockman was particularly outraged that he was not able to kill a $650 million-a-year program created by Carter in 1978. In Stockman's words, "If there was a single program in the 1981 budget we inherited that was both a statist abomination and something a Republican administration had a chance to kill outright, it was the Urban Development Action Grant Program [UDAG]."[81] This program required private industry to contribute $5 or $6 for every $1 in federal funds poured into its projects. When Stockman tried to eliminate this pork barrel program, Secretary of Housing and Urban Development Samuel Pierce mobilized hundreds of "distress calls" from local Republican officials and businessmen to the White House. These calls persuaded Meese that UDAG was really a Republican program and should be spared the budget ax. Reagan himself conveyed this decision to an audience of cheering mayors at the convention of the National League of Cities on March 5.[82] Stockman's failure to eliminate UDAG when he was at the peak of his power indicates both his limited influence and the constrained commitment of the Reagan administration to cut the budget when it negatively affected Republican constituents.

Stockman was also dismayed to find that although conservative Republican congressmen were demanding budget cuts, most of them had pet projects they wished to protect. For Senator Orrin Hatch, it was the Job Corps, which had a major facility in Utah; for Senator Jesse Helms, it was the tobacco subsidy; for Senator Howard Baker, it was the Clinch River Breeder Reactor; for former astronaut Senator Jack Schmitt, it was the space program. Senator Schmitt told Stockman that "technological progress is too important to be left to the free market." In response, Stockman later wrote, "Here was the premise of the Second Republic [Theodore Lowi's name for FDR's liberal regime] in a nutshell. Progress of *any* kind was too important to be left to capitalists. Only Washington could do it."[83] Even those espousing the ideas of the Reagan revolution were susceptible to the enticements of the liberal regime.

In brief, as Stockman desperately searched for places to cut the budget, he learned that each program was a sacred cow to some powerful figure. For Stockman, the dilemma was that in Washington, D.C., "sacred cows run in herds."[84]

As the number of real possibilities for cutting the budget diminished, the temptation to propose phony solutions increased. Both the administration and House Democrats rigged budget estimates and engaged in "gimmick wars" to escape from the dilemma of having to slice popular programs. One Democratic member of the House Budget Committee was quoted as saying, "It's our phony figures against Reagan's phony figures."[85]

The president's budget plan sailed through the Republican-controlled Senate with only minor problems. The Senate Budget Committee, with twelve

Republicans and ten Democrats and chaired by Senator Pete Domenici, began its deliberations on March 17. By March 19, the committee unanimously passed the reconciliation bill cutting FY 1982 expenditures by $36.4 billion, and by the first week in April, the bill passed the Senate by a whopping margin of eighty-eight to ten. After this success, the Senate Budget Committee went to work on the budget resolution and became embroiled over Stockman's use of a temporary plug of what had become $44 billion in future unspecified savings. Domenici, dedicated to balancing the budget (Stockman called him a Hooverite), wanted to list the $44 billion as a deficit, but he eventually succumbed to pressure from Stockman and Senator Robert Dole to label it as a future savings amount. Dole argued that this subterfuge was necessary to save the tax bill. Senate Majority Leader Baker then came up with the idea of designating the $44 billion plug with a magic asterisk.[86] On May 12, the Senate passed the 1982 budget resolution by a vote of seventy-two to twenty. Thus, the administration clearly communicated to Democrats in the House that it could obtain most of what it wanted in the Senate.

Politically, the LSG believed that the administration would eventually have to compromise on the tax bill, perhaps by jettisoning the third installment. With Reagan still recuperating from his gunshot wound, his advisers agreed that "the more ground given on spending cuts, the weaker the administration's position would be on the tax issue."[87] The strategy was to postpone any compromise on the budget cuts until the last possible moment. But Stockman was concerned that his political successes were not positively influencing the financial markets. Republican politicians may have been willing to be conned by a magic asterisk, but Henry Kaufman and the bond markets were not. The high bond yields of 15 percent that the administration had inherited in January had not declined by April, indicating that the financial world did not believe that the administration was going to be able to balance the budget.[88] However, in April, Stockman wrongly believed that this calamity could be averted by three adjustments: a more modest tax cut, a slower defense buildup, and major reforms in Social Security.[89] The budget director was not able to produce any of these adjustments.

In April, the spotlight shifted to the House Budget Committee, consisting of eighteen Democrats and twelve Republicans, and its new chairman, Jim Jones from Oklahoma. Jones was determined to block the Reagan juggernaut. He was willing to compromise in order to unite the Democratic majority in the House and create a responsible alternative to Reagan's budget. Before Reagan's victories in the Senate, Jones had talked about budget cuts of $25 billion, but afterward he mentioned figures closer to $35 billion. Jones understood that the key to attracting Boll Weevil votes was lowering the budget deficit and raising defense expenditures. After intense negotiations with his fellow Democrats, Jones produced a compromise bill that proposed a smaller tax increase, a more moderate defense buildup, and lower cuts in social spending (to attract liberal Democrats). Through some gimmicks (inflating revenue estimates and phantom savings of $6 billion from eliminating fraud, waste, and abuse), the Jones bill even promised to balance the budget one year earlier (in 1983) than the Reagan proposal. However, when one compares the two budgets, the Jones counterproposal was accepting 75 percent of what Reagan was demanding.[90]

Because it controlled the agenda and believed that it could entice enough southern Democratic votes to win, the administration was in no mood to split the difference and compromise. Instead, Stockman worked with Representative Phil Gramm, a conservative Democrat from Texas who would become a Republican senator in 1984, to produce a nominally bipartisan compromise budget proposal known as Gramm-Latta. Congressman Del Latta from Ohio, the senior Republican on the House Budget Committee, reluctantly accepted second billing. But Gramm-Latta was, in fact, *not* a compromise bill; it was virtually a replica of what the president had proposed in February and the Senate had passed early in April.[91]

In April, Jones managed to steer his budget resolution through the Budget Committee toward a showdown against Gramm-Latta on the floor of the House. In the key vote on May 7, the House accepted Gramm-Latta by a vote of 253 to 176. All 190 voting Republicans were joined by 63 defecting Democrats (mostly Boll Weevils) to give the president a surprisingly large victory. The president appeared to control an ideological majority in the House as well as a partisan one in the Senate. What Reagan achieved was a resolution directing House committees to cut $36.6 billion from the FY 1982 budget starting on October 1, 1981. By May 14, a conference committee had ironed out the minor differences between the House and Senate budget resolutions. The first concurrent resolution including reconciliation directions to the authorizing committees was then passed by both chambers. After this humiliating defeat, House Speaker O'Neill could see only one benefit for the Democrats: "I guess the monkey is off the Democrats' back. The cuts, as brutal as they are, are Reagan's cuts. The deficit is Reagan's deficit. The high interest rates . . . are Reagan's interest rates. The inflation rate—and most economists tell us it's going to soar—is Reagan's inflation rate."[92] In brief, political responsibility for the economy could no longer be foisted onto Carter; it was now Reagan's.

After the Gramm-Latta victory, several members of the Reagan administration felt that they had the momentum and opportunity to impose major reforms and cuts in Social Security. Both Reagan and Stockman viewed Social Security as an "intergenerational Ponzi game," where the workers of one generation were compelled to finance an increasing number of benefits to the retirees of the previous one. The structural dilemma of this arrangement was that the newer generations were producing fewer children, and medical advances were extending the life span of the elderly, which meant that the ratio of workers to retirees was declining. Politicians exacerbated this problem by periodically adding benefits to the Social Security program and underestimating their costs. Disability benefits were added in the 1950s, and early retirement (at age sixty-two with a 20 percent penalty in monthly benefits) was permitted in the 1960s. When automatic cost-of-living adjustments (COLA), tied to the Consumer Price Index, were added in 1972, expenditures accelerated. During the 1970s, old age and survivors' benefits soared by about 500 percent to $120 billion per year. Disability and Medicare costs went up even faster. By 1980, Social Security expenditures had risen to nearly $200 billion per year; but despite rising payroll taxes—including a major increase under Carter—the main trust fund was projected to go into deficit in 1983. The unfairness of the system was illustrated by the fact that whereas retirees in the next century were scheduled to receive far less in Social Security benefits than they had contributed, the average retired person in 1980 could look forward to receiving lifetime benefits five times as great as the total payroll taxes he or she had paid.[93]

According to Cannon, "Social security was always more tar baby than teflon for Reagan."[94] Stu Spencer (a campaign adviser) and James Baker considered Social Security to be Reagan's Achilles' heel and urged him to avoid the issue as much as possible. During the 1980 campaign, following instructions, Reagan repeatedly promised to protect the financial foundation of Social Security and to preserve the benefits for retirees already receiving them. He refrained from making explicit commitments concerning future retirees. Reagan's advisers understood that his libertarian streak made him critical of the compulsory nature of the Social Security system and open to the notion of a voluntary plan that would permit workers to select their own investments.

For Stockman, "No single issue was as critical to the success of the Reagan Revolution as social security reform. Spending on that program alone consumed nearly $200 billion per year, just under one-third of the entire domestic budget. It was therefore impossible to suppose that we could cut enough out of the budget to make our equation balance without touching it."[95] The issue for Stockman was not whether to cut Social Security benefits but when. Returning Social Security to actuarial discipline, whereby workers received back what they had contributed plus interest, meant that so-called unearned benefits would have to be stripped away. Such cuts would serve the twin purposes of symbolizing the revolutionary change from a liberal regime to a market-oriented, conservative one and providing the substantive reductions that would give meaning to the magic asterisk and balance the budget.

In March, Senator Domenici informed the White House that he and Democratic Senator Ernest Hollings had the outlines of a bipartisan compromise in the Senate Budget Committee to support a one-year freeze of Social Security COLA and other federal pension programs that could save $10 billion in FY 1982 and $25 billion by FY 1987. But James Baker strongly advised the president to reject the proposal, because to accept it would place Reagan in the position of appearing to renege on his campaign promise not to reduce Social Security benefits—an argument that Reagan always took seriously. Stockman also advocated a rejection of Domenici's offer; he had not yet had time to review the Social Security program, but he knew that he needed larger cuts in order to balance the budget. Stockman did not make clear to Reagan that he had a hidden agenda to cut Social Security later on. Hence, the president turned down Domenici's proposal at a meeting in Senator Howard Baker's office on March 17.[96] A major opportunity to reduce Social Security was thus squandered.

A few weeks later, the activities of Democratic Congressman J. J. "Jake" Pickle, chairman of the House Subcommittee on Social Security, forced the administration to reconsider its position on Social Security. Pickle informed Richard Schweiker, secretary of health and human services, that he was beginning to work on Social Security reforms and inquired about the Reagan position. On April 9, Pickle introduced a reform bill whose major feature was to raise gradually (over a ten-year period beginning in 1990) the normal retirement age from sixty-five to sixty-eight. As soon as Stockman heard about Pickle's bill, he was determined to derail it. In the budget director's words, "While I did not hope to cut the entire $44 billion per year out of social security, I did desperately need a reform plan that saved a lot more than Pickle's paltry proposal. And so the next day I set in motion a plan to get a lot more savings."[97]

On April 10, Stockman and a group of White House advisers met with Secretary Schweiker in the Roosevelt Room to discuss the administration's stance on Social Security. The participants agreed they had to come up with between $75 billion and $100 billion in savings over the next five years in order to make the system solvent. Schweiker argued for an expansionist solution, a proposal to add federal, state, and local government employees to the Social Security system. Stockman, aided by his ideological ally Martin Anderson, a White House domestic policy adviser, advocated a contractionist remedy that would reduce Social Security spending. The contractionist view prevailed. Schweiker was ordered by the White House to develop a number of options.

Within a few weeks, Schweiker and his department aides had come up with forty options presented in the obscure jargon of bureaucrats attempting to protect their interests. But Anderson understood the complexities of Social Security and Stockman had benefited from a crash tutorial on the subject from his staff. After much haggling, a one-hour meeting was set for 9 A.M. on May 11 at the White House in which several proposals would be presented to the president. At the meeting, Reagan quickly rejected Schweiker's option to expand the payroll tax. Stockman then presented his proposal—also camouflaged in arcane terminology—for a stiff increase in the penalty for early retirement. Since about two-thirds of retirees were taking early retirement, Stockman's proposal was economically appealing because it would save billions; but it was politically treacherous because it would seriously decrease the monthly income of many citizens planning to retire at the age of sixty-two. After a round of debate, Schweiker agreed to support a penalty of 45 percent (more than doubling the current penalty of 20 percent) for those retiring at sixty-two. The practical effect of this reform would have sliced the monthly check for an early retiree from $469 to $310. Anderson strongly supported Stockman's proposal on ideological grounds; it was authentic Reaganism to steer Social Security away from unearned benefits. Anderson also knew that Reagan had a disgust for Carter's 1977 rescue of Social Security, which had already demonstrated its deficiencies. Anderson encouraged the president to move quickly and decisively before his political advisers could dilute the reform proposal: "You'll be the first president in history to honestly and permanently fix social security. No one else has had the courage to do it."[98] The president took the bait so enthusiastically that he approved Stockman's package at the meeting, a rare occurrence.

Stockman was momentarily ecstatic; the president had agreed to Social Security budget cuts that would save $50 billion over the next five years. Not so James Baker and Richard Darman, who were caught off guard by this turn of events; together they agreed that this unforeseen decision was politically lethal for Reagan and that they should distance him from it as quickly as possible. Though Baker could not unilaterally reverse a presidential decision, by being in charge of White House operations, he could control how the decision was announced. He called an LSG meeting for 2 P.M. that very afternoon to discuss how the presidentially approved plan would be publicized, at which he expressed his concern that this decision might interfere with the administration's top priority, namely, the economic program. Stockman protested that Social Security cuts were not a peripheral matter but a vital component in ensuring a balanced budget. But when Darman asked whether the proposal had any support in Congress, Stockman and Schweiker had to concede that they had been so occupied working on options they had not consulted with legislators. Baker decreed that this proposal would not be proclaimed from the White House; it would be announced the next day from the Department of Health and Human Services and would be known as the Schweiker Plan. Both Schweiker and Stockman knew that this tactic would kill whatever chance the bill had; few Republican congressmen could be expected to fight for a controversial reform that the president was not willing to give his personal support to.[99]

Schweiker made the announcement on May 12, which elicited this headline in the May 13 edition of the *Washington Post*: "Reagan Proposes 10% Cuts in Social Security Costs." Tip O'Neill called the proposal "despicable." The media were filled with stories of workers who had planned an early retirement in 1982 and were now blindsided by the severe penalty. Stockman argued that only a Reagan television speech could save the situation, but Baker successfully urged a strategic retreat. When Democratic Senator Moynihan introduced a resolution defending Social Security, the LSG instructed Max Friedersdorf, the head of Reagan's congressional liaison staff, to negotiate a "face-saving" arrangement with Senators Baker and Dole. On May 20, the Senate voted ninety-six to zero against any bill that would "precipitously and unfairly penalize early retirees."[100]

After a string of victories, the Reagan presidency had suffered its worst defeat. The resilient administration would recover quickly and enjoy other political triumphs in 1981, but the opportunity for an authentic Reagan revolution was now ended. As a defeated revolutionary Stockman would later lament, "The truth was, from that day forward, social security, the heart of the United States welfare state, was safely back in the world of actuaries who had kept its massive expansion quiet over the decades. The centerpiece of the American welfare state had now been overwhelmingly ratified and affirmed in the white heat of political confirmation."[101] To Stockman's dismay, Reagan had proved to be less of a revolutionary—and more of a politician—than he had expected.

By early June, Stockman was shocked to discover that the administration's Gramm-Latta victory was in the process of being unraveled. The fifteen Democratic-controlled committees in the House were circumventing the guidelines of the first budget resolution. Under Gramm-Latta, the standing committees of the House were given reconciliation instructions to slash about $37 billion from the FY 1982 budget within thirty days. Some of the problems in meeting these requirements could be attributed to unfamiliarity with the reconciliation process, but the major reason for noncompliance was animosity to the proposed reductions. Carl Perkins, the Democratic chairman of the Education and Labor Committee, was the most candid in his rebellion, partly because his committee was ordered to cut $12 billion—more than any other committee. Perkins announced that he would not destroy in a day programs that had taken years to create, such as public service jobs under the Comprehensive Employment and Training Act and subsidized school lunches. To avoid the budget restrictions of Gramm-Latta, Democratic chairmen could select from a number of options: defy the Gramm-Latta mandate outright; make some cuts, but less than those required; or cut the specified amount, but not where the White House wanted cuts made. According to Stockman, "In combination, the fifteen committee bills amounted to a calamity. They claimed 1984 savings of $55 billion, of which about $25 billion was actually valid and taken from the 93 line-item instructions in the reconciliation mandate. That amounted to less than *one-fourth* of the $118 billion in cuts needed to achieve a balanced budget in 1984. And even the one-quarter loaf would be true only if Rosy Scenario held up—which she wouldn't."[102]

In response to this sabotage, Stockman in early June directed his OMB staff to secretly create "Gramm-Latta II," which would serve as a 1,000-page alternative to the budget bills the House Democratic committees were now preparing. Stockman viewed these chairmen as the "Politburo of the Welfare State," with an almost unlimited capacity for accounting gimmickry. His strategy was to bring about another up-and-down vote on Gramm-Latta II, which Stockman considered a valid version of the first reconciliation bill.

But Stockman's plan was hindered by several factors. First, Republican congressmen were becoming more sensitive about Democratic accusations that they had been reduced to "Reagan robots," mindlessly marching in lockstep to the numerical dictates of the abrasive Stockman. Many Republican congressmen were looking for opportunities to demonstrate their independence and their ability to gain special considerations for programs they supported. Second, with Speaker O'Neill pledging to renew the budget fights, the Reagan coalition needed every vote it could muster to reach the commanding majority of 218 in the House of Representatives. Stockman complained, "With none to spare, each vote became all the more precious—and all the more expensive. . . . Here was the nub of the problem: each committee had its pet project, and each bloc of GOP or Boll Weevils had enormous leverage on us. Each one could be the crucial bloc to put us over—or under—the magic 218."[103] And finally, Stockman did not have the full support of the president. What Stockman considered his "solo mission" in pushing for these budget cuts was made more so by the fact that Reagan did not understand the budget and, most important, was more committed to the tax cut and the defense buildup than to painful budget reductions.

By June 12, the fifteen House committees had completed their work on the reconciliation bills. At an LSG meeting on June 17, Max Friedersdorf reported that the administration lacked the necessary votes to pass the substitute bill. Because of defections from the Gypsy Moths (moderate Republicans) and Boll Weevils, support for Gramm-Latta II was under 190 votes. James Baker advocated going along with the House reconciliation bills, thus saving the tax cut legislation. For Baker, his reputation as a political strategist was at stake. Stockman, focusing on the goal of balancing the budget by 1984, argued, "The numbers in the House bills are so bad that we've got to go for broke. Put the president on the tube and beat them into submission."[104]

On June 18, the president met with his senior staff and his congressional supporters. Stockman was disappointed that only Gramm and Latta supported his strategy of forcefully opposing the House committee bills. Kent Hance, a Boll Weevil sponsor of the tax bill, urged compromise on the budget cuts. The president agreed and ordered Stockman to cooperate with Minority Leader Michel in creating a substitute bill that would concentrate on specific entitlement reforms and "incorporate as many of the committee bills produced by the House Democrats as possible."[105]

After this meeting, Michel and Stockman went to the minority leader's office and met with congressmen demanding specific budget increases in Gramm-Latta II. Over the next four hours, Stockman surrendered $20 billion in proposed three-year budget savings.[106] Northern Republicans won increases in expenditures for Amtrak, Conrail, energy subsidies to the poor, the National Endowments for Arts and Humanities, and nurses' training and a weaker cap on the growth of Medicaid spending. Southern Democrats gained budget increases on a sugar support program and the Fuel Use Act. Stockman publicly denied that any deals were made to buy votes, but Louisiana Democrat John Breaux, who agreed to support Gramm-Latta II in exchange for administrative backing of the sugar price support program, was more accurate when he said that his vote could not be bought but it could be rented.[107]

On June 25, the Senate passed Reagan's budget by a vote of eighty to fifteen. In the House, Budget Committee Chairman Jones and Reconciliation Task Force Chairman Leon Panetta, a Democrat from California, constructed a package that they claimed contained approximately 85 percent of Reagan's recommendations. The Democrats brought their bill to the floor under a rule calling for votes on separate parts of the proposal and preventing an up-and-down vote on the alternative of Gramm-Latta II. Before the key vote, Reagan telephoned twenty-nine congressmen, mostly Boll Weevils, urging them to vote to defeat the Democratic procedural motion. Most of them did. The Democratic proposal was defeated 217 to 210 on June 25, and Gramm-Latta II passed 232 to 193 the next day. Describing the frantic scene on June 26, Laurence Barrett wrote, "The omnibus bill [Gramm-Latta II] itself was a physical monstrosity because segments of it had been patched together so hastily. . . . Few members knew exactly what all the provisions meant. . . . Not merely numbers were involved, but alterations in benefit formulas that would have important impact for years to come. . . . The bill went through by a comfortable margin . . . even if no one, including David Stockman, could know exactly how many billions had been added and subtracted until O.M.B. computers reviewed all the changes."[108] Reagan had defeated the Democrats again, but he had been forced to make more compromises than was generally understood. Perhaps the most arresting symbol of the final House vote on June 26, reflecting the frenzy and lack of understanding concerning what was in the bill, was that Rita Seymour, a Congressional Budget Office staffer, had her name and telephone number enacted into law when they were scribbled on a page margin of the reconciliation bill.

Although Reagan's budget bills had passed both houses, Stockman was afraid that the administration would lose more budget savings if the bills fell victim to further compromises in a conference committee. (A conference committee, composed of selected members from the House and Senate, is designed to iron out the differences between House and Senate versions of a bill.) To avoid a conference committee, Stockman recommended that the Senate accept the House bill. The LSG and Reagan agreed with this suggestion, but the Senate Republican leaders, Baker and Domenici, angrily rejected Stockman's recommendation. Moreover, to demonstrate how fed up the legislators were with Stockman, OMB staffers were thrown out of the conference committee room. Gramm was also excluded. The conference committee, composed of 250 House and Senate members, then split into fifty-eight subconferences. Confirming the budget director's fears, in two weeks of meetings, the conference committee contributed to the retreat from a balanced budget. According to Stockman, "The conference produced valid budget savings lower than both the Senate and House bills. The resulting 1000 page document was replete with every loophole, every cut corner, every perversion of fine print in the considerable repertoire of the professional staff that dominated the conference."[109] The retreat from balancing the budget had become a rout.

The Omnibus Budget Reconciliation Act of 1981 passed the House and Senate on July 31 and was signed into law by President Reagan on August

13, 1981. It cut expenditures for FY 1982 by about $35 billion and over the 1982–1984 period by about $140 billion. More than 200 program alterations were squeezed into a single piece of legislation, and few of the changes were subjected to separate votes. The big budget winner was the Defense Department. Under Carter, the Pentagon had been allocated $180.7 billion for FY 1981; under Reagan, it received $199.7 billion for FY 1982. By FY 1986, military expenditures were projected to soar to $374.3 billion. Over the next five years, military spending authority was expected to reach $1.5 trillion.[110]

The big losers were social programs. Although the major middle-class entitlements, such as Social Security and Medicare, were generally protected and continued to increase expenditures, two-thirds of the budget cuts came from the human services area. Eligibility for the food stamp program was tightened, reducing the rolls (22 million people received food stamps in 1981) by about 1 million and cutting its $12.6 billion allocation by $1.66 billion. About $1.5 billion was cut from programs costing $4.4 billion in 1981 by reducing subsidies for school meals, tightening eligibility for free or reduced-price meals, and curtailing supplemental feeding programs for women, infants, and children. Public service employment (300,000 jobs) under the Comprehensive Employment and Training Act (CETA) was ended. Expenditures for other CETA programs, including training, Job Corps, and summer youth jobs, were reduced 20 percent. Additional unemployment benefits activated by national unemployment figures were terminated, and trade adjustment aid to workers was trimmed. Aid to Families with Dependent Children (AFDC) payments were reduced for those who work. The $30 billion authorized for public housing and rental subsidies in 1981 was slashed by $12 billion, cutting the number of planned new units from 254,000 to 154,000 and increasing the percentage of rent (from 25 to 30 percent) that poor tenants had to pay. Medicaid grants to the states were cut by about $1 billion.[111]

The Reagan administration had scored a great victory, defeating the Democrats and paving the way for its top goal, the tax cut. But the president had spent much of his political capital and had been forced to make many more compromises to keep his congressional coalition together. Too much of the budget had been granted political protection; there was no way the budget could be balanced by 1984. Budgetary truth was the victim of campaign-style rhetoric of both parties. As budget expert Allen Schick noted, "Both the Democrats and Republicans had reason to exaggerate the size of the reduction, the latter in order to claim more savings and the former in order to save more programs."[112] The stage was set for chronic budget deficits for the rest of the decade.

ECONOMIC RECOVERY TAX ACT (ERTA)

Helping to doom the effort to eliminate budget deficits was Reagan's personal commitment to cutting taxes. In terms of both rhetoric and behavior, Reagan demonstrated that significant reduction in tax rates was a strategic priority for him.[113] From Stockman's perspective, however, the president's engagement was a problem, because Reagan did not understand the tax code and its relationship to the budget. The president "could not grasp that to fiddle significantly with the former was to change the numbers in the latter—and for the worse."[114] Given Reagan's economic beliefs and optimism, he never accepted the fact that cuts in taxes meant reductions in revenue.

The problem for the administration was that many Republican congressmen, including leaders such as Howard Baker, Robert Dole, Pete Domenici, and Barber Conable, were not fully in support of the supply-side philosophy. Senator Baker was quoted labeling the tax cut "a riverboat gamble." A simple three-year tax reduction was an attractive campaign proposal; it was less appealing as a governing guide. Members of both parties feared that a tax cut would contribute to budget deficits, prevent the Federal Reserve from reducing interest rates, and fuel inflation. More experienced congressmen were skeptical about the administration's strategy of planning to pass two tax bills: the first being the simple tax cut bill introduced in February to deal with the economic emergency, and the second being a more complex tax reform bill. When Treasury Secretary Regan explained this strategy in February, Representative Rostenkowski, the new chairman of Ways and Means, interrupted and said: "Mr. Secretary, you know there might be only one train to Peoria this year. And if there is, everybody is going to want to get on it."[115] Rostenkowski's metaphor proved clairvoyant; many congressmen decided to get on board what they considered a gravy train.

In March, Rostenkowski announced that Reagan's tax bill was all but dead and that he would develop a Democratic substitute. As a new chairman with ambitions to be Speaker, Rostenkowski was anxious to be successful in his first shepherding of a tax bill. He was aware that the Republicans had more power on the floor of the House than in his Democratically stacked (two-to-one majority) committee. Rostenkowski wanted to make sure that any bill that emerged from his committee had enough Democratic and Republican support to win on the floor. Cobbling together such a coalition would be difficult, because many Democrats were opposed to a three-year tax cut and wanted to maintain the progressivity of the income tax.

In April, Rostenkowski announced the details of his committee's alternative to the Reagan bill. The chairman's proposal called for a single-year tax cut, aimed more at the middle class (defined as citizens earning $20,000 to $50,000 a year), and an expansion of the individual retirement account (IRA) program. According to tax expert John Witte, "This provision was supported by references to continuing concern over the national savings rate and by the argument that IRAs had become so widespread that it would be unfair if anyone were excluded from the program."[116] The most surprising component of Rostenkowski's bill was a supply-side–inspired measure to reduce "the top marginal rate on unearned income from 70 percent to 50 percent. This was an idea Reagan had reluctantly surrendered in February for fear of being charged with catering to the wealthy."[117] Over the next few weeks, the debate between the administration and Rostenkowski centered on the multiyear span of the tax reduction and on whether the reduction should be skewed (in favor of those who earned less than $50,000) or equal (each bracket receiving a 10 percent cut).

The bargaining situation changed drastically on May 7 as a result of the House vote on the administration's budget resolution, which demonstrated that the Republicans, with the aid of the Boll Weevils, could defeat the Democratic leadership on the floor. Rostenkowski recognized that he would have to make more compromises and began meeting with Senator Dole, the chairman of the Senate Finance Committee. The LSG met with the president on May 12 to discuss what changes would be needed to pass the bill. Donald Regan told the president that the administration's bill could not pass in its present, simple form and that compromises would have to made. Regan was jealous of all the publicity Stockman had received as the administration's "point man" on the budget bill, and he was determined to replace the budget director as the economic spokesman and to at least match Stockman's legislative victories. The ex-marine was not going to be outranked by an ex–divinity student. Baker and Darman were even more willing to compromise. "Their idea," according to Stockman, "was to achieve as much of the supply-side policy as you could without sacrificing the President's continuing capacity to succeed. As non-ideologues, they would have been happy to settle for a half loaf on the 30 percent rate cut—as long as it could be arranged so as to look like a 'win' for the President."[118] Baker and Darman recommended that the administration negotiate with the Boll Weevils to get a better compromise from Rostenkowski. An acceptable deal with Rostenkowski was the best solution, because it would avoid a bidding war and make it much easier to pass the tax cut in the House. Democratic Representative Kent Hance had lined up a number of Boll Weevils in support of delaying the first year's tax cut until 1982 and reducing its rate to 5 percent, while adding reductions in estate taxes and savings incentives. As an ex–union leader, Reagan was not averse to accepting compromises in his original pro-posal, especially when most of these additions—or "ornaments," as they were called—to his simple bill were tax cuts that were compatible with his philosophy. He was willing to delay the tax cut if that would help gain votes for both the budget reconciliation bill and his tax bill. But the president was adamant that he would not accept anything less than a 25 percent cut in tax rates over three years.[119]

Once Reagan specified his demand for a three-year 25 percent tax cut, Rostenkowski and his Democratic allies no longer wanted to negotiate with the administration; they wanted to fight. Reagan's advisers did not foresee that it would be better for Rostenkowski's political future to remain loyal to the Democratic Party and lose to Reagan than to betray his party (like Gramm) and accept most of the administration's bill. In early June, Rostenkowski did offer a two-year 15 percent tax cut plus ornaments, a proposal that was rejected by the president. The administration would now have to strike a deal with the Boll Weevils and then wage a bidding war against Rostenkowski's bill. By not reaching a compromise with Rostenkowski, the administration stumbled into a process that was driven by the need to buy votes in the House at the expense of rational tax and budget policy.

On June 4, Reagan announced that, in place of his original proposal, he would support a substitute bipartisan bill to be introduced by Republican Barber Conable of New York and Democrat Kent Hance of Texas. This compromise bill would delay the first installment of the tax cut from July 1 to October 1, 1981, and reduce it from 10 to 5 percent. The Conable-Hance bill would also reduce tax losses by revising the depreciation (10-5-3) formula, but at the same time it would increase IRA eligibility, lower gift and estate taxes, and reduce the rate on capital gains from 28 to 20 percent. Speaker O'Neill responded by accusing Reagan of stealing Democratic tax ideas and of not understanding the needs of working people, and he promised to lead the fight against the president's bill. The quest for a bipartisan compromise had now been replaced by a bidding war as each party tried to attain majority support for its legislation by adding ornaments.[120]

For different reasons, both sides were committed to a hectic pace in June and July. The Democrats wanted to schedule the votes quickly before the administration's powerful lobbying effort, which had already exhibited its persuasive capabilities in the House budget votes, could mobilize the public. The administration wanted to maintain its momentum and pass the tax cut before the August recess. The Democrats were determined not to lose again, and the administration was resolved to continue its victory string. Neither side was sure of winning, which created an ideal situation for tax lobbyists.[121]

The administration also lost more ground in its quest for a balanced budget as a result of a deal it made with Kent Hance. In return for the Boll Weevil's accepting October 1, 1981, as the starting date for tax reduction, the administration agreed to include Hance's request for a $2,500-per-year tax credit for small oil royalty owners against Carter's windfall profits tax. This provision would cost the Treasury only $700 million per year, but once this ornament was added to the administration's tax bill, it poisoned the political well, because it encouraged other congressmen to get their "fair share" for their constituents. According to Stockman, "Hance's $2,500 tax credit had triggered a trillion dollar bidding war."[122] That conflict demonstrated, contrary to what was being proclaimed in the media, that the Reagan revolution lacked majority support in Congress. The crucial margin of victory had to be bought the old-fashioned way. As a believer in the revolution, Stockman was disillusioned to discover that,

> When it came to taxes, the GOP's idea of tax reform consisted of opening up loopholes in the IRS code. They preferred to pump up the welfare state from its back end by means of tax subsidies rather than direct expenditures. Some championed the utilities industries; others shilled for smokestack manufacturers. Still others promoted tax breaks for the thrift industry, equipment leasing, small business, cattle feedlots, pharmaceuticals, waste water recycling plants, and countless more.[123]

The Senate Finance Committee began meeting in late May, while the House Ways and Means Committee began markup sessions on June 10. Dole expressed reservations that the bidding war was overwhelming the usual legislative constraints that kept tax cuts within reason. For example, the Democrats were not blocking Republican efforts to help business; instead, they were matching and sometimes raising the bid. Business lobbyists were astonished that the Democrats were now offering them more lucrative benefits (such as "expensing," a device that would allow immediate write-offs for the purchase of capital assets) than the Republicans. One disgruntled liberal Democrat, Representative David Obey, quipped, "It would probably be cheaper if we gave everybody three wishes."[124] The policy environment was accurately described in June by the economics columnist Leonard Silk: "What started out as a simple, clean tax cut is becoming, with the Reagan Administration's collaboration, a Christmas tree bill that outglitters any of the past. With Republicans and Democrats vying for the privilege of providing tax breaks to assorted groups, the bill is becoming a masterpiece of fiscal graffiti—a bonanza perhaps most of all for tax lawyers, tax accountants and investment advisers."[125]

On June 27, Senator Dole guided an amendment-laden bill through the Finance Committee by a surprisingly strong vote of nineteen to one. By including some tax increases and reducing the 10-5-3 write-offs, the bill's revenue losses came to approximately the administration's target of $150 billion in 1984. Both Stockman and Dole felt that the strong committee endorsement would be able to ward off amendments on the floor, but they were mistaken. Once it became known that the administration was dealing in the House, tax-sweetening ornaments began to multiply and pass in the Senate. For example, amendments by Republican Senator William Armstrong to institute tax indexing and by Democratic Senator Russell Long to create (with the aid of tax subsidies) employee stock ownership plans were passed and eventually reduced the 1986 revenue base by nearly $25 billion.

After the administration won the key House vote on the reconciliation bill on June 25, the Democrats became more obsessed with winning on the tax bill. Rostenkowski's bill even retreated from its two-year, 15 percent rate cuts to allow a third "trigger" year if economic objectives were achieved on the deficit, interest rates, and inflation.[126] Indeed, the Democrats had constructed a more generous package of tax cuts costing more in revenue reductions over the next two years than the Reagan bill. White House legislative aide Kenneth Duberstein told members of the LSG that "Conable-Hance isn't competitive— not even close."[127] In response, the administration held a long meeting on July 23 in the Cabinet Room to design Conable-Hance II into what Barrett would call a "cornucopia with something for almost everyone."[128] The president presided over this meeting in order to assure his three-year, 25 percent tax cut but was perplexed by most of the discussion. Conable insisted that tax indexing be incorporated, and it was, with a delayed effective date of 1985. Conable also won $6 billion worth of tax benefits for small businesses and an above-the-line charitable deduction for non-itemizers on individual income tax forms. New England Republicans gained a 15 percent subsidy for wood-burning stoves. The Boll Weevils received billions of dollars of benefits for the oil industry and oil royalty owners. After this meeting, a stunned Darman discussed with Stockman whether the administration might not be better off allowing this bill to die. The budget director quotes Darman as saying, "I don't know which is worse . . . , winning now and fixing up the budget mess later, or losing now and facing a political mess immediately." But after a few seconds of intense speculation, Darman blurted out, "I believe it finally has come down to the White House versus the Democrats. . . . Let's get at it. . . . We win it now, we fix it later."[129] No mention was made of whether there would actually be an opportunity to mend the mess later.

On Sunday, July 26, the president invited fifteen Democratic House conservatives to Camp David to discuss Conable-Hance II. Reagan's efforts were rewarded; twelve of the fifteen later voted for the administration's bill. On Monday evening, July 27, the president addressed the nation in a televised speech that Stockman characterized as "a masterpiece of propaganda." Reagan first played the role of a populist by stressing, "This is the first real tax cut for everyone in twenty years." But as a politician, he also pointed out that his bill contained benefits for select groups, such as farmers, small business owners, the savings industry, and small independent oil producers. Reagan enthusiastically endorsed indexing, because "bracket creep is an insidious tax." He then compared the two bills with the aid of a graph that portrayed taxes under the Democratic proposal going down for two years but then rising during the third year (apparently when the trigger failed), whereas under Conable-Hance II, taxes declined and stayed down. Reagan suggested that if citizens were planning to live longer than two years they should support his bill. The president finished this well-delivered speech by advising the public to contact their representatives in support of his bipartisan legislation.[130]

They did—in record numbers. The vote in the House was scheduled for July 29, and shortly before the tally, a shaken Speaker O'Neill said, "We are experiencing a telephone blitz like this nation has never seen. It's had a devastating effect."[131] What had appeared to be a close contest turned out to be a solid majority for the administration as the Conable-Hance II substitute for Rostenkowski's bill was passed by a vote of 238 to 195, with 48 Democrats abandoning their party's position, including 31 Boll Weevils. John Witte writes, "The final vote on the bill [again on July 29] was 323 to 107, allowing many more to claim a vote for tax reduction. On the same day, British Crown Prince Charles married Lady Diana Spencer, leading Speaker O'Neill to the cynical indictment: 'This has been quite a day for aristocracy: a royal wedding and a royal tax cut.' "[132] What O'Neill did not admit was how much of the Reagan tax cut philosophy was in the Democratic bill.

The slight differences between the House and Senate versions of the tax bill were ironed out by a conference committee in one day. The Economic Recovery Tax Act of 1981 was then passed by the Senate on August 3 by a vote of 67 to 8 and by the House on the following day by a vote of 282 to 95. It was signed into law by the president at his ranch in California on August 13.

ERTA was the largest tax cut in the history of the United States. It provided a tax cut of over $37 billion in 1982, increasing to about $267 billion in 1986, for a total five-year revenue loss to the Treasury of $750 billion. The rates on individual income taxes would be reduced by 5 percent on October 1, 1981, 10 percent on July 1, 1982, and 10 percent on July 1, 1983. The top tax rate was sliced from 70 percent to 50 percent on January 1, 1982. For individuals, ERTA included marriage penalty relief, indexing (beginning in 1985, there would be annual adjustments in personal exemptions, zero bracket amounts, and income brackets to offset bracket creep caused by inflation), a drop in the capital gains rate from 28 to 20 percent, and wider margins on tax breaks for home sellers. Business received generous depreciation write-offs for buildings, equipment, and vehicles; investment tax credits ranging from 6 to 10 percent; and reductions in the corporate tax rates. Savings incentives were increased by authorizing banks and savings institutions to issue one-year savers' certificates and expanding the number of people eligible to participate in IRA programs. The threshold for estate taxes was raised from $175,625 to $600,000, and the tax exemption for gifts from parents to children or between spouses was expanded to cover gifts up to $10,000 per year (previously $3,000). There were also numerous benefits for the oil industry and oil royalty owners. In brief, ERTA had two provisions that raised revenues and thirty that reduced them.[133]

CONCLUSION

The Reagan presidency achieved its goal of hitting the ground running upon assuming office in 1981. Members of the administration quickly focused on a limited number of economic goals and united behind a strategy to attain them. Reagan officials were also correct in their assumption that "how we begin will significantly determine how we govern." In retrospect, however, Reagan's first year looks different than it did to politicians, journalists, and scholars in 1981. His legislative victories still appear impressive, creating a new standard to replace FDR's first 100 days. Reagan had obviously met the leadership challenge of taking advantage of the honeymoon period. But a reexamination reveals that his administration engaged in much more compromising than contemporary observers noticed. Clearly, Reagan's initial success did not constitute a conservative revolution. The president succeeded in slowing the growth of the welfare state; he did not abolish it. This simple truth was hidden by the interaction between Reagan's revolutionary rhetoric and the partisan wailing of the Democrats, but it was recognized by a conservative, David Stockman, who wrote: "The borders of the American welfare state had been redefined, but they had been only slightly and symbolically shrunken from where they had stood before. The half-trillion-dollar per year domestic budget which remained now had incredible staying power, because in surviving the White House assault it had gained renewed political sanction."[134] What disturbed Stockman was that the president was not unhappy with this state of affairs, because Reagan was more of a politician willing to accommodate much of the system than a revolutionary leader committed to fundamentally changing the system.

The initial responses to Reagan's legislative triumphs was high praise. After several failed presidencies, Reagan had demonstrated that the office was not impossible to fill, and he was favorably compared with several legendary chief executives. A columnist wrote, "It has been years since America has had the kind of political leadership that Ronald Reagan is providing in the Oval Office. Reagan is a cross between John F. Kennedy (for style, grace, charms, looks and dash) and Franklin D. Roosevelt (for political insights and an uncanny reading of contemporary moods)."[135] Hedrick Smith suggested that "in 190 days President Reagan has not only wrought a dramatic conservative shift in the nation's economic policies and the role of the Federal Government in American life but has also swept to a political mastery of Congress not seen since Lyndon B. Johnson. With stunning victories today [July 29], the President has won Congressional approval for the largest budget and tax cuts in American history, changes that his partisans have termed 'the Reagan Revolution,' inviting comparisons to the early New Deal period of Franklin D. Roosevelt."[136] In August, a second-term Republican congressman from Georgia, Newt Gingrich, called Reagan "a realigning leader."[137] In brief, Reagan had restored confidence in the office of the presidency and was encouraging conservatives to believe that he was replacing a liberal regime with a conservative one.

Reagan's victories were also aided by the disarray of the Democratic Party. While the president energized and unified the Republican Party, Democratic congressmen were dispirited and undisciplined and could not agree on any strategy to oppose Reagan. The one Democratic victory was its defense of Social Security. Reagan's domination of the policy agenda was indicated by the fact that even if the House had voted for the Democratic tax cut, the bill was still largely a copy of the Republican proposal. "Me too" is not an inspiring battle cry to rally partisans. Most importantly, the Democrats had been defeated on issues that would place them on the defensive for the rest of the decade. By losing on the budget and the tax cut (including indexing), the Democrats were severely handicapped in their ability to propose new programs. Instead of expanding revenues, there was burdensome debt. As a conservative, Reagan did not need to recommend new legislation; liberal Democrats did.

As a political leader, Reagan was the beneficiary of an excellent advisory system. His staff efficiently transformed an electoral victory into an electoral mandate for Reagan's programs. During the first eight months of 1981, the president's staff operated as an effective blend of talent, with conservatives providing energy and ideological direction, pragmatists supplying experience and know-how about when to compromise, and public relations experts skillfully using the communications talents of Reagan. As the months went by, James Baker, the chief of staff, slowly eclipsed the authority of Edwin Meese, the counselor, a process that came about as critical decision making was shifted from Meese's Cabinet committees to the LSG, which met in Baker's office. The decline of Meese was also hastened by the alliance of Baker and Michael Deaver, deputy chief of staff in charge of public relations, who shared an appreciation of how important it was to fill media space with positive images of Reagan. To the dismay of conservatives, the stage was set for the Reagan presidency to be driven as much by public relations concerns as by conservative ideas. The staff also demonstrated the political skills to mobilize public opinion and congressional majorities to enact Reagan's programs. Finally, they exhibited a resilient capability that is vital for the success of a modern president. Thus, Reagan's staff helped him take advantage of the failed assassination attempt, recover quickly from the Social Security defeat, and construct substitute budget and tax bills when the original proposals were floundering.

As for Reagan himself, in his first few months in office, he displayed a commitment to the top priority on his presidential agenda—cutting taxes—courage after being shot, and an outstanding ability to communicate with the public. (The record also shows that although Reagan was skillful in marketing his few simple ideas, he was woefully uninformed about the details of his programs and how to implement them.) Finally, for most of 1981, he was a lucky leader.[138] The focus on the economic program was not distracted by any foreign or domestic crisis.

The accolades of August were replaced by a chorus of complaints in September. Richard Fenno's metaphor accurately described the shift: "The congressional recess of August 1981 marked the turning point in the Reagan domestic presidency. Before August, all was triumph; after August, all was struggle—from blitzkrieg to trench warfare."[139] Once it became clear that supply-side tax cuts were not going to magically resolve the economic and budgetary dilemmas the country was facing, bitter legislative struggles—sometimes characterized by gridlock—were inevitable for the rest of the decade.

The transformation of the political situation was caused by the first indications that the Reagan economic program was based on blatantly false estimates. By autumn 1981, the administration's economic forecasts were shown to be unreliable: inflation was declining faster than predicted, and unemployment was rising more quickly than anticipated. These two trends raised estimates of the budget deficit for FY 1982 from $42.5 billion to over $100 billion. In September, members of the administration began leaking to the press that the budget might not be balanced by 1984 but that lower deficits would be sufficient to drive down interest rates. Financial markets did not agree—interest rates remained high, and the stock market declined. On September 24, Reagan delivered his fifth prime-time television address, asking a bitter and weary Congress to slice an additional $13 billion in spending and add $3 billion in increased taxes for FY 1982. The reductions were based on 12 percent cuts in non-defense appropriations and additional restrictions on welfare entitlements. In late October, the national debt surpassed the symbolically significant figure of $1 trillion, which meant that the federal government would have to pay over $100 billion in interest charges in 1982. By the end of October, Treasury Secretary Regan admitted that the budget could not be balanced by 1984. On November 6, Reagan conceded the same point but denied that he was breaking a campaign promise to balance the budget, because "I've never said anything but that it was a goal."[140] This disingenuous remark may have assuaged Reagan's conscience, but it was widely ridiculed. When Congress passed a budget resolution that was higher than the president's request, Reagan issued his first veto on November 23. An outraged Speaker O'Neill accused the president of "political theatrics" and charged that Reagan "knows less about the budget than any other President in my lifetime."[141] In December, Congress finally accepted $4 billion of the $13 billion in reductions the administration had requested in September. Lance LeLoup describes how Congress finally resolved its budget dilemma, a scene worthy of the theater of the absurd: "The year ended with the House and Senate giving up on writing a realistic second resolution. Abandoning any pretense of completing the process, both houses simply ratified the figures in the first resolution, even though everyone knew they were wildly inaccurate."[142] Thus, a majority of Congress could only agree to accept illusionary numbers because the more accurate figures indicated frightening budget deficits that most members refused to vote for.

For those who believe in the rationality of policy making, an analysis of Reagan's first year is not encouraging. The evidence appears to support those who argue that the passage of legislation often resembles the unsavory process of making sausage. By the fall of 1981, it was obvious that the enactment of Reagan's economic program was at least partly based on an irrational policy process and on deception. How else can one explain why moderate Republicans and Boll Weevil Democrats, who were originally concerned that the tax cut was too big, eventually voted for it when ornaments were added that made the loss of revenue considerably larger? Moreover, winning the battles over the budget and the tax bills meant losing the war of balancing the budget, because the administration was forced into bidding wars to buy votes, resulting in shrinking budget reductions and expanding tax cuts, thus scripting at least a decade's worth of large deficits. Many of the flawed results of the policy decisions of 1981 were induced by the haste of the process, by misunderstandings of the defense budget by Stockman, and by personal jealousies between Regan and Stockman, Gramm and Hance, and Jones and Rostenkowski. But the biggest problem was Reagan's overly optimistic view of the effects of supply-side tax cuts and his lack of knowledge regarding basic budget trends.

Supply-side predictions that a tax cut would bring about a real economic growth rate of 5 percent in 1982 were denied by a recession that produced a decline in the growth rate of 1.5 percent for that year. Contributing to the gloom was the growing suspicion that deliberate deception had played a role in helping the Reagan program pass Congress. Particularly damaging was William Grieder's essay in the *Atlantic* in November 1981, which was based on eighteen tape-recorded interviews with David Stockman. The budget director was quoted as saying that no one understood the budget numbers, thus conceding the deviousness of the Rosy Scenario and the magic asterisk; he was also quoted as suggesting that the supply-side tax cuts were a "Trojan horse" to lower the top rates from 70 to 50 percent and a guileful means of selling the "trickle-down" theory.[143] Stockman survived this incident, but there was no doubt that the most committed and knowledgeable member of the administration concerned with balancing the budget was severely weakened and no longer capable of exerting major influence during his remaining five years in office.

The rapid change in the economy in the latter half of 1981 also wounded Reagan. Barrett points out that "during the first half of the year, Reagan was able to exploit his personal assets superbly—his skill as a public advocate, the quality of appearing firm but reasonable at the same time, his ability to convey confidence, his seemingly inexhaustible supply of luck. . . . During the next phase some of his faults came to the fore. His disdain of detail cost him, and so did his reluctance to impose discipline on his subordinates. What earlier appeared to be laudable consistency based on principle late came across, on occasion, as stubbornness resting on misconceptions."[144] Even after having been told by the CEA chairman of the likelihood of a recession and by his budget advisers that deficits were likely to increase, he was still prone to giving "chirpy statements" like the one he issued to the press on September 5: "I'm not sure that we might not have been . . . too conservative in our estimates on the tax program, because, remember, our proposals were based on the belief that the cut in tax rates would not mean a comparable cut in tax revenues, that the stimulant to the economy would be such that the Government might find itself getting additional revenues, as it did last year in the cut of the capital gains tax."[145] David Broder summarized the mixed evaluation of Reagan after one year in office by writing, "if Reagan was the first president since Johnson to accomplish his most important first-year goals, he is also the first since Warren Harding to end his first year with substantial and growing doubts that he is the master of his own mind and job. Indeed, as the year drew on, and the phrases honed in months of campaigning became less and less useful in defining and deciding the policy choices facing government, the sense of uncertainty about the president's grasp of policy grew apace."[146] The volatile political environment was demonstrated by journalists' comparing Reagan to FDR in August 1981 and to Harding in January 1982.

Hence, even though Reagan had successfully met the leadership challenge of exploiting the window of opportunity provided by the honeymoon period, the challenges of the presidency would test the resilience of Reagan and his staff again and again. Fortunately for the president, his administration had the capabilities to meet these tests, especially in the field of tax policy, which is the subject of the next chapter.

6

THE CONTRIBUTIONS
OF TAX POLICY TO REAGAN'S
POLITICAL SUCCESS

Given what we have learned about Ronald Reagan's decision-making style, one of the most perplexing problems for students of the presidency is explaining Reagan's political success. President Reagan and his supporters explain his success in terms of his ideological consistency. That is, after the uncertainties, ineptness, and flip-flops of the Jimmy Carter presidency, the American people were receptive to the leadership of a "conviction politician" who consistently adhered to a conservative philosophy. In one of Reagan's farewell addresses, the president stated, "History records a few significant turning points in the epic struggle [between those who shoulder the promise and burden of freedom and those who would . . . take us a mile or two more down . . . the road to serfdom], [but] surely . . . it will tell that one of those turning points came when, after a generation of gestation, a revolution of ideas became a revolution of governance on January 20, 1981."[1] Liberal opponents of Reagan account for his political success in terms of his luck, his communication skills, and the public relations capabilities of his staff—three aspects of his presidency that combined to fool the American public through the art of Hollywood illusion and the politics of unreality.[2] Neither of these explanations adequately elucidates Reagan's political achievements in overcoming the constraints of the imperiled presidency.

In this chapter, I suggest how Reagan's political leadership in one policy area—taxes—contributed to the success of his administration. Reagan was able to take the conservative idea of supply-side tax cuts, use the pragmatic skills of his staff to formulate and pass two major tax laws, and employ the techniques of his public relations staff to sell his idea about the universal benefits of his tax proposals. By concentrating on reducing tax rates, Reagan broadened his appeal as a conservative populist and controlled the domestic policy agenda for most of the decade.

152

REAGAN'S TAX PHILOSOPHY

Reagan's beliefs about taxes had a major impact on his administration's tax policy. As was typical of Reagan in policy matters, he did not understand much about the intricacies of the tax code, but his mind was dominated by the simple idea that tax rates were too high. What was atypical of Reagan in this policy area was that he was personally committed to reducing tax rates.[3]

The source of this commitment for Reagan was not philosophical but personal. Reagan was receptive to the "supply-side" reasoning that lower tax rates would encourage economic growth, because it was compatible with his Hollywood experience. The president frequently repeated the anecdote that after World War II he made only four movies a year because his income from those four alone put him in the top tax bracket of 91 percent. The highly progressive tax rates created a disincentive to make more movies.[4]

Reagan's belief in and commitment to tax reductions were revealed in his speeches. For him, government was essentially a wasteful tax spender that—with the exception of national defense—did little good. Reagan believed that high taxes threatened national security. In 1958, he warned that the graduated income tax, originally conceived by the communists, had the potential to tax the middle class out of existence and thus bring about socialism.[5] In his 1964 speech for Senator Barry Goldwater, he erroneously claimed, "No nation has ever survived a tax burden that reached a third of its national income."[6] Both as governor of California and as president, Reagan liked to picture himself as a hero protecting taxpayers from the voracious appetites of the tax-spending bureaucrats. During the 1980 presidential campaign, Reagan blamed the tax system for the major economic problems of the period. In his most important economic campaign speech, given on September 9, 1980, Governor Reagan stressed that "more than any simple thing, high rates in taxation destroy incentive to earn, to save, to invest. And they cripple productivity, lead to deficit financing and inflation, and create unemployment."[7]

To restore the economic health of the nation, candidate Reagan endorsed the Kemp-Roth tax cut and pledged that his top priority once elected would be to enact it. He also promised to support faster, less complex depreciation schedules for business in order to spur investment. In contrast to the current tax system, Reagan proclaimed that his tax program would encourage and reward economic success, not punish it. Once elected, Reagan emphasized that the tax burden had surpassed the ability and tolerance of the American people to bear it. On February 18, 1981, Reagan told the nation, "The taxing power of government must be used to provide revenues for legitimate government purposes. It must not be used to regulate the economy or bring about social change."[8] He declared buoyantly that tax rates could be reduced without resulting in a comparable cut in tax revenues because the economy would be positively stimulated to produce more growth, more jobs, more investment, and thus more tax revenue. Reagan strongly hinted that passage of his 1981 tax bill would lay the foundation for further rate reductions in the near future.[9]

Reagan become the spokesman of an incentive-oriented tax movement popularly known as supply-side economics. Supply-siders believed that taxes mattered—that is, that taxes strongly influenced behavior. From their rational economic choice perspective, supply-siders believed that tax rates influenced individual behavior to save, to invest, to consume, to work extra hours, to move, to get married, to have children. Supply-side economics was distinguished from Keynesian economic philosophy because the latter viewed tax cuts primarily as a means to increase the income of consumers and thus stimulate the demand side of the economy. Supply-siders claimed that their tax cuts, which would lower the rates for everyone and flatten the rates to dilute the disincentive effects of progressivity, would stimulate both demand and—especially—supply. As Lawrence Lindsey explained, "The supply-siders . . . focused on the supply-side, or incentive effects of tax policy. For them, tax policy represented the key to the problem of the 1970's and the solution for the 1980's. High tax rates discouraged people from working, saving, and investing and thereby caused the economy to slow and unemployment to rise. Sharp tax cuts aimed at restoring incentives would solve the stagflation dilemma."[10] In brief, Reagan and the supply-siders promised multiple benefits from the successful application of their tax cut program.

A major inconsistency in Reagan's tax philosophy emerges here. While he stated that the taxing authority should be used solely to provide revenues for legitimate government purposes, he also claimed that his tax policies would promote multiple benefits for the American people. While condemning the previous Keynesian-inspired tax code for trying to achieve such social goals as fine-tuning the economy or redistributing income, Reagan vowed that his tax policy would lead to healthier social consequences. Hence, Reagan seemed oblivious to the fact that he was manipulating the tax code to induce social change at least as much as the Keynesians were.

Changes in the tax rate structure from 1960 to 1980 had given the supply-side philosophy a populist appeal that Reagan was able to exploit brilliantly. As Thomas Edsall points out, in 1960, the progressivity of the tax system was targeted at the top 5 percent of the population. Only 3 percent of married couples earned as much as $15,000 a year in 1961; over 80 percent of the population made less than $8,000. For the bulk of the population, there was little or no tax disadvantage in receiving a major salary increase or from inflation-induced bracket creep. But as Edsall explains, "Between 1960 and 1979, however, the median family income grew from $5,620 to $19,684, in part from inflation and in part from real increases in spendable income. What had been a statistically exceptional income in 1960 became in 1978 the median income. . . . As a consequence of this process, the sharply rising marginal rates that had been targeted at the very affluent in the early 1960's—while most of the population faced what amounted to a flat tax—became a system in which the vast majority of taxpayers faced sharply increasing marginal tax rates as their income grew."[11] Thus, by 1980, the average taxpayer was paying rates that had been designed (by Democrats!) to tax the rich. This situation was exacerbated by inflation-driven bracket creep; inflation soared from 7.7 percent in 1978 to 13.5 percent in 1980.

From a supply-side point of view, the confiscatory level of the steeply progressive tax rates that had affected only a few taxpayers in 1960 was, by 1980, distorting the behavior of the majority of taxpayers. Being pushed up into higher tax brackets caused middle-class families to emulate the behavior of the affluent in seeking tax shelters, thus causing the tax base to shrink. Political pressures from middle-class voters caused Congress to reduce income taxes seven times in twenty years, but the average effective tax rates continued to climb. In Lindsey's words, "The income tax had been pushed beyond its limits both politically and economically. This time the excesses applied not just to a few elite taxpayers but to the vast majority."[12]

Reagan's populist response to this malaise was to design supply-side tax cuts that would promote economic growth and economic opportunity for the long term. Periodic fine-tuning of the tax code was derisively dismissed. It was asserted that sharply progressive tax rates neither gained appreciably more revenue from the rich nor redistributed income to the poor. Indeed, supply-siders claimed that "high tax rates help ossify the class structure rather than break it down. . . . The real losers from soak-the-rich taxation aren't the presently rich, but the would-be rich. High income tax rates bar access to the upper class."[13] No one was better than Ronald Reagan at bending the supply-side tax philosophy into a populist message of economic opportunity for all.

PRESIDENT REAGAN'S TAX POLICY

President Reagan's two major domestic policy achievements were the Economic Recovery Tax Act of 1981 (ERTA) and the Tax Reform Act of 1986 (TRA). ERTA was the top policy priority during the first year of Reagan's presidency; its passage, which fulfilled one of Reagan's major campaign promises, helped to establish his credentials as a leader who knew how to successfully wield presidential power. In 1981, Reagan "hit the ground running" by rolling over Congress with the passage of ERTA and $35 billion worth of budget cuts. The passage of the TRA in 1986 was the administration's major domestic success, and its passage prevented Reagan from being viewed as a lame duck in his second administration. By persuading Congress to pass ERTA and TRA, Reagan validated his credentials as a conviction politician.

From the administration's view, "Unlike many of the tax cuts of the postwar era, ERTA was designed as a fundamental restructuring of the tax system rather than as a temporary stimulus to aggregate demand."[14] In a modified form of the original Kemp-Roth proposal, individual income tax rates were reduced for all taxpayers in three stages: 5 percent on October 1, 1981, 10 percent on July 1, 1982, and 10 percent on July 1, 1983. The top rate, which was 70 percent in 1981, was reduced to 50 percent on January 1, 1982. The peak rate on capital gains was sliced to 20 percent, having earlier been reduced from 49 to 28 percent by the Steiger Amendment in 1978. According to economist Benjamin Friedman, ERTA "reduced personal income tax payments by $387 billion from 1982 through 1986 and $110 billion in 1986 alone, compared to what the government would otherwise have received."[15] Thus, the average family's marginal tax rate declined from 24 to 18 percent. To avoid the pernicious effects of inflation-induced bracket creep, ERTA also called for annual indexing of the personal exemption and income bracket to begin in 1985.

The 1981 tax cut also provided an estimated $350 billion of tax relief for business. One of the major goals of ERTA was to shift the burden of taxation away from capital income and thereby create greater incentives for personal savings and capital investments. A series of provisions provided more incentives through an accelerated cost recovery system (ACRS), an increase in the investment tax credit, and special incentives for small businesses to buy new equipment. The administration claimed that these changes would significantly augment business investment by increasing the after-tax return on new business projects. According to the president's 1982 *Economic Report,* "The ACRS will encourage business investments by shortening the period over which assets can be fully depreciated and by allowing firms to claim more of the depreciation early in the tax life of the asset. . . . The combined result of the ACRS and the investment tax credit will be a decline in effective tax rates on new investment over the period 1982 to 1987."[16]

ERTA was the largest tax cut in American history; far behind in second place was President Gerald Ford's $22.8 billion tax cut in 1975. A leading scholar of tax policy, John Witte, writes, "What is historically unique about the 1981 bill is the size of the tax reduction, its multiyear commitment in terms of rate reduction and indexation, and the overwhelming deference to business and upper-income 'savings groups.' Although these groups have benefitted from most postwar tax reductions, in earlier bills there was a degree of moderation that was simply lost in the summer of 1981."[17] The allure of Reagan's optimistic economic projections, the ineptness of the Democratic Party opposition, and the fiscally irresponsible bidding war between Republicans and Democrats in Congress combined to bring about a mammoth tax cut that was not tempered by concerns about its effects on the worsening budget deficit.

ERTA was also an overreaction to the social and policy concerns about equality that had prevailed in the 1960s. From the conservative point of view, the policies of the 1960s had proved to be totally counterproductive; they had produced nothing but economic decline and social despair. The progressive tax system that fueled the welfare state had to be radically changed. And it *was* changed by ERTA, which targeted over 35 percent of the personal tax cuts to only 5.6 percent of the population because of the assumption that these wealthy people were the most likely to save and invest. Reagan and the supply-siders had resurrected and modernized the nineteenth-century laissez-faire idea that any efforts to interfere with the free accumulation of wealth were likely to be counterproductive. As the supply-sider Norman Ture, undersecretary of the treasury, is quoted as saying in an August 1981 interview, " 'The touchstone for good tax policy in the contemporary era is its neutrality,' said Mr. Ture, who explained that, by 'neutral,' he meant preserving the distribution of income and wealth that would have taken place if there had been no tax system at all. 'This philosophy is what Mr. Reagan meant when he opposed using the tax system to bring about "social change," ' Mr. Ture said."[18]

The passage of ERTA did not end the debate over tax policy. Fears about soaring budget deficits and concerns about saving Social Security caused Congress to pass tax increases in 1982, 1983, and 1984, all of which were signed into law by Reagan. The most significant bill was the Tax Equity and Fiscal Responsibility Act of 1982 (TEFRA), which was designed to raise $98.3 billion over three years and thus effectively regain one-fourth of the tax benefits granted in 1981. As discussed in chapter 9, signing TEFRA was the price Reagan had to pay in order to persuade the Federal Reserve Board to lower interest rates and help the economy recover from the 1981–1982 recession.

Nevertheless, the net effect of the ERTA-TEFRA tax law was a significant cut in the effective tax rates on most investments. Indeed, the proportion of federal revenue supplied by corporate income taxes had been dropping for decades. Whereas corporate income taxes had provided about 25 percent of federal revenues in the 1950s, by 1983, corporations were contributing only 6.3 percent of federal revenues. In 1984, a report by Robert McIntyre for the Citizens for Tax Justice showed that 130 American corporations had legally "beat" the tax laws, paying no taxes from 1981 through 1985, even though they had earned $72.9 billion in pretax profits. In McIntyre's words, "The decline of the corporate tax is a direct result of the tremendous expansion in corporate loopholes—to an expected $87 billion in the current [1985] fiscal year, from $7 billion in 1970. President Reagan's 1981 tax act so expanded tax-avoidance opportunities that the corporate tax code is now more loop-hole than tax."[19]

Early in 1984, James Baker, mistakenly believing that Walter Mondale might agree to champion the Bradley-Gephardt tax bill, which would simplify the tax code and lower tax rates, suggested to Reagan that he direct the Treasury to develop comprehensive tax reform legislation. The president accepted Baker's advice, and in his 1984 State of the Union Address he ordered Treasury Secretary Donald Regan to conduct a study of tax reform and report back to him in December 1984. This maneuver essentially neutralized tax reform as an issue during the 1984 campaign. During the campaign, the focus was on the fact that Mondale wanted to raise taxes and Reagan did not.

After the 1984 election, the Treasury presented its recommended tax reform bill (called Treasury I) to Reagan. Early in 1985, James Baker and Donald Regan switched jobs. In reviewing Treasury I, Treasury Secretary Baker and his deputy, Richard Darman, decided that the proposal would have to be revised to make it more politically feasible before it could be introduced to Congress. This was done, and President Reagan presented his tax bill (known as Treasury II) to Congress in late May 1985. Unlike the situation in 1981, Reagan could not steamroll his opponents in 1985, but he was able to impose a major decision rule: any bill would have to be revenue neutral. That is, any new tax bill would have to raise the same amount of revenue as the existing tax law. Tax reform could not be a disguised tax increase. Still, each house of Congress significantly modified the bill. The Tax Reform Act was finally passed by Congress and signed by President Reagan on October 22, 1986.

The chief selling point of the 1986 law was that it reduced the fourteen rate brackets to two rates of 15 and 28 percent, with a complicated surtax that placed some upper-middle-class families (with joint income between $71,900 and $149,250) in a 33 percent bracket. An estimated 80 percent of American families fell in the 15 percent bracket. Thus, as Michael Boskin pointed out, "The top marginal tax rate in the personal income tax will have gone from 70 percent in 1980 to 28 percent by 1988, an astonishing reduction, making the *top* marginal tax rate in the United States lower than the *bottom* marginal tax rate in many countries."[20] By almost doubling the exemptions for self, spouse, and dependents, TRA removed approximately 6 million poor people from the tax rolls. This provision was supported by Democrats in terms of fairness and by Republicans for being pro-family. TRA eliminated the preferential treatment of capital gains income by raising the tax rate from 20 percent to the top individual rate of 28 percent. For many individuals, being able to take the standard deduction, which had been significantly raised, greatly simplified the filing of their tax returns. It was estimated that about 60 percent of all Americans paid slightly lower taxes (a few hundred dollars per year) because of this reform law, and another 25 percent paid what they had been paying before. The remaining 15 percent faced a relatively small tax increase.[21]

The most surprising feature of the TRA was that, between 1986 and 1991, it shifted an estimated $120 billion of the tax burden from individuals to corporations. As explained by Boskin, "This occurs despite the fact that the basic corporate tax rate is being reduced from 46 percent to 34 percent because of a very substantial increase in the corporate tax base, achieved through the elimination of the investment tax credit (common to all the reform proposals), much slower depreciation, and a stiff alternative minimum tax for corporations (to insure that no corporation that reports current profits to its shareholders will avoid paying taxes)."[22] The playing field for corporations may have been leveled by this tax reform, but it was now also more expensive to play.

The chief player in promoting the unlikely passage of the TRA was Ronald Reagan. He placed tax reform on the policy agenda by making it the symbol of his "Second American Revolution" in his 1985 State of the Union Address. He saved the bill in November 1985 when House Republicans were repelled by the modifications imposed by Dan Rostenkowski's Ways and Means Committee. He helped create an atmosphere in which no one wanted to appear responsible for killing the reform proposal. Witte stresses that "Reagan's support of tax reform amplified the unique political jockeying that the issue stimulated in both parties. In a bizarre political reversal of 1981, in deficit-plagued 1985 and 1986, tax reform acquired the same political momentum as wholesale tax reduction and loophole expansion had in 1981."[23] In a major study of the passage of the TRA, two *Wall Street Journal* reporters concluded that "Reagan wanted to go down in history as the president who cut that top tax rate at least in half, from 70 percent to 35 percent or lower. If abandoning business tax breaks and raising corporate taxes was the price he had to pay to achieve that goal, so be it."[24]

Despite Reagan's enthusiastic speechmaking in support of the TRA, it is likely that he was not knowledgeable about the major provisions in his own proposal. For example, in an interview following his 1985 State of the Union

Address, the president revealed that he did not understand that his Treasury II proposal included a 36 percent increase in corporate taxes.[25] In Albert Hunt's words, "The president's ignorance of the specifics of his own proposal was startling; throughout, he misrepresented or misunderstood the measure's tax increase on business, but President Reagan's attachment to lower rates was real and his commitment to the concept of this tax reform was even more powerful than his ignorance of the details. He never quite convinced the public but his political persona and communicative skills commanded such respect that they scared off a lot of potential opponents."[26]

By focusing on slicing the top rates on individual income taxes, Reagan failed to see how philosophically inconsistent ERTA and the TRA were.[27] Whereas ERTA had created a number of tax expenditures to encourage saving and investment, the TRA emphasized leveling the playing field by eliminating or reducing seventy-two tax expenditures. Tax breaks that had been designed to encourage specific economic activities were now removed because it was felt that they distorted the choices taxpayers were making. Whereas ERTA had compressed the tax lifetime for residential rental property from 32 to 15 years, the TRA lengthened the lifetime to 27.5 years.[28] Benjamin Friedman pointed out that, "On average for all types of equipment, a plausible estimate is that the 1986 legislation raised the effective tax rate applicable to income from new business investment by some twenty percentage points. For example, under the old law the effective tax rate on investment in industrial equipment was about 10 percent after taking account of all relevant credits and allowances. Under the new law it is 32 percent. . . . For research equipment the rate rose from 23 percent to 43 percent; for scientific instruments from 11 percent to 36 percent. It is hard to imagine a 'tax reform' more likely to blunt our efforts to compete in technologically oriented industries."[29] No wonder the TRA was publicly opposed by Murray Weidenbaum and Norman Ture, two prominent economic advisers to Reagan during the 1981 tax reduction battles who were no longer members of the administration.[30]

THE PUBLIC RELATIONS STRATEGY

Although Reagan liked to emphasize that his tax policies were determined by his conservative, market-oriented philosophy, those policies were also at least equally driven by public relations considerations. In the 1980 campaign, Reagan and his political advisers understood that it was easier to champion the supply-side philosophy—which allowed the candidate to promise tax cuts and a balanced budget—than it was to campaign under the austere constraints of traditional conservatism and monetarism. Similarly, in the 1984 campaign, Reagan did not stress tax reform because Richard Wirthlin's poll indicated that the issue was a loser. Many voters cynically viewed tax reform as code words for a tax increase. In a major study of the TRA, the authors point out that certain features of the legislation were "designed to suit the purpose of propagandists more than policy analysts. Public relations values, not economic ones, led Ronald Reagan to develop a 15-25-35 rate structure for Treasury II, rather than the more awkward sounding 16-28-37 [Treasury Secretary Regan said that this sounded like a quarterback's signals] devised by staff. Yet this slight change in enumeration had enormous fiscal consequences, forcing a sharp increase in business taxes and creating new tax cuts for many more individuals."[31] In this case, public relations concerns clearly outweighed supply-side beliefs.

There were also powerful political motivations propelling Reagan to support tax reform in 1985. The president had won a landslide victory in 1984, but under the direction of the cautious James Baker, he had run an issueless campaign. After the election, Reagan became increasingly concerned—as all presidents do in their second terms—about avoiding the impotency of lame-duck status and establishing his historical legacy. Before introducing his tax reform proposal to Congress in May 1985, Reagan had a dismal spring, suffering political defeats over the Pentagon budget, aid to the Nicaraguan Contras, and his trip to Bitburg, Germany. The success of Reagan's second administration would largely depend on his ability to pass tax reform legislation.

The partisan side of Reagan was also attracted to tax reform. Some of Reagan's political advisers, not including Lee Atwater, believed that tax reform had the potential to be a realigning issue. That is, tax reform could broaden the appeal of the Republican Party so that it could dominate both the presidency and Congress in much the same way that the Social Security issue gave the Democrats such domination during the 1930s. Republican partisans believed that tax reform could serve as a "symbol of the GOP's metamorphosis from country-club conservatism to a new coalition reaching out to a broader spectrum of Americans: workers, Catholics, new immigrants and entrepreneurs as well as old-style Republicans."[32] Shortly after Reagan introduced his bill to Congress, Hedrick Smith reported that the president "is daring to recast the image of the Republican Party with a hybrid tax proposal that is both populist and venture capitalist. For it offers lower tax rates to both the rich and poor, risks the disfavor of the established, capital-intensive industries in what was once the Republican heartland of the Middle West and casts the Republican lot more with the high-technology industries of the South and West."[33]

But there were two fatal flaws in the strategy of using tax reform as a realigning issue: first, it was too complex an issue for most voters to understand; second, Reagan needed Democratic support, especially in the Democratically controlled House Ways and Means Committee, to pass the legislation. Moreover, a significant number of Republican congressmen opposed the bill because it raised taxes on corporations. Obtaining the necessary Democratic votes required compromises that allowed the Democrats to impose some of their own thinking on the bill. As the TRA picked up bipartisan backing, its potential as a realigning issue evaporated.

Nevertheless, enactment of the TRA was a major victory for Reagan, and it was largely manufactured by his public relations skills. Reagan was successful in conveying the feeling to the public that he hated taxes as much as they did. He communicated an idea that seemed eminently reasonable to many voters: that they could spend their money more wisely than could bureaucrats in Washington. Reagan had the chameleon-like capability of identifying with and appealing to those who felt that taxes were too complex, those who felt that taxes were unfair, those who felt that the rich were not paying their fair share, and those who felt that taxes impeded their chances to move up. Reagan's major public relations achievement was in planting the idea that the progressive income tax was elitist; that flatter rates were egalitarian because they provided more opportunities for more people to do better. Echoing this theme, Reagan claimed, "We are not lowering the top tax rate to 35 percent [in the Treasury II proposal] so the rich will do better. We are lowering the top rate to 35 percent so that every working American will have a better chance to get rich."[34] In brief, Reagan was arguing that a high marginal tax rate was not a tax on the wealthy but rather a tax on those struggling to better themselves economically.

The administration's campaign to pass the TRA was composed of a legislative strategy, created by James Baker and Richard Darman, and a communications strategy, drafted by Patrick Buchanan. The overarching theme of the campaign was to frame President Reagan as championing the public interest against a Washington establishment that was aligned with narrow and selfish interests. In this perspective, Reagan was leading a "second American Revolution" to correct a long train of abuses that riddled the tax code with preferential treatment for special interests at the expense of the average, hardworking American citizen. The president's tax reform was portrayed as "profairness, profamily, and progrowth"; it epitomized Reagan's conservative populism. The White House trumpeted a politically appealing message: "Tax reform means a tax cut for average Americans."[35]

The administration's populist strategy was exemplified in a speech that Richard Darman delivered on tax day, April 15, 1985:

> The overwhelming majority of taxpayers eat lunch without being able to deduct their meals as business expenses. They buy baseball or hockey tickets without being able to enjoy the luxury of business-related sky-boxes. They talk of fishing boats, but don't take the tax deductions for ocean cruise seminars. They strain to pay interest on their home mort-gages and may take the tax deduction for their payments, but they can't quite figure out how others can invest in real estate shelters and get more back in tax benefits than is put at risk. They read that of those with gross income of over $250,000 before "losses," more than a fifth pay less than 10 percent or less in taxes.[36]

The president introduced his tax reform proposal in a nationally televised speech on May 28, 1985. The main theme of this address was that ordinary people pay too much in taxes because the privileged few do not pay their fair share. He criticized the existing tax code as an unwise and unwanted system that runs "roughshod over Main Street America," and he condemned it for being unfair, too complex, antigrowth, and antifamily. The system was anti-family, he said, because it took advantage of families being pushed by infla-tion into higher tax brackets and thus paying higher rates. Families also suffered because the personal exemption had failed to keep pace with infla-tion. In addition, families were forced to make up the revenue losses gained by the special interests through their loopholes. In the president's words, the tax system had become like Washington, D.C., itself: "complicated, unfair, cluttered with gobbledegook and loopholes designed for those with the power and influence to hire high-priced legal and tax advisors." Hence, Reagan char-acterized the tax code with the ultimate right-wing term of opprobrium: it was "un-American."[37]

Reagan continued his political offensive in support of tax reform in a series of speeches during the late spring and early fall of 1985. The offensive stressed that his proposal meant a tax cut for almost everyone, which would ensure families and firms the necessary incentives and rewards for hard work and risk taking. As was typical of Reagan's campaign style, he tried to frame himself as a champion of the people and his political opponents as tools for special inter-ests. From Reagan's perspective, tax reform was a "drama with heroes and vil-lains and a damsel in distress. The heroes are citizens . . . asking for tax justice. The villains are the special interests, the 'I got mine' gang. And the damsel in distress? A lass named Endless Economic Growth."[38] In this simplistic view, Reagan was the people's lobbyist, attempting to rally the public against selfish interests. These narrow interests were never specifically named, nor could they be, because many of them would turn out to be Republican constituencies taking advantage of Reagan's 1981 tax bill.

Reagan's public relations campaign did not mobilize public opinion in massive support of his tax reform proposal, but it did succeed in framing the issue in such a favorable manner that few congressmen wanted to assume the responsibility for killing it. The campaign launched a process that developed its own momentum. The Democrats were lured into cooperative participation; that is, the Democrats accepted that tax reform would have to be revenue neutral and that tax rates on both individuals and corporations would have to be lowered. Although the Democrats succeeded in making their mark on the TRA, the final result was certainly closer to the supply-side goal of a flat tax rate than to the liberal objective of a progressive income tax that possessed some redistributive capabilities.

CONCLUSION

This chapter has examined the role that tax policy played in the political success of President Reagan. The passage of ERTA in 1981 established Reagan's professional reputation as someone who could play and win in the big leagues. Reagan was more than an electoral phenomenon; his political leadership could formulate and achieve strategic priorities. The enactment of the TRA in 1986 constituted Reagan's major domestic policy success in the second term and helped him avoid the stigma of being considered a lame duck. Both these tax laws can be viewed as steps toward Reagan's goal of creating a less intrusive federal government. But unlike the other two means of achieving this goal— budget cuts in domestic spending and the deregulation of industry—the tax proposals were able to attain wider support and more success.

Neither Reagan nor his two major tax bills were philosophically consistent. A major contradiction in Reagan's tax philosophy was that, while he stressed that the taxing authority of the government must be used solely to provide revenues for legitimate government purposes, he also claimed that his tax proposal would provide multiple benefits for the American people. The irony of the 1986 tax reform was that it was designed to close many of the loopholes in ERTA, although it would be difficult to prove that Reagan understood that his 1981 bill had created many of those preferences or that his 1986 bill would eliminate many of them. John Witte wryly concludes, "Ronald Reagan thus has the unique historical position of supporting both the largest tax reform and the largest antitax reform legislation in the history of the United States."[39]

It should also be stressed that Reagan signed bills increasing taxes in 1982, 1983, and 1984. Nothing demonstrates better the skills of Reagan's public relations advisers and the ability of his administrative style to dissipate responsibility than the fact that despite his support of several bills raising taxes, he maintained his reputation as a tax cutter and a conviction politician.

Reagan achieved his success by focusing on reducing tax rates, which astutely served his political purposes throughout the decade. By championing tax cuts, Reagan was able to appeal to broad sectors of the American public as a conservative populist, substantiate his reputation as a conviction politician who fulfills his campaign promises, unite the Republican Party, attract a sufficient number of Democratic congressmen to pass two major pieces of legislation, and dominate the domestic policy agenda for most of the 1980s. But the price of this political success was that the president ignored the revenue needs of the government and discarded the limited redistributive capabilities of the progressive income tax. Reagan also created a legacy that has led conservative Republicans in the 1990s to be as prone to fling tax breaks at problems as liberal Democrats were to throw money at maladies in the 1960s.[40]

In brief, tax policy probably contributed more to the political success of the Reagan presidency than any other substantive policy. Thus we have a paradox: the president with the simplest ideas achieved some of his major political victories in one of the most complex policy fields. However, as we shall see in chapter 7, Reagan was less successful and more hindered by his ideology in dealing with the complexity of the savings and loan crisis.

7

UNLEASHING A DISASTER: THE REAGAN ADMINISTRATION'S ROLE IN THE SAVINGS AND LOAN DEBACLE

A favorite metaphor of President Reagan's was that the U.S. economy was shackled by the combination of high tax rates and stifling bureaucratic regulations. At his 1981 inaugural, Reagan explained, "If we look to the answer as to why for so many years we achieved so much, prospered as no other people on earth, it was because here in this land we unleashed the energy and individual genius of man to a greater extent than has ever been done before."[1] Reagan's remedy for the problems of the 1980s was to cut tax rates and eliminate many regulations and regulators, thus unleashing the great potential of the economy to expand. The president stressed the inefficiencies of government but seemed oblivious to the possible problems of deregulated industries. In Reagan's world, regulators were imbued with bureaucratic vices, and entrepreneurs were motivated by capitalistic virtues.

Usually, Reagan was able to enjoy the benefits and avoid most of the costs of being a conservative, conviction leader. But Reagan's ideology and deregulatory policies contributed to the savings and loan (S&L) crisis of the 1980s, which would eventually cost several hundred billion dollars to resolve. However, because Democratic congressmen shared responsibility for the S&L debacle, Reagan was able to avoid blame for the required bailout of insolvent institutions. The burden of cleaning up the mess fell to the Bush presidency.

A disaster as big as the S&L collapse in a political system characterized by checks and balances could not be blamed on any one person or institution. One suspects multiple villains, and there are. While recognizing the shared responsibilities of several participants in this financial scandal—the largest in American history—my focus is on the role played by the Reagan presidency.

This case study illustrates one of the few occasions on which the Reagan administration was obstructed by its conservative ideology, thus allowing a manageable problem of the mid-1980s to become, by the end of the decade, a multibillion-dollar disaster. The evidence indicates that the administration's ideology of deregulation contributed to the origins of the problem and that its partisan concerns were partly responsible for the costly neglect and deception that characterized the government's response, or lack thereof, to the growing number of S&L insolvencies that occurred during Reagan's years in office. Reagan's role in this story does not qualify as a profile in either courage or vision.

EVOLUTION OF THE S&Ls

The first American savings and loan institutions were created in 1831. They were originally called "thrifts" because they were designed to encourage savings among working people to finance the purchase of single-family homes. In 1932, President Herbert Hoover signed the Federal Home Loan Bank Act, which subjected the S&L industry to federal regulations. Two years later, Franklin Roosevelt signed a bill that created the Federal Savings and Loan Insurance Corporation (FSLIC), which pledged the full faith and credit of the U.S. government to guarantee deposits of up to $5,000 in an S&L. The system was monitored by the Federal Home Loan Bank Board (FHLBB), which consisted of a chairman selected by the president, usually from his own party, and two board members, one Democrat and one Republican. The FHLBB oversaw twelve regional banks that made low-interest loans to S&Ls. The reward for accepting federal supervision was the protection offered by federal deposit insurance. Deposit insurance for banks and S&Ls, according to F. Stevens Redburn, "corrects a potential market failure which, prior to its enactment, led to frequent financial panics caused by a tendency of depositors made nervous by one bank failure and unable to discriminate between solvent and insolvent banks to 'run' from healthy institutions, thus triggering a spreading pattern of failure and monetary contraction."[2] Fear of such meltdowns still influences regulatory behavior.

The two decades following World War II constituted a "golden age" for the S&L industry. From 1945 to 1964, interest rates were generally low, employment was high, and few families defaulted on their mortgage payments. An increasing proportion of American families owned their own homes, a trend that was enthusiastically endorsed by both Democrats and Republicans. It was believed that a healthy housing industry was dependent on thriving thrifts. Public policies to aid thrifts—such as the mortgage interest deduction and Regulation Q, which allowed S&Ls to offer a quarter of a point higher interest rates on savings accounts than commercial banks—were noncontroversial. Subsidizing thrifts was considered good policy and good politics because it helped business, labor, real estate agents, and families aspiring to buy their own homes. According to Michael Brintnall, "Thrifts were designed on the popular principle of local banks raising local funds to help local homeowners, and given a protected market. In their time, the thrifts created financing for housing where none existed before. Their capacity to do this was sustained by regulatory controls, tax policies, interest rate controls, and deposit insurance."[3] This sleepy, easy to regulate industry was sometimes summarized in the numbers 3-6-3. It was said that S&L executives offered 3 percent interest to attract deposits, lent the deposits out at 6 percent, and began playing golf at 3 P.M.

The thrifts had their own trade association, the United States League of Savings Institutions, which exerted considerable influence on Congress and on the FHLBB. S&Ls constituted a powerful pressure group because their executives lived in every congressional district, and they usually played major roles in making campaign contributions. The thrift industry was relatively united in its policy preferences and was therefore often able to "speak with one voice" to politicians and regulators. Thomas Romer and Barry Weingast stress that "the relative homogeneity of the industry . . . worked to its direct advantage with the relevant congressional committees and hence with the industry's chief federal regulator. . . . The absence of conflict among constituents led to an FHLBB that in many ways has looked like the paradigmatic captured agency: responsive for the most part to thrift industry interests, promulgating regulations that would increase industry rents, staving off competition from unwelcome poachers from commercial banking. Congress supported these policies both with active legislation, and—more generally—simply by not opposing them."[4]

This tranquil period came to an end beginning in the late 1960s and continuing into the 1970s. The causes were inflation, the fluctuation of the dollar, the oil crisis, Paul Volcker's monetary experiment, and rising interest rates. Rising interest rates destabilized the placid environment of the S&Ls by exposing a fatal flaw in the industry: thrifts borrowed short from depositors and lent long to mortgage holders. When inflation drove interest rates to higher levels, thrifts' interest costs surpassed their interest income from home mortgages. Here we must understand that, to an S&L operator, a loan is an asset because if it is paid off, it provides income in the form of interest payments, whereas a deposit is a liability because the S&L is obligated to pay interest to the depositor. The risks of "short-funding" are summarized by Edward Kane: "On average, the liabilities of thrifts turn over much faster than their assets do. This exposes their incomes and capital to loss from interest increases and from interest volatility. On the one hand, unanticipated increases in interest rates narrow spreads between accounting yields attributable to the assets already on the books and the institution's overall cost of funds. On the other hand, although unanticipated decreases in interest rates widen these spreads, they also encourage borrowers to prepay and refinance their debt. The wider the swings that occur in interest rates, the greater the chance that at some point enterprise-contributed capital can become exhausted."[5] Thus, in the new era of volatile interest rates, S&Ls could no longer be assured that the interest earned on mortgage loans would be higher than the rates paid on savings accounts.

By the end of the 1970s, deposits were flowing out of S&Ls (in a process called disintermediation) into money-market accounts created by banks and brokerage houses offering higher interest rates than thrifts were allowed to pay. To aid the S&Ls, Congress passed and President Carter signed the Depository Institutions Deregulation and Monetary Control Act in March 1980. This law phased out interest rate ceilings on savings accounts, outlawed state usury ceilings on mortgage loans, granted authority to federally chartered thrifts to establish statewide branches, allowed thrifts to allocate up to 20 percent of their assets in commercial loans and corporate-debt instruments, authorized S&Ls to offer interest-bearing checking accounts, allowed S&Ls to begin lending to consumers for personal purposes, and increased FSLIC and Federal Deposit Insurance Corporation (FDIC) insurance for accounts from $40,000 to $100,000. The provision raising federal insurance on deposits was not part of either the House or the Senate bill; it was added by friends of the S&Ls in the conference committee. It was not designed to protect most depositors, since the average savings account in 1980 was only about $6,000. The goal was to attract huge sums of money to the thrifts through a device called the "brokered deposit." L. J. Davis explains how the brokered deposit system worked:

> Wall Street brokerage houses and investment banks took billions of dollars they attracted from big-money investors (pension funds, insurance companies, oil-rich Arab nations, and eventually mobsters and other money launderers) and parceled this money into neat $100,000 packets. Each morning, these brokers scoured the nation for the highest rate being offered that day by the thrifts in their jumbo ($100,000) certificates of deposit—deposits fully insured by the federal government. . . .

The brokers moved their money around constantly from bank to bank (their deposits came to be called "hot" money), seeking the best rates for their clients, who owned shares in the funds. To attract these big deposits, the thrifts bid against one another, offering higher and higher rates of interest—rates they could not possibly afford to pay.[6]

In 1981, when the Reagan administration assumed office, 85 percent of the 4,600 S&Ls were losing money. The basic problem was that thrifts were collecting interest rates of approximately 8 percent or less on their thirty-year mortgages while paying double-digit interest to new depositors. For Reagan policy makers, the cure for this dilemma was deregulation, which would allow S&Ls to grow out of their unprofitability. In 1981, the Bank Board, now headed by Reagan appointee Richard Pratt, eliminated the rule that had forbidden thrifts to take more than 5 percent of their total deposits from money brokers. "By 1984," according to Davis, "there was more than $34 billion worth of brokered deposits held by the FSLIC-insured institutions. It was not uncommon for an S&L to have nearly half its deposits comprised of this 'hot' money; in a couple of thrifts, 'hot' money constituted the entire deposit base."[7]

S&Ls were also encouraged to shift their status from mutual associations, owned by their depositors, to joint-stock companies, owned by their investors. To liberate these joint-stock companies, the Bank Board eliminated a number of regulations. Under the old rules, "No thrift could have fewer than 400 stockholders, no single stockholder could own more than 10 percent of the shares, no control group or family could own more than 25 percent, and all stockholders had to live within 125 miles of the main office. Now, in 1982— its thinking addled by crisis and also by the deregulation zeitgeist of the 1980s—the Bank Board decided that anyone who had the money could buy or start a thrift. New S&Ls started springing up everywhere, and many others changed hands."[8] Some S&Ls were now dominated by a single stockholder. These changes attracted a new type of person and a more aggressive style of management to the S&L industry. The image of the S&L operator began to shift from Jimmy Stewart's portrayal in *It's a Wonderful Life* to the wheeling and dealing of a Charles Keating.

To aid the more assertive S&Ls, capital requirements were decreased. The capital in an S&L is the proportion of the money it uses that constitutes the investment of its owners. In October 1980, Jay Janis, Carter's head of the Bank Board, reduced capital requirements from 5 percent of assets to 4 percent. Two years later, Janis's successor, Richard Pratt, lowered it to 3 percent. With this stroke of a pen, a number of insolvent thrifts were now reclassified as solvent.

In terms of the viability of the FSLIC, "The capital of the S&L was the cushion that kept the insurance fund from being hit by an institution's losses."[9]

During Pratt's tenure (1981–1983) as head of the Bank Board, capital requirements were also reduced through revised accounting practices. The shift from generally accepted accounting principles (GAAP) to the lenient set of regulatory accounting principles (RAP) in 1982 was mockingly labeled creative accounting principles (CRAP) by government examiners. These accounting changes allowed—some would say "encouraged"—S&Ls to disguise their growing insolvency by misrepresenting their liabilities as assets. In Davis's words, "The [accounting] changes were hard to understand; they were almost impenetrable by laymen and by much of the financial press, who consequently ignored them. But by abandoning GAAP, which were themselves notoriously subject to a certain amount of creative manipulation, the board allowed a rapidly expanding S&L to show a handsome profit even if it was disastrously run, and the S&L could continue to show handsome profits until it was utterly looted by its owner."[10] Thus, through the hocus-pocus of creative accounting, a liability could be temporarily transformed into an asset, and a dying thrift could appear to be a thriving one.

With the S&Ls still suffering losses, Congress responded by passing the Garn–St. Germain Depository Institutions Act in October 1982. This law, named for the chairmen of the Senate and House Banking Committees, Senator Jake Garn and Representative Fernand St. Germain, further loosened constraints on S&L efforts to make investments and compete for deposits. The legislation was the result of consultations among officials of the FHLBB, the administration, and Congress and was enthusiastically endorsed by Reagan when he signed it into law. It ordered the phaseout of the savings interest rate differential by January 1, 1984, authorized the FSLIC to provide assistance for insured thrifts to raise net worth to required levels, and directed the twelve Federal Home Loan Banks to furnish loans to the FSLIC. The Garn–St. Germain Act also authorized S&Ls to invest up to 40 percent (up from 20 percent) of their assets in nonresidential real estate and commercial loans, make consumer loans up to 30 percent (up from 20 percent) of their assets, and make home and apartment loans without regard to appraisal values.[11] Martin Mayer argues that,

> Probably the single most damaging provision in this law was the elimination of all regulation of the ratio between what an S&L could lend to a developer and the appraisal value of the project for which the loan was made. The 1980 Deregulation Act had set limits of 66 percent of

appraised value for loans on unimproved land, 75 percent for loans on land with water and sewer systems or with frames beginning to rise, and 90 percent for low-income housing or in situations where insurance covered the risk of loss. The last was already a considerable loosening, because the Bank Board had asserted for years that no more than 80 percent of value should be lent on construction projects. Given the moral status of real estate appraisal as a profession, that was dangerous enough. Now . . . Garn–St. Germain was increasing greatly the proportion of their assets that S&Ls could have in commercial real estate—and at the same time eliminating all control over how much could be lent to build and carry commercial properties. And the Bank Board was permitting developers to buy S&Ls.[12]

The Garn–St. Germain Act induced even worse state laws. S&Ls can conduct their business only with a government charter, but that charter can be granted by either a state or the federal government. Thrift owners sought to operate under whichever had the loosest set of regulations. In California, where state officials had been closely regulating state-chartered S&LS, many of these thrifts switched to federal charters in the early 1980s. California legislators then became worried that they would be deprived of thrift campaign contributions if all the thrifts became federally chartered. In 1982, a Republican assemblyman, Pat Nolan, introduced a bill that virtually eliminated all limits on thrift investments; it passed with only one dissenting vote. The new legislation allowed California S&Ls to use noncash assets (usually land) to fulfill their capitalization requirements and permitted loans without demanding that borrowers put up any cash. Davis writes, "Under the Nolan Bill, a California-chartered thrift could invest 100 percent of its deposits in any venture it chose. . . . The California thrifts, in short, were permitted to become venture capitalists . . . but with full knowledge that beneath them spread the safety net of federal deposit insurance."[13] Similar bills were passed in Texas and Florida. Lou Cannon suggests, "This action enticed hordes of unscrupulous operators to open new state-chartered thrifts. Under such circumstances it is not surprising that state-chartered thrifts accounted for two-thirds of total S&L losses."[14] In 1984, Charles Keating bought an S&L in California.

In 1983, Pratt resigned as chairman of the FHLBB and went to work for Treasury Secretary Donald Regan's former firm, Merrill Lynch. President Reagan appointed Edwin Gray to be the new chairman. Gray was part of Edwin Meese's California group; he had worked as assistant press secretary for Governor Reagan in Sacramento and as deputy director of the Office of Policy Development in the White House. In 1982, however, Gray had returned to

California to go to work for an S&L in San Diego. According to Cannon, "Gray was then recruited by the thrift industry to replace Pratt. 'I was appointed because it thought I would be a patsy for the industry,' Gray said later. . . . Gray was a Reagan loyalist who believed in deregulation and was widely viewed as earnest, hardworking and not especially bright. 'The S&L industry wanted me, so I was automatic.' "[15] After Gray was sworn in, his first speech was entitled "A Sure Cure for What Ails You," in which the new chairman encouraged the managers of thrifts to take advantage of the deregulatory environment.

However, by September 1983, Gray was being informed by his staff that a potentially explosive problem was brewing. Despite declining interest rates, the plight of S&Ls was getting worse, not better. Davis writes, "Thanks to Garn–St. Germain, lax oversight, and liberalized state laws, the problem at the thrifts no longer centered on the negative spread between the cost of paying interest on deposits and the inadequate income derived from the mortgage portfolio. The problem, said the staff, now revolved around all the terrible loans . . . that the thrifts were making with their new brokered deposits. And the problem had suddenly become immense."[16] Beginning in 1984, Gray delivered several speeches warning that, because of the increasing number of insolvent S&Ls, the Treasury might have to financially rescue the FSLIC system. Insolvency can be defined as a situation in which the market value of a thrift's assets is less than the market value of its nonequity liabilities.[17] The number of insolvent institutions was steadily climbing—from 43 in 1980 to 445 in 1984—but the deposit insurance fund did not have the money to close these thrifts and pay off their depositors.[18] In 1985, according to an economist who worked for the FHLBB, the deposit insurance fund had about $4.6 billion in reserves, but it would have cost $5.8 billion to close all insolvent S&Ls.[19] The FSLIC fund was financed mainly by an annual premium of one-twelfth of 1 percent of a thrift's deposits. In 1985, an additional surcharge of one-eighth of 1 percent was added, bringing the total cost to five-twenty-fourths of 1 percent. Kane points out, "Because this explicit premium does not increase with the riskiness of an insured firm's operations, FSLIC insurance can simultaneously be unreasonably expensive for a conservatively run firm and unreasonably cheap for an aggressively run enterprise that has little of its own capital at risk."[20]

In 1984, after considerable resistance, Gray recognized that there was a major problem and began requesting increased funds from David Stockman's OMB for 750 new bank examiners. His requests, however, were rejected. Within the administration, Gray was condemned for being disloyal to the Reagan revolution by promoting "re-regulation." "Gray's transformation," according to Romer and Weingast, "was driven to a large extent by knowledge within the agency that disaster was impending—FSLIC was clearly going broke. If nothing were done, Gray and the agency would be blamed. Blame might be avoided if the problem were urgently brought to public attention."[21] Hence, Gray informed Congress in October 1985 that the FSLIC needed about $15 billion in new capital to close down the growing number of insolvent S&Ls. This request was as welcome as a thunderstorm at a picnic: Congress and the administration were presently negotiating the Gramm-Rudman mechanism to reduce soaring budget deficits, and the United States League of Savings Institutions vehemently opposed any governmental effort to close down bankrupt thrifts.

In July 1987, M. Danny Wall, who had been Senator Jake Garn's administrative assistant, replaced Gray as chairman of the FHLBB. Wall, who was very popular with the S&L industry and with Congress, spent most of his time in office underestimating the costs of bailing out insolvent thrifts. Whereas Wall estimated that $15 billion was sufficient in 1988, the FDIC estimated that it would take close to $60 billion, with the costs rising every day.[22]

In 1986, the Reagan administration had introduced a bill recommending a $15 billion increase in federal insurance funds to grapple with the increasing number of S&L bankruptcies. The bill was considerably diluted by Jim Wright and Tony Coelho, who had close political and economic ties to the S&L industry. After more than a year of difficult negotiations, President Reagan signed the Competitive Equality Banking Act in August 1987. Instead of $15 billion (which would have been insufficient), the law authorized only a $10.8 billion recapitalization bonding program for the FSLIC. The legislation also approved supervisory forbearance of up to three years for well-managed, capital-weak institutions in economically depressed areas. "Forbearance" essentially means a temporary suspension of the rules because of special circumstances; here, it was applied to economically depressed states such as Texas. Regulators exercised discretion in enforcing the rules because to do otherwise would have destroyed some thrifts financially. Romer and Weingast write, "The final legislation reinforced continued forbearance by allowing thrifts in farm and oil-patch states to continue to use the lenient regulatory accounting practices adopted in 1982. Thrifts in these areas . . . would also be allowed to stay open with a .5 percent capital-asset ratio. . . . Given the limited amount of new FSLIC funding relative to the magnitude of the thrift insolvency problem, the act ensured that many failing thrifts would have considerable more time to gamble for resurrection."[23] Thus, the cost of the crisis would continue to escalate.

Between 1984 and 1988, about 800 S&Ls, approximately one-fourth of the industry, became insolvent.[24] In March 1988, Alan Greenspan, chairman of the Federal Reserve Board, warned Congress that the $10.8 billion in borrowing authority that the FSLIC received in 1987 was inadequate to handle the expanding number of failed S&Ls. In May 1988, the General Accounting Office (GAO) alerted Congress that the FSLIC needed a new infusion of capital to cope with more than 500 failing thrifts. The GAO also reported that the FSLIC was insolvent by $13.7 billion, more than twice the level of the year before.[25] But Wall continued to support the Reagan administration's position that the problem could be resolved with the resources at hand and that no new tax revenues were needed. Wall's underestimation of the costs of a bailout, combined with Speaker Jim Wright's close ties with some corrupt Texas S&Ls, helped keep this issue out of the 1988 Bush-Dukakis election. Vice President Bush wanted to avoid this issue because he had headed a deregulatory advisory committee in the Reagan administration and because his son Neil was involved with an insolvent thrift in Denver.

After the 1988 elections, with the FSLIC lacking the funds to shut down bankrupt S&Ls, Wall supervised numerous deals with investors, such as Robert Bass and Ron Perelman, who received lucrative subsidies and tax incentives to buy 179 thrifts. These arrangements eventually cost the government about $70 billion.[26]

By the end of the Reagan presidency, Nathaniel Nash reported that the S&L industry was fragmented, "with about one-third of it healthy and profitable; one-third weakened but surviving; and one-third either hopelessly insolvent or moving quickly in that direction. These insolvent institutions are said to be adding $500 million to $1 billion each month to the industry's already huge losses."[27] By the end of 1988, it became clear that the bailout of the S&L industry would be the largest in American history, far exceeding the combined cost of the public assistance given to Chrysler, Lockheed, and New York City during the 1970s.

The cost of cleaning up the mess became the responsibility of the Bush administration. On August 9, 1989, President Bush signed the Financial Institutions Reform, Recovery and Enforcement Act. This law removed the FHLBB as the supervisor of the thrift industry and transferred that function to the FDIC. It also created the Resolution Trust Corporation (RTC), administered by the FDIC but under the policy guidance of the Treasury Department. The RTC was in charge of deposing the assets of the hundreds of S&Ls that had finally been closed down. The bill provided a $50 billion bailout, with $30 billion financed by thirty-year and forty-year bonds and $20 billion provided by the Treasury. According to Mayer, "The RTC is funded by the American taxpayer, who must carry the added debt burden of the bonds and bills sold by the Treasury for this agency. By summer 1990, the RTC . . . was the largest American financial institution, controlling assets with a face value of more than $200 billion, though their real value was much less. To the extent that the liabilities of the insured S&Ls under RTC direction exceed what the RTC gets for the assets, the taxpayer will be assessed for the losses."[28]

CAUSES OF THE S&L CRISIS

This brief history of the S&L crisis demonstrates that no one factor can explain what went wrong and no one villain can be blamed. Nash suggests that "there was not just one culprit, nor a single big mistake. Rather, from the late 1970s on, there was a confluence of error and ineptitude, at times compounded by fraud. Congress, regulators, and the industry, all failed. Together, they produced a maelstrom of legislation, regulatory measures and lending practices that were too lenient, shortsighted, poorly conceived, politically compromised or inadequate."[29] The usual capabilities of the political system to deal somewhat effectively with a problem, to "muddle through," were not operating. Irrational responses, instead of being checked and corrected by the policy process, were amplified. Until 1989, most attempts to cope with the declining fortunes of the thrifts only made conditions worse. Though we are prone to sing the virtues of bipartisan cooperation, the S&L story reveals a bipartisan disaster. Nor does the story highlight any heroes; indeed, the narrative uncovers the moral laxity of the 1980s.

One cause of the S&L breakdown was declining oil prices, which brought about major problems in Texas. When oil prices dropped from $40 a barrel in 1979 to less than $13 a barrel in 1986, that damaged the local economy. Texas thrifts had not lent much money to energy companies, but they were hurt by the ripple effects of vacant office buildings and home owners who defaulted on their mortgage payments. In 1987, the Houston metropolitan area had the highest rate of mortgage defaults in the nation. House prices fell in Houston, Dallas, Fort Worth, Austin, and San Antonio. These cities also suffered from a glut of unused office space.[30] By 1987, 60 percent of all the money in Texas's 280 thrifts came from brokered deposits, but 108 fell short of net-worth requirements and were technically insolvent, and 65 had negative net worth. Texas thrifts lost $6.9 billion in 1987.[31] Eventually, Texas S&Ls accounted for almost one-fifth of the thrifts that were closed—137 out of 747 institutions—giving Texas the dubious distinction of being the state with the highest number of thrift fatalities.[32] Some have argued that the risky lending practices of Texas thrifts should bear more responsibility than the drop in oil prices for the collapse of real estate. Mayer writes, "Apologists say the loss of value in real estate created the S&L crisis, but obviously it was the artificial inflation of such values by reckless lenders that produced the real estate collapse."[33] The crash of real estate prices was also evoked by the elimination of several subsidies in the Tax Reform Act of 1986.

Another major explanation for the S&L crisis is fraud. The colorful reports of widespread corruption among S&L owners—personified by Donald Dixon and Charles Keating—inevitably resurrected the old populist adage that the best way to rob a bank is to own one. The thrift regulatory system was unprepared for the explosive rise in chicanery that accompanied deregulation in the 1980s. When the Empire Savings and Loan Association in Mesquite, Texas, was closed by federal regulators on March 14, 1984, it was the first time that a thrift had been taken over because of fraud. In this case, over 100 people were indicted, and it eventually cost the FSLIC more than $500 million. Allan Pusey, who covered the S&L scandal for the *Dallas Morning News,* later wrote, "Although the disaster at Empire Savings gave federal regulators their first glimpse of fraud as a major cause of thrift failures, the role fraud played was consistently underrated—by regulators, by Congress, and certainly by the S&L industry itself."[34]

Corruption in the thrift industry was difficult to define, difficult to detect, and problematic to prosecute. "The deals at the heart of the alleged fraud," according to Richard Stevenson, "are often mind-numbingly complex, involving reams of paper, financing arrangements and jargon that is difficult for investigators, much less jurors, to understand."[35] It is little wonder that many prosecutors were reluctant to pursue S&L cases that were likely to be complex and time consuming and less likely to result in convictions. Consequently, only the most blatant cases of corruption were tried; unfortunately, there were many.

The deregulated environment of the 1980s provided opportunities and temptations for the new breed of S&L operators. For example, in 1983, Rambir Sahni, an Air India pilot, bought Tokay Savings and Loan Association in Lodi, California, and renamed it American Diversified Savings Bank. Sahni's thrift gave up granting mortgages and attracted brokered deposits by offering the highest return in the country. Between 1983 and 1985, the assets of American Diversified soared from $11.7 million to $1.1 billion. Sahni invested most of these assets in two "service corporations" that, in turn, invested in a number of speculative operations, such as windmill farms and a procedure to turn chicken manure into methane. For a short period, American Diversified was the fastest growing and most profitable S&L in the nation. The accounting firms of Touche Ross and Arthur Young both certified that American Diversified was making profits. But the investments Sahni was making were really loans that were not generating income. Mayer explains that "a lending institution that takes big fees for every loan it makes necessarily shows accelerating profits at times of accelerating growth. And in situations where the borrower pays the fees by taking a bigger loan, which means the S&L is paying itself, there aren't any real profits until the borrower begins to pay back what he borrowed, which in these situations never happens. Sahni was to some degree a partner in most of the 145 real estate developments to which American Diversified had lent money."[36] The Ponzi scheme financing of this enterprise was ended in December 1985 when California's S&L regulator prohibited American Diversified from accepting any more brokered deposits. The thrift was closed in June 1988 and cost the FSLIC about $800 million.

In reading about the fraudulent behavior of S&L owners, one is struck by the absence of any commitment to sound business practices. Each regarded his enterprise as a cash cow whose purpose was to be looted; each acted as if his charter to run an S&L was a license to gamble with depositors' money. Regulations were viewed as nuisances that should be circumvented. The owners paid themselves and their families extravagant salaries, lived luxuriously, and often traveled on their private jets. Profits were derived not from prudent lending but from the fees that large and numerous loans generated. Unscrupulous S&L owners developed the practice of land-flipping, in which a piece of property was sold rapidly within a short time at escalating prices. Mayer explains, "Such trades generated their own fake profits and gave appraisers whose main tool was the recent sales prices of compatible property an excuse to rocket up appraised values of all the land in the neighborhood. Then the S&Ls could peddle new deposits through money brokers . . . without violating capital restrictions. It should be remembered that each dollar of new capital created by reappraising owned property permitted an S&L to raise thirty-three dollars from the public in deposits the government insured."[37] When bad loans accumulated, corrupt S&Ls developed a mechanism whereby nonperforming loans were exchanged and refinanced (more fees); through creative accounting principles, the loans could then be reclassified as assets. This procedure was morbidly defined as "trading a dead horse for a dead cow."[38]

The most corrupt behavior was exemplified by Donald Dixon and Charles Keating. In July 1982, builder Donald Dixon bought Vernon Savings, with assets of $82 million, in the small town of Vernon, Texas (population 13,000), northwest of Dallas. By 1985, Dixon's practices had turned Vernon Savings into one of the most profitable S&Ls in the country, but federal regulators called the whole operation "Vermin Savings." Dixon used Vernon deposits to finance his own construction company. In 1983, Dixon and his wife toured Europe in a rented Rolls-Royce and Learjet and dined every night in a different Michelin three-star restaurant. This trip was paid for by Vernon Savings because it was labeled a market study for a French restaurant the Dixons were planning to create in Dallas. Dixon also spent $2.6 million for the sister ship to the presidential yacht. Dixon kept his boat anchored in the Potomac, where it was regularly used to entertain Democratic congressmen such as Jim Wright and Tony Coelho. Bank examiners reported significant regulatory violations, but Vernon Savings was not closed until November 1987. Wright had delayed the action for a year. When Vernon was taken over, its assets stood at $1.4 billion, but 96 percent of its loans were in default. Bailing out Vernon would cost taxpayers about $1.3 billion.[39] After being convicted on twenty-three counts of bank fraud and given a five-year jail sentence, Dixon conceded that he had made major errors, but he blamed Congress for sowing the seeds of destruction with its deregulatory policies. Dixon claimed, "It put too much money in the hands of too few people. . . . I found I could not handle the temptation that caused me to compromise my moral standards."[40] The devil and deregulation made him do it.

One person who claimed to have impeccable moral standards was Charles Keating. He had been appointed to an antipornography commission by President Nixon and was a financial supporter of Mother Teresa. Keating was chairman of a holding company, the American Continental Corporation (ACC), which bought the Lincoln Savings Corporation in Irvine, California, for $51 million in February 1984. The deal was supported by Drexel Burnham, Michael Milken's firm, which owned more than 10 percent of ACC's stock. Five of the top eight officers in ACC were Keating's kin: his son, daughter, and three sons-in-law. Over the next five years, ACC distributed about $34 million to Keating and his family.

After taking over Lincoln in 1984, the thrift grew from approximately $600 million in loans to nearly $6 billion in 1988. Lincoln largely withdrew from the home mortgage business and invested in high-yielding junk bonds handled by Milken and in speculative real estate. Mayer reports, "With the passage of time, as Keating reached further and further in search of high yields, Lincoln's junk bond portfolio got increasingly rancid. By . . . 1988, no less than 77 percent of it was in bonds that not only were not rated as 'investment grade' securities by Moody's or Standard and Poor's—they weren't rated at all! Lincoln's junk bond holdings have become a litany of bankrupt or troubled companies."[41] In brief, perhaps because Drexel Burnham controlled 10 percent of ACC's stock, Lincoln Savings was an excellent customer for Milken's junkiest bonds until federal authorities intervened in 1989.

Keating's most spectacular venture was the construction of the Phoenician Hotel, which cost over $300 million. When this 580-room hotel opened in

October 1988, with its $1.7 million art collection and a pool lined with mother-of-pearl tile, it was probably the most expensive hotel ever built in the United States. With various rooms named after Keating and his family, this "palace of unparalleled conspicuous consumption" was "a monument to Keating's ego."[42] However, its opulence guaranteed that there would be no profits for at least a decade.

Lincoln Savings was also involved in a number of high-risk real estate developments in Austin, Phoenix, and Tucson. Large amounts of undeveloped land would be bought for the purpose of creating planned communities. But most of these projects were years away from earning profits. And when real estate values collapsed in the latter half of the 1980s, most of these projects were doomed.

By the summer of 1986, bank board examiners in San Francisco urged their superiors in Washington, D.C., to admonish Lincoln because of its questionable accounting and loan practices. Keating responded with a sense of outrage, claiming that the local examiners did not understand Lincoln's sophisticated new investment strategies. Keating's appeals were buttressed by a warm endorsement in 1985 from Alan Greenspan, then a private consultant, to the Home Loan Bank Board in San Francisco. Greenspan extolled Lincoln as a "vibrant and healthy" institution that "presents no foreseeable risk" to the federal deposit insurance system.[43] Lincoln had also received a clean audit from Arthur Young and Company. However, it was later revealed that the accountant in charge of this audit, Jack D. Atchison, soon resigned from Arthur Young and went to work for Keating at four times his previous salary—$900,000. This sleazy arrangement eventually cost Arthur Young $400 million in its settlement with the federal government.[44]

As Gray began to tighten regulations in the summer of 1986, Keating tried to influence the chairman of the Bank Board by offering him a job as the head of an S&L. When this did not succeed, Keating advised Donald Regan, then White House chief of staff, to replace two retiring Bank Board members with two men who had ties to Keating. One of these recommendations was accepted, and on November 7, 1986, Lee Henkel, an Atlanta lawyer, was issued an interim appointment to the FHLBB by President Reagan. Keating and Henkel had been friends since they worked together in John Connally's presidential campaign in 1980. More importantly, Henkel had borrowed a considerable amount of money from Lincoln to finance land deals in South Carolina and Georgia that were in danger of defaulting. When Henkel attended his first FHLBB meeting, he proposed a rule change that would specifically benefit Lincoln Savings. When Henkel's ties to Keating were leaked to the press (probably by Gray), the new Democratic chairman of the Senate

Banking Committee, William Proxmire, demanded a criminal investigation. Henkel was forced to resign.[45]

After failing to gain control over the Bank Board, Keating decided to sue it on March 27, 1987, on the grounds that it had no authority to regulate state-chartered thrifts. Keating also sought legislative relief. On April 2 and 9, 1987, Gray was summoned to Senator Dennis DeConcini's office by Senators DeConcini, Alan Cranston, John Glenn, John McCain, and Donald Riegle (Riegle did not attend the April 2 meeting) to discuss the San Francisco Bank Board's investigation of Lincoln Savings. Keating had contributed $1.3 million to their campaigns and related causes, and it was now payback time. The senators urged Gray to be lenient toward Lincoln and stressed the Arthur Young audit. Gray was angered by what he considered unethical pressure, but he was polite because he desperately needed the senators' help in recapitalizing the FSLIC. When representatives from San Francisco said that they were considering criminal procedures against Lincoln, Senators McCain, Glenn, and Riegle began a hasty retreat. But Senators Cranston and DeConcini continued to support Keating, behavior that eventually ended their political careers.

Danny Wall kept Lincoln open until after the 1988 elections. On April 14, 1989, the government finally took control of Lincoln Savings. Keating was arrested and, in a series of federal and state trials, was convicted of ninety counts of fraud, racketeering, and conspiracy and sentenced to twelve years in prison. The most damaging charge was that Keating had authorized the sale of fraudulently marketed ACC junk bonds to thousands of Lincoln customers who had been led to believe that the bonds were backed by the federal government. Some retired customers of Lincoln lost their life savings in this swindle. The collapse of Lincoln cost taxpayers about $2.6 billion. Keating served over four years in prison, but because of legal technicalities, both his federal and state convictions were eventually overturned, and he was released.[46]

Colorful culprits like Dixon and Keating allowed the media to portray a complicated story in an entertaining fashion. The scandals personalized a complex system and shifted attention away from explaining the deeper reasons why this calamity was happening. What is most disturbing is that the two most notorious crooks in the S&L system were able to mobilize political support from top officials in the executive and legislative branches of government. The scandals also revealed that, due to the inadequacy of regulatory supervision during the 1980s, corrupt and reckless behavior could go on for years before it was discovered and stopped.

Recent evaluations of the S&L crisis have argued that early estimates exaggerated the role of fraud. One expert suggests that "although fraud and insider abuse appears to have contributed to many, if not most, thrift insolvencies, there are no reliable estimates to indicate what portion of the cleanup cost is due to criminal activity. My own guess . . . is that the figure is 20 percent or below."[47]

Lax regulation also contributed to the S&L crisis. In the naive fervor that accompanied deregulation, the need for increased vigilance was disparaged and obstructed. The regulatory system in the early 1980s was not prepared to deal with the new type of risk-taking S&L operators and the growing number of insolvencies. George Benston and George Kaufman write, "The sudden increase in allowable activities and risk-taking found [the regulatory system] greatly understaffed, undertrained, and underorganized. . . . Some associations were not examined for three or four years, and violators identified by field examiners frequently were not pursued by their supervisors. In addition, the FHLBB did not expand its examination staff to deal with the increasing scope and complexity of S&L operations, in part because of its own inadequacies and in part because it wanted to cooperate with Reagan administration efforts to restrain the growth of the federal government."[48]

Monitoring was reduced precisely when the danger of fraud was expanding. Examiners who had been trained to review mortgage loans were now confronted with analyzing junk bonds, land swaps, and development loans. "From 1980 to 1984," according to Steven Roberts and Gary Cohen, "the rate of bank examinations per billion dollars in assets dropped by 55 percent. In May 1983, the Home Loan Bank Board requested 38 fewer examiners than in the previous year."[49] At the end of 1983, the Bank Board had only 700 examiners to monitor 4,000 thrifts. Since their work was hard and their starting salary was low ($13,000 per year), turnover among examiners was exceptionally high (about 30 percent a year). The average examiner had only two years' experience. These problems were particularly severe in the ninth district, covering 510 thrifts in Mississippi, Louisiana, Arkansas, New Mexico, and Texas. In late 1983, the regional headquarters for the ninth district was shifted from Little Rock, Arkansas, to Dallas, Texas. Benston and Kaufman report that "only eleven of the 48 members of the supervisory staff were willing to make the move. As a result, the annual number of examinations in this district—which was in the heart of the problem area—declined from 261 in 1982–83 to 183 in 1983–84 and 173 in 1984–85 before increasing again to 283 in 1985–86."[50] In short, the region that required the most supervision experienced the least and ended up costing the Treasury the most.

In 1984, Gray recognized these problems and requested a larger budget to increase both the salaries and the number of bank examiners, but he was thwarted by Stockman and Regan. Gray circumvented OMB constraints in

July 1985 by transferring the examination staff to the twelve regional banks, where they could be paid higher salaries. He also appointed experienced regulators, such as H. Joe Selby to Dallas and Michael Patriarca to San Francisco, to monitor particularly tough situations.[51] The response to these efforts were leaks that Gray had accepted gifts (hotel rooms and meals) from the United States League of Savings Institutions.

When Gray was replaced as chairman of the Bank Board by Danny Wall on July 1, 1987, Wall responded to Keating's pressure by shifting the investigation of Lincoln Savings from the FHLBB in San Francisco to a more lenient group in Washington, which shattered morale among bank examiners. Wall was also committed to as much forbearance as the law would allow for insolvent S&Ls in economically depressed areas. He quickly announced, "By definition, we don't shut down Texas institutions."[52] Wall did not accept any gratuities from the S&Ls, but his deceptive efforts to camouflage the accelerating costs of the insolvent thrifts eventually cost the taxpayers billions of dollars.

Congress contributed to the S&L problem by its actions and inactions. Legislation in 1980 and 1982, according to Mayer, "deliberately altered deposit insurance from a protection for depositors to an engine of growth for . . . S&Ls."[53] In 1984, Congress did not support Gray's efforts to halt money brokers from placing jumbo sums of insured deposits at risk-taking thrifts. Congress also initially opposed Bank Board attempts to restrict S&Ls from placing more than 10 percent of their assets in risky real estate projects. The Bank Board was consistently pressured by Congress to practice leniency. Mayer bluntly states, "What congressmen wanted . . . was not honest accounting, a stable financial system, or the preservation of an insurance fund, they wanted what they called 'forbearance' for their constituents and especially for their contributors. They got it—reluctantly from Ed Gray, then enthusiastically from . . . Danny Wall, who was . . . a creature of the Senate."[54] And forbearance was virtually guaranteed when Congress made sure that the FSLIC lacked the funds to shut down most insolvent thrifts and pay off the depositors. With only slight exaggeration, Gray told a House banking subcommittee in January 1989 that "when it came to thrift matters in the Congress, the United States League and many of its affiliates were the de facto government. What the League wanted it got. What it did not want from Congress, it had killed. . . . Every single day that I served as Chairman of the Federal Home Loan Bank Board, the United States League was in control of the Congress as an institution."[55]

That control was based largely on campaign contributions and was symbolized by Keating's ability to line up five senators (four Democrats and one Republican) to plead his case against what he claimed was bureaucratic harassment.

When Keating was questioned about this unprecedented political intervention, he responded: "One question, among the many raised in many weeks, has to do with whether my financial support in any way influenced several political figures to take up my cause. I want to say in the most forceful way I can: I certainly hope so."[56] And Keating's efforts were rewarded when Wall shifted the investigation of Lincoln Savings from the FHLBB in San Francisco to bank examiners in Washington.

Congressman Jim Wright received $83,000 from Texas thrifts during the 1980s. Wright pressured Gray to ease the regulatory pressures on Craig Hall, a Dallas real estate syndicator who was more than $500 million in debt. Wright also complained that Joe Selby's Dallas office was dominated by homosexual lawyers engaged in a political vendetta to destroy Texas thrifts. To squeeze Gray, Wright pulled the bailout bill off the House floor in 1986 and was able to cut the administration's 1987 bill to only $5 billion. (The conference committee later raised it to $10.8 billion.)[57] Speaker Wright's behavior, along with that of other Democratic congressmen such as Tony Coelho, Fernand St. Germain, and Claude Pepper, inhibited Michael Dukakis from being able to raise the S&L issue against George Bush in the 1988 presidential campaign. Hence, the biggest issue before Congress in 1989 was ignored during the 1988 campaign.

The most comprehensive explanation of the S&L crisis is based on the concept of perverse incentives. In response to the inflation and interest volatility of the 1970s and early 1980s, an "incentive-incompatible" system was created among depositors, FSLIC-insured S&Ls, regulators, and politicians. Actors in this system were encouraged to behave in ways that eventually cost taxpayers billions. While extolling the virtues of deregulation and market rationality, these arrangements did not provide the incentives to induce markets or regulators to close down insolvent thrifts. In essence, the system in the 1980s subsidized failure and spurred recklessness. No powerful incentives were operating to protect taxpayers.

Since 1980, each depositor's account has been insured for up to $100,000 by the FSLIC. Given the nature of deposit insurance, savers have no incentive to search for prudently run S&Ls; they are motivated to find the thrift offering the highest interest rate for their deposits. During the 1980s, the thrifts advertising the most lucrative rates were often the most reckless in their operations.

The biggest fear among S&L regulators, especially top officials, was a panic in which depositors indiscriminately withdrew their savings from sick and healthy thrifts. In the early 1980s, the FHLBB was responsible for maintaining the stability of the $800 billion thrift industry with an FSLIC fund of only

$6 billion. Confronted with an increasing number of insolvent thrifts and hampered by a Congress and president who were not interested in providing the resources to identify and shut down insolvent thrifts, regulators were prone to follow lenient supervisory procedures. This behavior was compatible with a regulator's short-term responsibilities and post-government job ambitions. Kane stresses that "once a fund's unbooked losses become very large, it is hard for managers of a deposit-insurance bureau to tighten monitoring or insolvency resolution sufficiently without being perceived at least in part to be causing the industry the very problems they are seeking to cure. Fear of undermining public confidence in a weak fund and triggering a wave of contagious failures tends to inhibit strong supervisory action."[58] Redburn identifies the crux of the problem by pointing out that "the policy provided no external constituency for closing a failed institution and several for keeping it open."[59] In brief, effective regulation cannot be dependent on heroic, suicidal decision making.

The system also promoted perverse incentives for politicians. In the early 1980s, legislation designed to deregulate the S&Ls and help them grow appeared to be costless. When deregulation did not provide a costless solution, no major constituency could be aroused to support the required recapitalization. Recapitalization and stricter supervision were viewed by the S&L industry as threats that would result in the closing down of insolvent thrifts. This perspective was conveyed to congressmen, who in turn pressured regulators to practice forbearance. L. William Seidman, the head of the FDIC, writes, "Both parties were agreed on letting the industry run wild, but for entirely different reasons. For the Democrats, easy housing finance had always been a vote-getting ideology they fully endorsed. The Republicans agreed that nothing should be done to restrain the newly deregulated S&Ls' entrepreneurial zeal, which would demonstrate the superior economic efficiency of the market place."[60] When the numbers turned bad in the mid-1980s, no one was willing to take a leadership position on this issue; it offered no rewards, and it threatened painful costs. The effect of the prevailing incentives was to ignore and postpone dealing with the S&L problem.

The new system had its most perverse consequences on the behavior of many S&L operators. In the early 1980s, a series of federal and state decisions gave thrift owners greater discretion in choosing assets. It was assumed that allowing S&Ls to expand beyond mortgage lending and diversify their holdings would increase their profitability. What was *not* foreseen was that the changes would create irresistible incentives for a new breed of S&L owner to gamble with federally insured deposits. The FSLIC would create what economists call a "moral hazard," that is, "the tendency of those who are protected from the full costs of risks to take more risks."[61] Kane summarizes the S&L crisis by writing, "A decapitalized institution faces enormous incentives to undertake go-for-broke financial plays that load potential losses onto uninformed and insufficiently wary taxpayers, while depositors, regulators, and politicians have some incentives to look the other way."[62]

The decapitalized S&Ls of the 1980s that were allowed to keep functioning were called "zombie thrifts" by Kane. Instead of being closed down when their accumulated losses were recognized by federal auditors, zombie thrifts continued to function and to accelerate red ink. Their operations reduced the profits of healthy thrifts and threatened to turn them into zombies. For a period of time, by taking advantage of creative and sometimes fraudulent accounting principles, many decapitalized thrifts could post impressive growth figures. Mayer reports, "The Federal Home Loan Bank Board of San Francisco did some calculations in the mid-1980s and demonstrated that with a $2 million investment, a man with an S&L charter could grow his institution to $1.3 billion in deposits over five years without violating the capital requirements. Any self-proclaimed venture capitalist who got his hands on a state S&L charter with wide investment powers . . . could get the use of $99.85 of other people's money for every 15 cents he put in himself. And he could get it cheaply, because government insurance guaranteed his depositors that every penny they put in would be repaid, with the advertised interest."[63] It was rational for zombie thrifts to assume a casino mentality and gamble for resurrection by paying the highest interest rates to attract brokered deposits, and investing in the riskiest real estate developments and junk bonds.

THE REAGAN ADMINISTRATION'S ROLE

Although the Reagan presidency is justifiably proud that communism began to unravel during its watch, administration officials cannot avoid their responsibility for the S&L debacle during their years in office. Even one of the administration's most enthusiastic supporters, Robert Bartley, editor of the *Wall Street Journal,* concedes that the S&L crisis was "the most obvious blot on the Seven Fat Years."[64] The Reagan administration's final *Economic Report* treats the S&L problem as a challenge for the next administration, avoiding any explanation of why the problem was not resolved in the 1980s, and blaming Congress and regulatory agencies for creating incentives that encouraged "irresponsible management." Adopting a posture that frequently infuriated Democrats, the *Economic Report* blamed national policies for the S&L crisis while acting as if the Reagan administration was not one of the federal government's policy makers.[65] When Reagan wrote his memoirs, his editor, Michael Korda, could not persuade the ex-president to even mention the S&L problem in his book.[66]

In reality, the ideology of the Reagan presidency created a blind faith that deregulation would solve the problems of the S&Ls in the first term, and political calculations motivated the administration to postpone dealing with the growing number of insolvent thrifts in the second. The Reagan administration was not wrong in promoting a long overdue deregulation of the S&L industry, but it was impeded by ideology in not understanding the need for enhanced monitoring. The problems deriving from "moral hazard" were widely recognized by economists and regulators; a prudent administration would not have been blindsided by the predictable activities of zombie thrifts. Just as the deregulation of the airlines in terms of allocating routes did not decrease the obligation of the Federal Aviation Agency to monitor airline safety, the deregulation of thrifts should have been accompanied by increased concern about preventing S&L operators from gambling with depositors'—and ultimately taxpayers'—money.

Ideology and politics played major roles in whom Reagan appointed chairman of the Bank Board: Richard Pratt (1981–1983), Edwin Gray (1983–1987), and M. Danny Wall (1987–1989). Each of these political appointees was chosen because he believed in deregulation and was considered friendly to the S&L industry. Pratt had been an economist with the Savings and Loan League in the late 1960s and a professor of finance at the University of Utah before assuming the chair of the FHLBB in April 1981. He believed that the salvation of the S&Ls was for the larger members to absorb the smaller and poorly run two-thirds of the industry while at the same time diversifying their portfolios. This policy resulted in less burdensome regulations and fewer regulators. Because of Pratt's policies, according to Kane, "examination and supervisory resources declined in 1983 and 1984 . . . precisely when the economics of FSLIC's exposure to Zombie risk-taking was expanding and becoming harder to assess. This is true whether we measure these resources by the number of staff members or by the ratio of the bureau's examination-supervisory budget to the value of assets in FSLIC-insured institutions."[67] Mayer is particularly critical of Pratt: "it was during Pratt's two years as Chairman of the Bank Board that the road to hell was paved and polished. He wrote the worst of the regulations, and more than any other single person he wrote the Garn–St. Germain bill of 1982 that codified the perverse incentives the government gave the industry."[68] Pratt resigned from the Bank Board in 1983 and, with Secretary Regan's blessing, became vice chairman of Merrill Lynch Mortgage Trading.

In 1983, Reagan appointed Edwin Gray to replace Pratt. Gray was a protégé of Meese and had also worked for an S&L in San Diego. Initially, Gray was the "patsy" the S&Ls expected him to be. As Mayer explains, "The S&L industry was one where the Reagan Revolution had already occurred, and Gray's job was to preserve it and help the private sector garner the fruits."[69] But after Gray was informed by bank examiners in September 1983 that the flood of brokered deposits was encouraging S&Ls to behave recklessly, he underwent a metamorphosis, fearing a disaster that he might be blamed for. However, his attempts to monitor the S&Ls more closely—including his request for 750 more examiners, which was denied by Stockman—merely isolated him within the administration. In Seidman's words, "Anyone calling for more banking supervision was branded a 're-regulator' and by extension a disloyal Reaganite, the worst condemnation possible inside the Reagan administration."[70] Gray's efforts earned him the antagonism of Donald Regan, who complained that Gray was not a team player. Cannon reports that "by 1985, with Regan in the White House as Chief of Staff, . . . the word was sent to Gray by two Californians in the White House that Regan wanted him out. Gray refused to quit. He wanted to take his case to the President but was told that Reagan accepted Regan's advice on financial matters."[71] Regan's revenge was to nurture the scandal that Gray had accepted favors (meals and hotel rooms) from the S&L industry.[72]

When Gray's term was completed in mid-1987, he was replaced by M. Danny Wall. The new Bank Board chairman, a protégé of Senator Jake Garn and an optimistic believer in deregulation, immediately loosened several of the regulations imposed by Gray. Wall blamed Gray for obsessively concentrating on the few sick thrifts and stressed that he would focus on the healthy ones. He criticized GAO studies of the FSLIC as being the work of "morticians." According to Davis, "Wall repeated to anyone and everyone that whatever the problems of the S&L industry, there was no crisis and there be no need for tax money in the solution—an opinion that earned him the nickname, among officials at the Federal Deposit Insurance Corporation, of M. Danny Isuzu."[73] (Joe Isuzu was a lying car salesman in a television ad.) In early 1988, when bank examiners argued in private meetings that the bailout of sick thrifts would cost taxpayers more than $50 billion, they were condemned for being disloyal. Wall's Panglossian optimism served the political purposes of the Reagan administration by keeping the issue of the growing number of insolvent S&Ls out of the 1988 elections and helping Bush to be elected.

President Reagan never publicly acknowledged that the S&L problem was growing during the 1980s. When he signed the Garn–St. Germain bill in 1982, he boasted that "I think we hit a home run." A month later he delivered a speech to the United States League of Savings Institutions and declared that the problems of the thrift industry had been created "by people with noble intentions but without a solid grip on how the real world works." He bragged that his administration did not "suffer from paralysis by analysis" and claimed that Richard Pratt was "the best darn Chairman the Federal Home Loan Bank Board has ever had." Reagan predicted that the Garn–St. Germain law would be the "Emancipation Proclamation for America's saving institutions" and called on Congress to "go even further with financial deregulation."[74] Reagan's language and subsequent events suggest that more analysis was necessary, that deregulation was not a magic bullet, and that the president did not understand how the new world of thrift owners operated.

Cannon writes, "Reagan knew little about what was going on in the savings and loan industry except that the administration was trying to salvage the thrifts through his favorite remedy of deregulation. He did not raise the issue with anyone, and no one raised it with him."[75] Cannon's last statement is not completely true; the issue was raised by several officials. In the 1984 *Economic Report*, CEA Chairman Martin Feldstein warned, "The existence of Federal deposit insurance gives insured institutions an incentive to take undue risks in the hope of earning greater than normal returns. . . . As a practical matter, as the range of business activities increases, it may become much more difficult for regulators to thwart excessive risk-taking."[76] In response to the growing risk factors, the *Economic Report* recommended that policy makers consider such changes as relating insurance premiums to some measure of risk, strengthening capital requirements, increasing the risk exposure of large depositors, and privatizing all or part of the deposit insurance system. However, Secretary Regan urged Congress to ignore Feldstein's *Economic Report*, and the administration spent no capital in pursuing these proposals. When Feldstein's successor, William Niskanen, resigned from the CEA in March 1985, his final memorandum warned the president about the threat of the increasing number of bankrupt thrifts, but his memo had no effect.[77] Apparently neither Chief of Staff Regan nor Treasury Secretary James Baker felt that it was politically wise to attack this expensive problem when the budget was confronted with soaring deficits.

The irony of the S&L debacle is that one would have expected Reagan's market-oriented advisers to have been particularly skilled in foreseeing the probable negative effects of the incentive-incompatible system of federal deposit insurance. But the prevailing commitment to deregulation prevented most administration officials from discerning between an industry in which the risks were shared by investors and one in which the risks were foisted on to taxpayers. The Reagan administration contributed to a system driven by perverse incentives whereby S&L operators were encouraged to take greater risks, knowing that if they were successful they would reap the profits, and if they failed the FSLIC and eventually the taxpayers would pay most of the costs.

Charles Murray, a movement conservative, offers this criticism:

> The S&L fiasco is another example of the way in which the administration exhibited the ethical carelessness that lends credibility to the greed-and-selfishness indictment. The blame for the fiasco is complicated and diffuse, much of it antedating 1981. But a bedrock principle of Reaganism . . . is that people must bear the consequences of their actions. Giving S&L lenders license to make risky loans without incurring commensurate risk themselves should have caused instant consternation in every administration official who understood the specifics of deregulation. Apparently it didn't. Whatever the excuses, the result was that the Reagan administration permitted precisely the same error—government-created incentives for irresponsible behavior—concerning S&L bankers that it regarded with such horror when it saw criminals let off without punishment, teen-age girls rewarded for having babies, or students given diplomas without having to study.[78]

The S&L crisis should have caused Reagan to experience some cognitive dissonance. If he had looked carefully, several of his cherished beliefs would have been challenged and shown to be in need of revision. For example, the deregulation of the thrift industry motivated entrepreneurs to gain control of a number of S&Ls and engage in corrupt behavior. What Reagan did not understand was that allowing the S&Ls to engage in a broader range of enterprises should have been accompanied by more supervision, not less. Ideology blocked that option from being considered. In addition, Reagan's commitment to shifting responsibility to the states was impugned by the fact that state-chartered thrifts were responsible for two-thirds of total S&L losses. But Reagan never experienced any doubts about his beliefs because his administration decided to postpone dealing with the growing number of insolvent thrifts, he never sought information about the problem, and his political advisers blamed Congress for the mess.

CONSEQUENCES

In recent decades, the S&L industry has endured major changes. Economic developments and deregulation forced thrifts to decrease in number and increase in size. Between 1960 and 1990, the number of S&Ls was slashed from about 6,000 to 2,400. During the 1980s, over a thousand thrifts were either merged or closed down, and 27,000 jobs were cut.[79]

S&Ls have become less dominant in financing home mortgages. Whereas thrifts owned about 60 percent of the nation's mortgage debt in 1970, they held about 30 percent in individual mortgages in 1989 and an additional 12 percent in mortgage-backed securities. As a result of diversification, mortgage debt, which had represented 86 percent of the industry's total assets in 1970, declined to 70 percent in 1989.[80] Thrifts still originate half of the nation's home mortgages, and mortgage debt (nearly $3 trillion) still constitutes more than half of the private debt in the domestic economy. The surviving S&Ls are in a better position today than in 1980 because, with the securitization of the industry through mechanisms such as the Federal National Mortgage Association, thrifts can now make long-term mortgage loans, sell the loans to Fannie Mae, retain the fees for loan origination and collection of the payments, and transfer the interest risk to someone else.

Given Reagan's ideology, there were several unintended consequences of his inaction in the face of the growing S&L problem during his administration. First, the RTC gained control of about 680 thrifts with assets of $450 billion.[81] Ironically, the RTC became the largest real estate owner and the largest employer of lawyers in the world. Second, the S&L story revealed a moral rot that pervaded both the public and the private sectors. Reagan never understood that the deregulation of the S&L industry provided a window of opportunity for corrupt behavior. Entrepreneurial zeal could be combined with the search for the illicit angle, the dikes of professional ethics could be breached by greed. In Mayer's words, "The years 1980–89 witnessed an irrepressibly powerful confluence of the interests of fast-growing S&Ls, Wall Street broker dealers, gargantuan law firms, and elephantine accounting firms—all pressing to maintain and extend the incentives to waste and fraud implicit in what the government had done. Politics frustrated the cleansing action of the market, and those who profited from the market failure then prevented any change in policy."[82]

The most significant consequence of the S&L crisis was its cost; this was the most expensive financial scandal in U.S. history. Estimates of the final costs vary widely, from $100 billion to $500 billion, because there are a variety of assumptions (changes in interest rates and real estate values), calculation methods, and time periods employed in predicting these expenditures. Since much of the bailout was financed by the sale of bonds, the government will be paying about $15 billion a year in interest costs until 2020.[83] Although there is controversy about the final costs, there is little dispute that the problem could have been resolved at a much lower price if it had been dealt with honestly in the mid-1980s. But such courage was lacking in both the executive branch and Congress.

What is surprising is that the country could absorb such financial losses with so little pain. The billion-dollar losses of the S&L industry were not enough to shake the foundations of a $5 trillion economy. Fortunately, the adaptive and growing capabilities of U.S. capitalism can cover a multitude of public- and private-sector sins.

CONCLUSION

The S&L industry was threatened by high interest rates in the late 1970s; it was crushed by bad loans and shady practices by the end of the 1980s. When S&L executives, regulators, and politicians recommended that thrifts grow their way back to profitability, few foresaw that the new deregulated environment of perverse incentives would create a casino mentality that led a new breed of operators to gamble for resurrection at the taxpayers' expense. Nothing reveals the irrationality of the system more than the fact that the S&Ls with the most impressive growth and profits in the mid-1980s were the most likely to fail by the end of the decade. Ideology and politics created a system that subsidized failure and encouraged recklessness.

Most of the major players in this story displayed a "penchant for denial and deception."[84] For the Reagan administration, this meant championing deregulation as the magic bullet that would lead the S&Ls back to profitability in the first term and, when that did not happen, postponing the inevitable costs of dealing with the expanding number of insolvent thrifts in the second term. The denial and self-deception were driven in part by political calculations that it would be best to leave this problem for Reagan's successor. But more importantly, ideology prevented the administration from seeing that the deregulation of the S&L industry should have been accompanied by sharper supervision to protect taxpayers from operators such as Donald Dixon and Charles Keating. The certitude and vanity of the ideologue inhibit analysis and the search for solutions, since the answer is already predetermined by the belief system. The Reagan administration did not check the irrationality of Congress in handling S&L problems; instead, it contributed to the creation of perverse incentives that eventually cost billions to resolve. This was a rare example of the Reagan administration's being blinded by its ideology and not being helped by its pragmatists and public relations advisers, who preferred to use their skills to postpone dealing with the S&L issue. In this case, Reagan acted like a conventional politician, protecting a selfish interest group and his political position at the expense of the public interest.

The conservative claim for Reagan as a great moral leader is weakened by his role in the S&L crisis. By dodging the S&L problem, Reagan evaded painful responsibilities, but he cannot expect to elude the verdict of history. In the next chapter, we can observe the Reagan administration skillfully avoiding the snares of ideology and protectionist pressures in Congress and formulating a successful foreign economic policy.

8

THE REAGAN ADMINISTRATION COPES WITH GLOBAL INTERDEPENDENCE

When Ronald Reagan became president in January 1981, his administration was not primarily concerned with foreign economic policy. His chief domestic priorities were the supply-side tax cut and the defense buildup; his major foreign policy concern was to combat the evil empire of the Soviet Union. But inevitably, international economic problems became more salient and posed threats to both domestic and international politics. The purpose of this chapter is to explain how the Reagan administration responded to these unexpected challenges.

Some scholars initially assumed that the market-oriented administration would be unable to deal with the issues of global interdependence because of its ideological commitments. For example, Jeffrey Garten, a former member of President Nixon's Council of International Economic Policy, warned, "In the end, it is likely that eight years of Reaganomics will be seen as a time when a United States Administration took its own ideological instincts to extremes and was mesmerized by its own rhetoric."[1] A review of the Reagan record, however, reveals that his administration handled foreign economic policy with more pragmatic flexibility than most scholars saw during the 1980s. This is a story not of great victories but of how the administration was able to compromise just enough so as not to lose control of this policy area.

One of the great puzzles of the Reagan presidency is how it gained so many of the benefits of being an ideologically driven administration without suffering the expected costs. One answer to this riddle is that Reagan's pragmatic flexibility was often masked by some symbol of ideological rigidity that was repeatedly stressed in speeches. Thus, Reagan's willingness to do business with Gorbachev was protected by his commitment to the Strategic Defense Initiative. In domestic economic policy, Reagan's signing of several tax increases was concealed by his consistent commitment to cut tax rates. In foreign economic policy, Reagan's numerous violations of free trade were justified in terms of preserving free trade. With his reputation as a conviction politician, Reagan could sin to save virtue.

THE GOALS OF REAGAN'S FOREIGN ECONOMIC POLICY

The strategic priorities of the Reagan administration were to reassert both U.S. military power and U.S. economic power. This could be done by "unleashing" the awesome potential of our capabilities, which had been short-sightedly constrained, both domestically and internationally, by liberalism. Most of Reagan's advisers blamed the apparent decline of the United States on the policies of the Nixon, Ford, and especially Carter presidencies. These leaders had tried to guide the nation into a new world order in which the United States was "still pre-eminent but no longer predominant."[2] In this new environment, the country would have to adjust to the military power of the Soviet Union, the economic competitiveness of Japan and Western Europe, and the assertiveness of nationalistic Third World regimes. But Reagan's advisers believed that a vigorous unleashing of our economic and military capabilities could regain the power and autonomy the nation had enjoyed before losing the Vietnam War. According to Kenneth Oye, many Reagan officials believed that "the administration's two core programs—accelerated defense spending and Reaganomics—would restore American military and economic strength simultaneously. Over the long term, these programs were expected to reverse tendencies toward international diffusion and thereby obviate the need for adjustment and retrenchment. Over the short term, the Reagan administration explicitly repudiated the adjustments of the 1970s. The administration saw those adjustments as causes, not consequences, of the deterioration of the international position of the United States."[3]

This meant that our macroeconomic policies would not be restrained by international considerations.[4] Such bravado ignored the realities of increasing global interdependence. By the early 1980s, the export and import sectors of the economy constituted almost one-fourth of the GNP—a proportion that had doubled since 1970. Whereas a mere 7 percent of the U.S. economy had been subject to international competition in the 1960s, by the 1980s that proportion soared to 70 percent. And even though the dollar had been declining in value since President Nixon took the nation off the gold standard in the early 1970s, it remained the predominant reserve currency in international trade.

In 1981, C. Fred Bergsten pointed out that "one of every six U.S. manufacturing jobs depends on markets abroad. One of every three acres of U.S. farmland produces for export. Almost one of every three dollars of U.S. corporate profit derives from the international activities—investment as well as exports—of American firms."[5] Whereas the Reagan administration saw these facts as measures of U.S. economic power, they were also reflections of interdependence. In brief, the ideological pretensions of the administration were likely to conflict with the realities of global economic interdependence.

The economic recovery program Reagan espoused in 1981 virtually ignored international economics. The president's economic advisers assumed that what was best for America would be good for the rest of the world. Reaganomics would bring about an expanding U.S. market for our trading partners and increase the competitiveness of our exports. The dollar would appreciate in value, decrease in volatility, and become more attractive as the primary international trading currency. "This strategy," according to Oye, "was predicated on the assumption that domestic Reaganomics would increase savings and investment, boost American productivity, and stimulate noninflationary growth. Greater American competitiveness would negate the need for governmental defense of American commercial interests, and noninflationary growth would eliminate many of the international financial and monetary problems that seemed to require multilateral management during the stagflationary 1970s. This laissez-faire economic strategy departed sharply from the managerial policies of the Nixon, Ford, and Carter administrations."[6]

Initially, Reagan and his advisers were more opposed to international economic institutions than to domestic ones. They wanted international economic markets to handle the problems of coordination rather than international policy management. They were particularly skeptical about monetary authorities intervening in foreign exchange markets to reverse market trends. Reagan's Council of Economic Advisers (CEA), in its first annual report, argued that there was no hard evidence that such interventions had achieved their goals and some indications that they were counterproductive. The new president's CEA criticized the Carter administration for intervening in currency markets and proudly announced that the Reagan administration had scaled back these activities. Reagan's CEA proclaimed, "In conjunction with a strong emphasis on economic fundamentals, this Administration has returned to the policy of intervening only when necessary to counter conditions of severe disorder in the market."[7]

REAGAN'S FOREIGN ECONOMIC POLICY

1981–1985

If the Reagan administration had adhered to its free-trade credo, there would be little story to tell. As it was, although the president often repeated his commitment to such an economic strategy, in practice, this was not a field in which Reagan was personally involved; rather, trade was largely relegated to the secretaries of treasury and commerce and the U.S. trade representative (USTR). The lack of presidential participation meant that officials such as Secretary of Treasury James Baker (1985–1988) and Trade Representatives William Brock (1981–1985) and Clayton Yeutter (1985–1989) had a fair amount of autonomy in formulating the administration's foreign economic policy.[8]

The Reagan administration violated its commitment to free trade within its first few months in office by providing protection for the U.S. auto industry from Japanese imports. Gasoline prices had doubled in 1979, causing a shift in demand toward small, high-mileage cars, a change for which Detroit was unprepared. Japanese imports largely filled this demand, leaving Ford and General Motors to suffer record losses; Chrysler required a federal bailout to avoid bankruptcy. With 300,000 of the 1 million autoworkers unemployed in 1980, candidate Reagan promised Detroit that his administration would help the U.S. auto industry by getting the Japanese to restrict their exports.[9] That year, cars imported from Japan totaled 1.9 million, constituting over one-fifth of the U.S. market. In December 1980, the U.S. auto industry's petition for escape-clause relief (such as the raising of a tariff to help domestic industries suffering serious injury from unfair foreign competition) was rejected by the International Trade Commission (ITC), causing the automakers to turn to Congress for relief. In early 1981, Senator John Danforth, the new Trade Committee chairman in the Republican-controlled Senate, introduced an auto import quota bill that would restrict Japanese imports to 1.6 million units per year through 1983.

The Reagan administration devoted a Cabinet meeting to the subject on March 3, 1981, and immediately found itself split on the issue. Transportation Secretary Drew Lewis argued that the administration had to honor Reagan's campaign promise to limit Japanese auto imports. Lewis was supported by Commerce Secretary Malcolm Baldridge, Labor Secretary Raymond Donovan, and William Brock. Brock employed the classic metaphor for justifying compromise by suggesting, "There are times when you have to take some steps backward in order to go forward." Murray Weidenbaum, the chairman of the CEA, was opposed, believing that providing protection for the auto industry would violate the administration's free-trade principles, set a bad precedent that would encourage demands by other industries for protection, and hinder the administration's anti-inflation program.[10]

The official most opposed to providing such protection was David Stockman, the director of the Office of Management and Budget (OMB). For Stockman, free trade was a vital component of the free-enterprise system; he was disappointed that protectionist sentiments could be expressed so openly in an administration that was supposedly devoted to free markets. But Stockman was shocked when he heard Reagan say, "Yes, we believe in free trade, but there's something different here. Government regulation is responsible for this."[11] In his memoirs, Stockman explained, "The President was a strong free trader, but he was also a politician, and his political antennae could be tuned to the desired frequency. In this case, Lewis and the others had cooked up a theory that the auto industry had been so overregulated and crippled by air bags, pollution control devices, safety standards, and other government-imposed Ralph Naderite schemes that it was now up to the government to undo the damage. . . . The President was being convinced that the government *owed* it to Detroit to get back at Ralph Nader by attacking the Japanese."[12] This was a specious argument, because in order to sell their vehicles in the United States, Toyota, Honda, and Nissan were subject to the same regulations as General Motors, Ford, and Chrysler.

The administration escaped this dilemma with the aid of a subterfuge. Under the threat of congressional action, the Japanese were pressured to "voluntarily" restrict their auto imports. On May 1, with Brock in Tokyo, the Japanese government announced its decision to limit exports to 1.68 million vehicles for several years. Brock immediately promised the Japanese that they would no longer have to worry about Senator Danforth's bill. A bitter Stockman later wrote, "And so the essence of the Reagan Administration's trade policy became clear: Espouse free trade, but find an excuse on every occasion to embrace the opposite. As time passed, we would find occasions aplenty."[13] Stockman's ideological rigidity led him to write this exaggerated evaluation, but it does contain a kernel of truth. He had discovered that his president and his administration were less ideologically driven and more politically motivated than the OMB director had initially believed.

The Japanese extended this voluntary export restraint (VER) on cars throughout the decade and into the 1990s.[14] The annual limit of 1.68 million units lasted until 1985 and then was expanded to 2.3 million units per year. This agreement raised import prices and provided an opportunity for U.S. automakers to regain profitability. But it also created incentives for the Japanese to export more expensive cars to the United States (with higher profit margins) and to set up manufacturing plants here. Thus, according to Mike Mochizuki, "the Japanese share of the American auto market has not declined, staying in about the 20 to 22 percent range; and automobile trade with Japan accounted for more than one-third of America's bilateral trade deficit."[15]

For the next four years, Reagan's trade policy was difficult to character-ize. He continued to support the principle of free trade in his speeches and would sometimes back up that commitment with policy decisions. In July 1981, for example, Reagan terminated four years of protection begun when President Carter had decreed import quotas on shoes from Taiwan and South Korea. However, in late October 1982, during the congressional election campaign and in the midst of a recession, the president announced that Euro-pean steel producers had "voluntarily" agreed to restrict steel exports to the United States. This VER was obviously designed to take the steam out of steel quota legislation that was being considered in Congress. James Shock suggests that, "as 1982 came to an end, a pattern of strategic interaction be-tween the two parties had begun that would continue throughout the decade. Democratic attempts to exploit the trade issue regularly prodded the White House to take moderately tough trade actions, especially just before elections on key congressional votes, resulting in a racheting up of U.S. trade policy during the 1980s."[16]

Meanwhile, the Democratic Party and many of its presidential candidates were becoming far more associated with protectionism than was the Reagan presidency. The United Auto Workers (UAW) advocated legislation that would impose a "domestic content" requirement on cars sold in the United States, and this bill was passed twice by the Democrat-controlled House of Representatives—in December 1982 and in November 1983. However, this protectionist legislation was never able to reach the floor of the Republican-controlled Senate. Democratic presidential hopefuls Ted Kennedy, Walter Mondale, Alan Cranston, John Glenn, and Ernest Hollings supported the domestic content bill and were positioning themselves to exploit the trade issue in the 1984 election. When the economy was suffering from the reces-sion of 1981–1982, some Democratic leaders and policy intellectuals (Lester Thurow, Robert Reich, and Felix Rohatyn) argued that a politically potent response to the growing trade deficit and to the country's apparent compet-itive decline was "industrial policy." In early 1983, Senator Kennedy stressed that, "historically, the unifying issue for the Democratic Party has been the economic issue. We need the restoration of our economy. The basis of that restoration is the development of an industrial policy."[17]

But there was intellectual resistance to industrial policy because of expec-tations that politicians would not have the wisdom to pick winners, and the policy would inevitably degenerate into quixotic and futile attempts to protect declining industries (losers). The catastrophic consequences of the 1930 Smoot-Hawley tariff had tainted protectionism for policy elites. In January 1983, David Broder wrote, "It is part of Reagan's insistence, in both public speeches and private meetings, that government policy must assist—and not resist—the great transition of the American manufacturing base from heavy industry to high technology. And it comes at a time when the Democratic Party and most of its leading presidential hopefuls are lashing themselves ever more tightly to the very protectionist measures Reagan has rejected. Here we have the makings of a great political-economic debate—and one in which Reagan is clearly on the side of change. However resistant he may be on other fronts, here he is clearly on the offensive, moving with history and not against it."[18] Hence, this attempt to use industrial policy as a big idea to unify the Democrats against Reagan's perceived strategy of relying on free trade quickly petered out as the economy, in 1983 and 1984, recovered strongly from the recession of the two previous years.

For the next few years, according to I. M. Destler, Reagan continued to extol the virtues of free trade in principle, but he was concerned with "protecting his political flanks in practice."[19] In 1983, the president increased export subsidies (against the advice of Stockman) and restricted motorcycle, specialty steel, and Chinese textile imports. On June 12, 1984, the ITC unexpectedly ruled that five categories of steel imports were damaging the domestic industry. In July, the ITC submitted recommendations for quotas and tariffs to protect the steel industry. By law, the president was bound to respond to this advice by mid-September—just two months before the election. Reagan's political advisers did not have to be reminded that the nine major steel-producing states had 225 electoral college votes. On September 18, Reagan announced voluntary restraint agreements (VRAs) with the European Community, Japan, Canada, Argentina, Mexico, Brazil, and South Africa designed to limit steel imports to about 20 percent of U.S. production. Shock writes, "In opting for V.R.A.s rather than more restrictive tariffs, Reagan achieved something of a political miracle. . . . He managed to at least partially appease steel state interests while simultaneously allowing himself to defend his credentials as a free trader, cooling foreign tempers and allaying fears among farmers and steel users."[20] This adroit maneuver helped to defuse the trade issue in the 1984 presidential election.

Reagan was also fairly successful in dealing with a trade bill that was winding its way through Congress in 1984. With the trade deficit projected to exceed $100 billion in 1984, free traders were definitely on the defensive. The Reagan administration was most concerned with renewing the Generalized

System of Preferences (GSP), which provided trade preferences for developing countries. This provision had been part of the Trade Act of 1974 and was scheduled to end on January 3, 1985. Labor was opposed to the GSP, but its extension was important to the administration for the purpose of bargaining with Third World countries in order to gain intellectual property protection and access to their markets.[21]

By early October 1984, the House and Senate had each passed protectionist bills, and a conference committee was created to reconcile the differences. Both bills called for the administration to negotiate a free-trade agreement with Israel, so there was no difficulty in including that provision in the final compromise. Operating under the time constraint of the end of the session and under threats of a Reagan veto if the bill was too protectionist, the conferees quickly reached agreement on other provisions to be included in the final bill, and the Trade and Tariff Act of 1984 was passed by both houses on October 9. Destler writes, "It had proved possible for Congress to pass a general trade bill that extended an unpopular program (GSP), while omitting or gutting most protectionist provisions. Language designed to benefit copper, ferroalloys, shoes, and dairy products was deleted or neutralized. On preferences, in fact, the bill represented a move in the liberal-internationalist direction . . . by encouraging the administration to negotiate with the NICs [newly industrializing countries] for market access and intellectual property rights, and offered the NICs inducements as well as penalties."[22] However, the legislation also reflected a bipartisan compromise pressuring the administration to reduce steel imports below 20 percent of the U.S. market within a reasonable period of time. Protectionist pressures were obviously growing.

Another foreign economic issue emerged in 1982 that would challenge the Reagan administration and its successor, the Bush presidency, throughout the decade and into the 1990s. In August 1982, it became clear that Mexico could no longer service its skyrocketing foreign debt. By the end of the year, virtually every Latin American nation had interrupted the paying of its foreign debt and was seeking new and more lenient terms for meeting its loan obligations. Between 1960 and 1980, as measured by constant 1980 U.S. dollars, the region's external debt increased from about $18 billion to over $150 billion. Since the 1973 and 1979 oil crises, the rate of increase in external debt had accelerated, with a growing proportion of the debt owed to private U.S. banks. These banks were flush with petrodollars from oil-rich Middle Eastern countries and were thus eager to make development loans to Latin American governments. The sudden crisis in 1982 was caused by several factors, including an anti-inflation rise in interest rates in the United States and Western

Europe, an economic recession in the United States, and a sluggish international economy that stifled Latin American export growth. By September 1982, Mexico had the largest external debt in the Third World, owing in U.S. dollars about $80 billion, of which $56 billion was obligated to private foreign banks. By early 1983, Brazil's external debt was about $90 billion. By the end of 1983, Latin American nations had accumulated over $300 billion in foreign debts, half the total of all foreign debts owed by Third World nations.[23] As chairman of the Federal Reserve in 1982, Paul Volcker was concerned about a potential Latin American default on debt obligations to U.S. banks, because "for the nine US money center banks, loans to Mexico alone averaged about 45 percent of their capital. Loans to all of Latin America averaged close to twice their capital."[24]

The Latin American debt crisis held the potential for a number of catastrophes. Demagogues such as Cuba's Fidel Castro were calling for the creation of a debtors' cartel, a move that would threaten the financial stability of Western banking. In attempting to meet their debt obligations, many governments faced the prospect of collapse and of being replaced by left-wing leaders who would repudiate their countries' IOUs. In addition, the collapse of the Mexican political system would have created enormous immigration problems for the United States. As it turned out, although millions of Latin Americans suffered terribly during the "lost decade" of the 1980s, none of these possible calamities occurred.

Such potential disasters were avoided by the skill and cooperation of Volcker, the International Monetary Fund (IMF), the commercial banks, Latin American leaders, and several members of the Reagan administration (luck also may have played a major role). Volcker singles out Jacques Larosiere, the director of the IMF, for preventing this crisis from causing a panic. In Volcker's words, "Larosiere's role between the debtor countries and the banks resembled . . . that of a bankruptcy judge on a grand international scale. But it was an area in which there was no settled law practice, so he had to work out new rules as he went along. He did so with great skill and persistence."[25] In dealing with the Mexican situation, Larosiere was largely responsible for creating the standard procedures that administered the debt crisis. "He insisted," according to Volcker, "that no Fund program or loan for Mexico would be approved without the commercial banks first committing to a 'critical mass' of the needed bank financing, which was set at 90 percent of the total loans that commercial banks would be expected to produce ($5 billion in that first Mexican program). The effect was to force a high degree of solidarity among the lending banks. They launched lengthy negotiations over how the new loans should be fairly shared among themselves and the negotiations among them often seemed as difficult as the ones they had with the Mexicans."[26]

To qualify for new loans, debtor nations were required to sign agreements that they would devalue their currencies, earn surplus dollars by decreasing imports and increasing exports, balance their budgets, and jettison money losing public corporations by privatizing. The IMF claimed that this package of steps would stabilize these nations' economies (by taming inflation), but many Latin Americans feared that this market-oriented strategy would destabilize their political systems by bringing about recessions. The IMF package, eventually agreed to by most Latin American countries, did cause recessions, but not political instability. For the United States, however, this IMF policy brought about a reduction in exports and an increase in imports from Latin America, a region where we had traditionally enjoyed a trade surplus. The debt crisis forced many Latin American countries to expand their exports to the United States in order to earn the dollars necessary to service their debt. Growing Latin American exports significantly contributed to our soaring trade deficit.

Volcker was initially worried that the Reagan presidency would not comprehend the steps that would have to be taken to avert a meltdown of the banking system. He feared that ideologues within the administration would view this crisis as a dispute between Latin American debtors and private creditors and would advocate that the U.S. government avoid becoming a participant. The most conservative ideologues might also object to the growing role of the IMF in handling the debt problem, which meant increasing the financial resources of that disliked institution. Volcker submitted a memorandum to the president explaining the problem and stressing that Mexico's debt difficulties would inevitably be followed by others. James Baker, the chief of staff, called for a policy meeting on this subject. According to Volcker, "There really was not much discussion; the case for helping to coordinate rescue efforts seemed clear enough on foreign policy and economic grounds as well as financial ones."[27]

Thus, the Reagan administration was not blocked by its ideological beliefs in responding to the debt crisis. Emergency loans were quickly provided for Mexico and Brazil. Reagan conveniently forgot his previous criticisms of the IMF and successfully implored Congress to expand U.S. contributions to that institution at a time of increasing concern about the budget deficit. Hence, C. Fred Bergsten could write in 1985, "When Mexican debt difficulties threatened the world financial system in mid-1982, the administration promptly abandoned laissez faire policies and put together a short-run rescue package. It subsequently provided similar assistance to several other key debtors. . . . The administration thereby showed its pragmatic ability to switch policies when the need is urgent."[28] This pragmatic approach helped prevent the Latin American debt from becoming a dire problem during Reagan's first term. But the debt burden continued to fester and would require more initiatives in the second term.

After recovering from the 1981–1982 recession and winning the 1984 presidential election by a landslide, Reagan felt very confident starting his second term. But several officials, including Martin Feldstein (chairman of the CEA, who replaced Murray Weidenbaum in 1982), Stockman, and Volcker, were sounding alarms that the overvalued dollar was causing a negative trade balance that would eventually stifle the economic recovery. The ever-optimistic Reagan was prone to say that "a strong dollar means a strong America," but sanguinity was blinding the president from seeing that the overvalued dollar was crippling many American manufacturers by pricing their products out of foreign markets and even the domestic market. In December 1984, Nicholas Kristof wrote:

> The ballooning trade deficit is an example of how economic policy making has become more difficult in a world of floating exchange rates and highly mobile capital. . . . American budget deficits force the Government to borrow funds, and so the greater demand in the credit markets drive interest rates up. Attracted by these rising interest rates, foreign investors change their holdings into dollars and deposit them in the United States. This, in turn, increases the demand for dollars, and pushes up the dollar against other currencies. That makes foreign goods cheaper when paid for in dollars, and imports flood into the country.[29]

Volcker was pleased to see *some* increase in the value of the dollar, because that contributed to restraining inflation by keeping import prices low. But by early 1985, the dollar had appreciated against the German mark by about 45 percent above 1980 levels. This rapid growth, according to Volcker, "had gone from something constructive to a potential catastrophe. The competitive position of our industry was being undermined in a way that might do lasting damage. Sooner or later, I thought, there would all too likely be a sickening fall in the dollar, undermining confidence, as had happened so often in the 1970s. Yet there was an administration that simply didn't seem to care. . . . the strength of the dollar came to be cited by some officials [in Reagan's Treasury Department] as a kind of Good Housekeeping Seal of Approval provided by the market, honoring sound Reagan economic policies."[30]

Many of Reagan's economic advisers saw the country rejoicing in its largest surge in consumer demand since the Korean War and simply refused to accept that this phenomenon was unsustainable. In 1983 and 1984, the United States was recovering faster from the global recession than any other industrialized country and was therefore generating a very strong import demand. Garten points out that "in 1983, increased U.S. imports accounted for one-half of the net growth in world trade, and in 1984, imports were running at a 25 percent higher rate. The United States was by far the principal market for other nations' new export sales."[31] But by 1985, it was becoming obvious that the U.S. economy could no longer play the role of a locomotive pulling other Western economies into a more vigorous recovery.

The U.S. trade deficit rose from about $28 billion in 1981 to a record deficit of $148.5 billion in 1985. During that same period, the U.S. trade deficit with Japan climbed from $16 billion to $49.7 billion. In response to these figures, an increasingly hostile Congress proposed over 300 pieces of trade-restricting legislation. This growing chorus of congressional Japan-bashing was actually aimed at Reagan and was designed to shake the president from his complacency about the overvalued dollar.[32]

At the same time, an uneasy Congress was becoming increasingly aware that the United States was shifting from a creditor to a debtor nation, a status we had not held since 1914. Toyoo Gyohten, a former official in Japan's Ministry of Finance, explains that, "until 1980, . . . the savings of Americans were enough to finance their government's overspending, and it was not necessary to borrow from foreigners to finance the budget deficit. But after 1980, the balance between savings and investment of the private sector deteriorated, and the federal deficit increased further. The combination of these developments contributed to a higher interest, a stronger dollar, and a large external deficit. The deficit turned the United States from a creditor in 1981 with net assets abroad of $141 billion to a debtor with net liabilities in 1985 of $111 billion, a swing of $250 billion in just four years."[33] There was no prestige in replacing Mexico and Brazil as the world's largest debtor nation. As a debtor, we could consume more than we produced for only a short time; eventually we would have to live on less than what we produced in order to repay our foreign debts.

The root cause of this turn of events was that Reagan's supply-side tax cut in 1981 was supposed to increase domestic savings, but it did not. The problem was exacerbated by the $200 billion budget deficits in the mid-1980s, which were absorbing nearly three-fourths of our private savings.[34] We inevitably became more dependent on foreign savings drawn to the United States by favorable interest rates, which in the mid-1980s averaged 2 percent above those in Europe and Japan. In Volcker's words, "As time passed, the shortage of domestic savings was compensated in substantial part by an enormous inflow of mainly borrowed capital from abroad. That inflow was at one point running at a greater rate than all the personal saving in the United States and turned out to be far larger than I had thought possible. I remember . . . chiding the Fed staff for making a presentation sometime around 1983 that suggested that capital inflow might need to reach and even exceed $75 billion a year in order to cover a growing account deficit. . . . In fact, in the peak year of 1985, the recorded net capital inflow was $103 billion."[35]

In short, although it appeared as though there was an equilibrium between the United States as the world's largest debtor and Japan as the largest creditor, in reality, this relationship was unsustainable because it was causing too much economic damage to the United States. The disequilibrium in the global economy had to be corrected. The political challenge was to make this correction in as orderly a manner as possible.

1985–1989

At the beginning of Reagan's second term, James Baker and Donald Regan switched jobs. Baker announced that he was "ecstatic" about leaving the White House chief of staff position to become secretary of treasury. He brought along his former White House assistant, Richard Darman, who became deputy secretary of treasury. Darman assumed the international tasks that had previously been handled by Beryl Sprinkel, who was now chairman of the CEA. Paul Volcker was pleased to see Sprinkel removed from the Treasury Department, because he considered Sprinkel to be a rigid monetarist who was opposed to most forms of international coordination. According to Volcker, "we now had a pragmatic political team in the Treasury. From the start, it was obvious that Baker and Darman were more concerned about the dollar than their predecessors had been. . . . they were old Washington hands, with finely honed political antennae and instincts. And among the things worrying them at the time was the degree of protectionist pressure in Congress and in the United States generally. They didn't need to be Ph.D. economists to relate that pressure to the strength of the dollar, which in their new positions they actually might be able to do something about."[36] Volcker was sure that Baker and Darman, being activists, would attempt to make their mark on the world stage. He was right.

Baker and Volcker established closer contacts than had existed between the Federal Reserve and Treasury Secretary Regan by instituting a private breakfast every Thursday at 7:30 A.M., alternately at the Federal Reserve and the Treasury. Senior officials of the Treasury and the Federal Reserve, usually excluding Baker and Volcker, met every Wednesday for lunch. Baker also had a weekly breakfast meeting with Secretary of State George Shultz, Commerce Secretary Baldridge, and Sprinkel.

Upon assuming office, Baker's top priority was to pass the tax reform legislation that was introduced in the spring of 1985. Finally passed in 1986, this bill was designed to cut tax rates and simplify the tax code by eliminating many loopholes, but it probably would *not* stimulate the economy (which had begun to sag at the end of 1984), because Reagan had conceived it to be "revenue neutral"—that is, to raise approximately the same amount of revenue as had the tax system it replaced.

In 1985, several of Reagan's economic advisers were worried that the economic growth the nation had enjoyed since 1982, which had been fueled by the 1981 supply-side tax cut (implemented over a three-year period), the rise in consumer spending, and the military buildup, was now losing momentum. Whereas the GNP had expanded by over 6 percent in 1984, it had grown at a sluggish annual rate of only 1 percent during the first six months of 1985. A new stimulus for the economy was needed, and Baker believed that expanding exports was the best feasible choice.

But to augment exports, the value of the dollar would have to be decreased. Between October 1979 and February 1985, export growth had been stifled because the value of the dollar had risen by over 80 percent against a package of eleven major currencies.[37] On February 25, 1985, the dollar peaked against the Japanese yen at 263.65 yen to the dollar. The overvalued dollar was contributing to the trade deficit, and the trade deficit was retarding economic growth.

Yet even if it were decided that reducing the value of the dollar was the best answer to economic stagnation, such a course was clouded by uncertainty. Few economists were sure how the dollar might behave once it started to decline in value—especially if it was pushed in that direction by a policy decision. If panic set in, a falling dollar might become a collapsing dollar, which would mean higher inflation in the United States. The uneasiness about what to do was captured by Peter Kilborn, writing in March 1985: "Little in the behavior of the dollar of the 1980s . . . has much precedent in history. In rising more than 70 percent since the middle of 1980, the dollar has climbed far beyond the boundaries of normal currency behavior, defying one nugget of conventional wisdom after another."[38] Currencies are expected to decline when the trade of the economies behind them descends into deficit, but the United States had experienced two consecutive years of record trade deficits, and still the dollar rose. Currencies are expected to decline when the economies behind them are more inflationary than those of their trading partners, but even though the U.S. inflationary rate was higher than Japan's, the dollar kept rising against the yen. In brief, these were uncharted waters.

This uncertainty was reflected in the Federal Reserve Board's decision making. Normally, domestic considerations determined the Federal Reserve's monetary decisions, but it cited the continued strength of the dollar as a justification for lowering the discount rate in November and December 1984. In this new era of interdependence, the Federal Reserve Board had to factor in the effects of its decisions on foreign exchange rates and the ability of the Third World to meet its debt obligations. Volcker was particularly anxious about the ability of international policy makers to bring about a "soft landing" for the dollar because of the size and volatility of foreign exchange markets. Since navigating such a soft landing for a highly overvalued currency was historically unprecedented, some questioned whether it could be done. In July 1985, Volcker warned Congress that if the dollar fell too quickly, it would reignite the fires of inflation. The challenge facing economic policy makers in the summer of 1985 was how to respond to the nation's trade deficit without causing more serious problems for the domestic economy. The policy context was described by Leonard Silk: "Clearly the Fed is walking a tightrope between keeping the economy moving ahead—important not only for domestic reasons but to keep the world economy, and especially the Third World debtor countries, recovering—and not increasing the money supply so fast as to raise inflationary expectations, push up interest rates, aggravate the trade deficit and intensify protectionist pressures."[39] Embarking on such a course would require skillful navigation indeed.

In 1985, Democratic congressmen believed that Reagan was politically vulnerable on the trade issue. They echoed Bergsten's accusation that "the Achilles heel of Reaganomics has turned out to be this failure to take into account the international repercussions of domestic policies."[40] Many Democrats and some Republicans believed that an out-of-touch Reagan was refusing to face the reality that the overvalued dollar was causing major problems for the country. When the Japanese Ministry of Trade and Industry announced in March 1985 that Japan would continue voluntary auto restraints, but at a level 25 percent higher than in 1984, Congress exploded. Both the Senate and the House passed resolutions by overwhelming majorities (92 to 0 in the Senate and 394 to 19 in the House) calling for retaliation against Japan unless Tokyo seriously reduced its trade imbalances with the United States. In April 1985, Clyde Farnsworth, the international trade correspondent for the *New York Times,* wrote, "Tensions over world trade conditions rose last week to a level unmatched since the 1930s."[41] There was a danger that the administration would lose control over the trade deficit issue.

The trade issue, restimulated by the release of negative trade balance statistics each month, provided Democrats with the hope that they could recover from Reagan's forty-nine-state electoral landslide in 1984. Current trade deficit figures could be used to refute the president's assertions that his policies had provided a long-term recipe for economic growth and "standing tall" internationally. Reagan's policy mix was unsustainable because it ignored the fact that debtor nations can't stand tall; inevitably, they must bow to their creditors. In the summer of 1985, the Democrats won an election in east Texas largely because of the effect of the trade deficit on jobs. In September 1985, Democratic Congressman Richard Gephardt charged that Reagan's trade policies had turned "Uncle Sam into Uncle Sap."[42] In short, Democrats hoped that the trade issue would renew their credentials as protectors of jobs and defenders of the national interest.

Perhaps the best solution to reversing the rise of the dollar after 1984 would have been a deal with Congress to reduce the budget deficit by some combination of expenditure cuts and tax increases. But Reagan's campaign pledge not to raise taxes precluded that scenario. How to wiggle out of this box became a puzzle that intrigued Baker and Darman. The answer would turn out to be the Plaza Accord.

During the spring of 1985, Darman had been educated in international economics by C. Fred Bergsten, a former assistant secretary of the treasury under Carter. It had become clear to Darman and Baker that the overvalued dollar was causing the trade deficit and that something must be done to drive down its worth. They also understood that the Reagan administration could not accomplish this alone; the cooperation of both the Federal Reserve and our major allies would be required. Baker initiated secret negotiations with European and Japanese finance ministers, and in early August he outlined his plan to Volcker. The discussions with Volcker were delicate because, on the one hand, Baker's strategy required the support of the Federal Reserve, and on the other hand, as an independent regulatory agency, the Federal Reserve was sensitive about its political autonomy. Because Baker understood that his objective of bringing about a decline in the dollar could be undercut if the Federal Reserve raised interest rates, he wanted assurances that this would not happen. Volcker could not provide such guarantees for the long term, but he explained that, with the economy slowing down and inflation under control, there would be no need to tighten monetary policy over the next few months.

Baker probably recognized that this response was the most he could get from Volcker, and it was sufficient to proceed with international negotiations. Volcker later explained his feelings by writing, "Getting the dollar down from its extreme heights in 1985 made sense, but I didn't want to end up with so abrupt and disturbing a decline that worries about inflation would reappear, followed by higher interest rates. . . . After considerable discussion, we . . . agreed that we ought to aim at a decline of 10 or 12 percent over a period of time, and then the whole thing could be reconsidered."[43]

Baker had to keep his plan to drive down the value of the dollar secret, because if currency speculators found out about it, they could wreck his strategy. But the need for secrecy also helped Baker circumvent the usual decision-making procedures of the administration, where his proposal to intervene in international currency markets would inevitably arouse intense opposition from market-oriented officials such as Beryl Sprinkel and provoke heated debates in front of Reagan. As a skilled and cautious operator, Baker undoubtedly cleared his proposal with the president, but one wonders whether Reagan, with his usual lack of interest in asking for more information, understood how much Baker's proposal reversed previous policy.

Yoichi Funabashi explains that "President Reagan might have changed the course of United States economic policy-making had he chosen to become more involved. Instead, when Baker informed him of the Plaza plan only a few days before the Plaza meeting, the President 'supported it and had no problems with it,' recalled a Reagan administration official. Thereafter his involvement was minimal."[44]

On Sunday, September 22, 1985, Baker secretly met with Paul Volcker and the finance ministers and central bankers of Japan, West Germany, Great Britain, and France (known as the G5 countries) at the Plaza Hotel in New York. That same day, they publicly announced an international agreement (the Plaza Accord) to intervene in foreign markets to depress the dollar and elevate the value of other currencies. In other words, the G5 ministers promised that their central banks would sell dollars and buy the currencies of other countries. Unnamed Treasury officials explained to the press that the administration was still philosophically committed to having markets, rather than governments, determine exchange rates, but that this agreement was a necessary exception to usual policy. According to anonymous Treasury spokesmen, the fact that markets were not reacting properly to correct the enormous U.S. trade deficit and the large Japanese trade surplus necessitated this concerted international action.[45] Years later, Volcker was more blunt: "The whole episode represented the most aggressive and persistent effort to guide exchange rates on both a transatlantic and transpacific scale since floating had begun more than a decade earlier."[46] It is important to note, however, that the Plaza Accord was designed to work *with* market trends, not against them. The dollar was already declining against the yen after hitting its peak in February 1985.

For Baker, the Plaza Accord reflected a short-term strategy to block protectionist legislation in Congress, a medium-term strategy to maintain global economic growth by stimulating demand in Japan and West Germany, and a long-term strategy to lessen the burden of Third World debt service (in depreciated dollars).[47] The Plaza Accord also demonstrated Baker's political style and motivation. He wanted to stage a media event to publicize that the G5 could work together and reach mutually beneficial agreements. Business confidence was now dependent on international cooperation. Baker's new style drew this comment from Nigel Lawson, the British chancellor of the exchequer:

> By the standards of the G5, which normally met in secret and had never issued a communique at all until the January meeting in Washington, the publicity that came after the Plaza agreement was astonishing. Although I recognized the immense pressure the Reagan Administration was under from the protectionist lobby in the Congress, I had not realized the extent to which Jim Baker had envisaged the Plaza agreement as a great domestic political event in the United States. At the conclusion of the meeting all the . . . media were summoned to a hastily convened televised press conference. . . . In order to impress Congress that there was an alternative to protectionism as a way of solving the world's and especially America's problems, the hitherto secret society of the G5 went public in a big way.[48]

Since most currency experts believe that it takes eighteen to twenty-four months before the results of significant changes in exchange rates can be charted, the Plaza Accord bought time for the administration with Congress. Protectionist pressures noticeably subsided in Washington as legislators waited to measure the effects of the reduced dollar. As it turned out, the results of the accord were decidedly mixed.

The dollar's decline began immediately. On the day after the Plaza Accord was announced, "the dollar fell 4.29 percent, the largest single-day's drop ever recorded."[49] What happened later was explained by Volcker: "There was some heavy intervention in the ensuing weeks to make sure the trend continued, and by the end of October, after more than $3 billion of intervention by the United States alone, the dollar had fallen by more than 12 percent against the yen and close to 9 percent against European currencies. Then the dollar continued to decline without much additional intervention, and by January 1986 it stood on average a full 25 percent below the peak it had hit about one year before."[50] A dollar that could buy 240 yen in September 1985 could buy only 171 yen at the end of May 1986.

On September 23, 1985, the day after the Plaza Accord was announced, President Reagan delivered a major speech to 200 businessmen at the White House. Bentley Elliott, the conservative head of the president's speechwriters, wrote the original draft of this speech, but it was rejected by Chief of Staff Donald Regan. Elliott's draft was a ringing defense of free-trade principles that Regan and his political advisers believed would only antagonize a Congress concerned about the rising trade deficit. Regan's objective was to "derail" the train of protectionist legislation in Congress. He directed Alfred Kingon, the White House Cabinet secretary, to rewrite the speech, and the result was a vintage Reagan oration that blended ideological conviction and pragmatic compromise. The president began by stating, "I, like you, recognize the inescapable conclusion that all of history has taught: The freer the flow of world trade, the stronger the tides for human progress and peace among nations. I certainly don't have to explain the benefits of free and open markets to you. They produce more jobs, a more productive use of our nation's resources, more rapid innovation, and a higher standard of living. They strengthen our national security because our economy . . . is stronger."[51]

But after touching this ideological base, Reagan went on to suggest that the United States could not single-handedly bring about a free trading system; it needed the help of its allies. He stressed that free trade is fair trade and listed a number of unfair practices of our trading partners (with specific references to Japan, the European Community, South Korea, and Brazil). Reagan pledged that he would fight against discriminatory trading practices abroad that caused domestic businesses to fail and workers to lose their jobs. The president outlined a new action plan that called for the USTR to initiate unfair trade practice investigations, the creation of a $300 million war chest to support up to $1 billion in loans to aid businesses harmed by unwarranted foreign trade procedures, and the creation of a strike force (composed of officials from State, Commerce, and the USTR) charged with uncovering unreasonable trading practices. Shock writes, "the White House was . . . resorting to an old tactic—'export politics'—in order to defuse protectionist pressures. But rather than isolating protectionist firms by harnessing exporters in support of multilateral negotiations to lower global trade barriers, as in years past, the White House this time was forced to try to split newly-aroused exporters off from companies seeking outright protection by supporting 'fair trade' and 'reciprocity' policies."[52]

After dealing with the dollar in the Plaza Accord and trade policy in Reagan's fair-trade speech, the administration shifted its attention to the Third World debt problem at the IMF meeting in Seoul on October 6, 1985. As explained earlier, the IMF and the Reagan administration had been successful in containing the debt crisis that had erupted in August 1982. But by 1985, conditions were deteriorating, and a new policy, one that would generate hope for a better future in Latin America, was clearly needed. Many Latin American countries were suffering from falling prices on their commodity exports and negative growth rates. In attempting to service their debts, these nations were exporting more capital than they were attracting. For example, from 1980 to 1987, Brazil paid out $50 billion more in debt payments than it received in new loans.[53] Latin American politicians were complaining that they could not continue to meet their debt obligations when their own populations were suffering from declining standards of living.

Baker's response to this dilemma was to recommend that fifteen debtor nations be supported with $29 billion in new loans from the World Bank, the Inter-American Development Bank, and private commercial banks, on the condition that these countries employ market-oriented development policies. The Baker Plan was intended to pressure bankers into lending enough new capital to debtor nations so that they could make the interest payments on their old debt and also have a surplus to finance economic growth. Publicly, the Baker proposal was based on the idea that these nations could grow out of their debt problems; realistically, the plan was designed to give banks and Latin American governments more time to manage this burden. For the banks, according to Howard Wiarda, this meant "continuously rolling over the debt, foregoing fees, lowering interest charges, ignoring due dates, making new loans available, and even forgiving some debts." For Latin American governments, managing the crisis meant "some belt-tightening, some compliance with I.M.F.-imposed austerity, continuous promises to repay the loans, and constant renegotiations over debt restructuring."[54] The Baker Plan did not solve the debt problem, but it did keep it under control.

Despite the Plaza Accord, the trade problem worsened in 1986. Baker's Plaza strategy was successful in contributing to the decline of the dollar and increasing U.S. exports, but not in reducing the U.S. trade deficit. The rising yen had two unanticipated consequences. First, it pressured Japanese industries to become more efficient and to lower profit margins in order to maintain market shares in the United States. Second, the increasing value of the yen allowed investors to buy American real estate and financial assets. These consequences fueled the exaggerated fear in the latter part of the 1980s that the United States could no longer compete against the Japanese and was declining economically. One liberal wrote, "whatever the defense buildup has done to restore America's stature in the world, the nation is not standing tall among its trading partners. The United States may be winning the arms race but losing the economic marathon."[55]

Baker and Darman wanted to build on the Plaza process of political bargaining among finance ministers and central bank officials to bring about greater economic cooperation. Their goal was to expand beyond cooperating on exchange rates to coordinating monetary and fiscal policy among the G7 countries (Canada and Italy had joined the group since the Plaza Accord). Under this new system, the leading industrial countries would also negotiate and set mutually agreed upon target indicators, such as economic growth, employment, inflation, interest rates, budget deficits, and trade balances. In March 1986, Peter Kilborn wrote, "The plan the Administration is developing is founded on the view that countries, while politically independent, are nevertheless economically interdependent. They have become more and more so with the growth of world trade, and a thriving world economy is better for all countries . . . than one in which some countries prosper while others struggle."[56] Within the administration, Baker was able to gain the support of George Shultz and Donald Regan for his proposal.

The United States and its economic allies agreed that each member would be better off in a steadily expanding global economy, but they disagreed about what each should do to achieve that goal. The Japanese and the Europeans (especially the Germans) believed that the problems of trade imbalances were caused mainly by the Reagan administration's budget deficits. They felt that the United States had failed to deliver on its (implicit) part of the Plaza agreement—namely, to decrease the budget deficit while the Japanese and Europeans accepted the decline of the dollar. One observer explained, "The German diagnosis of external imbalances and currency misalignment boiled down to the mistakes of U.S. macroeconomic policy and the trade problem between the United States and Japan. . . . From [the German] point of view, the potential for inflation caused by a cheaper deutsche mark necessitated modest currency realignment, but they rejected out of hand the notion that coordination of macroeconomic policies beyond that extent was required."[57] Baker urged the Japanese and Germans to cut both their taxes and their interest rates in order to stimulate domestic demand, which he believed would then spur global growth. Nigel Lawson later wrote, "This dance [among the Germans, Japanese, and Americans] was more like a scherzo than a stately minuet; it was to be repeated many times with small variations for the next six years."[58]

Foreign officials were fearful that the United States, as a debtor nation, had more incentives to encourage the continuing depreciation rather than the stabilization of the dollar. They were suspicious that Baker's new system of expanded international cooperation would be exploited by Washington to coerce them into accepting policies to correct problems caused by U.S. budget deficits. As one Japanese official explained, "From the Japanese and German viewpoints, the whole process was frustrating because we thought that the United States was trying to gain political concessions from the surplus countries of Japan and Germany by using the threat of talking down the dollar and the threat of protectionism, knowing that both could really damage the economies of the surplus countries. . . . As a result the surplus countries were obsessed by a deep suspicion that in introducing policy coordination and exchange rate management, the United States was trying to impose upon them a system that would benefit only itself. Our response therefore was defensive and displayed a lack of willingness to contribute positively to the global economic benefit."[59] In brief, the representatives from Japan and Germany were wary that Baker was exploiting U.S. strengths and weaknesses to force them to bear the costs of Reaganomics.

At the Tokyo Summit, which met on May 4 and 5, 1986, major parts of Baker's proposal were nominally accepted by our economic allies. The new cooperative strategy called for the G7 finance ministers to meet regularly between the annual summits of the G7 heads of state. The Tokyo Declaration also called for the members to use a set of economic indicators to monitor the performance of the G7 nations. How Baker hoped that this system would operate is explained by Funabashi: "these indicators included GNP growth rates, inflation rates, interest rates, unemployment, fiscal deficit ratios, current account and trade balances, monetary growth rates, reserves, and currency rates. The indicators would exercise a disciplinary influence upon the seven finance ministers and central bank governors, in their conduct of 'multilateral surveillance,' and facilitate discussion of 'appropriate remedial measures' whenever the indicators showed a substantial deviation."[60] A harbinger of why this system did not work is revealed by the British chancellor of the exchequer:

The description "indicator" was chosen carefully after much haggling, to distinguish them from objectives. But even in the improved form in which they eventually emerged, they were essentially a device to put pressure on the Japanese and Europeans to take "expansionary measures" and in this way to take the heat off the falling dollar. There was never any agreement—or even proper discussion—of what to do if the various indicators pointed in different directions, or even any analyses of the relationships of the different indicators to each other. I found it impossible to take the exercise very seriously—and it certainly played no part, for all James Baker's combination of nagging and enthusiasm, in the subsequent course of world economic policy.[61]

The policy context changed in the beginning of 1987. The U.S. trade figures continued to worsen; also, the Democrats had gained control over the Senate, which meant that sentiments for protectionist legislation were likely to increase. In addition, foreigners understood that Reagan, weakened by the Iran-Contra scandal, would have difficulty blocking protectionist legislation from passing in the new 100th Congress. Baker's response was to increasingly pressure Japan and West Germany to stimulate their economies. The treasury secretary was now struggling with President Reagan over fiscal policy, with Volcker over interest rates, with Congress over protectionism, and with our allies over growth.

On February 21 and 22, 1987, Baker met with the finance and banking leaders of our allies at the Louvre in Paris. At this meeting, economic policy makers were attempting to establish what macroeconomic policies might be developed to correct trade imbalances, as well as the extent to which our allies could accommodate Baker's proposal to institutionalize procedures for coordinating economic policies among the members, and what position the participants should take on exchange rates.

As is true of most international conferences, the differences among the members were papered over in the final communiqué. The Louvre Accord acknowledged the necessity of altering the balance between savings and investments in both surplus and deficit countries, which meant an increase in public spending in Japan and a reduced budget deficit in the United States. The members also agreed on a new system of surveillance, which required each nation "to make a medium term projection, and economic indicators would be used to monitor whether it was on track. . . . If they showed a country's economy was heading off the track to the target, all agreed they would then discuss their individual situation with the rest of the G7."[62]

Finally, the representatives agreed to try "to maintain the [current] exchange rate within a 5 percent band—2.5 percent on either side. If the rate went beyond that, countries were expected to launch concerted market intervention, and if the market rate diverged by 5 percent in either direction, [the members] would consult on the possibility of changing the range. To defend the rates, the Seven pledged that a total of $12 billion would be made available until the next meeting in the spring."[63] The actual numbers of this part of the agreement were kept secret.

Whereas at the Plaza meeting the finance ministers and central bank governors had agreed that the dollar should decline, at the Louvre they agreed that there should be currency stability. Japanese representatives were under great domestic political pressure to make sure that the yen would not rise above 150 yen to the dollar. On Friday, February 20, 1987, the exchange rate was 153.50 yen to the dollar. The Louvre Accord was essentially Baker's offering to stabilize the dollar in return for our economic allies' agreeing to stimulate their economies.

The Louvre Accord was plagued by major problems. First, it contained an obvious contradiction by claiming in its communiqué that the current exchange rates were in line with economic fundamentals. "But at the same time," according to Gyohten, "the Seven recognized that their external payments were badly out of balance and conceded that this imbalance was unsustainable. But if a payments situation is unsustainable, the exchange rate cannot really be in line with economic fundamentals. The only way these mutually contradictory statements could be reconciled would be for each country to take the steps it promised, and this would bring its economic fundamentals in line with the existing exchange rate regime."[64] However, the fulfillment of such promises was not likely.

Second, the agreement required the members to consult if, for example, the dollar declined more than 5 percent against the deutsche mark, without specifically setting out what was to be done under such circumstances. Thus, when the dollar weakened against the deutsche mark, the Germans believed that the United States should raise its interest rates—a response Washington rejected because of fears of recession. Baker argued that the Germans should lower *their* interest rates—a response the Germans opposed because of their fears of inflation. Nigel Lawson later wrote, "The weakness of the Accord, which eventually undermined it, was its failure to bolster the pledge to intervene in the foreign exchange markets with an undertaking to adjust domestic monetary policies to validate the agreed ranges."[65]

By April 1987, the yen had risen to 138 to the dollar. Because of opposition by Japan and West Germany, the indicator system was not developed enough to connect exchange rate realignments to macroeconomic policy accommodations. Throughout most of 1987, the dollar continued to fall, and Baker continued to pressure the Germans and the Japanese to stimulate their economies. The treasury secretary became particularly piqued at the Germans, whom he claimed were not living up to their international agreements and responsibilities. When the dollar fell below its Louvre trading range against the deutsche mark early in October, Baker refused to advocate an increase in interest rates, fearing that it might cause the American economy to slide into a recession. The open squabbling demonstrated that the international cooperation that had characterized the Plaza and Louvre meetings was breaking down. On October 14, 1987, investors responded to a disappointing U.S. trade report, and the Dow-Jones industrial average dropped a record ninety-five points. The following Sunday, on *Meet the Press,* Baker repeated his complaints that German interest rates were too high and implied that if Germany did not stimulate its economy, the United States would allow the dollar to decline further. The next day, Black Monday, October 19, the Dow-Jones fell 508 points. Since the bull market was fifty-nine months old and most analysts believed that stocks were overvalued, the stock market was ripe for a correction or temporary reversal. Nevertheless, Baker was widely criticized for making inappropriate remarks that only added anxiety to already skittish markets. In Hobert Rowen's words, "To be sure, no single factor can ever explain a break of 508 points on the Dow Jones industrial index. The crash on Black Monday . . . also represented investors' reactions to the huge run-up in stock prices to the point where dividend yields on stocks were, on the average, only a fraction of the return on bonds—a sure sign that stocks would turn down. But Baker's words indicated that the major powers, who clearly would have to act together to stem a financial crisis, might be too far apart."[66]

Fearing a recession, the Reagan administration discarded the Louvre ranges and allowed the dollar to decline for a while after the stock market meltdown. No G7 meeting was called because of fears that if no agreement was reached, business confidence might be shattered again. Funabashi concludes, "The Louvre range agreement fell victim to the inaction both on fiscal and monetary coordination."[67]

On October 21, two days after the stock market crash, House and Senate conferees met for the first time to discuss the Omnibus Trade and Competitiveness Bill. This legislation had been introduced in January 1987 by the new Democratic Speaker Jim Wright; its title reflected a shift in the emphasis of the Democrats' attacks on Reaganomics, from "industrial policy" to competitiveness. The 1,000-page bill had made slow and painful progress through forty House and Senate subcommittees as both political parties, as well as the Reagan administration, attempted to influence its contents.

The Democrats believed that Reagan was vulnerable on the trade deficit; here was an issue—protecting jobs against unfair foreign trading practices—that could make them look patriotic and also help them regain the labor vote from the Republicans. What they sought was to reduce the president's discretion by dictating what he must do in response to unfair practices of our trading partners. Representative Richard Gephardt and Senator Joseph Biden were both seeking the Democratic nomination for president in 1988 by championing economic nationalism. Electorally sensitive Republican congressmen, after losing control of the Senate in 1986, felt that they had to support a more aggressive trade policy. The administration wanted to win authority to negotiate a new multilateral agreement in the Uruguay round of trade talks. Reagan's negotiators also demanded that the president maintain maximum flexibility in trade negotiations concerning how to retaliate against unfair foreign trading practices.

The effect of the Wall Street crash was to increase the incentive for compromise. With pundits commenting about the catastrophic consequences of the Smoot-Hawley Tariff of 1930, and with both parties fearful about the outcomes of their decisions on the economy, a more cooperative atmosphere for serious negotiations was created. The chances for success increased in March 1988 when Gephardt's campaign collapsed after defeats in the "Super Tuesday" primaries. In late April 1988, the conference committee completed its reconciliation efforts, which were passed by the House 312 to 107 and by the Senate 63 to 26. In May, Reagan vetoed the bill, citing a provision (supported by Senator Ted Kennedy) requiring businesses with over 100 employees to give sixty days' notice before plant closings and another section forbidding certain oil exports from Alaska. After Reagan's veto was sustained, the Democrats removed both sections, and the president signed the bill, on August 23, 1988. The Democrats then reintroduced the plant-closing provision as a separate bill, which was rapidly passed in the House and Senate and became law without Reagan's signature.[68]

The Omnibus Trade and Competitiveness Act of 1988 was the first legislatively initiated comprehensive trade bill since the Smoot-Hawley Act in 1930. The administration won its fast-track authority to negotiate the Uruguay round of trade negotiations. Democratic and Republican congressmen replaced the Gephardt amendment, which required the president to impose quotas on countries running large bilateral surpluses with the United States, with a section labeled "Super 301," which "spelled out procedures for identifying countries with unfair trade barriers, for negotiating an end to these barriers, and for United States retaliation when negotiations failed."[69] Super 301 was a skillfully crafted compromise, in that it allowed congressmen to vote *for* opening up external markets and *against* unfair foreign trade practices while providing the chief executive enough discretionary authority to permit Reagan to sign the bill.

The trade act also included creation of a $1 billion retraining program, with most of the money going to the states; measures to encourage broader recognition of U.S. patents, copyrights, and other property rights protections; and the creation of a Competitiveness Policy Council charged with analyzing the economic and social problems that affect the nation's ability to compete successfully in the global economy. Destler adds: "There were two important things the bill did not do: it did not impose statutory protectionism, and it did not impose direct congressional control over trade. Rather, it passed the policy ball back to the statutorily enhanced USTR with multiple provisions aimed at setting the USTR's agenda and stiffening its spine."[70] In brief, the Reagan administration had withstood the Democratic challenge on trade issues by making compromises and by adopting a more aggressive export-expanding policy.

Results

The results of Reagan's foreign economic policy can be briefly summarized. By 1989, the total Third World debt had ballooned to $1.3 trillion. The largest debtor was Brazil, which owed $110 billion, followed by Mexico with $107 billion; other major debtors were Argentina, $50 billion, and Venezuela, $33 billion. This debt burden caused hardships in most Latin American countries and probably reduced U.S. exports to the region to about half of what they might have been without the debt problem. But the key point is that none of the worst-case scenarios occurred. Instead, by opening up their markets, many Latin American governments were in a better position to promote economic growth at the end of the 1980s than they had been at the beginning. U.S. banks were pressured to make new loans, but most of this money was used by the debtors to service their previous debts. "From the point of view of the banks," according to Wiarda, "the process was decidedly successful, as debtors generally kept up interest payments, to the extent that they have almost all paid out more in interest than the original amounts of their loans."[71]

With the support of the Reagan administration, banks opposed any consideration of debt forgiveness, even though virtually everyone understood that there was no way they would ever be repaid in full. This reality was recognized in financial markets, where one could buy Third World debt at considerable discounts. But the banks were now better prepared to endure losses than they had been in 1982. Gyohten adds that there was also a clandestine transfer of risk from private to public lenders. Whereas in 1984 public lenders were responsible for 38 percent of all Third World debt and private lenders held 62 percent, by 1990 the proportions had shifted to fifty-fifty. In Gyohten's words, "The entire process of cooperation toward the common goal of working down the debt steadily without bankrupting a country or crippling the world financial system is bound to continue."[72]

As for the trade deficit, the Reagan administration believed that a decline in the dollar, by making American goods cheaper and imports more expensive, would bring about a rise in exports and a decrease in imports. From 1985 to 1990, the dollar's foreign exchange value fell by over 40 percent. In 1985, a dollar could buy 240 yen; in 1988, only 120 yen. This strategy worked for exports, as they expanded by over 20 percent a year from 1985 to 1990 and contributed to sustaining economic growth, but it did not work for imports. The U.S. trade deficit hit a record high of $159 billion in 1987 and then declined to $108 billion in 1990. The bilateral deficit with Japan also decreased—from $56 billion in 1987 to $41 billion in 1990.[73] In 1981, cars imported from Japan had 20 percent of the U.S. market; by 1990, Japanese imports and cars built in Japanese factories in the United States held about 30 percent of the domestic market.[74]

Many Americans blamed the unfair trading practices of our partners, especially the Japanese, for our chronic trade deficits. Rowen reports, "While 'Japan-bashing' may have been popular, it was counterproductive; it lulled the American public into thinking that if only the Japanese would behave themselves, our economy would magically revive. . . . As former USTR William Brock quipped: 'My nightmare is that Japan does everything I ask it to do, then I wake up, and our deficit stays the same.' But even Representative Richard Gephardt . . . admitted . . . that no more than 20 percent of the trade deficit with Japan could be attributed to their unfair trading practices."[75] Reaganomics never cured the fundamental source of our trade deficit, which is that we consume more than we produce.

Finally, the Reagan administration's efforts to create a system of international cooperation through regular meetings of G7 finance ministers and central bankers met with only modest success. Baker and Darman recognized that the Reagan-Sprinkel strategy of relying solely on the market to determine the value of the dollar was no longer serving the economic and political interests of the Reagan presidency. At the Plaza and Louvre meetings, Baker was able to work with our allies and with foreign exchange markets to bring about a soft landing for the dollar. However, when a higher level of international cooperation was attempted in terms of coordinating fiscal and monetary policies, the system broke down. Funabashi concludes, "With respect to the substance of policy coordination, . . . the Plaza strategy did not overcome three delays: the delay in cutting the U.S. budget deficit; Japan's delay in opening markets; and West Germany's and Japan's delay in stimulating demand."[76] The failure of this effort should not blind us to the irony of the Reagan administration's quest to institutionalize a new international political regime that would engage in considerable market meddling.

CONCLUSION

In the mid-1980s, the Reagan administration discovered, but never formally acknowledged, that the U.S. economy was far more intertwined with the world economy than had been realized, and for the remainder of Reagan's presidency, it was forced to cope with the consequences of that reality. Reagan's economic recovery program of 1981 ignored the international repercussions of its domestic economic policies, and by 1985, the country was faced with massive trade deficits and a demotion in status from a creditor to a debtor nation. An aroused Congress threatened to succumb to protectionist temptations that could trigger trade wars and thus inhibit the economic growth of the world economy. Reagan's pragmatic secretary of the treasury, James Baker, and his deputy, Richard Darman, recognized this danger and sought to reverse the administration's laissez-faire policy by successfully negotiating the Plaza Accord to drive down the value of the dollar with the help of our economic allies. With Paul Volcker's assistance, this policy succeeded in guiding the descent of the dollar to a "soft landing" and encouraged the export growth that helped fuel economic expansion for the United States in the second half of the 1980s. The deepening immersion of the U.S. economy into the global economy helped control inflation by increasing competitive pressures to keep prices down, which, as I discuss in Chapter 9, was essential for prolonging periods of economic growth. However, the declining dollar did not work as planned in terms of rectifying our trade deficit or balancing our trade with Japan. By 1989, the United States had a net debt of over $600 billion.

The Latin American debt crisis was the second unforeseen economic challenge faced by the Reagan administration. The debt problem was never resolved, but it was successfully managed in terms of preventing a collapse of U.S. banking and avoiding political instability in Latin America. The ironic outcome of meeting this challenge was that the Reagan administration became heavily dependent on the IMF—which was exactly the type of international organization despised by movement conservatives—to manage the negotiations with the Latin American countries needing to restructure their debt obligations. These negotiations were used by the Reagan administration to pressure Latin American governments into accepting market-oriented reforms that, although they initially caused a great deal of pain for Latin Americans, eventually helped many countries recover economic solvency. The Baker Plan, launched in October 1985, did not cure the debt problem, but it did buy more time for markets and banks to adjust to this predicament, and it symbolized the Reagan administration's commitment to assuming some political responsibility for dealing with this issue. Success for the Reagan presidency in handling the Latin American debt quandary was probably defined in terms of the problem never careening out of control.

In evaluating Reagan's foreign economic policy, it is important to remember that this was not a top priority for his administration. The aim here was not to gain big victories but to guard one's flanks against the Democrats and prevent the collapse of markets. The administration might have suffered some major setbacks if it had allowed its ideological predispositions to block its pragmatic skills. Thus, the administration kept the protectionist proclivities of Congress under control by negotiating VERs with a number of countries; it successfully navigated the historically unprecedented soft landing of the dollar; and, in 1982, it responded quickly to help Mexico deal with its debt crisis. Efforts by Baker to bring about more international cooperation to stabilize foreign exchange rates and coordinate monetary policy were not successful. The one time the administration stumbled occurred in October 1987, when the public conflict with Germany may have contributed to a stock market collapse, resulting in a drop of 508 points in the Dow. But this panic was short-lived, and the stock market soon recovered.

In dealing with the global economy of the 1980s, the Reagan administration had to make as many adjustments as the presidencies of the 1970s. Unlike the Old West heroes Reagan played in the movies, the United States could stand tall only with the cooperation of its trading partners. One wishes that Reagan had used his rhetorical skills to educate the public about the realities of economic interdependence, but this was not his style. The president did not like to talk about limits, complexity, and sacrifice. Nor did Reagan like to clean up his messes. Since Reagan knew that his intentions were good, he simply could not acknowledge that some of his policies had unanticipated negative consequences and that he bore some responsibility for rectifying them. He would deny the truth of Richard Rose's charge that "the legacy of the Reagan administration includes budget and trade deficits that have made the dollar a global problem."[77]

In reviewing the Reagan administration's foreign economic policy, the president himself does not seem to have been a major player. Based on what we know today, the one issue in which he might have played a major role was his 1981 decision to honor his campaign pledge to seek voluntary export restraints on Japanese cars. In most other cases, he appears to have played the role of Neustadt's "clerk"; that is, Reagan ratified the decisions made by officials such as Baker and Volcker. But as he floated above foreign economic policy issues, Reagan was able to maintain his reputation as a free trader and a supporter of competitive markets while making a number of decisions that violated these principles. He could justify these breaches of the conservative credo for any number of reasons: to win an election; to preempt more protectionist proposals by Congress, to defend national security, to compensate industries for having to obey government regulations, and to assure U.S. technological preeminence. With many Democratic congressmen and presidential candidates adopting protectionist positions, it was easier for Reagan to maintain his reputation as a free trader.

In brief, Reagan's maintenance of his reputation as a conviction politician did not inhibit him or his administration from exercising the pragmatic flexibility that increased his ability to achieve political success. A major source of that success was the Reagan administration's ability to enhance the ability of the U.S. economy to grow for an extended period without suffering the threat of inflation. This economic growth is the subject of Chapter 9.

9

CONSTRUCTING A
CONSERVATIVE REGIME
FOR ECONOMIC GROWTH

The Reagan administration came into office motivated to fulfill an ambitious agenda. Its political project was not only to destroy much of the old liberal regime but also to construct a conservative one. The Reagan presidency failed to abolish most liberal programs and was not successful in passing constitutional amendments outlawing abortion, allowing prayer in public schools, or requiring a balanced budget. But during the 1980s, it did succeed—partly by design, partly by compromise, partly by muddling through—in creating a policy regime that was capable of promoting long-term economic growth with low inflation. The malaise and stagflation of the 1970s were replaced in the 1980s by an adaptive economy that generated millions of new jobs and discredited the thesis that the United States was a declining superpower. To explain how this regime was built, I examine the following topics: the 1981–1982 recession, economic growth, jobs, savings and investment, and inflation and monetary policy.

THE 1981–1982 RECESSION

The Reagan administration predicted that the passage of the $750 billion tax cut in August 1981 would generate rational exuberance in financial markets. Supply-siders believed that even before the tax cuts took effect (5 percent in October 1981, 10 percent in July 1982, and 10 percent in July 1983), the depressed stock and bond markets would quickly react with brisk rallies. Instead, both markets declined in August and September 1981.[1] Rather than enjoying a burst of prosperity, Reagan found himself challenged by a recession.

A recession is usually defined as two consecutive quarters of declining gross domestic product (GDP). There had been a short recession in the first half of

1980, but the economic downturn that began in August 1981 proved to be more severe and would last longer. The 1981–1982 slump was the eighth recession the United States had suffered since the end of World War II. In the last quarter of 1982, factory utilization averaged only about 68 percent of capacity, the lowest figure on record since these measures were first compiled in 1948. High mortgage rates caused the number of housing starts to drop to 1,061,000, the fewest since 1946. There were over 25,000 business failures in 1982, the second-highest number since the depression of 1933. In November 1982, more than 9 million Americans were unemployed, a number that would climb to a peak of 11.5 million in January 1983. Whereas the seven postwar business cycles before 1982 averaged unemployment rates at the trough of 7.1 percent, the eighth one hit a peak of 10.8 percent at the end of 1982. About 2.3 million manufacturing jobs were lost in the recession, which fueled fears about the deindustrialization of the United States. The one encouraging statistic was that prices rose only 3.9 percent in 1982, the smallest increase since 1972, when Nixon's wage and price controls were in effect.[2] The pathology of the recession was curing the disease of inflation.

After a decade of bad economic news in the 1970s, the length and depth of the 1981–1982 recession caused fear among economists about the future. They were concerned that, even with a declining rate of inflation, interest rates remained high. Historically, the cost of borrowing money was usually about two to three points above the rate of inflation, but in 1982, interest rates were more than six points higher than the inflation rate. Many economists predicted that such high interest rates would restrict the recovery. Even more worrisome was that some economists feared that they no longer understood how to cure the problems of the economy. A Yale economist lamented, "To those who follow developments in economics, the paralysis should come as no surprise, given the demise of the earlier Keynesian consensus. Economists are today a shellshocked army, barraged by criticism because of poor forecasts, confused because of divided intellectual leadership, unsure of which way to retreat."[3] Another economist wrote, "given the current state of the economy, an all-but-unthinkable question arises. Do we know how to prevent a deep recession from spiraling into a depression? It may be that the nation has arrived at a new spot on the economic map where the old remedies—or what we thought were remedies—have lost their power and the economic wise men have lost their magic."[4]

Reagan handled this trial by recession fairly well. When Murray Weidenbaum, the chairman of the Council of Economic Advisers (CEA), told Reagan in late July 1981 that a recession was about to begin, the normally amiable president reacted with a cold stare of disbelief.[5] By October, he admitted publicly that the economy was suffering from a "slight recession," but he predicted a fast recovery if we had the courage to "stay the course" and continue his policies. While supply-siders and Treasury Secretary Regan blamed the recession on Federal Reserve Board Chairman Paul Volcker's "excessive" tightening of the money supply, the president did not. He viewed the recession as stemming from the fact that his original supply-side proposal for cutting taxes by 10 percent for three successive years beginning on January 1, 1981, had been delayed and watered down.

As economic conditions steadily worsened in 1982, Reagan consistently played the role of cheerleader, encouraging citizens not to lose faith. He condemned the media for emphasizing "doom and gloom" stories, which he believed were delaying the recovery. In his 1982 *Economic Report* to Congress, Reagan declared, "I am convinced that our policies . . . are the appropriate response to our current difficulties and will provide the basis for a vigorous economic recovery this year. It is of the greatest importance that we avoid a return to the stop-and-go policies of the past. The private sector works best when the Federal Government intervenes least. The Federal Government's task is to construct a sound, stable, long-term framework in which the private sector is the key engine to growth, employment, and rising living standards."[6] In public speeches, Reagan depicted his administration as the "cleanup crew" tidying up the mess caused by a forty-year "nonstop binge" (a significant metaphor for the son of an alcoholic). This recession provided conclusive evidence that the economic policies of previous presidencies did not work. He exhorted Americans to increase their savings rate by two percentage points, which would add about $60 billion a year to the nation's capital pool to combat high interest rates and to finance investments, mortgages, and new jobs. In a national radio address in September 1982, he angrily condemned the Democrats for "the most cynical form of demagoguery" in suggesting that progress in lowering the inflation rate was contributing to the rise in unemployment, a relationship that had been accepted by Reagan's recently appointed CEA chairman Martin Feldstein. But Reagan vehemently denied that his policy was to fight inflation by increasing unemployment.[7]

In a nationally televised speech before the 1982 congressional elections, Reagan painted the best possible face on his policies. He stressed that when he came into office, the country faced five critical problems: high taxes, runaway government spending, inflation, high interest rates, and unemployment. Reagan claimed progress in dealing with the first four of these problems. As for his lack of success in raising employment, he pointed out that employment is always a lagging indicator during a recovery. He assured the nation that his policies were not based on "quick fixes" but on dealing with the "root causes" of the economic problems and that by taming inflation, which eventually led to unemployment when unabated, he was constructing a recovery that was "built to last."[8]

The recession helped the Democrats pick up twenty-six seats in the House of Representatives in the 1982 congressional elections, thus ending Republican aspirations to control both chambers during the 1980s. Reagan's public approval ratings declined from a high of 67 percent in April 1981 to the mid-30s in early 1983. But exit polls in the 1982 elections indicated that voters were more likely to blame the Democrats, rather than Reagan, for economic problems.[9] Historian Alonzo Hamby suggests that "it was a measure of the depth of public dissatisfaction with Carter and the Democrats that Reagan was able to survive the worst economic trough since the Great Depression with little damage."[10] Lou Cannon wrote, "Later in his presidency, after Reagan had become a remote and disengaged monarch, first-term aides would recall the grim months of recession as if they were a golden age. They would remember Reagan scoffing at his critics and the polls and defiantly proclaiming that he would 'stay the course' with his economic program. 'The greatest show of his leadership was then,' said speechwriter Bentley Elliott."[11]

The irony of this episode is that the success of the Reagan administration's economic policies was not due to "staying the course" but to changing it significantly. Although Reagan had initially hoped that his fiscal and monetary policies would complement each other, with tax cuts promoting economic growth and a tight monetary policy lowering inflation, it turned out that stringent controls over the growth of the money supply overpowered the stimulative effects of the tax cuts and rising budget deficits. In early 1982, administration officials and supporters pressured Volcker to loosen the money supply; by that summer, Volcker had ended the monetarist experiment and was allowing the money supply to expand at a faster pace in order to lower interest rates. In August 1982, Reagan signed the Tax Equity and Fiscal Responsibility Act (TEFRA), which was designed to prevent soaring budget deficits by raising $98.3 billion over the next three years. It appears that an implicit compromise was negotiated—the administration accepted a tighter fiscal policy in exchange for the Federal Reserve's pursuing a looser monetary policy.

These changes in fiscal and monetary policy bore quick rewards. In August 1982, the stock market began the longest bull market in U.S. history. On August 17, the Dow-Jones index experienced its highest single-day rise in its history (38.81 points) to finish at 831.24, with a near record trading volume of over 92 million shares.[12] Between July and October 1982, the Federal Reserve allowed the M1 money supply (currency in circulation and checking accounts) to grow by 15 percent. This growth in the money supply frightened strict monetarists such as Milton Friedman and Beryl Sprinkel, who predicted that it would lead to rising inflation in 1983 and 1984. Instead, the economy grew strongly in those two years, and inflation remained under control.

In 1983, with a more accommodating monetary policy, the Reagan tax cuts were finally stimulating economic growth, but—more in line with a Keynesian perspective than a supply-side one—they were producing increases in consumption rather than in savings and investment. According to James Tobin, a Nobel laureate in economics, "By pure serendipity, the Administration carried out a classic well-timed Keynesian antirecession fiscal policy complementary to the countercyclical change in monetary policy in late 1982, when the Fed moved to rescue the economy from worsening unemployment."[13] Most of the public was not interested in the academic debate of whether the recovery was brought about by Keynesian or supply-side policies; what pleased them was that a long period of healthy economic growth had begun in 1983. And Reagan, because of his consistent conservative rhetoric camouflaging changing policies, reaped the political benefits of this prosperity. In Sidney Blumenthal's words, "By projecting an unchanging ideology throughout the economic crisis, he had been able to convince voters that his policies had not undergone any substantial revision and were actually the cause of the recovery. A majority of the voters gave him credit for the upturn. Between January and May 1983, he gained eleven points in the ABC-*Washington Post* poll. His interpretation of the recent past was prevailing—a triumph of ideology."[14] Democrats might not like how he had done it, but Reagan had successfully dealt with a major recession and had set the stage for his reelection in 1984.

ECONOMIC GROWTH

The political success of the Reagan administration was largely based on its economic performance. As indicated in Table 9.1, below the economy began a long-lasting recovery from the recession in 1983, with the GNP increasing 3.6 percent in that year and a whopping 6.8 percent during the presidential election year of 1984. From 1983 to 1990, the economy grew at about 3.5 percent a year, and the GNP expanded by 32 percent. The Dow-Jones industrial average went up 32.8 percent in Reagan's first term and 71 percent in the second. From 1982 to 1989, the Standard and Poor's index of 500 stocks went up almost 300 percent. Reagan had fulfilled his 1980 campaign promise to rejuvenate the economy. The United States could no longer be accurately viewed as a declining superpower.[15]

Table 9.1. The Reagan Administration's Economic Record

Year	GNP in 1982 Dollars (Billion)	Percent Change from Preceding Year	Gross Private Investment (Billion) of 1982 Dollars	Unemployment Rate	Yearly Change CPI	Federal Budget Deficits (Billions)
1980	3,187.1	-.2	509.3	7.0	13.5	-73.8
1981	3,248.8	1.9	545.5	7.5	10.3	-78.9
1982	3,166.0	-2.5	447.3	9.5	6.2	-127.9
1983	3,279.1	3.6	504.0	9.5	3.2	-207.8
1984	3,501.4	6.8	658.4	7.4	4.3	-185.3
1985	3,618.7	3.4	637.0	7.1	3.6	-212.3
1986	3,717.9	2.7	639.6	6.9	1.9	-221.2
1987	3,845.3	3.4	669.0	6.1	3.6	-149.7
1988	4,016.9	4.5	705.7	5.4	4.1	-155.1
1989	4,117.7	2.5	716.9	5.2	4.8	-153.4

Source: Council of Economic Advisers, *Economic Report of the President, January 1991* (Washington, D.C.: U.S. Government Printing Office, 1991), pp. 288, 289, 305, 330, 355.

The most remarkable attribute of this period of economic growth was its durability. It lasted 92 months, which was more than twice the average length of expansions since 1945 and was exceeded only by the 106-month growth period from February 1961 to December 1969, which was partly fueled by the Vietnam War. A new and more resilient economy emerged in the 1980s, one that was able to grow despite fears raised by budget and trade deficits, by the 508-point drop in the Dow-Jones index in October 1987, and by all the technological changes that seemed to be accelerating.

Supply-siders exaggerated the success of Reagan's economic policies. They evaluated Reagan's performance using data from 1983 to 1990, blaming the 1981–1982 recession on Carter and the 1991 recession on President Bush's decision to raise taxes. But productivity, which averaged a growth rate of almost 3 percent annually from 1948 to 1973, did not pick up in the 1980s, during which it averaged about 1.1 percent a year.[16] Nor did the tax cuts expand the economy's capacity to grow beyond its natural potential of approximately 3 percent a year. As Charles Schultze points out, "After the deepest recession of the postwar period in 1982, the GNP did rise rapidly for some years, but this change reflected a period of aggregate demand catching up to potential GNP. The growth of potential GNP, and in particular, the growth of productivity—that is, output per worker—did not speed up during the 1980s."[17] In terms of annual GDP growth, Presidents Truman (5.9 percent), Kennedy/Johnson (4.9 percent), and Johnson (4.4 percent) had better records than Reagan (2.3 percent in his first term and 3.2 percent in his second).[18] What made Reagan's record look so good was comparisons to the last two years of the Carter presidency.

A number of factors should be credited for the Reagan growth period's longevity. The combined effects of a severe recession in 1981–1982 and increased competition from abroad compelled American businesses to grow leaner and more efficient. The oil shocks of 1973 and 1979, which sent energy prices soaring, had forced the business sector to make painful adjustments; in the 1980s, business was rewarded with lower energy costs. The private sector, which had also adjusted to many of the costly environmental regulations of the 1970s, felt freer in the 1980s to concentrate more on raising profits. Whereas the adult population had increased at an annual rate of 2.4 percent during the Carter administration, it slowed to 1.8 percent in the Reagan years. Thus, in the 1970s, the absorption of 20 million new and inexperienced workers—the big surge of the baby boom generation—probably acted as a drag on productivity. In the 1980s, these workers were more experienced and productive, and the economy had fewer new workers to assimilate.

What maintained living standards during the 1980s was the increase in the number of women working outside the home. Whereas about half the female adult population worked in 1980, by 1988 about 57 percent did. With 50 million women in the labor force, the traditional family of the father as bread-winner and the mother as housewife was becoming a shrinking minority of American households.[19] These were changes being generated not by the counterculture of the 1960s (as alleged by the conservative movement) but by capitalism.

Most importantly, the United States was experiencing a rapid metamor-phosis from a manufacturing economy to a more flexible information-based, service-providing economy created by computers, revolutions in shipping (UPS), just-in-time ordering, efficiency-minded reorganizations and plant closings, outsourcing, and the increasing use of temporary workers. The result was that corporations could better control their inventories, lower their over-head expenses, and generate higher profits. According to Joel Kurtzman, "In their efforts at greater efficiency, companies have jettisoned layers of middle management, reduced the number of production workers, and cut down the time it takes to bring new products to market. As a result, they are better posi-tioned to deal with the upsets of a recession and able to design new products more quickly to suit the times."[20] In the 1980s, there was greater acceptance of the strategy that markets must be allowed to bring about change even though much of the change—considerably more than Reagan ever acknowl-edged—will cause pain to portions of society and the economy. But because this transformation bolstered American corporations to compete successfully in the global economy, more people benefited from the changes than suffered from them. In brief, public policy and private initiatives had a new formula and a greater capability to prolong the growth stage of the business cycle.

This in no way suggests that the new economy, as it was called in the mid-1990s, was immune from recessions and inflation. The dynamics of capital-ism assured that there was no permanent recipe for sustaining prosperity. And although the effects of the global economy were generally favorable for the United States, our growing interdependence with other nations subjected us to greater risks when even distant economies (e.g., Thailand, South Korea) floundered.

JOBS

The political success of the Reagan presidency was largely dependent on the fact that the American economy produced over 18 million new jobs during the 1980s. In 1980, over 99 million Americans had jobs, and the unemploy-ment rate stood at about 7 percent; by 1990, almost 118 million workers were employed, and the unemployment rate had dropped to 5.4 percent.[21] Apologists for Reagan skip over the point that 1.9 million jobs were lost between April 1981 and November 1982 and stress that in the twenty-seven months after November 1982, 7.6 million jobs were produced. Reagan supporters also neglect to report that the economy produced more jobs in the 1970s than in the 1980s. In the administration's final *Economic Report*, the CEA declared, "this remarkable expansion has benefitted all segments of the population. While civilian employment has increased by more than 17 percent, Hispanic employment has grown by more than 45 percent, black employment by nearly 30 percent, and female employment by more than 20 percent."[22]

The United States' record in producing jobs during this period was impressive compared with Western Europe's. Until the late 1970s, unemployment rates in the United States were usually higher than in Western Europe. But by 1988, the unemployment rate in Western Europe was twice that in the United States, with Spain's rate at more than 20 percent, Italy's at more than 14 percent, and France's at 11 percent. Even in West Germany, Europe's strongest economy, the jobless rate in January 1988 was over 9 percent.[23] Paul Krugman points out that "the United States has been the great job engine of the advanced world, with a 38 percent increase in employment from 1973 to 1990, compared with 19 percent in Japan and only 8 percent in Europe."[24] From 1980 to 1995, the U.S. economy produced 24 million new jobs, while the European Union, with a one-third larger population than America, added less than 9 million.[25]

The success of American capitalism in producing more jobs than Western Europe destroyed the argument that the United States was a declining economic power. Clearly, American capitalism adapted more successfully to the requirements of competing in the global economy than did European capitalism. While European nations responded to economic changes by maintaining high wages (because of powerful unions), they were suffering from lack of job growth; in contrast, the United States had much slower growth in real wages and a much higher rate of growth in the creation of new jobs. American families maintained their standard of living by placing more women in the workforce; in addition, more workers were absorbed into the labor force by their willingness to accept part-time and temporary jobs.[26] Unfortunately, many of these temporary or part-time jobs were at lower wage levels and did not include health coverage.

While the economy was adding 18 million new jobs, Fortune 500 corporations were employing fewer workers (4 million fewer in 1991 than in 1981). Two-thirds of the manufacturing jobs lost in the 1981–1982 recession were never regained. The 1980s was the first decade in the twentieth century in which the number of Americans laboring in manufacturing declined. Yet during this period, productivity in manufacturing grew at a robust 3.1 percent a year, compared with 1 percent a year in nonmanufacturing jobs. Within the manufacturing sector, there was a shift from heavy industry to efficient high-tech industries such as telecommunications.

These "leaner and meaner" corporations paid their executives higher salaries and earned the type of profits that encourage rising stock prices. But since factory jobs paid higher wages than service-sector jobs, the decrease in blue-collar employment limited the economic prospects of relatively uneducated workers. Unions were particularly hard hit by this phenomenon. The United Auto Workers lost nearly 40 percent of its membership between 1980 and 1992, dropping to about 850,000 from 1.4 million. During the same period, the steelworkers' union membership dropped from 1 million to 500,000, and the International Ladies Garment Workers Union membership fell from 350,000 to 150,000.[27]

The decline in manufacturing jobs was partially offset by Reagan's military buildup. As military spending rose from $157 billion in fiscal-year 1981 to over $300 billion in fiscal-year 1989, the number of people occupying jobs dependent on defense expenditures grew by 45 percent, to a total of 3.2 million.[28] Between 1981 and 1989, the United States spent over $2.1 trillion on defense. Supporters of Reagan claim that these expenditures helped the United States win the Cold War. (In the 1990s, the decline in the Pentagon budget caused painful adjustments for many defense industries and for regions of the county, such as California, that were dependent on these federal funds. By 1997, there were fewer than 1 million military-related manufacturing jobs.)

The big surge in jobs during the 1980s came in the service sector. Just as earlier in this century laborers who were pushed off the farm found employment with the railroads, the steel industry, the automobile manufacturers, and in highway construction, during the 1980s, new workers and displaced blue-collar laborers migrated to retailing, health care, restaurants, finance, and security occupations. According to Sylvia Nasar, "In the 80s, the services added a stunning 19 million new jobs, $800 billion worth of new technology, 16,000 new shopping malls, and three billion square feet of new office space (nearly as much again as existed in 1980)."[29] In the early part of the decade, most of these service jobs were low paying, but by the end of the 1980s and into the 1990s, salaries significantly improved. In the dawning information-age economy, about two-thirds of new service jobs were in the managerial and professional ranks.[30] However, although service jobs proliferated, their productivity gains were sluggish, averaging only about a third as high as the productivity increases of the manufacturing sector. By 1990, the bloated ser vice sector was ripe for a major streamlining. There were few service job reductions during the 1981–1982 recession, but in the 1990–1991 slump, 570,000 service jobs were lost.[31] This later recession hit the middle class particularly hard and prevented President George Bush from being reelected. But just as the adjustments to the 1981–1982 recession helped American factories compete successfully with those in Japan and Europe, the adaptation to the 1990–1991 downturn, which included finding new ways to use computers to give businesses a competitive edge, made the service sector more efficient and more capable of fueling steady economic growth in the years ahead. By the mid-1990s, unemployment was below 5 percent, with no signs of inflationary pressures.

SAVINGS AND INVESTMENT

The Reagan presidency had less success in increasing Americans' propensity to save and invest than it did in providing jobs. Its disappointing record in encouraging higher rates of savings by lowering tax rates was not a potent political issue, but many economists were concerned about its long-range effects on competitiveness and standards of living. A nation that does not make sacrifices today, in terms of holding down consumption by augmenting savings and investment, is less likely to enjoy a prosperous tomorrow. Fortunately for the administration's pro-growth policy, however, the capital-short, consumption-driven U.S. economy was bailed out by an unforeseen boost in foreign investment, which was attracted to our low-inflation, high-interest safe haven.

In 1981, the Reagan administration's program for economic recovery stressed that, in contrast to the inflationary, demand-led expansions of the past, growth in the 1980s would be based on the supply side of the economy. Increases in savings and investment would allow the economy to flourish without anxiety about capacity-induced inflation pressures. Administration supply-siders such as Norman Ture predicted that tax cuts would significantly increase gross private savings (which are composed of personal and business savings). Personal savings as a proportion of disposable personal income were projected to rise from an average of 5.4 percent in 1977–1980 to 7.9 percent in 1986. Business savings, which generally account for slightly more than two-thirds of total private savings, were forecast to climb above the 17 percent of GDP rate that had been maintained since 1956.[32]

These goals were not achieved. Personal savings, instead of rising to 8 percent of disposable income, fell and averaged only 4.5 percent during the 1980s. Gross national savings declined from 19.2 percent of GDP in 1980 to 15.6 percent in 1989.[33] From 1971 to 1980, the net national saving ratio averaged 8.9 percent of the GDP; from 1981 to 1988, it averaged only 3.7 percent.[34] Changes in the tax code did not cause the American people to give up their inclination to consume. Instead, we continued to be a buy-now, pay-later society. Consumer debt, as a proportion of personal income after taxes, climbed from 62.7 percent in 1970 to 74.9 percent in 1980 and reached 96.9 percent in 1990.[35] Increased consumption accounted for over two-thirds of the growth during the economic expansion from 1982 to 1990.[36] To the dismay of supply-siders, the evidence of the 1980s indicates that culture and demographics had a greater impact on saving rates than did alterations in the tax code.

The decline in savings meant disappointing rates of private investment. According to a Harvard economist writing in 1993, "After allowance for replacement of buildings and machines that wore out or became obsolete, business investment in new productive facilities averaged 3.6 percent of U.S. national income in the 1960s and 3.7 percent in the 1970s. Since 1980, the average net investment rate has been just 2.6 percent."[37] From 1974 to 1980, gross investment averaged 18.8 percent of the GDP; from 1981 to 1991, it averaged 17 percent.[38] There was no supply-side revolution in the 1980s.

Economists believe that private investment equals the sum of three kinds of savings: private savings, government savings, and net inflows of capital from foreign nations. With private savings down and with the enormous federal budget deficits in the 1980s cutting into national savings, the United States became more dependent on foreign sources of capital. Between 1982 and 1989, foreigners increased the value of their U.S. government security holdings from $132.5 billion to $265.9 billion. During the same period, direct foreign investment in the United States expanded from $124.7 billion to $400.8 billion.[39] During the 1980s, the United States continued to be the leading source of foreign investment, and it also became the largest recipient of foreign investment. Although some scholars and political opponents of the Reagan presidency warned that these trends indicated that the United States was losing its independence and limiting future standards of living, the growing supply of foreign capital helped reduce interest rates and increase investment capital. If foreign capital had not filled the gap caused by the lack of domestic savings, the budget deficits would have absorbed a much higher proportion of funds needed for business investment and led to much higher interest rates. And one of the keys to a long period of economic growth is avoiding higher interest rates.

INFLATION AND MONETARY POLICY

When Reagan assumed office in 1981, inflation appeared to be a chronic disease, a scourge that democratic governments lacked the understanding and discipline to handle successfully. By the time he left office, inflation was considered a manageable problem. Credit for taming inflation should be shared between the administration and Paul Volcker's Federal Reserve Board. During the decade, the Consumer Price Index (CPI) was reduced from 13.5 percent in 1980 to 4.1 percent in 1988 (see Table 9.1). Inflation averaged about 3.6 percent between 1983 and 1989, which helped to lower interest rates. Since inflation has corrosive effects on both the value of money and incentives to promote economic growth, lowering inflation rates was an essential ingredient in promoting long-term expansion. In the past, growth periods have been derailed by severe inflation that led to the imposition of high interest rates by the Federal Reserve. Cannon correctly argues that "the long period of low inflation had a stabilizing effect in the United States and was of enormous political benefit to Reagan. . . . [T]he Reagan-Volcker legacy of treating inflation as Public Enemy No. 1 . . . may well prove the most enduring and popular of Reagan's conflicting economic legacies."[40]

The monetarist leg of the administration's economic recovery policy was based on the Federal Reserve's targeting the supply of money rather than interest rates. In 1981, Treasury Undersecretary Beryl Sprinkel suggested that M1 should decrease by one percentage point per year, from seven in 1981 to three in 1985. Despite these specific recommendations, the administration claimed to respect the autonomy of the Federal Reserve Board, which, as an independent regulatory agency, has the legal responsibility to regulate the money supply. The administration's initial anti-inflation strategy was based on Milton Friedman's theory, which assumed that there was a direct relationship between the quantity of money in the economy and the level of output. Hence, when the money supply decreased, there was a recession; when it expanded moderately, there was sustainable economic growth; and when it grew too fast, there was inflation. Obviously, the correct choice was to have the Federal Reserve provide a slow, steady increase in the supply of money; but this alternative, so easy to select in theory, proved impossible to implement in practice.

Monetary policy proved to be essential for Reagan's success in the 1980s, but not as originally planned by the administration. The key strategist in the battle against inflation was Paul Volcker, who had been appointed chairman of the Federal Reserve Board in 1979 by President Carter. Just as Reagan was attempting to restore confidence in the presidency, Volcker was trying to restore confidence in the Federal Reserve Board after its failure to control inflation in the late 1970s. During Volcker's Senate confirmation hearings, he labeled himself a "pragmatic monetarist," which signaled that he would not rigidly adhere to Friedman's doctrine. Volcker strongly believed that inflation was a growing menace threatening the health of the economy and that only a hard-nosed monetary policy could free us from its insidious effects. He saw that inflation had become deeply entrenched in our economic expectations and behavior. By the end of the 1970s, the inflationary process was feeding on itself and distorting economic incentives. In Volcker's words, "Too much of the energy of our citizens was directed toward seeking protection from future price increases and toward speculative activity, and too little toward production."[41] Unlike Reagan, he felt that only a prolonged and painful process would be successful in combating an inflationary system that had grown too large to be harnessed by moderate means. The repeated failures since the late 1960s bred skepticism as to whether policy makers had the knowledge, commitment, and courage to subdue inflation.

With inflation appearing to be out of control, Volcker led the seven-person Federal Reserve Board into a Friedman-inspired monetary experiment in October 1979. Instead of trying to control interest rates, the Federal Reserve would set specific money supply goals and employ its authority over bank reserves to achieve them. This shift in focus from interest rates to restricting the growth of the money supply was designed to signal markets that a new and far more serious effort was under way to combat inflation. The plan was to establish a target for M1 growth and then "hit" it by manipulating bank reserves. Bank reserves can be influenced by the activities of the Federal Open Market Committee (FOMC). The FOMC is composed of the seven members of the Federal Reserve Board and five of the twelve Federal Reserve Bank presidents. It always includes the president of the Federal Reserve Bank of New York; the other members rotate. The FOMC determines open market policy—that is, it decides whether to buy or sell government securities (bills, notes, and bonds). FOMC directives to ease or tighten the money supply are implemented by the Open Market Desk of the Federal Reserve Bank in New York. To stimulate monetary growth, the Federal Reserve buys government securities; conversely, to tighten the money supply, it sells government securities. As Albert Rees explains, "When the Federal Reserve buys securities, it pays for them by creating deposits for the sellers in the Federal Reserve Banks; these deposits serve as additions to reserves for commercial banks. The added reserves permit commercial banks as a group to expand their loans and deposits by a multiple of the new reserves; this multiple is the inverse of the reserve ratio. For example, if reserves of 10 percent are required against all deposits, an additional dollar of reserves could ultimately support $10 of additional deposits."[42] When the Federal Reserve sells government securities, it has the opposite effect.

With inflationary expectations so embedded in pricing and wage behavior, and with politicians refusing to make the compromises necessary to prevent soaring budget deficits, Volcker knew that it would take a long period of tight money to slow down inflation. Not operating in a campaign mode, Volcker never promised a quick or easy victory over inflation. As the Federal Reserve tightened the money supply and allowed interest rates to float, the economy slowed down and then went into a severe recession in the autumn of 1981. Historically, high interest rates cause record-high business failures and rising unemployment rates. Volcker's cure for inflation seemed to be causing more pain than the disease. Inevitably, a wide variety of congressmen—House Majority Leader Jim Wright, Congressman Jack Kemp, Senator Ted Kennedy, and Senator Howard Baker—condemned the chairman. While supply-siders criticized Volcker for tightening the money supply too much, some monetarists complained that the controls were producing erratically wide swings in the quantity of money. Within the Reagan administration, Volcker was reprimanded by Treasury Secretary Donald Regan and Treasury Undersecretary Beryl Sprinkel (a former student of Milton Friedman), who vaguely threatened the Federal Reserve Board by talking about administration studies that would reduce its independence. Yet Reagan generally supported the Federal Reserve Board. In Volcker's words,

> President Reagan must have received lots of advice to take on the Fed himself, but he never did despite plenty of invitations at press conferences. . . . I never saw him often, as I had Mr. Carter, nor did I ever feel able to develop much personal rapport or indeed much influence with him. He was unfailingly courteous, but he plainly had no inclination either to get into really substantive discussions of monetary policy or, conversely, to seek my advice in other areas. But I had the sense that, unlike some of his predecessors, he had a strong visceral aversion to inflation and an instinct that, whatever some of his advisers might have thought, it wasn't a good idea to tamper with the independence of the Federal Reserve.[43]

As inflation rates declined in 1982, Volcker acknowledged that stabilizing prices during the most severe recession in forty years was not a great victory. The real challenge was to promote a noninflationary recovery and sustained economic expansion. His goal was to use monetary policy to make the 1980s a "mirror image of the 1970s," reversing the debilitating trends of the past decade.[44]

In July 1982, after establishing its credibility as an inflation fighter, and seeing that Congress was about to pass a $98 billion tax increase that would lower future budget deficits, the Federal Reserve began to loosen the money supply by raising money targets. On July 19, 1982, it lowered the discount rate from 12 to 11.5 percent, and the stock market began to recover. In October, Volcker supported further easing. The FOMC also announced that it was temporarily suspending money supply targeting. Donald Kettl explains why: "More than $31 billion of special tax-free All-Savers certificates were about to come due and would suddenly pour into checking and saving accounts, and that sudden flood of money would cause the Fed to overshoot its target of M1. . . . Volcker announced the Fed's action as a temporary change: it would 'de-emphasize' . . . the most narrow measure of money (M1) and focus instead on broader measures (M2 and M3) that included savings accounts and certificates of deposit as well as cash and checking accounts."[45] Markets interpreted these changes as a harbinger of easier money; banks lowered their prime rate, and the stock market surged. Volcker had both initiated and ended Friedman's monetarist experiment and set the stage for a long period of noninflationary economic growth.

The 1980s were not kind to Friedman's theory. After the Federal Reserve tightened the money supply in 1981 and 1982, it allowed M1 to grow by 11 percent in 1983 and 7 percent in 1984. James Alt reports, "For the 1980s as a whole, M1 growth [was] just under 8 percent per annum, two points higher than in the 1970s, while M2 growth averaged just over 8 percent, the same as it was in the 1970s."[46] Despite this growth in the money supply, inflation rates in the 1980s were considerably lower than in the 1970s. In the early 1980s, Milton Friedman forecast a rise in inflation followed by a recession in 1984, predictions that were way off.[47] Benjamin Friedman (no relation to Milton) pointed out that "since 1980 the relationship between money growth and the growth of either income or prices in the United States has collapsed. . . . Further, because the mid-1980s brought both the fastest money growth of the postwar period and the greatest *dis*inflation, the correlation between money growth and price inflation calculated in the way recommended by Milton Friedman (using two-year averages to smooth out short-run irregularities, and a two year lag between the money growth and the inflation) is now *negative* for postwar samples including this decade."[48]

Friedman's theory was also wounded by the fact that, with the government deregulating the banking system, it became more difficult, perhaps impossible, for the Federal Reserve to control the growth of the money supply. There were months when the Federal Reserve sought to restrict M1, yet it expanded. At other times, the opposite occurred. Arthur Schlesinger lampooned Friedman's monetary experiment by writing, "Friedmaniaism, with its spurious claim to precision, received its obituary from Sir Ian Gilmour at last year's Conservative Party conference when, evoking Oscar Wilde's description of fox-hunting as 'the unspeakable in pursuit of the uneatable,' he called monetarism 'the undefinable in pursuit of the uncontrollable.' "[49]

One reason that Friedman's theory did not work as predicted was that there was an unforeseen change in what is called the "velocity" of money. Velocity is the economist's concept that describes the relationship between the money supply and the GNP. As Kettl explains, "It is based on the willingness of consumers to hold or spend money. The same dollar is spent over and over again during any year; the faster consumers spend a given dollar, the more any given level of the money supply increases economic growth."[50] In the early 1980s, the Federal Reserve's money targets were generating less economic growth than that predicted by monetarist models, because beginning in the summer of 1981, the velocity of money unexpectedly slowed down. As inflation slackened, consumers were less inclined to spend their money quickly before prices climbed. As interest rates declined, this also slowed down the velocity by lowering the opportunity costs of keeping assets in the form of currency and demand deposits. William Niskanen argues, "The most probable reasons for the reduction in velocity were the increase in financial wealth and the combination of declining market interest rates and the higher rates on bank deposits allowed by deregulation, the latter conditions reducing the cost of holding assets in the form of bank deposits."[51]

Milton Friedman's theory concentrated on the slow, steady growth of the supply of money and did not consider interest rates and unemployment to be important. Since most of the public is affected by interest rates and unemployment and has no understanding about the quantity of money, it is not surprising that political support for Friedman's monetarism disintegrated during the early 1980s. After Volcker ended Friedman's monetarist experiment in 1982, Reagan reappointed him chairman in 1983. Thus, Friedman experienced the reward of being awarded the Nobel Prize for economics and the humiliation of having his theory prove unworkable when applied to national monetary policy.

The success of Volcker's pragmatic, discretionary monetary policy, as opposed to Friedman's automatic monetary policy, played an indispensable role in supporting Reagan's presidency. Volcker helped Reagan construct a vital component of a new policy regime that was able to promote economic growth that was less susceptible to inflation. Because the old system based on the Phillips curve (whereby the Federal Reserve allowed inflation to inch up in order to bring down unemployment), had broken down by the end of the 1970s, a new strategy was required in the 1980s. Instead of using Federal Reserve control over the money supply to balance levels of inflation and unemployment, the new system stressed the strategic importance of preventing inflation. The new strategy held that sustained economic growth was derived from an effective anti-inflationary policy, which meant hiking interest rates in response to the first signs of inflation. Given the rigidities of the budget and the frequent gridlock between the president and Congress, fiscal policy was playing a declining role in controlling inflation and in stabilizing the business cycle. With the federal government, private corporations, and individuals piling up debts, and increasing international mobility of private capital seeking higher interest rates, the role of monetary policy had grown rapidly and had become preeminent in promoting prosperity. By 1986, even a Keynesian economist could write that "the monetary policy of the Federal Reserve has become the dominant instrument of macroeconomic management. If any fine or coarse tuning of the economy is done, it's the Fed that calls the tune, through its control of money and interest rates. After all, Chairman Volcker and his colleagues can make nine or ten moves a year. The budget makers in the executive and Congress can make only one, and in recent years their procedures, politics, and conflicts have become so complex that national economic prospects and strategies play little role in the outcome."[52] In brief, the chairman of the Federal Reserve has become the most important economic policy maker in the United States.

Volcker's success was dependent on some deviousness. He was probably less of a Friedmanite and more of a pragmatist than he appeared to be in 1979. By engaging in the experiment of targeting the money supply instead of interest rates, Volcker most likely knew what the results were going to be. When the Federal Reserve tightened the money supply by more than had been recommended by the Reagan administration, interest rates soared, businesses failed, and millions of workers lost their jobs. Volcker had launched a chain of predictable events that led to a recession, but he correctly, if disingenuously, claimed that he was targeting money aggregates, not throwing people out of work. With interest rates so elevated in 1981, Volcker could not announce that he planned to raise them higher without stimulating a political backlash that might threaten the very independence of the Federal Reserve Board. So he "camouflaged" his goal of raising interest rates to throttle inflation by restrictively targeting money aggregates.[53] Once the recession had killed inflation and Friedman's experiment, he could implement his preferred, pragmatic monetary policy of targeting interest rates. There were no specific rules to guide Federal Reserve decision making (as there are in Friedman's "High Church" monetarism), but there was a grim determination to prevent inflation from breaking loose again.

William Niskanen, a member of Reagan's CEA, asks and answers a question that may provide further insight into Volcker's motivation. Niskanen asks, why did the Federal Reserve limit the growth of the money supply more than the initial Reagan recommendations? He answers that, just as Defense Secretary Weinberger decided to exploit the window of opportunity to finance a huge military buildup because he believed that political support would soon fade, Volcker concluded that the Federal Reserve would have to subdue inflation quickly through a recession because there would not be enough political backing to sustain a multiyear struggle. In Niskanen's words, "My judgment is that Volcker believed that the consensus for monetary restraint was temporary and that the American political system would not tolerate the slow, steady reduction in money growth recommended by the initial Reagan guidance. He may have wanted to reduce inflation as rapidly as possible, despite the temporary adverse effects on the economy."[54]

The success of Volcker's policies causes some problems for Reagan's ideological supporters. First, Volcker was originally appointed chairman of the Federal Reserve by Carter, the personification of failed liberalism. After much debate within the Reagan administration, Volcker was reappointed in 1983 but was replaced by Alan Greenspan in 1987. Second, Volcker's monetary policy, which was largely followed by his successor, was a national policy, formulated by a centralized political institution, that successfully muzzled inflation without inhibiting job creation and economic growth. The Federal Reserve's goal was to navigate an overheated economy into a "soft landing," where growth remained positive, thus avoiding a "hard landing," where the economy contracted. Such metaphors sounded suspiciously like the Keynesian concept of "fine-tuning" the business cycle that had so offended conservatives in the 1960s. The Volcker-Greenspan success story weakens the conservative assertion that discretionary government policies cannot improve market outcomes. And finally, the record indicates that Volcker did more of the "heavy lifting" in fighting inflation that Reagan did. While the president ran large budget deficits, Volcker bore the political heat of keeping interest rates fairly high. The self-serving conservative narrative is that Volcker's policies caused the recession, and Reagan's policies brought about noninflationary economic growth. This chapter suggests that Reagan deserves credit for not attacking Volcker during the dark days of the 1981–1982 recession and for reappointing him in 1983, but Volcker was clearly the architect of the anti-inflationary strategy that has proved to be so essential for promoting a prolonged economic expansion.

CONCLUSION

Emerging from the uncertainty and despair of the 1970s, the United States in the 1980s constructed a new framework for economic growth. This new regime had less confidence in what government could accomplish and more faith in the efficiency of markets. By the end of the 1980s, the economy resembled the mirror image of itself at the end of the 1970s: corporate profits were strong, unemployment low, jobs multiplying, inflation negligible, and the stock market flourishing. By reducing the number of permanent employees and relying more on outside sources and temporary workers, corporations were able to lower their fixed costs and increase their capacity to maintain profits by contracting during slowdowns and expanding during periods of growth. The revolution in computer technology caused painful adjustments but eventually made both the manufacturing and the service sectors more efficient. "After years of travail," according to Louis Uchitelle, "this country has finally fielded the right formula for generating wealth and prosperity in the highly competitive global economy. . . . The essence of the American formula . . . is this: Business must be free to innovate, restructure, relocate. These are necessary ingredients for baking an ever larger pie, however distasteful the downsizing and wage inequality that are part of the process."[55]

President Reagan made major contributions to the creation of this policy regime. He never succumbed to the malaise of the 1970s, always remaining optimistic that his remedies would restore health to the economy. Reagan's tax cuts for both individuals and corporations stimulated the prosperity that, except for a short, mild recession in 1990–1991, has continued into the 1990s. However, this framework for economic growth was not simply a function of fulfilling Reagan's original vision in 1980. Contrary to Reagan's speeches and conservative myth spinners, the president's success was not based on "staying the course"; rather, it derived from his skill in shifting policy directions while maintaining rhetorical consistency. By 1982, it was apparent that there was a fundamental incompatibility between Reagan's fiscal and monetary policies. An implicit compromise was arranged whereby the administration accepted a tighter fiscal policy by acquiescing to tax increases, and Paul Volcker's Federal Reserve Board agreed to implement a looser monetary policy. Volcker ended Friedman's experiment in 1982, was reappointed chairman in 1983, and then skillfully directed monetary policy to constrain inflation. Low levels of inflation were an essential ingredient in prolonging the growth stage of the business cycle. Ironically, then, Reagan's success was partly dependent on the skill and courage of a pragmatic bureaucrat originally appointed by President Carter.

Chapter 10 postulates that Reagan's political success was not dependent on overcoming the growing trend of income inequality in the United States, a fact that future scholars are likely to weigh heavily in evaluating the historical significance of his presidency.

10

THE REAGAN PRESIDENCY, GROWING INEQUALITY, AND THE AMERICAN DREAM

A discussion about equality in the United States literally invites partisan polemics. The concept of equality is so difficult to define and is so susceptible to a variety of measurements that one can "prove" diametrically opposing arguments. Throughout the 1980s, the Democrats attacked Reagan's economic policies for being unfair in promoting the interests of the rich at the expense of the poor. Given how important the value of equality is within the United States' political culture, one might have expected the Democratic charges, accompanied by supporting statistics, to have wounded the Republican president more than they did. But even though there was evidence of widening income and wealth disparities throughout the decade, Reagan was able to win two landslide elections, maintain fairly high public approval ratings, and hand over the presidency to his vice president, George Bush.

This chapter seeks to explain why the growing inequalities of the 1980s did not threaten the political success of the Reagan administration. To accomplish this, I briefly discuss the concept of equality in the United States, describe the growing inequalities in the nation, and analyze how the Reagan administration successfully coped with this issue.

EQUALITY IN THE UNITED STATES

Along with liberty and individualism, equality has long been understood as a fundamental component of the American political culture. The French political philosopher Alexis de Tocqueville begins *Democracy in America* by writing, "No novelty in the United States struck me more vividly during my stay there than the equality of conditions. It was easy to see the immense influence of this basic fact on the whole course of society. . . . the more I studied American society, the more clearly I saw equality of conditions as the creative element from which each particular fact derived, and all my observations constantly returned to this nodal."[1] From de Tocqueville's perspective, the equalitarian ethos of the democratic revolution bloomed more rapidly in the United States than elsewhere because the United States had been "born free" of feudalism. Careers were more open to talents in the United States (except in the South, because of slavery) than in most other countries. He also believed that equality in America was both a source of dynamism (promoting mobility and prosperity) and a chronic source of discontent. In de Tocqueville's words,

> It is odd to watch with what feverish ardor the Americans pursue prosperity and how they are ever tormented by the shadowy suspicion that they may not have chosen the shortest route to get it. . . . They have abolished the troublesome privileges of some of their fellows, but they come up against the competition of all. . . . No matter, therefore, how democratic the social conditions and political constitution of a people may be, one can be sure that each and every citizen will be aware of dominating positions near him, and it is a safe guess that he will always be looking doggedly just in that direction. . . . Hence, the more equal men are, the more insatiable will be their longing for equality.[2]

In brief, de Tocqueville came to the melancholy conclusion that equality generates needs that can never be satisfied.

The fact that the United States is committed to equality has not meant that disputes over it have been avoided. Equality issues have been deeply involved in most of the great dramas in American history: the Revolution, the Jacksonian era, the Civil War and Reconstruction, the Populist-Progressive period, the New Deal, and the civil rights struggles of the 1960s and 1970s. According to Sidney Verba,

> In each period, challenging groups sought both political and economic equality, for themselves and on the behalf of others. Inevitably, each battle led to some progress toward egalitarianism on both fronts. In the end, however, each upheaval did relatively little to redress inequalities in the distribution of income and wealth. The enduring and significant result of these historical battles was rather the achievement of greater political equality through the expansion of political rights or the dispersion of political influence. In other words, the principal legacy of the drives for equality in the United States has been a steadily increasing democratization.[3]

However, this democratization has not prevented a steadily increasing inequality in income distribution.

Americans' commitment to equality has always been tempered by their support of liberty, individualism, self-reliance, limited government, and federalism. These values often restrict public policies designed to promote equality (such as affirmative action).

There has also been a split among Americans concerning competing visions of equality—equality of opportunity versus equality of outcome. These two views appeared to be similar at the time of the American Revolution because, as Gordon Wood wrote, "it was widely believed that equality of opportunity would necessarily result in a rough equality of station, that as long as the channels of ascent and descent were kept open, it would be impossible for artificial aristocrats or overgrown rich men to maintain themselves for long."[4] Individuals pursuing their economic interests in unregulated markets would produce prosperity and equality.

In the twentieth century, most egalitarians no longer believe that equal opportunity is a sufficient condition for achieving equal results. Richard Ellis contends that "today, it is widely believed that the opportunity to compete creates unconscionable inequalities, and that the call for equal treatment is often little more than an excuse to perpetuate existing inequalities."[5] Thus these two visions of equality, which were mutually supportive in our earlier history, have become more contentious in the latter half of the twentieth century.

Egalitarian notions are also associated with what we call the "American dream." Economists operationalize the American dream when they point out that in much of our history the standard of living has doubled roughly every thirty years. Each generation expects to live considerably better than the previous one. When egalitarianism merges with American optimism, we become a society of haves and will-haves. Our history and myths suggest that we can all hope to share in America's prosperity. For leftist radicals, the American dream has had a stifling effect on their efforts to mobilize the poor in support of redistributive programs because so many of the poor do not want to eliminate the rich—they want to join them.

A major turning point for liberals in their orientation toward equality was reflected in Lyndon B. Johnson's announcement in June 1965 that equal opportunity was not enough to overcome the inequalities caused by racism. President Johnson proclaimed, "We seek . . . not just equality as a right and a theory but equality as a fact and equality as a result."[6] Ellis concludes, "In the contemporary period, it has been the attempt to help blacks and other minorities that has perhaps contributed most to the collapse of the belief that securing equal process is sufficient to achieve more equal results."[7] This shift has been electorally costly for liberal Democrats because the idea of equality of opportunity has more public support and appears to be more compatible with the American political heritage than equality of results. To bring about an equality of results would require a far more intrusive government than most Americans want or are willing to finance.

In response to growing income disparities, many liberals talk of progressive income taxes and welfare policies to redistribute income from the rich to the poor. Although they rarely mention a ceiling on income for the rich, liberals frequently talk of the moral need (in terms of fairness) to raise the living standards of the poor. The specific results liberals are aiming for are left vague. Mickey Kaus, a neoliberal, argues that liberals have created a whole repertoire of "fudge phrases" to avoid specifying the income distribution they prefer: "They want 'to tilt the balance in favor of ordinary people'; they want 'a good deal more equality than we now have'; they believe 'the strong owe a duty to the weak'; they favor—in F.D.R.'s early evasion—the 'underprivileged' over the 'overprivileged.' "[8] When liberals refuse to define the kind of equality they want, however, it arouses conservative suspicions that liberals have a secret agenda.

Liberals concede that competitive markets are efficient, but they claim that government interference may be necessary to ensure more social justice. Without social justice, modern political systems cannot sustain their legitimacy. If capitalism continues to expand inequalities and increase personal insecurities, liberals fear that our democratic political system will be undermined. The economist Lester Thurow warns, "Since accurate data have been kept, beginning in 1929, America has never experienced falling real wages for a majority of its work force while its per capita GDP was rising. In effect, we are conducting an enormous social and political experiment—something like putting a pressure cooker on the stove over a full flame and waiting to see how long it takes to explode."[9] Robert Reich, Clinton's first secretary of labor, suggests that, "unlike the citizens of most other nations, Americans have always been united less by a shared past than by the shared dreams of a better future. If we lose that common future, we lose the glue that holds our nation together."[10] In brief, growing inequalities are stifling the hopes nurtured by the American dream.

American conservatives value individual freedom far more than equality. Whereas liberals believe that equality and liberty can be reconciled, conservatives do not. Whereas liberals claim that by extending equality you are expanding freedom, conservatives assert that attempts to augment equality constitute lethal threats to individual freedom. While liberals tend to think of equality as promoting social justice, conservatives believe that equality brings about stifling uniformity, leveling, and bureaucratic oppression. For conservatives, according to Conrad Waligorski, "Any attempt to apply [equality] to groups or to consider the conditions for equality, beyond identical treatment by the law and equal right to attempt to compete in free markets, is illegitimate and must destroy freedom. Beyond these narrow limits, freedom and equality are mutually exclusive."[11]

The modern conservative is essentially arguing that America's yearning for equality should be pacified by the condition of equality of opportunity. Liberals worry that the unequal resources of the participants in markets will prevent them from being able to compete effectively, while conservatives argue that market rationality will produce the best results in the long run. Liberals scoff at how conservatives employ the concept of equality of opportunity by quoting R. H. Tawney's gibe that it signifies "the equal right to be unequal." The conservative polemicist R. Emmett Tyrrell responds, "Our only safeguard . . . from all the baseness that issues from equalitarians is reverence for personal liberty as the ultimate political value. . . . The intelligent quest is for the free society with equality of opportunity. The quest for equality of result is the path to the widest inequality of all: despotism."[12] Similarly, the conservative monetarist Milton Friedman cautions, "A society that puts equality— in the sense of equality of outcome—ahead of freedom will end up with neither equality nor freedom."[13] However, as conservatives have attempted to enlarge their electoral popularity, they have argued that their ideology of freedom first will produce more equality than liberalism.

These different perspectives toward equality cause increasing hostility between liberals and conservatives. For liberals, equality is a moral incentive leading to a more socially just society; for conservatives, it is economically counterproductive, politically dangerous, and a demagogic appeal to envy. Whereas liberals believe that freedom will be threatened by growing inequalities, conservatives have no doubt that freedom will be sacrificed if government attempts to reduce disparities.

GROWING INCOME INEQUALITY IN THE UNITED STATES

Evidence from the Census Bureau, the Federal Reserve Board, the Internal Revenue Service, the Congressional Budget Office, and numerous academic studies demonstrates that inequality is growing in the United States. Republican denials of this mountain of evidence are reminiscent of tobacco companies' denials that smoking constitutes a health threat. But Democratic accusations that Reagan's tax and budget policies were the major cause of increasing inequality are also inaccurate. America was becoming more unequal before Reagan came to office in January 1981, and the inequality trend has continued since he left office in January 1989.

Following World War II, economist Simon Kuznets argued that inequality in income increased as nations developed economically and decreased after they industrialized. Data from the United States supported Kuznets's theory. During the 1950s and 1960s, income growth was equalizing, as the average adjusted family income of the lowest two quintiles of households increased faster than that of the other three. But in the 1970s, this equalizing trend began to slow down. For example, between 1950 and 1960, family income of the lowest quintile increased by 117 percent, and that of the highest quintile increased by 51.4 percent. However, between 1970 and 1980, the lowest quintile raised its income by 7.9 percent, and the highest quintile's income went up by 10.3 percent.[14]

In 1991, a Census Bureau study of 24,000 households chosen to be representative of the nation's 92 million households concluded that the wealth of the most affluent Americans increased substantially during the 1980s while the net worth of other citizens barely kept pace with inflation. The Census Bureau defines wealth, or net worth, as the value of savings and checking accounts, real estate, stocks and bonds, and other assets, minus debts. Wealth is more concentrated than income because it reflects not one year's income but the lifetime accumulation of assets. After adjusting for inflation, wealth of the richest one-fifth of all households increased 14 percent from 1984 to 1988, while the remaining four-fifths of households did not experience any significant change in net worth.[15]

In 1970, the richest 1 percent of households possessed about 20 percent of the nation's wealth. Data from a 1995 Federal Reserve study showed that the wealthiest 1 percent of households—with net worth of at least $2.3 million each—now owned nearly 40 percent of the nation's wealth.[16] In 1996, a University of Michigan study found that the most affluent 10 percent of American households held 61 percent of the country's wealth in 1989 and over 66 percent in 1994.[17] A 1996 Census Bureau report indicated that during the first two years of the Clinton administration, despite a progressive tax increase, the share of national income obtained by the richest 5 percent of households expanded at a faster rate than during the eight years of the Reagan presidency. The Census Bureau study concluded that, from 1968 to 1994, the share of the nation's aggregate income earned by the top 20 percent of households increased to 46.9 percent from 40.5 percent. During the same period, the proportion of income attained by the other quintiles decreased or remained stationary. While the average income of households in the bottom 20 percent of earners rose from $7,702 to $7,762, the average in the top 5 percent of earners surged from $111,189 to $183,044.[18]

Apparently, the opportunity to become richer has expanded in recent decades. In 1980, there were 4,414 millionaires in the United States; by 1987, there were 34,944; and by 1994, there were about 65,000.[19] In 1982, there were twenty-one billionaires in the nation; by 1991, there were seventy-one.[20] The top 1 percent of households own a lopsided proportion of many types of assets: 49 percent of publicly held stock, 62 percent of business assets, 78 percent of bonds and trusts, and 45 percent of nonresidential real estate. Controlling these assets has meant that these affluent households have attracted three-fourths of the gain in pretax income from 1977 to 1989. Sylvia Nasar concludes, "By 1989, the one percent (834,000 households with about $5.7 trillion of net worth) was worth more than the bottom 90 percent of Americans (84 million households with about $4.8 trillion in net worth)."[21] Thurow adds, "By the early 1990s, the share of the wealth (more than 40 percent) held by the top one percent of the population was essentially double what it had been in the mid-1970s and back to where it was in the late 1920s, before the introduction of progressive taxation."[22] In terms of growing income inequality, we appear to be headed back to the future.

There is no agreement and much controversy concerning why inequality has been expanding in the United States. The usual suspects include declining wages for unskilled workers as automation spreads, the shift in the economy from manufacturing jobs to service jobs, the decline in the numbers of workers who are unionized, the increasing use of part-time workers, global competition, the rapid expansion in the 1980s of the stock and bond markets, and the low tax rates on the affluent during the 1980s. Whatever the causes, "United States wage distribution is more unequal than in other countries, and we do less in terms of tax and transfer policy to cushion the disparities."[23]

Comparative data suggest that "rather than being an egalitarian society, the United States has become the most economically stratified of the industrial nations."[24] We have more poor and more rich than other industrialized nations. America's chief executive officers (CEOs) are paid two to three times more than Germany's or Japan's. George Will writes, "In Japan, the compensation of major CEOs is 17 times that of the average worker; in France and Germany, 23–25 times; in Britain 35 times; in America, between 85 and 100 times. The American CEO-worker disparity doubled during the 1980s—while the top income tax rate was cut and workers' tax burden increased because of social security taxes."[25] What disturbed Will, a conservative, about these figures was not the questionable justice of this growing inequality but the possibility that these statistics would be exploited by liberals to launch an antibusiness campaign.

There is also a greater stratification within the workforce. In 1979, a male college graduate could expect to earn 49 percent more than a man with only a high school diploma. This was a sizable difference, but the high school graduate could still reasonably hope to participate in the middle-class standard of living, such as being able to buy a house. By 1992, the gap in earning had expanded to 83 percent, and the working-class expectation of being able to realize the American dream had been reduced. After rising in every decade from 1940 to 1980, the home ownership rate for all households declined in the 1980s from 65.6 percent in 1980 to 63.9 percent in 1989. There has been a similar divergence in benefits. According to Robert Reich, "Employer-sponsored health coverage has declined only slightly for workers with college degrees, covering 79 percent in 1979 and 76 percent in 1993. But the rate for high school graduates has fallen from 68 percent to 60 percent, and among high school dropouts, from 53 percent to 36 percent. Nearly two-thirds of workers with college degrees have employer sponsored pension plans, but fewer than a quarter of high school dropouts do."[26]

Inequality has increased in recent decades because so many of the poor appear to be anchored to a life of poverty. A rising tide of economic growth does not lift all social sectors. The optimism of the 1960s that the number of families living at or beneath the poverty level could be significantly reduced and possibly eliminated has been replaced by the pessimism and neglect of the 1980s and 1990s.

The concept of the poverty level was first operationalized in the Johnson administration in 1964 at three times the amount of money a family would need to feed itself adequately and is adjusted annually to reflect changes in the Consumer Price Index (CPI). In 1960, there were about 39.5 million poor people, or about 22 percent of the population. By 1973, the poverty rate had decreased to 11.1 percent, the lowest percentage ever recorded. After 1978, the poverty rate steadily ascended and, because of the 1981–1982 recession, reached 15.2 percent in 1983. At the end of the Reagan administration in 1989, the poverty rate was 12.8 percent, which meant that 31.5 million persons were classified as poor.[27] What is most depressing about these figures is that 1983 to 1990 (years of impressive economic growth) was the first period of economic expansion since World War II in which the poverty rate demonstrated such immovability.[28] It will obviously require something more than economic growth to cut the poverty rate.

The face of poverty has also changed; it has become younger, more female, and more concentrated. Because of Social Security (indexed to the CPI since the early 1970s) and Medicare, the poverty rate for the elderly decreased from 35.2 percent in 1959 to 11.4 in 1989. This success in public policy was matched by a failure—the poverty rate for children rose from 15 percent in 1970 to about 20 percent in 1989. Felicity Barringer reports that "one in four of new entrants into the ranks of the poor in the 1980s was under 18 years of age; one in 25 was 65 or older."[29] In 1990, the poverty rate for whites was about 10 percent, for Hispanics about 26 percent, and for blacks about 32 percent. Forty-four percent of black children lived in poverty in 1990. Poverty has also become more entrenched and concentrated. The number of people living in concentrated poverty areas (where at least 40 percent of the population is poor) grew from 3.7 million in 1970 to 5.6 million in 1980 to 10.4 million in 1990.[30] Life in these subcultures is characterized by unemployment, female-headed families, welfare dependency, crime, and alcohol and drug abuse. The American dream is not likely to flourish here. Neither is equality of opportunity.

Poverty is a particularly dangerous threat for women. From 1940 to 1956, the rate of illegitimate births in the United States was about 4 percent. After 1956, the rate began to climb and has not declined since 1970. By 1990, over 30 percent of births were to single mothers, with estimates that illegitimate births will reach 50 percent by the beginning of the new century. In 1980, there were 6.2 million families headed by single women; at the end of the decade, the number had climbed to 8.4 million. In 1980, 17 percent of female heads of households had never been married; by 1990, that figure had soared to 33 percent. More than half the children in households headed by single women are poor. Two-thirds of black children born in 1990 had unmarried mothers.[31] Such female-headed families are not likely to escape from the culture of poverty.

Several conclusions can be derived from these trends. First, a nation that was considered the most egalitarian has become considerably less so. There are powerful factors that have promoted inequality through periods of economic growth and recession, price stability and inflation, and Republican and Democratic presidencies. Not even the longest peacetime expansion on record (from 1983 to 1990) could deter this inegalitarian trend—and may even have accelerated it. Second, America is still a land of outstanding opportunities, as evidenced by the nation's attraction for immigrants and the growing number of millionaires. Third, the very factors that have upgraded the more educated and powerful—increasing use of computers, flexible production, global competition—have not benefited over 40 percent of the population. An improving economy no longer means that the bulk of the citizens will be better off. Even more disturbing, a public mood has been created that suggests that we are more proud of our millionaires than we are concerned about how many millions are trapped in the prison of poverty.

COPING WITH INEQUALITY

A successful president has to be able to handle a variety of issues. On certain strategic issues he has to go on the offensive and win; on others he might be content to wage a defensive campaign that blocks his opponents from scoring. Reagan came to the presidency largely because he promised to rejuvenate the American dream, which he believed could be done if tax rates were lowered, inflation was controlled, and entrepreneurship was unleashed. Promoting economic growth was a strategic issue for Reagan, and when the economy recovered from the 1981–1982 recession and began a long period of expansion, his political prospects brightened considerably. The decline of Reagan's public approval rating to 35 percent during the recession and the loss of twenty-six House seats in the congressional elections of 1982 suggest that when there was no growth, there was no Teflon.

Since Reagan was not elected to bring about more equality, the growth of inequality during the 1980s did not create a lethal problem for him. Although his more pragmatic advisers, along with his public relations team, understood that the president might be vulnerable to Democratic accusations that his policies stimulated inequality and were, therefore, unfair, they reasoned correctly that, even as evidence mounted that inequality was increasing, they could neutralize the publicity of such disparity as long as the economy continued to grow.

Still, given the equalitarian heritage of the United States, one might have predicted that such inequalitarian trends would have caused the administration more political problems than they did. Certainly the Democrats hoped that they would. The Democrats continually blasted the Reagan presidency for its tax policies, which benefited the rich, and its budget cuts, which hurt the poor. They condemned it for its "moral meanness" in its disregard for black civil rights and for its lack of concern in promoting the equal rights of women. The Democrats also attacked the Reagan administration for trying to cut Medicare while proposing high increases in the defense budget and for posing as the champion of family values while slashing programs that benefited education, child nutrition, health, and job training.

Lane Kirkland, president of the AFL-CIO, described Reagan's policy in 1981 as "economic Darwinism, that is, the survival of the richest."[32] Thomas P. O'Neill, the Speaker of the House, proclaimed, "This has been a program of the rich, by the rich, and for the rich."[33] During the 1984 presidential election, Democratic Party advertisements maintained: "It isn't fair. It's Republican." Hodding Carter, a political appointee in the Carter administration, responded to Reagan's 1982 proposals to shift policy responsibilities for the poor from the federal government to the states by writing, "Rather than nurturing a more perfect union, they would instead produce a confederacy of inequality, in which the obligations of shared national community are submerged in the rush by states and individuals to beggar their neighbors."[34] What Reagan extolled as encouragement for individuals to take advantage of the expanding opportunities in a dynamic economy were condemned by the Democrats as appeals to avarice. For Democrats, vain and arrogant millionaires such as Charles Keating, Michael Milken, Leona Helmsley, and Donald Trump personified the "go for it" greed of the 1980s.

Carter or Mondale might have been perceived as being more concerned about the poor than Reagan, but they were also seen as ineffective political leaders. After the failures of the 1970s, few believed that liberal sensitivities about poverty could be transformed into competent policies to help the poor. Nor could the Democrats receive credit for their rhetoric about social justice when much of their motivation appeared to be electoral payoffs to special interests. By election day of 1984, according to Thomas Cavenagh and James Sundquist, "The Democratic Party was seen not as the traditional defender of the middle class but as tax collector for the welfare state, the Republican Party not as the tool of Wall Street and the rich but as the instrument to bring about widespread economic growth and opportunity."[35] For many Americans, the limited improvements made under Reaganomics appeared better than the painful losses suffered under Carter. And for the many who had not yet received increases in real income, the long period of growth nurtured hopes that they would eventually share in the prosperity.

The Democratic Party's dilemma was painfully revealed in its own studies in 1985, which showed that white middle-class and white working-class voters equated the word "fairness" with "giveaways" to blacks. The studies demonstrated how difficult it would be for the party to construct messages that would regain the support of disaffected white middle- and working-class voters without alienating blacks.[36] With the increasing emphasis on affirmative action, civil rights now meant preferential treatment for minorities and women rather than equality under the law. The result was less support for civil rights among whites, especially white working-class men. Peter Applebaum reports, "*New York Times* polls indicate significant slippage in support for any preferential employment practices. When respondents were asked in May 1985 if they favored preferences in hiring or promotion for blacks in areas where there had been discrimination in the past, 42 percent said 'yes' and 46 percent said 'no.' Asked the same question in December 1990, 32 percent said 'yes' and 52 percent said 'no.' "[37]

The Reagan administration countered Democratic attacks based on the growing inequality issue with conventional conservative arguments, effective use of the White House public relations capabilities, and utilization of Reagan's political skills. The conservative case against the liberal welfare state can be analyzed using Albert O. Hirschman's book *The Rhetoric of Reaction.* Hirschman claims that conservatives employ three basic rhetorical arguments to criticize and ridicule attempts to promote equality. In his words, "According to the *perversity* thesis, any purposive action to improve some feature of the political, social, or economic order only serves to exacerbate the condition one wishes to remedy. The *futility* thesis holds that attempts at social transformation will be unavailing, that they will simply fail to 'make a dent.' Finally, the *jeopardy* thesis argues that the cost of proposed changes or reform is too high as it endangers some previous, precious accomplishment."[38]

The futility argument, backed up by the jeopardy thesis, is stressed by market economists. For them, the laws of supply and demand are immutable. It is as pointless to try to alter the natural outcome of markets as it would be to order a change in the tides. All nations have unequal wealth and income distribution, and it is foolhardy to criticize any degree of market determined inequality where inequality is the natural order of things. On top of that, any attempt to bring about greater equality is likely to jeopardize freedom. The jeopardy thesis is best articulated in the books of Friedrich Hayek and Milton Friedman.[39]

Hirschman claims that the argument conservatives use most often to delegitimize efforts to foster equality is the perversity thesis. Liberal reformers are "world worseners" because their attempts to improve conditions inevitably backfire. Any liberal attempt to reduce unemployment actually increases it; liberal efforts to help families with dependent children encourage mothers on welfare to have more children, thus creating their own prison of poverty. In *Losing Ground,* the conservative author Charles Murray argues, "We [the United States] tried to provide more for the poor and produced more poor instead. We tried to remove the barriers to escape poverty and inadvertently built a trap."[40] White House counselor Edwin Meese stressed in a 1984 speech that "the broken families, dependent mothers and fatherless children that were spawned by a decade of aimless spending are the real victims of a well-meaning but misguided system of government aid and regulations."[41] In brief, although conservatives might occasionally concede that liberal policies are well-intentioned, they generally argue that such efforts produce negative consequences.

The perversity thesis postulates that a liberal activist government generates more problems than solutions. Waligorski explains the conservative position by writing, "If equalization policies, whether affirmative action or minimum wage laws, necessarily fail to attain their end but cause inequality, then refusal to intervene, while seemingly anti-egalitarian, is in fact egalitarian because it forces people onto the market which rewards them according to their contribution to the welfare of others, thereby producing whatever equality is possible."[42] Milton and Rose Friedman add that "a society that puts freedom first will, as a happy by-product, end up with both greater freedom and greater equality."[43] Hence, in the ultimate irony, conservatives have argued that their emphasis on freedom will eventually produce more equality than liberalism. This reflects the ideologues' propensity to believe that all good things go together.

Reagan's White House public relations machine was also utilized to ward off Democratic attacks. The bluntest responses came from conservatives, such as Meese, who considered Democratic concerns about inequality a bogus issue. Conservatives claimed that liberals were demagogues and engaged in the politics of envy; they ridiculed the idea that poor people are poor because rich people are rich. David Stockman, director of the Office of Management and Budget, was particularly active in defending the administration against Democratic charges of unfairness. For Stockman, the active pursuit of equality inevitably brought about a tyrannical state and an inefficient economy. In his words, "I don't accept that equality is a moral principle. . . . That's the overlay, the idea around the welfare state. A safety net is different—it's the minimum to which you'll allow anyone to fall. To go beyond that and seek to level incomes is morally wrong and practically destructive."[44]

At a more profound level, the Reagan administration was trying to change the policy context by substituting its conservative public philosophy for welfare-state liberalism. Whereas the New Deal and the Great Society had tried to make the public aware of what government could do *for* them, the Reagan administration was attempting to make citizens fear what the government could do *to* them. Using the jeopardy argument, the administration played upon the taxpayer's fear of higher taxes, the businessman's fear of stifling regulations, the white male worker's fear of affirmative action, and of religious groups' fear of an expanding secular state. Democratic Senator Daniel Patrick Moynihan complained, "There is a movement to turn Republicans into Populists, a party of the people arrayed against the party of the state."[45] Judging by the presidential elections of the 1980s, this Republican strategy had considerable success.

Reagan's public relations specialists, such as Michael Deaver and David Gergen, and his politically sensitive advisers, led by James Baker and Richard Darman, made sure that the administration could respond to Democratic attacks with facts and figures. In the spring of 1983, the White House compiled a 286-page briefing book to aid officials in defending the Reagan presidency against charges of unfairness.[46] The president and his spokesmen continually stressed that their budget cuts had not destroyed the social safety net that protected the old, sick, poor, and disabled. Moreover, the administration's tax cuts in 1981 and 1986 were fair because they removed 6 million poor families from the tax rolls and resulted in the rich paying a higher proportion of the nation's taxes at the end of the decade than at the beginning. Reagan's supporters also argued that, in a dynamic capitalist society, income inequality statistics of quintiles were meaningless. According to Paul Craig Roberts, a supply-sider who served in Reagan's Treasury Department, "The reason is the extremely high rate of income mobility in the United States. The poor and the rich will always be with us, but they are not the same people from year to year. The poor move up over time and the rich fall off their high peaks."[47] For example, only 171 of the original 400 richest Americans listed in *Forbes* magazine in 1982 were listed in the magazine's 1991 issue. For conservatives, it was about as significant to analyze income inequality statistics as it was to probe which soap bubbles rose to the top in a washing machine.

But the Reagan White House believed that its strongest defense against charges of unfairness was that its policies had ended the stagflation of the 1970s and were providing sustainable economic growth. Economic expansion fueled opportunities for investors to increase their wealth on Wall Street and for workers to improve themselves in the job market. Conservatives characterized the 1980s as a decade in which both the poor and the rich got richer. After the 1981–1982 recession (labeled the Carter recession by Reagan's supporters), the White House was constantly publicizing statistics that proved that Reaganomics was producing more growth and jobs than the policies of our European and Japanese allies. The Reagan growth period lasted ninety-two months, until July 1990, which was more than twice the average period of expansion since 1945. Between 1982 and 1990, real disposable income per capita increased by 18 percent, and the economy added 18.4 million jobs.[48] Reagan believed that the poor would be better off with a soaring economy rather than an expanding bureaucracy. When a Census Bureau report indicated a drop in the poverty rate in 1984, Reagan announced, "I believe these numbers are further proof that the greatest enemy of poverty is the free enterprise system. The success of 1984 does not mean that the battle against poverty in this country is over; it does mean that America, after a difficult decade, is once again headed in the right direction."[49]

In explaining Reagan's landslide victory over Mondale in the 1984 election, Richard Wirthlin, the president's pollster, indicated that economic prosperity had shielded the administration from Democratic fairness assaults. In Wirthlin's words, "Growth is the best alternative we can offer to the Democrats' state welfarisms."[50] Given the policy context of the 1980s and 1990s, the Republicans had immunized themselves from accusations of unfairness as long as they were producing economic growth. However, during periods of economic contraction, such as 1981–1982 and 1990–1991, Democratic attacks were more likely to draw blood—and voters.

The administration's stress on promoting growth was analogous to the conservatives' emphasis on liberty. Economic expansion would bring higher standards of living for almost everyone. To express this idea, Reagan often borrowed President Kennedy's maxim that a rising tide lifts all boats. Hence, a focus on economic growth would produce more equality in the long run than if there were more emphasis on liberal distributive policies.[51]

The most effective asset the Republicans had to neutralize the inequality issue was Ronald Reagan. Born poor in the Midwest, moving west to become a rich movie star, and then achieving the presidency, Reagan was the personification of the American dream. The White House publicized every aspect of Reagan's life that might deflect Democratic attacks. Thus stories were disseminated about how Reagan's mother, Nelle, aided the poor; how Reagan's father, Jack, worked for the Civil Works Administration under Franklin Roosevelt; and how Reagan befriended a black football player on his Eureka College team.[52] Deaver made sure that the president was frequently pictured promoting charities, education, the Special Olympics, and the like.[53] Reagan presented a softer and gentler image than most other conservatives. As an inclusive political leader, Reagan was proud of his past affiliation with the Democratic Party, and he used it effectively to invite Democrats to join him in the new Republican Party.[54] While Democrats were trying to portray Reagan as a tool of the rich, Reagan was declaring, "The secret is that when the left took over the Democratic Party, we took over the Republican Party. We made the Republican Party into the party of the working people, the family, the neighborhood, the defense of freedom, and, yes, the American flag and the Pledge of Allegiance to one nation under God. So, you see, the party that so many of us grew up with still exists except that today it's called the Republican Party, and I'm asking all of you to come home and join me."[55]

Since Reagan did not intend for his policies to bring about more inequality, it was sufficient for him to believe that it was not happening. But Reagan's budget, tax, and antiregulatory policies did nothing to thwart the inequality trends that preceded his administration, and they may have accelerated wealth disparities. For the first time since the New Deal, the federal government ceased attempting to constrain the propensity of capitalism to generate inequality. Nevertheless, Reagan was able to avoid being wounded by the fairness issue by framing himself as a conservative populist. The president was also successful in delegitimizing most Democratic Party proposals to deal with inequality by labeling them not as sincere efforts to remedy social injustice but as selfish attempts by liberal elitists to reward special interests and federal bureaucrats.

The combination of Carter's political failures in the 1970s and Reagan's political success in the 1980s meant that it would become more difficult to propose policies to aid the poor and promote equality. Reagan helped create an atmosphere in which it was easier for the public to approve increased funding for the military, the police, and prisons rather than for education, health, or housing. His political success and his insensitivity to equality arguments created a model for today's politicians that may delay endeavors to deal with growing inequality problems. New York's Democratic Governor Mario Cuomo voiced a telling criticism when he said, "At his worst, Reagan made the denial of compassion respectable."[56] By the end of his presidency, nearly one in five children was suffering from poverty, but with the exception of Jesse Jackson, no serious presidential candidate would take the risk of trying to change this situation with a major new initiative. According to Jason De Parle, "In the millions of words uttered on the topic, none linger more convincingly in the public mind than Ronald Reagan's perfect-pitch quip: 'We fought a war on poverty, and poverty won.'"[57] He considered the Vietnam War a "noble cause," but not the war on poverty. Reagan's ridicule was aimed at the failure of poverty and welfare programs, and he conveniently ignored abundant evidence of corruption and waste in the Pentagon ($435 hammers and $600 toilet seats).

It is certainly reasonable to subject social welfare policies, like any other proposals, to serious scrutiny as to whether they will achieve their objectives for a reasonable cost. It is less reasonable—and perhaps immoral—to erect new barriers to promoting a more socially just society by denying the success of previous policies and automatically maligning new projects for being motivated by selfish purposes. In evaluating the Reagan presidency on this issue of equality, David Broder wrote, "History will not deal kindly with his administration's deliberate efforts to slow down or reverse the two previous decades of steady progress in reducing poverty and discrimination. . . . [Reagan] was neither heartless nor biased personally, but he was deaf to calls for justice. The Great Communicator used all his rhetorical tools to advance the causes he cared about; unfortunately, justice was not one of them."[58]

CONCLUSION

For reasons that are not entirely clear, indices of inequality have increased since the 1970s. These changes are altering the nature of the United States from one of the most equalitarian industrialized nations to one of the least. The evidence indicates that the policies of the Reagan administration were not the origin of the growing inequality, but it does suggest that they contributed to that trend. More importantly, Reagan's policies did nothing to inhibit inequality, and his administration attempted to delegitimize any governmental endeavors to promote equality. By adding barriers to the already Herculean task of initiating policies to help the poor, Reagan served his partisan purposes but not necessarily the nation's good. The claims of Reagan's supporters that he was a great moral leader can be seriously challenged because he contributed to poisoning the policy milieu against proposals to bring about a socially just nation.[59] Our greatest presidents were all instrumental in bringing about greater equality to the nation.

In a country that has traditionally prided itself on its early and continuing commitment to equality, one would have expected the inequalitarian trends that began in the 1970s and accelerated in the 1980s to have caused more political problems for the Reagan presidency. Increasing inequality means a narrowing of opportunity for those hoping to share in the American dream. The unique and sustaining myth of the American dream is that it is achievable by the many and not by just the select few. As conservatives have tried to expand their electoral popularity, they have argued that their ideology of emphasizing freedom will eventually produce more equality than liberalism will. The statistical trends of the 1980s do not support their contention. Their policy of relying on competitive markets produced powerful incentives for efficiency and economic growth, but not equality.

In brief, the political skills of the Reagan administration, combined with the residual effects of the Democratic Party's failures in the 1970s, meant that as long as the economy was growing, Reagan's presidency was relatively immune to attacks about the lack of fairness in its policies. But such "success" served to nullify one of the dynamic and progressive forces in our political culture—the quest for equality.

11
CONCLUSION

This book has evaluated the political leadership of Ronald Reagan. No attempt has been made to summarize the performance of the entire Reagan presidency; instead, the focus has been on economic policy making, which, as stressed in Chapters 1 and 5, was a strategic priority of his administration. To make the political leadership of a president more than an abstract, academic concept, a scholar has to relate it to areas of substance. For Reagan, the core area of his leadership was economic policy. Confident that he knew how the economic world worked, he wanted to lead the United States—which, in 1980, was suffering from a high misery index (a combination of the unemployment and inflation rates)—to a sustainable prosperity based on low tax rates, market rationality, the encouragement of entrepreneurial activities, and deregulation. Reagan's economic performance was crucial to his political success because his election in 1980 was largely due to President Carter's inability to cure the stagflation of the late 1970s.

In trying to portray the true contours of the Reagan era, I was determined to move beyond those ideological arguments of liberals and conservatives that have distorted the vices and virtues of the Reagan administration. Because many conservatives see Reagan as their movement's leader, they have not been interested in an objective analysis of his leadership. They are more concerned with creating a mythical view of Reagan as the great leader who came to power after a long march to change the United States and who, once in office, went on to change the world.[1] From the conservative perspective, criticism of Reagan is frequently rejected as betrayal (kiss-and-tell memoirs) or as the perceived bias of the liberal establishment in the media and universities. Liberals often ridicule Reagan, explaining his political success in terms of luck and the public relations skills of his staff.[2]

For several reasons, even some presidential scholars have underestimated Reagan's leadership. First, Reagan was a far cry from Richard Neustadt's FDR-inspired model of a leader.[3] Reagan was not his own intelligence adviser, scanning issues to locate where his personal power stakes lay, asking his advisers to clarify questions to uncover the crucial details that would give him the bargaining leverage to persuade more effectively. Second, in a rush to judgment, several major evaluations of the Reagan presidency were published before he was out of office.[4] These premature studies not only overestimated the damage of the Iran-Contra scandal but also came out before Reagan successfully negotiated the Intermediate Range Nuclear Force Treaty with the Soviet Union, helped elect his vice president as his successor (called by some Reagan's third term), and stepped down in January 1989 with a 65 percent approval rating.

Several other scholars have recognized Reagan's political skills. Journalist Lou Cannon suggests that Reagan "has always been more complex as a person and as a political leader than either his cheerleaders or his critics believed."[5] Most observers of Reagan, according to Cannon, underestimated him because they failed to see that his "genial demeanor and genuine modesty shielded a hard, self-protective core that contained both a gyroscope for maintaining balance and a compass pointing toward success. . . . Most of those who dealt with Reagan in public life saw the soft surface instead of the hard core, and underrated him."[6] James McGregor Burns made a similar point by drawing an analogy between Walter Lippmann's famous error in failing to perceive the steel behind Franklin Roosevelt's genial facade and the media's inability in the 1980s to recognize the tenaciousness beneath Reagan's amiable exterior.[7]

Samuel Kernell treats the Reagan presidency as being potentially as important in the evolution of the office as was Franklin Roosevelt's. According to Kernell, in a political system characterized by individualized pluralism (more candidate-oriented elections, a more decentralized Congress, more single-issue constituencies outside of Washington, D.C.), Reagan "was ideally suited by experience, temperament, and ideology to capitalize on going public."[8] After a series of failed presidencies, Reagan's "going public" skills helped revitalize the institution.

Much of Reagan's political success can be attributed to his ability to deliver a speech.[9] In analyzing his speeches through decades, one is struck by how little they changed over time. A typical Reagan oration was composed of humor, heroes, nostalgia, anecdotes, statistics, symbols, and mythic visions. He used simple sentences and stark choices (slavery or freedom) to convey his message. Reagan was particularly effective at boiling abstractions down to concepts that the public could understand: the United States was threatened externally by communism and internally by the seductive appeal of big government, but the nation could thrive if we only adhered to the traditional values that made us great. Norman Rockwell's values would take us back to the future.

Reagan did not teach us difficult truths about hard choices in governing because he did not believe there were any. In Reagan's mind, the eternal truths of individual liberty and limited government had been verified again and again throughout our nation's history. He could sell his vision because he was a skilled actor and an effective salesman who thoroughly believed in what he was marketing. As Cannon suggests, "even when he was exasperatingly wrong or misinformed, he was so thoroughly convincing and self-assured that others believed him. . . . Reagan was not believable because he was the Great Communicator; he was the Great Communicator because he was believable."[10] And being believable, he could sell his persuasive narrative that he was rescuing the country from the malaise of the 1970s.

Given Reagan's ideology, the intellectual burdens of communication were not too heavy. His cheerful brand of conservatism, based on tax cuts, did not ask the public to endure sacrifices in order to succeed. In essence, Reagan's style of leadership was to stress simple truths and simple solutions, and the simplest solution was to elect Reagan.[11]

By repeating the same simple messages for so many years, Reagan became the embodiment of those messages. One Reagan speechwriter claimed that his function was to "plagiarize the president's old speeches," and George Will wrote that "it is hard for Reagan to avoid sounding like an echo of echo."[12] But by repeating himself, Reagan solidified his credentials as a conviction politician—a rare breed among the poll-driven politicians of the period. And by identifying himself with such popular symbols as patriotism, religion, and the family, Reagan placed his opponents in the awkward position of appearing to assault fundamental American values whenever they attacked him personally.

Reagan's success was not determined solely by his media talents; it was also based on the substance of his message. His message expanded the electoral appeal of conservatism by adding populism. The old populism of the early twentieth century had feared big business; Reagan redefined it to mean that the major threat to people's lives now came from big government. Liberal policies, according to Reagan, foster big government; big government restricts individual liberty. Reagan promised tax cuts for everyone and asked rhetorically who could best decide how to spend the nation's wealth: citizens or federal bureaucrats? Championing fundamental values also increased Reagan's populist appeal.

Under Reagan's leadership, the Republican Party became far more capable of successfully challenging the Democrats. Ironically, led by the oldest president ever elected, the Republicans in the 1980s appeared to be the party of ideas, appealing to younger voters and attracting young conservative activists. Supply-side economics was certainly oversold and may have been "voodooish," but it helped Reagan project his optimistic and populistic image onto his party. The Republican Party was no longer constrained by its old arguments regarding balancing the budget; it was now the party of economic growth and opportunity. By prolonging the growth stage of the business cycle, the administration was multiplying the opportunities for many more people to raise their standards of living.

Reagan was especially skillful in putting the Democrats on the defensive. He ridiculed their calls for social justice, their concerns about the environment and "limits to growth," their complex proposals, their prophecies of "gloom and doom." The American people were confronted with a choice between pessimism and optimism, and Reagan clearly represented the latter. From Reagan's perspective, his proposals called for no sacrifices, no painful trade-offs; in his mythical "magic of the marketplace," we would all be winners because we could rely on our entrepreneurial talents, feel secure that our hard work would be suitably rewarded, and enjoy the support of our families, churches, and communities. These ideas and the young activists to whom they appealed ensure that the Reagan presidency was not merely a brief interlude but will significantly affect the policy agenda for years to come.

One intriguing aspect of Reagan as campaigner was his continuing role identification as an "outsider," challenging the pathologies of the federal government (such as budget deficits) even *after* he was elected to office. By playing the role of the crusading outsider, a citizen (not a politician) who had heeded his country's patriotic call to clean up the stable, Reagan often succeeded in avoiding the disadvantages of a president in office while exploiting the powers that the office afforded him. He handled the logical inconsistency of this position by defining the government as Congress and the bureaucracy.

Reagan also handled the challenge of creating an advisory system that he was comfortable with and that could help him make decisions to promote his political purposes. Reagan's political successes—and a few of his disasters—can be explained by his ability to attract and utilize the talents of three types of personnel: conservatives, pragmatists, and public relations experts. The interaction of these three groups proved conflictive, but it was also effective because each group provided the president with vital services. By providing ideological direction and energy, conservatives helped Reagan appear to be a conviction politician. Pragmatists supplied the Washington insights and know-how that helped Reagan fulfill his visions. And the public relations experts furnished the skills to maintain the president's high approval ratings. Thus, Reagan's presidency oscillated between conservative consistency and pragmatic compromise without suffering the negative label of "flip-flopping" as Carter's presidency had.

Reagan's public relations staff helped him pursue Kernell's leadership strategy of going public, while the pragmatists gave him the ability to follow Neustadt's bargaining path, and the conservatives provided the ideological commitments that, as long as they were constrained by political realities, served to increase the president's bargaining leverage. Through it all, whether consciously or not, Reagan was able to play both outsider and insider, both the conservative hero living up to his moral convictions and the former union negotiator who understood the need for compromise.

The most intriguing paradox about Reagan was that he was often a passive, uncurious, and detached man who was also tenaciously committed to a few basic goals—a combination not found in any other president. Whereas Neustadt believed that an effective president had to master the details of policy and politics in order to have a personal impact, Reagan never felt that way, even about issues he claimed to be interested in. For Reagan, his rhetoric pointed out the direction he wished policy to go, and it was the responsibility of his subordinates to compete among themselves to fill in the details. Although it is true that Reagan knew little about the tax code, the budget, or the Strategic Defense Initiative, it is also evident that his leadership had a personal impact in reducing tax rates, raising defense expenditures, and negotiating the INF Treaty. Most importantly, Reagan's personal commitments were exceptionally effective in serving his political purposes.

The most unexpected political skill Reagan demonstrated in office was his ability to enjoy the advantages of being a conviction politician, leading and uniting the multiple sects of the conservative movement while avoiding the pitfalls outlined in Chapter 3. Avoiding being dragged down by the treacherous currents of ideological politics while maintaining majority approval required a political finesse that few observers attributed to Reagan. Reagan dodged the minefields that had wounded conservatives in the past, namely, isolationism, anti-Semitism, racism, and conspiratorial fantasies. He succeeded in becoming the focus of the conservative movement while also appealing to nonconservatives, a feat that neither Barry Goldwater in the 1960s nor Newt Gingrich in the 1990s could accomplish.

Reagan was a politician who was willing (perhaps unknowingly) to bend his conservative principles; a competitive man who wanted to win more than he wanted to be consistently conservative; an inspirational leader who was not willing to risk political capital for lost causes, or sometimes even for difficult ones. Cannon described a key truth about Reagan's leadership when he wrote

that "on nearly all issues, Reagan was simultaneously an ideologue and a pragmatist. He complained to aides that true believers on the Republican right
such as Jesse Helms preferred to 'go off the cliff with all flags flying' rather
than take half a loaf and come back for more."[13] George Shultz wrote, "the
right thinks they have enormous influence in the White House, but the president just goes on making them furious. Ronald Reagan was a hardliner, but
with a major difference from most of his hard line supporters: he was willing
to negotiate with his adversaries and was confident in his ability to do so."[14]

Reagan's conservatism was uniquely his own. He violated traditional conservative sentiments and reflected his optimism when he often approvingly
cited Tom Paine's line: "We have it in our power to begin the world over
again." Reaganism was not intellectual enough for traditional conservatives,
not angry enough for the New Right, not single-minded enough for supply-
siders, not grim enough for neoconservatives, and too fun-loving for the Religious Right. Each faction of the conservative movement strove to capture
Reagan's mind, but he retained his autonomy to pursue his political purposes.
He was indispensable to the movement, but each of its components was dis-
pensable as far as he was concerned, because he had the ability to reach out
beyond the movement. In Cannon's words, "Like his first political idol,
F.D.R., Reagan had proved a master in using the militant fringe when it served
his purpose and isolating it when it did not."[15]

The crucial point is that Reagan's conservatism did not prevent him from
being a flexible and effective politician. His adroitness was demonstrated in
the way he maintained the allegiance of the conservative movement by granting it some of what it wanted, at the same time asserting enough autonomy
to pursue his own political objectives and preserve his popularity. By initially
stressing economic issues, Reagan unified the Republican Party, got Congress
to pass his tax cuts, and, after the 1981–1982 recession, was able to claim
credit for a record-long economic recovery. By proposing constitutional
amendments to ban abortion, allow prayer in the public schools, and ensure a
balanced budget, Reagan kept liberals on the defensive and maintained the
loyalty of conservative voters; yet he enacted only a portion of his social policy into law. The president maintained the support of most conservatives by
employing more consistently conservative rhetoric than policy. Hearing their
ideas expressed in elegant phrases was particularly effective in keeping the conservatives, who believed that they had been deprived of the status they de-
served for so many years, "on the reservation." As a result, their major
criticisms were aimed at Reagan's administrative style and his pragmatic appointees, who allegedly inhibited his predilection to act conservatively. But
the conservative mantra, "Let Reagan be Reagan," was a rationalization. It

maintained their illusion that Reagan was a totally committed conservative and prevented them from considering that the candidate they had brought to the dance (the presidency) was a promiscuous politician.

It is more accurate to describe Reagan the politician as the resilient president than as the Teflon one. Given the number, range, complexity, and uncertainty of the decisions a modern president has to make, it seems certain that he (someday she) will make a number of mistakes. The challenge for a chief executive is to avoid lethal blunders such as Vietnam and Watergate and to be capable of recovering from lesser errors. Reagan was an effective leader not because he avoided mistakes and gaffes but because he weathered them. When the economy suffered a recession in 1981–1982, or when the administration was hit by the Iran-Contra scandal at the end of 1986, the president was not able to escape blame for these problems. In both cases, Reagan's approval ratings plummeted, just as they would for any president. In recovering from both of these blows, Reagan was aided by his likable personality, his communication skills, his campaign abilities, his dexterity in being flexible while appearing decisive, and the talents of his advisers, who were exceptionally good at identifying and taking advantage of windows of opportunity. Larry Berman reports, "When Reagan left office in January 1989, 68 percent of the American people approved his overall job performance, 71 percent approved his handling of foreign relations, and 62 percent gave approval to his handling of the economy."[16] Clearly, Reagan had successfully met the challenge of being resilient.

Blessed with a unique set of political skills (and instincts), Reagan enjoyed a successful presidency. He did not provide what some conservatives call the Reagan revolution because, by constitutional design, our political system seriously restricts political leadership. What Reagan's politics did bring about was a hybrid regime that was a mixture of conservative values and liberal commitments. Tax rates were lowered and flattened, but Social Security, Medicare, Medicaid, and federal laws to protect the environment were not eliminated. In the perceptive words of a political scientist, "Ronald Reagan did not reduce government to nearly the same extent as Lyndon Johnson expanded it. But he created the policy conditions for a contractive politics that had never been played before."[17] However, when one compares conditions at the end of the 1970s with those at the close of the 1980s, it is obvious that Reagan restored confidence in the presidency, the economy, and the nation.

By focusing on the economy, the Reagan administration, with the help of Paul Volcker, increased the capability of our economic system to provide long-term growth with low inflation and to compete successfully in international markets. Still, Reagan's presidency and legacy are most vulnerable to the liberal accusation that many Americans did not share in the prosperity of the 1980s. Struggling to reverse growing inequalities and fighting the war on poverty are noble causes that should not be ridiculed and blocked, as they were by Reagan and officials in his administration. Reagan delegitimized reform proposals by stigmatizing them as partisan attempts by liberal elitists to reward an unholy alliance of special interests and federal bureaucrats. By raising the threshold for acceptance of new programs to deal with inequality, Reagan was lowering the capability of the federal government to promote social justice.

Many scholars have criticized Reagan for making it more difficult for public policy to promote social justice not only because of their own liberalism but also because the quest for equality has been a vital component of American political culture. Nevertheless, the net effects of Reagan's policies, both domestically and internationally, were very positive. The country was better off because of Reagan's eight years in office. But, in opposition to what Reagan proclaimed in his 1981 inaugural speech, effective government was an essential component in resolving the nation's problems. It is ironic, and a tribute to both the adaptive capabilities of American capitalism and the resources available to the modern presidency, that such a passive man provided such effective leadership during the 1980s.

NOTES

1. CONTRASTING EVALUATIONS OF THE REAGAN PRESIDENCY

1. Richard E. Neustadt, *Presidential Power: The Politics of Leadership* (New York: John Wiley, 1960); Fred I. Greenstein, *The Hidden Hand Presidency: Eisenhower as Leader* (New York: Basic Books, 1982).

2. Aaron Wildavsky, "What Was So Bad about the 80's Anyway?" *New York Times Book Review,* May 17, 1992, p. 9.

3. Martin Anderson, *Revolution* (New York: Harcourt Brace Jovanovich, 1988).

4. *New York Times,* August 17, 1992.

5. Alonzo L. Hambey, *Liberalism and Its Challengers from F.D.R. to Bush,* 2d ed. (New York: Oxford University Press, 1992), p. 339.

6. William Ker Muir, Jr., *The Bully Pulpit: The Presidential Leadership of Ronald Reagan* (San Francisco: ICS Press, 1992), p. 18; William K. Muir, Jr., "Ronald Reagan: The Primacy of Rhetoric," in *Leadership in the Modern Presidency,* edited by Fred I. Greenstein (Cambridge, Mass.: Harvard University Press, 1988), p. 262.

7. Muir, *The Bully Pulpit,* p. 184.

8. George F. Will, *Suddenly: The American Idea Abroad and at Home, 1986–1990* (New York: Free Press, 1992), p. 149.

9. Muir, *The Bully Pulpit,* p. 18.

10. Bernard Weinraub, "The Reagan Legacy," *New York Times Magazine,* June 22, 1986, p. 14.

11. Edwin J. Feulner, *New York Times,* January 22, 1989.

12. Edwin Meese III, *With Reagan: The Inside Story* (Washington, D.C.: Regnery Gateway, 1992), p. 148.

13. Robert L. Bartley, *The Seven Fat Years: And How to Do It Again* (New York: Free Press, 1992), pp. 135–149; Lawrence Lindsey, *The Growth Experiment: How the New Tax Policy Is Transforming the U.S. Economy* (New York: Basic Books, 1990), pp. 53–81.

14. *New York Times,* September 26, 1991. See also Patrick Buchanan, *Houston Chronicle,* May 17, 1991.

15. R. Emmett Tyrrell, Jr., *The Conservative Crack-Up* (New York: Simon and Schuster, 1992), p. 170.

16. Dilys Hill and Phil Williams, "The Reagan Presidency: Style and Substance," in

The Reagan Presidency: An Incomplete Revolution? edited by Dilys Hill, Raymond Moore, and Phil Williams (New York: St. Martin's Press, 1990), p. 13.

17. *U.S. News and World Report,* January 9, 1989, p. 20.

18. William Randolph Hearst, Jr., *Houston Chronicle,* April 21, 1991.

19. Meese, *With Reagan,* p. 334.

20. David Boaz, "Introduction," in *Assessing the Reagan Years,* edited by David Boaz (Washington, D.C.: Cato Institute, 1988), p. 3.

21. George Will, *Newsweek,* January 9, 1989.

22. Boaz, "Introduction," p. 5.

23. Paul M. Weyrich, "The Reagan Revolution That Wasn't: Why Conservatives Have Achieved So Little," *Policy Review* 41 (Summer 1987), p. 50.

24. Tyrrell, *The Conservative Crack-Up,* pp. 197–212.

25. William Safire, *New York Times,* January 12, 1989.

26. George Will, *Newsweek,* January 9, 1989, p. 15. *The Economist* (January 21, 1989, p. 21), reaches a similar conclusion: "Mr. Reagan promised a revolution and delivered a dinner party."

27. William Safire, *New York Times,* January 12, 1989.

28. Ibid.

29. Arthur M. Schlesinger, Jr., *The Cycles of American History* (Boston: Houghton Mifflin, 1986).

30. Irving Howe, *New York Times,* January 20, 1993.

31. Garry Wills, "Mr. Magoo Remembers," *New York Review of Books,* December 20, 1990, p. 3.

32. *New York Times,* January 19, 1989.

33. Robert Wright, *New Republic,* January 9 and 16, 1989, p. 6.

34. Ibid.

35. Michael Kinsley, *New Republic,* October 7, 1991, p. 4.

36. C. Michael Aho and Marc Levinson, "The Economy after Reagan," *Foreign Affairs* 67 (Winter 1988/89), p. 11.

37. Benjamin Friedman, "Reagan Lives!" *New York Review of Books,* December 20, 1990, p. 29.

38. Bill Mintz, *Houston Chronicle,* August 16, 1992.

39. Donald Kaul, *Houston Chronicle,* November 21, 1991.

40. Daniel Patrick Moynihan, "Reagan's Bankrupt Budget," *New Republic,* December 26, 1983, pp. 19–20.

41. David Broder, *Houston Chronicle,* January 15, 1989.

42. Jesse Jackson, *Newsweek,* January 9, 1989, p. 15.

43. Mark Green, *New York Times,* January 22, 1988.

44. Leonard Silk, *New York Times,* May 8, 1992.

45. Friedman, "Reagan Lives," p. 29. See also *New York Times,* September 26, 1991.

46. Robin Toner, *New York Times,* January 28, 1992.

47. Hendrick Hertzberg, "The Child Monarch," *New Republic,* September 9, 1991, p. 33.

48. Paul Kennedy, *The Rise and Fall of the Great Powers* (New York: Random House, 1987); Richard Rosecrance, *The Rise of the Trading State: Commerce and Conquest in the Modern World* (New York: Basic Books, 1986); Lester Thurow, *Head to Head: The Coming Economic Battle among Japan, Europe, and America* (New York:

William Morrow, 1992); Steven Schlosstein, *The End of the American Century* (Chicago: Congdon and Weed, 1989).

49. Charles L. Schultze, *Memos to the President* (Washington, D.C.: Brookings Institution, 1992), p. 100.

50. Arthur Schlesinger, Jr., *Houston Chronicle,* May 22, 1988.

51. Wright, *New Republic,* p. 7.

52. Hodding Carter, *The Reagan Years* (New York: George Braziller, 1988), pp. 10–11.

53. Charles W. Dunn and J. David Woodard, "Ideological Images for a Television Age: Ronald Reagan as Party Leader," in *The Reagan Presidency: An Incomplete Revolution?* edited by Dilys Hill, Raymond Moore, and Phil Williams (New York: St. Martin's Press, 1990), p. 130.

54. Maureen Dowd, *New York Times Book Review,* November 18, 1990, p. 44. See also Christopher Hitchens, *Nation,* January 9 and 16, 1989, p. 42.

55. Jeffrey Tulis, *The Rhetorical Presidency* (Princeton, N.J.: Princeton University Press, 1987), p. 189; Michael Schaller, *Reckoning with Reagan* (New York: Oxford University Press, 1992), p. 181; Larry Berman, "Looking Back at the Reagan Presidency," in *Looking Back at the Reagan Presidency,* edited by Larry Berman (Baltimore: Johns Hopkins University Press, 1990), p. 4; and Mary E. Stuckey, *Getting into the Game: The Pre-Presidential Rhetoric of Ronald Reagan* (New York: Praeger, 1989), p. 76.

56. Haynes Johnson, *Sleepwalking through History: America in the Reagan Years* (New York: W. W. Norton, 1991), p. 447.

57. Laurence Barrett, *Time,* January 23, 1989. See also John Kenneth White, "How Should Political Science Judge Ronald Reagan?" *Polity* 22 (Summer 1990), p. 714.

58. Lou Cannon, quoted in *Newsweek,* January 9, 1989, p. 21.

59. Carter, *The Reagan Years,* p. 1.

60. David Mervin, quoting Arthur Schlesinger, "Ronald Reagan's Place in History," *Journal of American Studies* 23 (August 1989), p. 283.

61. Robert Samuelson, *New Republic,* January 9 and 16, 1989, p. 22.

62. Stuart Eizenstat, quoted in Welnraub, "The Reagan Legacy," p. 20.

63. David Broder, *Houston Chronicle,* January 17, 1993; Stephen S. Rosenfield, *New York Times,* January 16, 1989.

64. Lou Cannon, *President Reagan: The Role of a Lifetime* (New York: Simon and Schuster, 1991), p. 831.

2. PREPARING THE STAGE FOR REAGAN

1. Peggy Noonan, *What I Saw at the Revolution: A Political Life in the Reagan Era* (New York: Random House, 1990), p. 270. See also Theodore Lowi, "An Aligning Election and a Presidential Plebiscite," in *Election of 1984,* edited by Michael Nelson (Washington, D.C.: Congressional Quarterly Press, 1985), p. 279.

2. Michael Foley, "Presidential Leadership and the Presidency," in *The Reagan Years,* edited by Joseph Hogan (New York: Manchester University Press), p. 42.

3. Stephen Skowronek, *The Politics Presidents Make: Leadership from John Adams*

to George Bush (Cambridge, Mass.: Belknap Press of Harvard University Press, 1993), p. 20.

    4. Ibid., p. 37.

    5. Ibid., p. 39.

    6. Ibid., p. 40.

    7. Ibid.

    8. Ibid.

    9. Ibid., p. 366.

    10. Council of Economic Advisers, *Economic Report of the President* (Washington, D.C.: U.S. Government Printing Office, 1989), p. 39. See also Herbert Stein, *Presidential Economics: The Making of Economic Policy from Roosevelt to Reagan and Beyond* (New York: Simon and Schuster, 1984), p. 219; Michael J. Boskin, *Reagan and the Economy: The Successes, Failures, and Unfinished Agenda* (San Francisco: Institute for Contemporary Studies, 1987), p. 13.

    11. Boskin, *Reagan and the Economy,* p. 13.

    12. James E. Alt, "Leaning into the Wind or Ducking out of the Storm? US Monetary Policy in the 1980s," in *Politics and Economics in the Eighties,* edited by Alberto Alesina and Geoffrey Carliner (Chicago: University of Chicago Press, 1991), p. 66. See also Charles L. Schultze, *Memos to the President* (Washington, D.C.: Brookings Institution, 1992), p. 140.

    13. Boskin, *Reagan and the Economy,* p. 139.

    14. Kenneth Bacon, *Wall Street Journal,* January 22, 1981.

    15. Stein, *Presidential Economics,* p. 221.

    16. Steven M. Gillon, *The Democrat's Dilemma: Walter F. Mondale and the Liberal Legacy* (New York: Columbia University Press, 1992), p. 199.

    17. Ibid., pp. 135, 148.

    18. Ibid., p. 295.

    19. Skowronek, *The Politics Presidents Make,* p. 116.

    20. Alonzo Hamby, *Liberalism and Its Challengers: From FDR to Bush,* 2d ed. (New York: Oxford University Press, 1992), p. 386. See also Gillon, *The Democrat's Dilemma,* p. 297.

    21. E. J. Dionne, *Why Americans Hate Politics* (New York: Simon and Schuster, 1991), p. 144.

    22. Charles O. Jones, *Separate but Equal Branches: Congress and the Presidency* (Chatham, N.J.: Chatham House Publishers, 1995), p. 44.

    23. Lowi, "An Aligning Election," p. 278.

    24. Skowronek, *The Politics Presdients Make,* pp. 121–122.

    25. Gillon, *The Democrat's Dilemma,* pp. 170, 180.

    26. Erwin C. Hargrove, *Jimmy Carter as President: Leadership and the Politics of the Public Good* (Baton Rouge: Louisiana State University Press, 1988), p. 5.

    27. James Sterling Young, "Foreword," in ibid., p. xx.

    28. John P. Burke, *The Institutional Presidency* (Baltimore: Johns Hopkins University Press, 1992), p. 119. See also Walter Williams, *Managing America: The Rise of the Anti-Analytic Presidency* (Lawrence: University Press of Kansas, 1990), p. 54.

    29. Hargrove, *Jimmy Carter,* p. 164.

    30. Sidney M. Milkis and Michael Nelson, *The American Presidency: Origins and Development, 1776–1990* (Washington, D.C.: Congressional Quarterly Press, 1990),

p. 327. See also Hamby, *Liberalism,* p. 354.

31. Burke, *The Institutional Presidency,* p. 119.

32. Zbigniew Brzezinski, *Power and Principle: Memoirs of the National Security Adviser, 1977–1981* (New York: Farrar Straus Giroux, 1985), p. 71.

33. Interview with Stuart Eizenstat, White Burkett Miller Center of Public Affairs, University of Virginia, Project on the Carter Presidency, vol. XIII, January 29–30, 1982, p. 58, Jimmy Carter Library (hereafter cited as PCP). See also Burke, *The Institutional Presidency,* pp. 120, 122, 130.

34. Emmet John Hughes, "The Presidency vs. Jimmy Carter," *Fortune* 98 (December 4, 1978), p. 52. See also Colin Campbell, S.J., "The White House and Cabinet under the 'Let's Deal' Presidency," in *The Bush Presidency: First Appraisals,* edited by Colin Campbell, S.J., and Bert Rockman (Chatham, N.J.: Chatham House Publishers, 1991), p. 92.

35. Hargrove, *Jimmy Carter,* p. 190. See also James Fallows, "The Passionless Presidency, Part I," *Atlantic Monthly,* May 1979, pp. 42–43.

36. Stephen Hess, *Organizing the Presidency,* 2d ed. (Washington, D.C.: Brookings Institution, 1988), p. 145. See also James Fallows, "For Old Times Sake," *New York Review of Books,* December 16, 1982, p. 9.

37. Dionne, *Why Americans Hate Politics,* p. 119.

38. Gary W. Reichard, "Early Returns: Assessing Jimmy Carter," *Presidential Studies Quarterly* 20 (Summer 1990), p. 616.

39. James David Barber, *The Presidential Character: Predicting Performance in the White House,* 4th ed. (Englewood Cliffs, N.J.: Prentice-Hall, 1992), p. 432.

40. Jones, *Separate but Equal Branches,* p. 153.

41. Hargrove, *Jimmy Carter,* p. 188.

42. Interview with Landon Butler, part of the Hamilton Jordan interview, PCP, vol. VI, November 6, 1981, p. 36.

43. Robert Strong, "Recapturing Leadership: The Carter Administration and the Crisis of Confidence," *Presidential Studies Quarterly* 16 (Fall 1986), p. 643. See also Hargrove, *Jimmy Carter,* pp. 173–174.

44. Thomas P. O'Neill with William Novak, *Man of the House: The Life and Political Memoirs of Speaker "Tip" O'Neill* (New York: Random House, 1987), pp. 297, 308. See also Paul Quirk, "Presidential Competence," in *The Presidency and the Political System,* edited by Michael Nelson (Washington, D.C.: Congressional Quarterly Press, 1990), pp. 135–136.

45. Interview with Hamilton Jordan, PCP, vol. VI, November 6, 1981, p. 27. See also Jones, *Separate but Equal Branches,* p. 189.

46. Interview with Hamilton Jordan, PCP, p. 28. See also Gillon, *The Democrat's Dilemma,* p. 188.

47. Interview with Stuart Eizenstat, PCP, pp. 63, 102.

48. Gillon, *The Democrat's Dilemma,* p. 207.

49. Ibid., p. 255.

50. Dionne, *Why Americans Hate Politics,* p. 131.

51. Hargrove, *Jimmy Carter,* p. 187.

52. Marcia Lynn Whicker and Raymond Moore, *When Presidents Are Great* (Englewood Cliffs, N.J.: Prentice-Hall, 1988), p. 80.

53. Hargrove, *Jimmy Carter,* pp. 107, 80.

54. Interview with Stuart Eizenstat, PCP, p. 88. See also Burton I. Kaufman, *The Presidency of James Earl Carter, Jr.* (Lawrence: University Press of Kansas, 1993), p. 100.

55. Dionne, *Why Americans Hate Politics,* p. 141.

56. Richard Neustadt, *Presidential Power and the Modern Presidents: The Politics of Leadership from Roosevelt to Reagan* (New York: Free Press, 1990), p. 208. See also Bert Rockman, *The Leadership Question: The Presidency and the American System* (New York: Praeger, 1985), p. 186.

57. James L. Sundquist, "The Crisis of Competence in Our National Government," *Political Science Quarterly* 95 (Summer 1980), pp. 183–208.

58. Foley, "Presidential Leadership," p. 28.

59. James A. Baker III, *The Politics of Diplomacy* (New York: G. P. Putnam, 1995), p. 261.

60. Norman Podhoretz, "The New American Majority," *Commentary,* January 1981, p. 24.

61. Skowronek, *The Politics Presidents Make,* p. 366.

3. RONALD REAGAN AND THE CONSERVATIVE MOVEMENT

1. Alan Wolfe, "An Open Letter to Republican Conservatives," *Commonweal,* September 12, 1980, p. 497.

2. Leslie H. Gelb, "Memorandum to the President," *New York Times Magazine,* January 18, 1981, p. 15.

3. Clinton Rossiter, *Conservatives in America: The Thankless Profession,* 2d ed. (New York: Vintage Books, 1962), p. 24.

4. Louis Hartz, *The Liberal Tradition in America* (New York: Harcourt, 1955). See also Stephen L. Newman, "Liberalism and the Divided Mind of the American Right," *Polity* 22 (Fall 1989), pp. 75–96.

5. George Will, *Houston Chronicle,* January 11, 1988.

6. Norman C. Thomas, "Public Policy and the Resurgence of Conservatism in Three Anglo-American Democracies," in *The Resurgence of Conservatism in Anglo-American Democracies,* edited by Barry Cooper, Alan Kornberg, and William Mishler (Durham, N.C.: Duke University Press, 1988), p. 98.

7. Conrad Waligorski, *The Political Theory of Conservative Economists* (Lawrence: University Press of Kansas, 1990), p. 154.

8. Richard A. Viguerie, *The New Right: We're Ready to Lead* (Falls Church, Va.: Viguerie Company, 1980), p. 55.

9. *Time,* May 4, 1981, p. 21.

10. Joseph Sobran, "Pensees: Notes for the Reactionary of Tomorrow," *National Review,* December 31, 1985, p. 37.

11. Ibid., p. 53.

12. R. Emmett Tyrrell, Jr., *The Liberal Crack-Up* (New York: Simon and Schuster, 1984), p. 20.

13. Quoted in Sidney Blumenthal, *The Rise of the Counter-Establishment: From Conservative Ideology to Political Power* (New York: Harper and Row, 1986), p. 287.

14. Tyrrell, *The Liberal Crack-Up,* p. 21.

15. Blumenthal, *Rise of the Counter-Establishment,* pp. 32–37.

16. William Schambra, "The Roots of the American Public Philosophy," *Public Interest* (Spring 1982), p. 36.

17. Viguerie, *The New Right,* pp. 15–16.

18. Quoted in Michael Lienesch, "Right-Wing Religion: Christian Conservatism as a Political Movement," *Political Science Quarterly* 97 (Fall 1982), p. 410.

19. J. David Hoeveler, Jr., *Watch on the Right: Conservative Intellectuals in the Reagan Era* (Madison: University of Wisconsin Press, 1991), p. 15.

20. Ibid., p. 24.

21. Ibid., pp. 23–53.

22. Newman, "Liberalism," pp. 84–85.

23. Viguerie, *The New Right,* pp. 241–242.

24. Ibid., p. 15.

25. Quoted in Hoeveler, *Watch on the Right,* p. 224.

26. Blumenthal, *Rise of the Counter-Establishment,* p. 167.

27. Ibid., p. 169.

28. Quoted in ibid., p. 151.

29. Norman Podhoretz, "The New American Majority," *Commentary,* January 1981, p. 20.

30. Quoted in Nigel Ashford, "The Neo-Conservatives," *Government and Opposition* 16 (Summer 1981), p. 357.

31. Norman Podhoretz, "The Neo-Conservative Anguish over Reagan's Foreign Policy," *New York Times Magazine,* May 2, 1982, p. 31.

32. Francis Fitzgerald, "A Disciplined, Charging Army," *New Yorker,* May 18, 1981, p. 64.

33. Jerry Falwell, "Introduction," in Viguerie, *The New Right,* p. 1.

34. Quoted in Dinesh D'Souza, "Out of the Wilderness: The Political Education of the Christian Right," *Policy Review* (Summer 1987), p. 57.

35. Quoted in Lienesch, "Right Wing Religion," p. 404.

36. Ibid., p. 408.

37. Ibid., p. 403.

38. Newman, "Liberalism," p. 85.

39. Kevin Phillips, "Hubris on the Right," *New York Times Magazine,* May 12, 1985, p. 62.

40. Blumenthal, *Rise of the Counter-Establishment,* p. 329.

41. E. J. Dionne, *New York Times,* October 13, 1987.

42. Arthur Schlesinger, *Houston Chronicle,* May 22, 1988.

43. John Lukacs, "The American Conservatives," *Harper's,* January 1984, p. 48.

44. Thomas S. Langston, *Ideologues and Presidents: From the New Deal to the Reagan Revolution* (Baltimore: Johns Hopkins University Press, 1992), p. 210.

45. Blumenthal, *Rise of the Counter-Establishment,* pp. 35–37.

46. Quoted in ibid., p. 315.

47. Quoted in Hedrick Smith, *New York Times,* August 26, 1982.

48. David Boaz, "Introduction," in *Assessing the Reagan Years,* edited by David Boaz (Washington, D.C.: Cato Institute, 1988), p. 3.

49. Quoted in Denis Farney, *Wall Street Journal,* February 3, 1981.

50. *Time,* August 23, 1982, p. 8.

51. *Time,* January 31, 1983, p. 26.
52. Richard Viguerie, *Houston Chronicle,* March 25, 1987.
53. Patrick Buchanan, *Philadelphia Inquirer,* July 13, 1981.
54. Albert Hunt, *Wall Street Journal,* February 17, 1982.
55. *Time,* August 16, 1982, p. 24.
56. William F. Buckley, "On the Right," *National Review,* August 13, 1982, p. 7.
57. *Time,* January 25, 1982, p. 23.
58. Norman Podhoretz, "The Reagan Road to Detente," *Foreign Affairs* 63 (Fall 1984), pp. 459, 461, 463. See also Irving Kristol, *Wall Street Journal,* January 11, 1982.
59. Quoted in Hedrick Smith, "The Right against Reagan," *New York Times Magazine,* January 17, 1988, p. 38.
60. William Buckley, *Houston Chronicle,* December 30, 1987.
61. R. Emmett Tyrrell, Jr., *The Conservative Crack-Up* (New York: Simon and Schuster, 1992), p. 118.
62. Joel Brinkely, *New York Times,* December 20, 1987.
63. Douglas Hallett, *Wall Street Journal,* September 8, 1982.
64. Paul H. Weaver, "The Intellectual Debate," in Boaz, *Assessing the Reagan Years,* p. 415.

4. PRESIDENT REAGAN'S ADMINISTRATIVE
FORMULA FOR SUCCESS

1. Richard Neustadt, *Houston Chronicle,* April 7, 1986; Alexander George, *Presidential Decision-Making in Foreign Policy* (Boulder, Colo.: Westview Press, 1980); Nicole Woolsey Biggart, "Management Style as Strategic Interaction: The Case of Governor Ronald Reagan," *Journal of Applied Behavioral Science* 17, no. 3 (1981), pp. 291–308; Joseph A. Pika, "Management Style and the Organization Matrix: Studying White House Operations," *Administration and Society* 20, no. 1 (May 1988), pp. 3–24.
2. Fred I. Greenstein, "Ronald Reagan—Another Hidden-Hand Ike?" *PS: Political Science and Politics* 23, no. 1 (March 1990), p. 17.
3. Sidney Blumenthal, *The Rise of the Counter-Establishment: From Conservative Ideology to Political Power* (New York: Harper and Row, 1986), p. 274.
4. Quoted in Bob Schieffer and Gary Paul Gates, *The Acting President* (New York: E. P. Dutton, 1989), p. 90.
5. Ibid., p. 64.
6. Lou Cannon, *Reagan* (New York: G. P. Putnam, 1982), pp. 372–373. For William Casey's view of Reagan's passivity, see Bob Woodward, *Veil: The Secret Wars of the CIA, 1981–1987* (New York: Pocket Books, 1987), p. 463.
7. Peggy Noonan, *What I Saw at the Revolution: A Political Life in the Reagan Era* (New York: Random House, 1990), p. 268.
8. David S. Broder, *Houston Chronicle,* September 2, 1985.
9. Gary Wills, *Reagan's America: Innocents at Home* (Garden City, N.Y.: Doubleday, 1987).
10. Noonan, *What I Saw,* pp. 150–151. Martin Anderson wrote, "Reagan may be

unique in that he is a warmly ruthless man." Martin Anderson, *Revolution* (New York: Harcourt Brace Jovanovich, 1988), p. 288.

11. Noonan, *What I Saw*, p. 168.

12. Ibid., p. 240. Jack Nelson, *Houston Chronicle,* January 6, 1985.

13. Noonan, *What I Saw*, p. 213.

14. Nancy Reagan with William Novak, *My Turn: The Memoirs of Nancy Reagan* (New York: Random House, 1990), p. 240.

15. Taylor Branch, "James A. Baker III, Politician," *Texas Monthly,* May 1982, p. 258.

16. Alexander Haig, *Caveat: Realism and Foreign Policy* (New York: Macmillan, 1984), p. 83.

17. Dick Kirschten, "Decision Making in the White House," *National Journal,* April 3, 1982, p. 585; *New York Times,* October 4, 1981; "The President's Men," *Time,* December 14, 1981, p. 18.

18. William Niskanen, *Reaganomics: An Insider's Account of the Policies and the People* (New York: Oxford University Press, 1988), p. 301.

19. *New York Times,* April 15, 1985.

20. Branch, "James A. Baker III," p. 264.

21. Donald Regan is one of the most difficult staff aides to classify. He had no personal ties to Reagan and was not a movement conservative. In an interview (*New York Times Magazine,* January 5, 1986, p. 31), he defined himself as "a pragmatist, but definitely on the conservative side." However, he had no previous Washington experience, and he possessed few skills in public relations. And he certainly failed to make the key alliance with Nancy Reagan.

22. Frances X. Clines, "James Baker: Calling Reagan's Re-Election Moves," *New York Times Magazine,* May 20, 1984, p. 53.

23. Branch, "James A. Baker III," p. 256.

24. Ibid., p. 263.

25. Clines, "James Baker," p. 58.

26. Niskanen, *Reaganomics,* p. 300.

27. *Time,* January 21, 1985, p. 21.

28. Clines, "James Baker," p. 60.

29. Branch, "James A. Baker III," p. 249. For reporters' negative views toward Meese, see Jane Mayer and Doyle McManus, *Landslide: The Unmaking of the President, 1984–1988* (Boston: Houghton Mifflin, 1988), p. 324.

30. Helene Von Damm, *At Reagan's Side: Twenty Years in the Political Mainstream* (New York: Doubleday, 1989), pp. 292–294.

31. *New York Times,* April 21, 1988.

32. *Houston Chronicle,* April 15, 1984.

33. Noonan, *What I Saw*, p. 143.

34. Mark Hertsgaard, *On Bended Knee: The Press and the Reagan Presidency* (New York: Farrar Straus Giroux, 1988), pp. 19–20.

35. Ibid., pp. 5, 32, 34, 37.

36. Gary Wills, *New York Review of Books,* June 16, 1988, p. 4.

37. Reagan, *My Turn,* p. 17.

38. *New York Times,* February 3, 1988.

39. Ibid.

40. Hugh Sidey, "A Conversation with Ronald Reagan," *Time,* August 5, 1985, p. 22.

41. Bert A. Rockman, "The Style and Organization of the Reagan Presidency," in *The Reagan Legacy,* edited by Charles O. Jones (Chatham, N.J.: Chatham House, 1988), p. 8.

42. Steven R. Weisman, "Can the Magic Prevail?" *New York Times Magazine,* April 19, 1984, p. 46.

43. Ann Reilly Dowd, "What Managers Can Learn from Manager Reagan," *Fortune,* September 15, 1986, p. 35; Leslie H. Gelb, "The Mind of the President," *New York Times Magazine,* October 6, 1985, p. 112.

44. David Stockman, *The Triumph of Politics: Why the Reagan Revolution Failed,* (New York: Harper and Row, 1986), p. 366.

45. Noonan, *What I Saw,* p. 171.

46. Haig, *Caveat,* p. 57.

47. Gelb, "The Mind of the President," p. 103.

48. Mayer and McManus, *Landslide,* pp. 189–271.

49. *Time,* February 6, 1984, p. 23.

50. Von Damm, *At Reagan's Side,* p. 188.

51. Stockman, *Triumph of Politics,* p. 76.

52. Donald T. Regan, *For the Record: From Wall Street to Washington* (New York: Harcourt Brace Jovanovich, 1988), pp. 142, 146.

53. Haig, *Caveat,* p. 5.

54. Noonan, *What I Saw,* p. 165.

55. Terrel H. Bell, *The Thirteenth Man: A Reagan Cabinet Memoir* (New York: Free Press, 1988), p. 32.

56. Stockman, *Triumph of Politics,* p. 76.

57. Noonan, *What I Saw,* p. 169.

58. Terry L. Deibel, "Reagan's Mixed Legacy," *Foreign Policy* 75 (Summer 1989), p. 47.

59. Douglas Hallett, "The Problem with Reagan," *Wall Street Journal,* September 8, 1982. See also Hedrick Smith, *New York Times,* August 26, 1982.

60. Clines, "James Baker," p. 58.

61. Noonan, *What I Saw,* p. 175.

62. "How Reagan Decides," *Time,* December 13, 1982, p. 14.

63. Regan, *For the Record,* p. 188.

64. *Time,* December 8, 1986, p. 34.

65. David Broder, *Houston Chronicle,* October 16, 1984.

66. Reagan, *My Turn,* p. 266.

5. THE FIRST YEAR

1. Elisabeth Drew, "A Reporter at Large," *New Yorker,* March 16, 1981, p. 84. See also Wallace Earl Walker and Michael R. Reopel, "Strategies for Governance: Transition and Domestic Policymaking in the Reagan Administration," *Presidential Studies Quarterly* 16 (Fall 1986), pp. 735–736.

2. Quoted in Mark Hertsgaard, *On Bended Knee: The Press and the Reagan Presidency* (New York: Farrar Straus Giroux, 1988), p. 107.

3. Drew, "Reporter at Large," p. 84.

4. *New York Times,* December 14, 1981.

5. David Stockman, *The Triumph of Politics: Why the Reagan Revolution Failed* (New York: Harper and Row, 1986), pp. 71–74; Lou Cannon, *President Reagan: The Role of a Lifetime* (New York: Simon and Schuster, 1991), p. 107; Laurence I. Barrett, *Gambling with History: Reagan in the White House* (New York: Doubleday, 1983), pp. 134–135.

6. Cannon, *President Reagan,* pp. 107–108. See also *Wall Street Journal,* January 9, 1981.

7. Drew, "Reporter at Large," p. 84.

8. Cannon, *President Reagan,* p. 101.

9. Ibid., p. 108.

10. Richard E. Neustadt, *Presidential Power and the Modern Presidents: The Politics of Leadership from Roosevelt to Reagan* (New York: Free Press, 1990), p. 325.

11. Allen Schick, "How the Budget Was Won and Lost," in *President and Congress: Assessing Reagan's First Year,* edited by Norman J. Ornstein (Washington, D.C.: American Enterprise Institute for Public Policy Research, 1982), p. 40.

12. Alan Greenspan, *Wall Street Journal,* January 16, 1981.

13. Stockman, *Triumph of Politics,* p. 75.

14. Ibid., p. 74.

15. Ibid., p. 76.

16. Ibid., p. 83.

17. Ibid., pp. 70–71.

18. Ibid., p. 82.

19. Ibid., p. 124.

20. Ibid., p. 125.

21. Caspar Weinberger, *Fighting for Peace: Seven Critical Years in the Pentagon* (New York: Warner Books, 1991), pp. 5, 18–21.

22. Stockman, *Triumph of Politics,* p. 107.

23. Hedrick Smith, *The Power Game: How Washington Works* (New York: Random House, 1988), p. 387.

24. Stockman, *Triumph of Politics,* p. 108.

25. Ibid., pp. 108–109.

26. Ibid., p. 278.

27. Ibid., p. 131.

28. Ibid., p. 96.

29. Ibid.

30. Ibid., p. 97.

31. *America's New Beginning: A Program for Economic Recovery* (Washington, D.C.: White House, February 18, 1981), p. 10.

32. *New York Times,* February 19, 1981.

33. Ibid.

34. Ibid.

35. Herbert Stein, *Presidential Economics: The Making of Economic Policy from Roosevelt to Reagan and Beyond* (New York: Simon and Schuster, 1984), p. 19.

36. Smith, *The Power Game,* p. 386.

37. Drew, "Reporter at Large," p. 96.

38. Cannon, *President Reagan,* p. 236.

39. *Public Papers of the Presidents of the United States, Ronald Reagan 1981* (Washington, D.C.: U.S. Government Printing Office, 1982), p. 139.

40. Henry Aaron, *Wall Street Journal,* February 27, 1981.

41. George Will, *Washington Post,* February 22, 1981.

42. Christopher Conte, *Wall Street Journal,* February 27, 1981.

43. Lester Thurow, "How to Wreck the Economy," *New York Review of Books,* May 14, 1981, p. 6. See also Leonard Silk, *New York Times,* February 20, 1981.

44. Rudolph Penner, *New York Times,* February 22, 1981.

45. Walker and Reopel, "Strategies for Governance," p. 747.

46. Schick, "How the Budget Was Won and Lost," p. 28.

47. Barrett, *Gambling with History,* p. 89; James P. Pfiffner, *The Strategic Presidency: Hitting the Ground Running* (Chicago: Dorsey Press, 1988), p. 31.

48. Hedrick Smith, "Taking Charge of Congress," *New York Times Magazine,* August 9, 1981, p. 17.

49. Thomas P. O'Neill with William Novak, *May of the House: The Life and Political Memoirs of Speaker Tip O'Neill* (New York: Random House, 1987), p. 345.

50. Richard F. Fenno, Jr., *The Emergence of a Senate Leader: Pete Domenici and the Reagan Budget* (Washington, D.C.: Congressional Quarterly Press, 1991), p. 51.

51. Pfiffner, *The Strategic Presidency,* p. 131; Fenno, *Emergence of a Senate Leader,* p. 52.

52. Allen Schick, "The Budget as an Instrument of Presidential Policy" in *The Reagan Presidency and the Governing of America,* edited by Lester Salamon and Michael S. Lund (Washington, D.C.: Urban Institute Press, 1985), p. 103.

53. Barbara Kellerman, *The Political Presidency: Practice of Leadership* (New York: Oxford University Press, 1984), p. 239.

54. Quoted in Fenno, *Emergence of a Senate Leader,* p. 49.

55. Quoted in Hedrick Smith, *New York Times,* March 28, 1991.

56. Charles O. Jones, "Ronald Reagan and the U.S. Congress: Visible-Hand Politics," in *The Reagan Legacy: Promise and Performance,* edited by Charles O. Jones (Chatham, N.J.: Chatham House, 1988), p. 40. See also Norman Ornstein, "Introduction," in *President and Congress: Assessing Reagan's First Year,* edited by Norman Ornstein (Washington, D.C.: American Enterprise Institute for Public Policy Research, 1982), p. 10.

57. Smith, *The Power Game,* p. 481.

58. Carl Rowan, *Washington Star,* February 26, 1981.

59. Cited by Kellerman, *The Political Presidency,* p. 228.

60. Walter Heller, *Wall Street Journal,* June 12, 1981.

61. Kellerman, *The Political Presidency,* p. 229.

62. *New York Times,* December 14, 1980.

63. Quoted in Norman Miller, *Wall Street Journal,* February 26, 1981.

64. Kellerman, *The Political Presidency,* pp. 232, 244.

65. Ibid., p. 245.

66. Quoted in Smith, "Taking Charge of Congress," p. 17. See also Stephen J.

Wayne, "Congressional Liaison in the Reagan White House," in Ornstein, *President and Congress,* p. 88.

67. Quoted in Smith, "Taking Charge of Congress," p. 18.

68. Charles H. Stuart III, "The Politics of Tax Reform in the 1980s," in *Politics and Economics in the Eighties,* edited by Alberto Alesina and Geoffrey Carliner (Chicago: University of Chicago Press, 1991), p. 154.

69. Kellerman, *The Political Presidency,* p. 249.

70. Pfiffner, *The Strategic Presidency,* p. 128; Schick, "How the Budget Was Won and Lost," p. 23.

71. Cannon, *President Reagan,* p. 110.

72. Samuel Kernell, *Going Public: New Strategies of Presidential Leadership* (Washington, D.C.: Congressional Quarterly Press, 1986), p. 126.

73. George Edwards III and Alec M. Gallup, *Presidential Approval: A Sourcebook* (Baltimore: Johns Hopkins University Press, 1990), p. 91.

74. Cannon, *President Reagan,* p. 156.

75. Quoted in Smith, "Taking Charge of Congress," p. 47.

76. Stockman, *Triumph of Politics,* p. 127.

77. Ibid., p. 129.

78. Ibid., p. 38.

79. Ibid., p. 140.

80. Ibid., p. 141.

81. Ibid., p. 142.

82. *New York Times,* March 6, 1981.

83. Stockman, *Triumph of Politics,* p. 151.

84. Ibid., p. 147.

85. Dennis Farney, *Wall Street Journal,* April 6, 1981. See also Walter Williams, *Managing America: The Rise of the Anti-Analytic Presidency* (Lawrence: University Press of Kansas, 1990), p. 78.

86. Stockman, *Triumph of Politics,* pp. 164–166. See also Albert Hunt, *Wall Street Journal,* March 20, 1981.

87. Barrett, *Gambling with History,* p. 151.

88. Stockman, *Triumph of Politics,* p. 179.

89. Ibid.

90. Barrett, *Gambling with History,* p. 151.

91. Stockman, *Triumph of Politics,* p. 175.

92. *Wall Street Journal,* May 8, 1981. See also Pfiffner, *The Strategic Presidency,* p. 131.

93. Cannon, *President Reagan,* p. 242; Barrett, *Gambling with History,* p. 155.

94. Cannon, *President Reagan,* p. 243.

95. Stockman, *Triumph of Politics,* p. 181.

96. Cannon, *President Reagan,* pp. 244–247.

97. Stockman, *Triumph of Politics,* p. 181.

98. Ibid., p. 188.

99. Ibid., pp. 187–190; Cannon, *President Reagan,* pp. 250–251.

100. Stockman, *Triumph of Politics,* p. 192.

101. Ibid., p. 193.

102. Ibid., p. 198. See also Barrett, *Gambling with History*, p. 326; Dennis Farney, *Wall Street Journal*, June 1, 1981.

103. Stockman, *Triumph of Politics*, pp. 209–210.

104. Ibid., p. 211.

105. Ibid., p. 214.

106. Ibid.

107. Smith, "Taking Charge of Congress," p. 47.

108. Barrett, *Gambling with History*, p. 163.

109. Stockman, *Triumph of Politics*, p. 227.

110. James Pfiffner, "The Reagan Budget Juggernaut," in *The President and Economic Policy*, edited by James Pfiffner (Philadelphia: Institute for the Study of Human Issues, 1986), p. 124.

111. Ibid., p. 128. See also Dennis S. Ippolito, *Uncertain Legacies: Federal Budget Policy from Roosevelt through Reagan* (Charlottesville: University Press of Virginia, 1990), p. 221.

112. Schick, "The Budget as an Instrument of Presidential Policy," p. 104.

113. Stockman, *Triumph of Politics*, pp. 229–230.

114. Ibid., p. 234.

115. Steven R. Weisman, "Reaganomics and the President's Men," *New York Times Magazine*, October 24, 1982, p. 85.

116. John F. Witte, *The Politics and Development of the Federal Income Tax* (Madison: University of Wisconsin Press, 1985), p. 223.

117. Barrett, *Gambling with History*, p. 166.

118. Stockman, *Triumph of Politics*, p. 235.

119. Ibid., p. 239.

120. Witte, *Federal Income Tax*, p. 225.

121. Stockman, *Triumph of Politics*, 248.

122. Ibid., p. 249.

123. Ibid., p. 231.

124. Ibid., p. 256.

125. Leonard Silk, *New York Times*, June 12, 1981.

126. Witte, *Federal Income Tax*, p. 227.

127. Stockman, *Triumph of Politics*, p. 256.

128. Barrett, *Gambling with History*, p. 169.

129. Stockman, *Triumph of Politics*, p. 263.

130. Ibid. See also Witte, *Federal Income Tax*, p. 229.

131. "Tax Cut Passed by Solid Margin in House, Senate," *Congressional Quarterly Weekly Report* 39 (August 1, 1981), p. 1374.

132. Witte, *Federal Income Tax*, p. 230.

133. Ibid., pp. 232–233; *New York Times*, August 2, 1981.

134. Stockman, *Triumph of Politics*, p. 228. See also Paul Light, "Presidential Policy Making," in *Researching the Presidency*, edited by George C. Edwards, John H. Kessel, and Bret A. Rockman (Pittsburgh: University of Pittsburgh Press, 1993), pp. 188–191; Stephen Skowronek, *The Politics Presidents Make: Political Leadership from John Adams to George Bush* (Cambridge, Mass.: Belknap Press of Harvard University Press, 1993), p. 421.

135. Tom Fox, *Philadelphia Inquirer*, August 9, 1981.

136. Hedrick Smith, *New York Times,* July 30, 1981.

137. *New York Times,* August 2, 1981.

138. Hedrick Smith, *New York Times,* May 29, 1981.

139. Fenno, *Emergence of a Senate Leader,* p. 58.

140. Cannon, *President Reagan,* p. 346.

141. Hedrick Smith, *New York Times,* November 24, 1981.

142. Lance T. LeLoup, "After the Blitz: Reagan and the U.S. Congressional Budget Process," *Legislative Studies Quarterly* 7 (August 1982), p. 327.

143. William Grieder, "The Education of David Stockman," *Atlantic* 248 (December 1981), pp. 27–41. See also Cannon, *President Reagan,* p. 261.

144. Barrett, *Gambling with History,* p. 174.

145. *Public Papers of the President,* p. 710.

146. David Broder, *Houston Chronicle,* January 20, 1982.

6. THE CONTRIBUTIONS OF TAX POLICY
TO REAGAN'S POLITICAL SUCCESS

1. "Remarks to Administration Officials on Domestic Policy," December 13, 1988, in *Public Papers of Ronald Reagan, 1988* (Washington, D.C.: U.S. Government Printing Office, 1989), p. 1615. See also Edwin Meese, *With Reagan: The Inside Story* (Washington, D.C.: Regency Gateway, 1992).

2. See, for example, Mark Hertsgaard, *On Bended Knee: The Press and the Reagan Presidency* (New York: Farrar Straus Giroux, 1988); Haynes Johnson, *Sleepwalking through History: America in the Reagan Years* (New York: W. W. Norton, 1991); and Bob Schieffer and Gary Paul Gates, *The Acting President* (New York:. E. P. Dutton, 1989).

3. David A. Stockman, *The Triumph of Politics: Why the Reagan Revolution Failed* (New York: Harper and Row, 1986), pp. 229–230, 235.

4. Lou Cannon, *President Reagan: The Role of a Lifetime* (New York: Simon and Schuster, 1991), pp. 90–91.

5. Betty Glad, "Reagan's Midlife Crisis and the Turn to the Right," *Political Psychology* 10 (December 1989), p 613.

6. Johnson, *Sleepwalking through History,* p. 67.

7. Ronald Reagan, "Let's Get America Working Again," speech delivered before the International Business Council, Chicago, Ill., September 9, 1980, *Vital Speeches of the Day* 46 (October 1, 1980), p. 739. For an excellent analysis of how Reagan's ideology affected his economic policy making, see M. Stephen Weatherford and Lorraine M. McDonnell, "Ideology and Economic Policy," in *Looking Back on the Reagan Presidency,* edited by Larry Berman (Baltimore: Johns Hopkins University Press, 1990), pp. 122–156.

8. "Address Before a Joint Session of Congress on the Program for Economic Recovery," February 18, 1981, in *Public Papers of the Presidents, Ronald Reagan, 1981* (Washington, D.C.: U.S. Government Printing Office, 1982), p. 110.

9. Address to the Nation, February 5, 1981, in *Public Papers of Ronald Reagan, 1981* (Washington, D.C.: U.S. Government Printing Office, 1982), p. 82. See also Hedrick Smith, *The Power Game: How Washington Works* (New York: Random House, 1988), p. 384.

10. Lawrence Lindsey, *The Growth Experiment: How the New Tax Policy Is Transforming the U.S. Economy* (New York: Basic Books), 1990, p. 7.

11. Thomas Edsall, *The New Politics of Inequality* (New York: W. W. Norton, 1984), pp. 210–211.

12. Lindsey, *The Growth Experiment*, p. 43.

13. Ibid., pp. 89–90.

14. Council of Economic Advisers, *Economic Report of the President, January 1989* (Washington, D.C.: U.S. Government Printing Office, 1989), p. 87.

15. Benjamin Friedman, *Day of Reckoning: The Consequences of American Economic Policy under Reagan and After* (New York: Random House, 1988), p. 293.

16. Council of Economic Advisers, *Economic Report of the President, January 1982* (Washington, D.C.: U.S. Government Printing Office, 1982), p. 122.

17. John F. Witte, *The Politics and Development of the Federal Income Tax* (Madison: University of Wisconsin Press, 1985), p. 234.

18. *New York Times,* August 2, 1981.

19. Robert S. McIntyre, *Houston Chronicle,* November 4, 1984. See also Cathie Jo Martin, "Corporate Taxation in Pursuit of Growth," *American Politics Quarterly* 19 (October 1991) p. 471; and John F. Witte, "The Tax Reform Act of 1986: A New Era in Tax Politics," *American Politics Quarterly* 19 (October 1991), p. 446.

20. Michael J. Boskin, *Reagan and the Economy: The Success, Failures, and Unfinished Agenda* (San Francisco: Institute for Contemporary Studies, 1987), p. 158.

21. *New York Times,* September 28, 1986. For an excellent analysis of the TRA, see Ronald F. King, "Introduction: Tax Reform and American Politics," *American Politics Quarterly* 19 (October 1991), pp. 417–425.

22. Boskin, *Reagan and the Economy*, p. 158.

23. Witte, "The Tax Reform Act of 1986," p. 447.

24. Jeffrey H. Birnbaum and Allan S. Murray, *Showdown at Gucci Gulch: Lawmakers, Lobbyists and the Unlikely Triumph of Tax Reform* (New York: Vantage Books, 1988), p. 286.

25. Ibid., p. 73. See also Timothy J. Conlan, Margaret T. Wrightson, and David R. Beam, *Taxing Choices* (Washington, D.C.: C2 Press, 1990), p. 71.

26. Albert S. Hunt, "Introduction," in Birnbaum and Murray, *Showdown at Gucci Gulch*, p. xiv.

27. For analysis of philosophical inconsistencies, see Paul E. Peterson and Mark Rom, "Lower Taxes, More Spending, and Budget Deficits," in *The Reagan Legacy,* edited by Charles O. Jones (Chatham, N.J.: Chatham House Publishers, 1988), pp. 218, 220; and Boskin, *Reagan and the Economy*, pp. 159, 163.

28. James M. Poterba, "Taxation and Housing Markets: Preliminary Evidence on the Effects of Recent Tax Reforms," in *Do Taxes Matter? The Impact of the Tax Reform Act of 1986,* edited by Joel Slemrod (Cambridge, Mass.: MIT Press, 1990), p. 146.

29. Friedman, *Day of Reckoning*, p. 291.

30. Murray Weidenbaum, *New York Times,* August 24, 1986; Norman Ture, "The Tax Reform Act of 1986: Revolution or Counterrevolution?" in *Assessing the Reagan Years,* edited by David Boaz (Washington, D.C.: Cato Institute, 1988), pp. 30, 39.

31. Conlan et al., *Taxing Choices*, p. 245.

32. *Wall Street Journal,* May 23, 1985. See also Smith, *The Power Game*, p. 552.

33. Hedrick Smith, *New York Times,* May 31, 1985.

34. Reagan speech in Indianapolis, June 19, 1985, and reported in the *New York Times,* June 20, 1985.

35. Hedrick Smith, *New York Times,* May 31, 1985.

36. Quoted in Birnbaum and Murray, *Showdown at Gucci Gulch,* p. 9.

37. *New York Times,* May 28, 1985.

38. Conlan et al., *Taxing Choices,* p. 103.

39. Witte, "The Tax Reform Act of 1986," p. 443.

40. Dennis S. Ippolito, "Tax Policy and Spending Policy," *American Politics Quarterly* 19 (October 1991), p. 463.

7. UNLEASHING A DISASTER

1. *New York Times,* January 21, 1981.

2. F. Stevens Redburn, "The Deeper Structure of the Savings and Loan Disaster," *P.S.* (September 1991), p. 439. See also L. J. Davis, "Chronicle of a Debacle Foretold," *Harper's Magazine* 281 (September 1990), pp. 50–52.

3. Michael Brintnall, "Political Science and the S&L Crisis," *P.S.* (September 1991), p. 432.

4. Thomas Romer and Barry R. Weingast, "Political Foundations of the Thrift Debacle," in *Politics and Economics in the Eighties,* edited by Alberto Alesina and Geoffrey Carliner (Chicago: University of Chicago Press, 1991), p. 185.

5. Edward J. Kane, *The S&L Insurance Mess: How Did It Happen?* (Washington, D.C.: Urban Institute Press, 1989), pp. 72–73.

6. Davis, "Chronicle of a Debacle Foretold," pp. 53–54.

7. Ibid., p. 54.

8. Ibid., p. 55. See also Martin Mayer, *The Greatest-Ever Bank Robbery: The Collapse of the Savings and Loan Industry* (New York: Collier Books, Macmillan, 1990), p. 65.

9. Mayer, *Greatest-Ever Bank Robbery,* p. 65.

10. Davis, "Chronicle of a Debacle Foretold," p. 55.

11. Anthony S. Campagna, *The Economy in the Reagan Years: The Economic Consequences of the Reagan Years* (Westport, Conn.: Greenwood Press, 1994), p. 141; Kane, *S&L Insurance Mess,* p. 36.

12. Mayer, *Greatest-Ever Bank Robbery,* pp. 97–98.

13. Davis, "Chronicle of a Debacle Foretold," p. 56. See also Steven V. Roberts with Gary Cohen, "Villains of the S&L Crisis," *U.S. News and World Report,* October 1, 1990, p. 55.

14. Lou Cannon, *President Reagan: The Role of a Lifetime* (New York: Simon and Schuster, 1991), p. 826.

15. Ibid., p. 827.

16. Davis, "Chronicle of a Debacle Foretold," p. 60.

17. Kane, *S&L Insurance Mess,* p. 98.

18. Ibid., p. 25.

19. R. Dan Brumbaugh, *New York Times,* March 15, 1991.

20. Kane, *S&L Insurance Mess,* p. 6–7.

21. Romer and Weingast, "Political Foundations of the Thrift Debacle," p. 188.

22. L. William Seidman, *Full Faith and Credit: The Great S&L Debacle and Other Washington Sagas* (New York: Random House, 1993), p. 112.

23. Romer and Weingast, "Political Foundations of the Thrift Debacle, pp. 200–201.

24. Kane, *S&L Insurance Mess,* p. 3.

25. Nathanial Nash, *New York Times,* May 20, 1988.

26. Roberts and Cohen, "Villains of the S&L Crisis," p. 59; Stephen Laboton, *New York Times,* September 19, 1990; and Mayer, *Greatest-Ever Bank Robbery,* pp. 254–256.

27. Nathanial Nash, *New York Times,* October 31, 1988.

28. Mayer, *Greatest-Ever Bank Robbery,* p. xi.

29. Nathanial Nash, *New York Times,* June 12, 1988.

30. Thomas C. Hayes, *New York Times,* March 24, 1988.

31. John M. Barry, *The Ambition and the Power* (London: Viking, 1989), p. 222; Christine Gorman, *Time,* August 29, 1988, p. 55.

32. Pamela Yip, *Houston Chronicle,* December 10, 1995.

33. Mayer, *Greatest-Ever Bank Robbery,* p. 4.

34. Allan Pusey, "Fast Money and Fraud," *New York Times Magazine,* April 23, 1989, p. 32.

35. Richard W. Stevenson, *New York Times,* December 15, 1991.

36. Mayer, *Greatest-Ever Bank Robbery,* p. 7.

37. Ibid., p. 70.

38. Ibid.; and Davis, "Chronicle of a Debacle Foretold," p. 59.

39. N. R. Kleinfield, *New York Times,* March 17, 1991; Davis, "Chronicle of a Debacle Foretold," p. 62; and Mayer, *Greatest-Ever Bank Robbery,* pp. 9–11.

40. Thomas Hayes, *New York Times,* April 3, 1991.

41. Mayer, *Greatest-Ever Bank Robbery,* pp. 184–185.

42. Seidman, *Full Faith and Credit,* pp. 229–230.

43. Roberts and Cohen, "Villains of the S&L Crisis," p. 59.

44. Seidman, *Full Faith and Credit,* p. 231.

45. Mayer, *Greatest-Ever Bank Robbery,* pp. 194–197.

46. Adam Zagoria, *Time,* February 3, 1997.

47. Robert E. Litan, "Comment," in *Politics and Economics in the Eighties,* edited by Alberto Alesina and Geoffrey Carliner (Chicago: University of Chicago Press, 1991), p. 210. See also Mayer, *Greatest-Ever Bank Robbery,* p. 53; and Albert Karr, *Wall Street Journal,* September 2, 1994.

48. George J. Benston and George G. Kaufman, "Understanding the Savings and Loan Debacle," *Public Interest* 99 (Spring 1990), p. 85.

49. Roberts and Cohen, "Villains of the S&L Crisis," p. 55.

50. Benston and Kaufman, "Understanding the S&L Debacle," p. 85.

51. Davis, "Chronicle of a Debacle Foretold," p. 63.

52. Mayer, *Greatest-Ever Bank Robbery,* p. 235.

53. Ibid., p. 321.

54. Ibid., p. 156.

55. Ibid., p. 32.

56. Ibid., p. 221.

57. Davis, "Chronicle of a Debacle Foretold," p. 63; Roberts and Cohen, "Villains of the S&L Crisis," p. 58.

58. Kane, *S&L Insurance Mess,* p. 103.

59. Redburn, "Deeper Structure of the S&L Disaster," p. 434.

60. Seidman, *Full Faith and Credit,* p. 191.

61. Redburn, "Deeper Structure of the S&L Disaster," p. 439.

62. Kane, *S&L Insurance Mess,* p. 67.

63. Mayer, *Greatest-Ever Bank Robbery,* p. 66.

64. Robert L. Bartley, *The Seven Fat Years: And How to Do It Again* (New York: Free Press, 1992), p. 145.

65. Council of Economic Advisers, *Economic Report of the President, January 1989* (Washington, D.C.: U.S. Government Printing Office, 1989), pp. 200–204.

66. Michael Korda, "Prompting the President," *New Yorker,* October 6, 1997, p. 93.

67. Kane, *S&L Insurance Mess,* p. 100.

68. Mayer, *Greatest-Ever Bank Robbery,* p. 61.

69. Ibid., p. 118.

70. Seidman, *Full Faith and Credit,* p. 180.

71. Cannon, *President Reagan,* pp. 827–828.

72. Suzanne Garment, *Scandal: The Crisis of Mistrust in American Politics* (New York: Random House, 1991), p. 248.

73. Davis, "Chronicle of a Debacle Foretold," p. 66.

74. Remarks at the Annual Convention of the United States League of Savings Institutions in New Orleans, November 16, 1982, in *Public Papers, Administration of Ronald Reagan, 1982* (Washington, D.C.: U.S. Government Printing Office, 1982), pp. 1482–1483.

75. Cannon, *President Reagan,* p. 826.

76. Council of Economic Advisers, *Economic Report of the President, February 1984* (Washington, D.C.: U.S. Government Printing Office, 1984), p. 160.

77. William Niskanen, *Reaganomics: An Insider's Account of the Policies and the People* (New York: Oxford University Press, 1988), p. 201.

78. Charles Murray, "The American 80s," *Commentary,* September 1990, p. 21.

79. Kane, *S&L Insurance Mess,* p. 32; Jerry Knight, *Houston Chronicle,* November 25, 1990; Barbara Rudolph, *Time,* February 20, 1989, p. 73; Peter Kilborn, *New York Times,* February 1, 1992.

80. Nathanial Nash, *New York Times,* February 19, 1989.

81. Andrew Taylor, *Congressional Quarterly,* November 21, 1992, p. 3670; Pamela Yip, *Houston Chronicle,* December 10, 1995.

82. Mayer, *Greatest-Ever Bank Robbery,* pp. 2–3.

83. Robert Kuttner, *Everything for Sale: The Virtues and Limits of Markets* (New York: Alfred A. Knopf, 1997), p. 22; Mayer, *Greatest-Ever Bank Robbery,* p. 2; Stephen Labaton, *New York Times,* September 18, 1991; and James Flanagan, *Houston Chronicle,* December 8, 1996.

84. Roberts and Cohen, "Villains of the S&L Crisis," p. 58.

8. THE REAGAN ADMINISTRATION COPES
WITH GLOBAL INTERDEPENDENCE

1. Jeffrey E. Garten, "Gunboat Economics," *Foreign Affairs* 63 (Fall 1984),
p. 588.
2. Benjamin J. Cohen, "An Explosion in the Kitchen? Economic Relations with
Other Advanced Industrial States," in *Eagle Defiant: United States Foreign Policy in
the 1980s,* edited by Kenneth A. Oye, Robert J. Lieber, and Donald Rothchild (Boston:
Little, Brown, 1983), p. 109.
3. Kenneth A. Oye, "Constrained Confidence and the Evolution of Reagan's Foreign Policy," in *Eagle Resurgent? The Reagan Era in American Foreign Policy,* edited
by Kenneth Oye, Robert J. Lieber, and Donald Rothchild (Boston: Little, Brown,
1987), p. 5.
4. Council of Economic Advisers, *Economic Report of the President, 1982* (Washington, D.C.: U.S. Government Printing Office, 1982), p. 167.
5. C. Fred Bergsten, "The Costs of Reaganomics," *Foreign Policy* 44 (Fall 1981),
p. 36.
6. Oye, "Constrained Confidence," p. 5. See also CEA, *Economic Report of the
President, 1982,* p. 8.
7. CEA, *Economic Report of the President, 1982,* p. 173.
8. Clyde Farnsworth, *New York Times,* September 29, 1988.
9. I. M. Destler, *American Trade Politics,* 2d ed. (Washington, D.C.: Institute
for International Economics, 1992), p. 77. See also *Time,* March 23, 1981, p. 69.
10. Kenneth Bacon, *Wall Street Journal,* March 5, 1981.
11. David A. Stockman, *The Triumph of Politics: Why the Reagan Revolution Failed*
(New York: Harper and Row, 1986), p. 155.
12. Ibid.
13. Ibid., p. 158.
14. Destler, *American Trade Politics,* p. 178.
15. Mike Mochizuki, "The United States and Japan: Conflict and Cooperation,"
in Oye et al., *Eagle Resurgent?* p. 344.
16. James Shock, "Party Competition, Divided Government, and U.S. Trade Policy in the 1980s," American Political Science Convention, New York, September 1994,
p. 14.
17. Quoted in Sidney Blumenthal, "Drafting a Democratic Industrial Plan," *New
York Times Magazine,* August 28, 1983, p. 40.
18. David Broder, *Houston Chronicle,* January 28, 1983.
19. Destler, *American Trade Politics,* p. 177.
20. Shock, "Party Competition," p. 16.
21. Destler, *American Trade Politics,* p. 84.
22. Ibid., p. 87.
23. John W. Sloan, *Public Policy in Latin America* (Pittsburgh: University of Pittsburgh Press, 1984), pp. 148–149.
24. Paul Volcker and Toyoo Gyohten, *Changing Fortunes: The World's Money and
the Threat to American Leadership* (New York: Random House, 1992), p. 198.
25. Ibid., p. 205.
26. Ibid., p. 206.

27. Ibid., p. 207.

28. C. Fred Bergsten, "Reaganomics: The Problem?" *Foreign Policy* 59 (Spring 1985), p. 139.

29. Nicholas Kristof, *New York Times,* December 19, 1984.

30. Volcker and Gyohten, *Changing Fortunes,* p. 180.

31. Garten, "Gunboat Economics," p. 540.

32. Destler, *American Trade Politics,* p. 124; Mochizuki, "The U.S. and Japan," pp. 341–342.

33. Volcker and Gyohten, *Changing Fortunes,* p. 248.

34. Benjamin Friedman, *Day of Reckoning: The Consequences of American Economic Policy under Reagan and After* (New York: Random House, 1988), p. 10.

35. Volcker and Gyohten, *Changing Fortunes,* pp. 178–179.

36. Ibid., p. 241.

37. Stephen Grubaugh and Scott Summers, "Monetary Policy and the U.S. Trade Deficit," in *The Reagan Years,* edited by Joseph Hogan (New York: Manchester University Press, 1990), p. 243.

38. Peter Kilborn, *New York Times,* March 3, 1985.

39. Leonard Silk, *New York Times,* July 19, 1985.

40. Bergsten, "Reaganomics: The Problem?" p. 136.

41. Clyde Farnsworth, *New York Times,* April 7, 1985.

42. Steven Roberts, *New York Times,* September 29, 1985; Destler, *American Trade Politics,* p. 177.

43. Volcker and Gyohten, *Changing Fortunes,* p. 243.

44. Yoichi Funabashi, *Managing the Dollar: From the Plaza to the Louvre,* 2d ed. (Washington, D.C.: Institute for International Economics, 1989), p. 79. See also Volcker and Gychten, *Changing Fortunes,* p. 243; and Hobert Rowen, *Self-Inflicted Wounds: From LBJ's Guns and Butter to Reagan's Voodoo Economics* (New York: Times Books, 1994), p. 308.

45. Peter Kilborn, *New York Times,* September 23, 1985.

46. Volcker and Gyohten, *Changing Fortunes,* p. 229.

47. Funabashi, *Managing the Dollar,* p. 216.

48. Nigel Lawson, *The View from No. 11: Memoirs of a Tory Radical* (London: Corgi Books, 1992), p. 537.

49. Rowen, *Self Inflicted Wounds,* p. 307.

50. Volcker and Gyohten, *Changing Fortunes,* p. 246.

51. "Remarks at a White House Meeting with Business and Trade Leaders," September 23, 1985, in *Public Papers of the Presidents of the United States, Ronald Reagan, 1985* (Washington, D.C.: U.S. Government Printing Office, 1986), p. 1127. See also Robert Merry, *Wall Street Journal,* September 24, 1985.

52. Shock, "Party Competition," p. 20.

53. James Brooks, *New York Times,* July 26, 1989.

54. Howard Wiarda, "The Politics of Third World Debt," *Political Science* 23 (September 1990), p. 412.

55. Isabel Sawhill, "Reaganomics in Retrospect," in *Perspectives on the Reagan Years,* edited by John L. Palmer and Isabel Sawhill (Washington, D.C.: Urban Institute, 1986), p. 106.

56. Peter Kilborn, *New York Times,* March 15, 1986.

57. Funabashi, *Managing the Dollar,* p. 109.
58. Lawson, *View from No. 11,* p. 546.
59. Volcker and Gyohten, *Changing Fortunes,* p. 263.
60. Funabashi, *Managing the Dollar,* p. 130.
61. Lawson, *View from No. 11,* p. 547.
62. Volcker and Gyohten, *Changing Fortunes,* p. 266.
63. Ibid., p. 268.
64. Ibid., p. 267.
65. Lawson, *View from No. 11,* p. 555.
66. Rowen, *Self-Inflicted Wounds,* p. 319; Volcker and Gyohten, *Changing Fortunes,* p. 268; Lawson, *View from No. 11,* p. 556.
67. Funabashi, *Managing the Dollar,* p. 210.
68. Destler, *American Trade Politics,* p. 95.
69. Shock, "Party Competition," p. 32.
70. Destler, *American Trade Politics,* p. 95.
71. Wiarda, "Politics of Third World Debt," p. 421.
72. Volcker and Gyohten, *Changing Fortunes,* p. 226.
73. Destler, *American Trade Politics,* p. 224.
74. Steven Greenhouse, *New York Times,* April 6, 1992.
75. Rowen, *Self-Inflicted Wounds,* p. 322; Paula Stern, "A Burdensome Legacy: The Reagan Administration's Trade Policy," *Brookings Review* (Fall 1991), p. 43.
76. Funabashi, *Managing the Dollar,* p. 220.
77. Richard Rose, *The Postmodern President,* 2d ed. (Chatham, N.J.: Chatham House Publishers, 1991), p. 288.

9. CONSTRUCTING A CONSERVATIVE REGIME FOR ECONOMIC GROWTH

1. John Brooks, "The Supply Side," *New Yorker,* April 19, 1982, p. 11.
2. *Time,* January 31, 1983; Alfred Malabre, *Wall Street Journal,* January 17, 1983; Charles L. Schultze, *Memos to the President: A Guide through Macroeconomics for the Busy Policymaker* (Washington, D.C.: Brookings Institution, 1992), p. 21; and Lou Cannon, *President Reagan: The Role of a Lifetime* (New York: Simon and Schuster, 1991), p. 232.
3. William D. Nordhaus, *New York Times,* December 26, 1982.
4. Benjamin Stein, "A Scenario for a Depression?" *New York Times Magazine,* February 28, 1982, p. 36. See also Robert Heilbroner, "Does Capitalism Have a Future?" *New York Times Magazine,* August 5, 1982, p. 20.
5. Sidney Blumenthal, "Letter from Washington," *New Yorker,* July 19, 1993, p. 30.
6. Council of Economic Advisers, *Economic Report of the President, January 1982* (Washington, D.C.: U.S. Government Printing Office, 1982), pp. 9–10.
7. Steven Weisman, *New York Times,* September 26, 1982; *Public Papers of the Presidents of the United States, Ronald Reagan, 1982* (Washington, D.C.: U.S. Government Printing Office, 1983), pp. 27, 28, 53.
8. *New York Times,* October 14, 1982.

9. Mark Peffey and J. T. Williams, "Attributing Presidential Responsibility for National Economic Problems," *American Politics Quarterly* 13 (October 1985), p. 414.

10. Alonzo L. Hamby, *Liberalism and Its Challengers: From F.D.R to Bush,* 2d ed. (New York: Oxford University Press, 1992), p. 368.

11. Cannon, *President Reagan,* p. 275.

12. Alexander Haines, *New York Times,* August 18, 1982.

13. Quoted in Leonard Silk, *New York Times,* May 26, 1984.

14. Sidney Blumenthal, *The Rise of the Counter-Establishment: From Conservative Ideology to Political Power* (New York: Harper and Row, 1986), p. 277.

15. Paul Kennedy, *The Rise and Fall of the Great Powers: Economic Change and Military Conflict from 1500 to 2000* (New York: Random House, 1987).

16. Peter Passell, *New York Times,* August 24, 1996.

17. Schultze, *Memos to the President,* p. 220.

18. *Barron's,* August 12, 1996, p. 30.

19. Karen Arenson, *New York Times,* April 8, 1984; Peter Kilborn, *New York Times,* September 4, 1988.

20. Joel Kurtzman, *New York Times,* August 12, 1990.

21. Council of Economic Advisers, *Economic Report of the President, January 1991* (Washington, D.C.: U.S. Government Printing Office, 1991), p. 322.

22. Council of Economic Advisers, *Economic Report of the President, January 1989* (Washington, D.C.: U.S. Government Printing Office, 1989), p. 7.

23. Steven Greenhouse, *New York Times,* January 25, 1988.

24. Paul Krugman, *Peddling Prosperity: Economic Sense and Nonsense in the Age of Diminished Expectations* (New York: W. W. Norton, 1994), p. 262.

25. John Tagliabue, *New York Times,* June 20, 1996.

26. Barbara Presley Noble, *New York Times,* May 8, 1994; Robert Kuttner, *Everything for Sale: The Virtues and Limits of Markets* (New York: Alfred A. Knopf, 1997), p. 106.

27. E. J. Dionne, *Houston Chronicle,* November 29, 1993.

28. Robert Pear, *New York Times,* October 1, 1987.

29. Sylvia Nasar, *New York Times,* January 2, 1992. See also Louis Uchitelle, *New York Times,* March 22, 1994.

30. Sylvia Nasar, *New York Times,* October 17, 1994.

31. Louis Uchitelle, *New York Times,* January 8, 1992.

32. *America's New Beginning: A Program for Economic Recovery* (Washington, D.C.: White House, February 18, 1981), p. 10. See also Edward Cowan, *New York Times,* May 3, 1981.

33. Schultze, *Memos to the President,* p. 259; Krugman, *Peddling Prosperity,* p. 158.

34. Andrew Dean, Martin Durand, John Fallon, and Peter Hoeller, "Saving Trends and Behavior in DECD Countries," *OECD Economic Studies* 14 (Spring 1990), p. 9.

35. Leonard Silk, *New York Times,* November 29, 1991.

36. Keith Bradsher, *New York Times,* June 17, 1994.

37. Benjamin M. Friedman, "The Clinton Budget: Will It Do?" *New York Review of Books,* July 15, 1993, p. 37.

38. Krugman, *Peddling Prosperity,* p. 158.

39. CEA, *Economic Report of the President, January 1991,* p. 401.

40. Cannon, *President Reagan,* p. 278.

41. *New York Times,* February 11, 1982.

42. Albert Rees, *Striking a Balance: Making National Economic Policy* (Chicago: University of Chicago Press, 1984), p. 71.

43. Paul Volcker and Toyoo Gyohten, *Changing Fortunes: The World's Money and the Threat to American Leadership* (New York: Random House, 1992), p. 175.

44. Quoted in Kenneth Bacon, *Wall Street Journal,* April 19, 1982.

45. Donald F. Kettl, *Leadership at the Fed* (New Haven, Conn.: Yale University Press, 1986), p. 183.

46. James E. Alt, "Leaning into the Wind or Ducking out of the Storm? U.S. Monetary Policy in the 1980s," in *Politics and Economics in the Eighties,* edited by Alberto Alesina and Geoffrey Carliner (Chicago: University of Chicago Press, 1991), p. 46.

47. Alfred L. Malabre, *Lost Prophets: An Insider's History of the Modern Economists* (Cambridge, Mass.: Harvard Business School Press, 1994), p. 163.

48. Benjamin Friedman, "Comment," in Alesina and Carliner, *Politics and Economics in the Eighties,* pp. 82–83.

49. Arthur Schlesinger, *Wall Street Journal,* March 16, 1982.

50. Kettl, *Leadership at the Fed,* p. 147.

51. William Niskanen, *Reaganomics: An Insider's Account of the Policies and the People* (New York: Oxford University Press, 1988), p. 315.

52. James Tobin, "How to Think about the Deficit," *New York Review of Books,* September 25, 1986, p. 44.

53. Kettl, *Leadership at the Fed,* p. 177; Peter Kilborn, *New York Times,* June 3, 1987; and Krugman, *Peddling Prosperity,* p. 173.

54. Niskanen, *Reaganomics,* pp. 168–169.

55. Louis Uchitelle, *New York Times,* April 27, 1997.

10. THE REAGAN PRESIDENCY, GROWING INEQUALITY,
AND THE AMERICAN DREAM

1. Alexis de Tocqueville, *Democracy in America,* translated by George Lawrence, edited by J. P. Mayer (New York: Harper and Row, 1988), p. 9.

2. Ibid., pp. 536, 537, 538.

3. Sidney Verba, *Elites and the Idea of Equality: A Comparison of Japan, Sweden and the United States* (Cambridge, Mass.: Harvard University Press, 1987), p. 44.

4. Gordon S. Wood, *The Creation of the American Republic 1776–1789* (Chapel Hill: University of North Carolina Press, 1969), p. 72. See also Richard J. Ellis, "Rival Visions of Equality in American Political Culture," *Review of Politics* 54 (Spring 1992), p. 258.

5. Ellis, "Rival Visions," p. 256.

6. Quoted in John Kenneth White, *The New Politics of Old Values,* 2d ed. (Hanover, N.H.: University Press of New England, 1990), p. 65.

7. Ellis, "Rival Visions," p. 265.

8. Mickey Kaus, *The End of Equality* (New York: Basic Books, 1992), p. 12.

9. Lester Thurow, "The Rich: Why Their World Might Crumble," *New York Times Magazine,* November 19, 1995, p. 78.

10. Robert B. Reich, *New York Times,* August 31, 1994.

11. Conrad Waligorski, *The Political Theory of Conservative Economists* (Lawrence: University Press of Kansas, 1990), p. 29.

12. R. Emmett Tyrrell, Jr., *The Liberal Crack-Up* (New York: Simon and Schuster, 1984), p. 219.

13. Milton Friedman, *Capitalism and Freedom* (Chicago: University of Chicago Press, 1962), p. 195.

14. Committee on Ways and Means, U.S. House of Representatives, "Overview of Entitlement Programs," 1991 Greenbook, 102nd Congress, 1st session, May 7, 1991, pp. 1261–1262.

15. Robert Pear, *New York Times,* January 11, 1991.

16. Andrew Hacker, "The Rich: Who They Are," *New York Times Magazine,* November 19, 1995, p. 70. See also Keith Brasher, *New York Times,* April 17, 1995; Edward N. Wolff, *Top Heavy: A Study of Increasing Inequality of Wealth in America* (New York: Twentieth Century Fund Press, 1995), p. 7.

17. Keith Bradsher, *New York Times,* June 22, 1996.

18. Steven Holmes, *New York Times,* June 20, 1996.

19. Michael Lewis, "The Rich," *New York Times Magazine,* November 19, 1995.

20. Sylvia Nasar, *New York Times,* August 16, 1992.

21. Sylvia Nasar, *New York Times,* April 21, 1992. See also Sylvia Nasar, *New York Times,* March 5, 1992; 1991 Greenbook, p. 1336.

22. Thurow, "The Rich," p. 78.

23. Keith Bradsher, *New York Times,* April 17, 1995. See also Wolff, "Top Heavy," pp. 21–31.

24. Keith Bradsher, *New York Times,* April 17, 1995.

25. George Will, *Houston Chronicle,* September 5, 1991.

26. Robert B. Reich, *New York Times,* August 31, 1994. See also Benjamin M. Friedman, "Reagan Lives!" *New York Review of Books,* December 20, 1990, p. 29.

27. 1991 Greenbook, p. 1135.

28. "Reinventing America," *Business Week,* January 19, 1993, p. 35.

29. Felicity Barringer, *New York Times,* May 29, 1992. See also Jason De Parle, *New York Times,* January 27, 1991.

30. Robert Pear, *New York Times,* October 10, 1993. See also Jason De Parle, *New York Times,* September 2, 1991.

31. David Broder, *Houston Chronicle,* June 22, 1994; Jason De Parle, *New York Times,* January 10, 1992; and Jason De Parle, *New York Times,* March 22, 1994.

32. *Time,* September 14, 1981, p. 14.

33. Robert Pear, *New York Times,* July 25, 1983.

34. Hodding Carter, *Wall Street Journal,* February 11, 1982.

35. Thomas E. Cavenagh and James L. Sundquist, "The New Two Party System," in *The New Direction In American Politics,* edited by John E. Chubb and Paul E. Peterson (Washington, D.C.: Brookings Institution, 1985), p. 37.

36. Paul Taylor, *Washington Post,* November 23, 1985; Paul Taylor, *Washington Post,* December 14, 1985.

37. Peter Applebaum, *New York Times,* April 3, 1991.

38. Albert O. Hirschman, *The Rhetoric of Reaction: Perversity, Futility, and Jeopardy* (Cambridge, Mass: Belknap Press of Harvard University Press, 1991), p. 7.

39. Friedrich A. Hayek, *The Road to Serfdom* (Chicago: University of Chicago Press, 1976); Milton Friedman, *Capitalism and Freedom* (Chicago: University of Chicago Press, 1962).

40. Charles Murray, *Losing Ground: America's Social Policy, 1950–1980* (New York: Basic Books, 1984), p. 9.

41. Edwin Meese quoted by Frances X. Clines, *New York Times,* December 16, 1983.

42. Conrad Waligorski, "The Economic Justification of Inequality," Southwest Social Science Convention, March 1995, p. 14.

43. Milton Friedman and Rose Friedman, *Free to Choose: A Personal Statement* (New York: Avon, 1979), p. 139.

44. Quoted in Sidney Blumenthal, *The Rise of the Counter-Establishment: From Conservative Ideology to Political Power* (New York: Harper and Row, 1986), p. 222.

45. Quoted in White, *The New Politics,* p. 53.

46. William A. Niskanen, *Reaganomics: An Insider's Account of the Policies and the People* (New York: Oxford University Press, 1988), p. 279.

47. Paul Craig Roberts, *Houston Chronicle,* June 8, 1992.

48. Robert L. Bartley, *The Seven Fat Years: And How to Do It Again* (New York: Free Press, 1992), pp. 135–149; Lawrence Lindsey, *The Growth Experiment: How the New Tax Policy Is Transforming the U.S. Economy* (New York: Basic Books, 1990), pp. 53–91.

49. Robert Pear, *New York Times,* August 28, 1985.

50. Quoted in John K. White, *The New Politics,* p. 70.

51. Kate Walsh O'Beirne, *Houston Chronicle,* September 9, 1988.

52. Garry Wills, *Reagan's America: Innocent at Home* (Garden City, N.Y.: Doubleday, 1987).

53. Michael K. Deaver, *Behind the Scenes* (New York: William Morrow, 1987). See also Francis X. Clines, *New York Times,* December 13, 1983.

54. Lou Cannon, *Washington Post,* October 13, 1988.

55. Kaus, *The End of Equality,* p. vi.

56. Quoted in Lou Cannon, *President Reagan: The Role of a Lifetime* (New York: Simon and Schuster, 1991), p. 24.

57. Jason De Parle, *New York Times,* November 7, 1993.

58. David Broder, *Houston Chronicle,* January 15, 1989.

59. William Ker Muir, Jr., *The Bully Pulpit: The Presidential Leadership of Ronald Reagan* (San Francisco: ISC Press, 1992).

11. CONCLUSION

1. Martin Anderson, *Revolution* (New York: Harcourt Brace Jovanovich, 1988); Edwin Meese, *With Reagan: The Inside Story* (Washington, D.C.: Regnery Gateway, 1992); William Ker Muir, Jr., *The Bully Pulpit: The Presidential Leadership of Ronald Reagan* (San Francisco: ICS Press, 1992); Dinesh D'Souza, *Ronald Reagan: How an Ordinary Man Became an Extraordinary Leader* (New York: Free Press, 1997).

2. Mark Hertsgaard, *On Bended Knee: The Press and the Reagan Presidency* (New York: Farrar Straus Giroux, 1988); Haynes Johnson, *Sleeping through History: Amer-*

ica in the Reagan Years (New York: W. W. Norton, 1991); Bob Schieffer and Gary Paul Gates, *The Acting President* (New York: E. P. Dutton, 1989).

3. Richard Neustadt, *Presidential Power and the Modern Presidents: The Politics of Leadership from Roosevelt to Reagan* (New York: Free Press, 1990).

4. Charles Jones, ed., *The Reagan Legacy: Promise and Performance* (Chatham, N.J.: Chatham House Publishers, 1988); Jane Mayer and Doyle McManus, *Landslide: The Unmaking of the President, 1984–1988* (Boston: Houghton Mifflin, 1988).

5. Lou Cannon, "A Journalist's Perspective," in *Leadership in the Reagan Presidency*, Part 2, edited by Kenneth W. Thompson (Lanham, Md.: University Press of America, 1993), p. 53.

6. Lou Cannon, *President Reagan: The Role of a Lifetime* (New York: Simon and Schuster, 1991), p. 217.

7. James MacGregor Burns, *The Power to Lead: The Crisis of the American Presidency* (New York: Simon and Schuster, 1984), p. 57.

8. Samuel Kernell, *Going Public: New Strategies of Presidential Leadership* (Washington, D.C.: Congressional Quarterly Press, 1992), p. xv.

9. Mary Stuckey, *The President as Interpreter-in-Chief* (Chatham, N.J.: Chatham House Publishers, 1991), p. 117; Robert E. Denton, Jr., *The Primetime Presidency of Ronald Reagan: The Era of the Television Presidency* (New York: Praeger, 1988), pp. 65–66; Roderick Hart, *Verbal Style and the Presidency* (Orlando, Fla.: Academic Press, 1984), pp. 215–228.

10. Lou Cannon, *Reagan* (New York: G. P. Putnam, 1982), p. 371.

11. Mary Stuckey, "Rhetoric and Power: The Reagan Candidacies," paper delivered to the American Political Science Convention, August 28–31, 1986, p. 15.

12. Tony Dolan quoted in William K. Muir, "Ronald Reagan: The Primacy of Rhetoric," in *Leadership in the Modern Presidency*, edited by Fred I. Greenstein (Cambridge, Mass.: Harvard University Press, 1988), p. 278; George Will, *Houston Chronicle*, January 28, 1983.

13. Cannon, *President Reagan*, p. 185.

14. George Shultz, *Turmoil and Triumph: My Years as Secretary of State* (New York: Charles Scribner and Sons, 1993), pp. 963–964.

15. Cannon, *Reagan*, p. 316.

16. Larry Berman, "Looking Back on the Reagan Presidency," in *Looking Back on the Reagan Presidency*, edited by Larry Berman (Baltimore: Johns Hopkins University Press, 1990), p. 4; James Ceaser, "The Reagan Presidency and American Public Opinion," in Jones, *The Reagan Legacy*, p. 209.

17. Charles Jones, "Ronald Reagan and the U.S. Congress," in Jones, *The Reagan Legacy*, p. 56.

INDEX